JOUR for the ONE

Thanks for being the One,

Monty Joyner ⊕

Steve White Eagle

John Peterson

Books by Monty Joynes

Naked Into The Night
(1997)

Lost In Las Vegas
(1998)

Save The Good Seed
(1999)

Dead Water Rites
(2000)

The Celestine Prophecy: The Making of the Movie
(2005)

Conversations With God: The Making of the Movie
(2006)

Journey For The One: The Biography of
Jeanne White Eagle and John Pehrson
(2008)

JOURNEY
for the
ONE

The Biography *of* Jeanne White Eagle *and* John Pehrson

MONTY JOYNES

One Journey Publications
Asheville, North Carolina, USA

Cover design by Frame 25 Productions

One Journey Publications
Asheville, North Carolina, USA

If you are unable to order this book from your local bookseller, you may order directly from the publisher. Quantity discounts for organizations are available.

Library of Congress Control Number 2008926999

ISBN 978-0-615-20911-1
10 9 8 7 6 5 4 3 2 1

Printed on acid-free paper in Canada.

TABLE OF CONTENTS

2005

2006

2007

FOREWORD

When someone intimately, quietly, and sincerely shares with us their personal experiences with divine energy in an eye-to-eye, heart-to- heart, long-term encounter, how should we respond if we are grounded in intellectual logic and the scientific method of proofs? Knowing what we do of human psychology and the ego's constant need to feel special or important, how can we accept the testimony of individuals who have crossed the mind-body barriers into metaphysics? And since the quest for enlightenment has produced so few masters over the course of human history, how can we trust the appearance of prophets in our contemporary world? Who and what are we to believe in an age of justifiable skepticism? How are we to accept that a woman and a man who are so much like us are truly transformed by a divine vision—a vision that not only includes us but embraces us without resorting to the dogma of a theology? How are we to respond when their goal is for us to have the experience of divine vision, divine energy for ourselves, and that the method for this transformation is not a catechism but merely an invitation to sing and to dance the songs of our soul connection?

Journey For the One is an opportunity to travel the path of our common humanity with a married couple—Jeanne White Eagle Pehrson and John Pehrson—and to have a very intimate perspective on how they came to be realized and honored as the bringers of inner peace to diverse, and sometimes conflicting, cultures on six continents.

My function is to be with Jeanne and John as the reader's alter ego and to record their life experience for the sake of sharing it as clearly and as forthrightly as I am able. At the conclusion of this story, the reader will have to deal with all the rational asides that have emerged in consciousness along the way; and in a very personal and private way, the reader will then have to decide if the moment has arrived for joining the universal singing and dancing that unites us in ceremony as the reality of the divine soul. In *Journey For the One*, you, too, are not separate from the One.

Monty Joynes
4 March 2005

THE DANCE

I f life is not linear, but a circle, then one can join the circle at any point and be on the right path. To begin this story, let us enter the circle at a point in April of 2005, where Jeanne White Eagle Pehrson is thanking the dancers and crew of a March "For the One" Dance in Tennessee. It is perhaps as good an introduction as any to understand the process of the couple's journey. Later, we will see how Jeanne and John come together, and we will travel the total arc of the circle that contains their lives. But first, hear Jeanne's words as an insight to where we are going.

"To Dancers and Crew of the recent 'For the One' Dance in TN:

First, we both want to thank you for your courage and wisdom in 'showing up and saying yes.' We continue to be amazed and in awe at the power of Spirit inside this beautiful dance 'For the One.' You've heard us say before, it is all beyond our comprehension . . . which, indeed, it is, at least to the part of us that has forgotten how extraordinarily perfect each of us is and how connected each of us is to each other. Thus, the mission of the dance . . . to help us remember that very thing . . . there is no separation. There is only Love.

"The impact that you had not only on yourselves and those immediately present, but on the world and all existence as we perceive it, is more than any of us can imagine. We can only hope to understand and experience Love at this level through the changes we begin to go through in our everyday lives, in how we perceive ourselves and those around us, and particularly in how we then treat ourselves and those around us, including the land and the more than two-leggeds.

"Some of you experienced firsthand the various creation energies that come into the dance as the sound and movement birth a vibration that literally takes us all to the point from which all creation comes. This energy gets experienced in a variety of ways. It may even feel sexual at times, or simply be a feeling of pure elation and joy . . . and it may feel chaotic and confusing, even fearful at times, all of which is part of natural birth. Whatever it is, it is perfect . . . It is Life creating Life, Love remembering itself.

"What occurred in this particular dance at the Center for Peace was something that moved us all to the next level. We got a glimpse of what will happen when the thousands physically come and participate. Several of us saw with spiritual eyes the Ancient Ones come forth to dance and sing with us . . . again, the thousands. And it isn't even about the numbers . . . it is about the part of the larger Self coming into a time and space where the memory that there is only One of us here, that there is only Love, is beginning to surface into mass consciousness.

"Just know that you did something very powerful in your dance, whether it was inside the arbor or on the outside . . . the circle was made complete.

"So thank you, dear ones. We walk humbly in our appreciation and love for each of you."

Since 1993, when Jeanne and John began their relationship, they have traveled all over the world as spiritual seekers to fulfill the persistent call to be of healing service to a violently separated human family. Mexico, Russia, Guatemala, Germany, Denmark, Norway, Australia, New Zealand, Canada, Scotland, Croatia, Bolivia, India, Israel, England, Ireland, South Africa, and Brazil are some of the places along the way. In addition, Jeanne and John have criss-crossed the United States many times.

The circle of this Journey for the One continues as we see it reflected in the lives of two daring individuals who are as much us as we are them.

NELDA JEAN LANE

Her Beginning

Jean Lane was the first of three children born to Perry and Catherine (Kit) Lane. (*Jean* became *Jeanne* later in life.) Jean was born while her father was at war in the Pacific as a bombardier in B-25's. Her mother recalls, "Jean was born while Perry was in New Guinea during World War Two. I had prayed for a child before he went overseas, and for a child that would sing. My prayers were answered. This is the reason Jeanne was given a 'ringing name' at birth—Nelda Jean Lane."

Perry graduated with a degree in mechanical engineering at the University of Tennessee; and after the war, the couple had two more children—Tom (four years Jean's junior), and Jill (eight years her younger sister). The Lane family had deep roots in Tennessee, and Jeanne was raised in the upper middle class of well-mannered, church (Methodist) going Southerners in Chattanooga. In 1974, Perry started Tel-A-Train, a video-based training company that became very successful. As an adult, Jean would eventually work in the company as its Human Resources Director.

Jean was a very bright, if headstrong, little girl. As her mother remembers, "When Jean enters a room, it is like a tornado has hit." Even as a child, Jean must have had that explosive, staccato laugh that she has today.

"I think I got the impression that Jean wanted to travel when she was about six years old," Kit remembers. "We were living in Chattanooga at the time. I went looking for Jean one cold, winter day, but I couldn't find her anywhere. Then, I found an open window in her room, and I knew that I was in trouble. I got in my car and started looking for her. Sure enough, on one of the busiest streets in Chattanooga, I spotted her walking along the side of the road with a knapsack on her back. When she saw me, she jumped in a ditch to hide, but I saw her and told her to get in the car, which she did, reluctantly. When we arrived home, to escape the oncoming consequences, she pretended to faint. It was very creative, but it didn't work. Actually the only thing that happened was a stern but loving talk from her father. I was just thankful to have found her." With humor, Kit adds, "Jean was quite a challenge and still is."

Jean remembers her early school years with this vignette.

"I was a real handful. Maybe it was my dimples that helped me through most of my messes. I was always being sent to the principal's office for instance (in the first and second grades) for talking too much. I became pretty good friends with the principal, and every once in a while, when another child was being disciplined as well, I proudly would comfort them because I was so 'familiar with the territory.' In the first grade, my seat was always being moved from my regular desk to the inverted trash can, where I would sit on top of the trash can to do my work, again as part of a disciplinary measure. I remember once, Mom picked me up at the school to go to the dentist. She then brought me straight back to the class itself. I was thrilled and relieved to find that the teacher had moved my seat back to my regular desk so that I wouldn't be embarrassed. It was hilarious when I think back on it, because I really did like to explore things with 'words.' I was grateful that the teachers and the principal seemed to love me and were always gentle, regardless of my garrulous mouth. And here's the thing. I was only five years old!"

There is another childhood story that the Lane family likes to tell about Jean. When she was around eight years old, her daddy brought a huge watermelon into the kitchen and plopped it down on the kitchen counter. While he and her mom were unloading groceries, little, impetuous Jean declared that the watermelon was not so huge that she couldn't carry it, and before her parents could stop her, she tried. It must have seemed like slow motion to Perry and Kit as Jean pulled the ponderous green giant off the cliff of the kitchen counter, wobbled mightily with it, and then see it slip from her small arms and explode into a "gazillion" pieces, thereby "repainting" the kitchen and everybody standing in it. Watermelons were a favorite summer treat for the Lanes, but no melon was served thereafter without reference to Jean's watermelon lifting fiasco. Jean admits that she lost her taste for watermelons throughout most of her adult life, only to have a craving return later.

In the ninth grade, while singing in the school chorus, the recognition of Jean's powerful voice came to her family, although she had already been singing in public since the sixth grade, including the adult church choir. At the age of fourteen, she was given professional voice lessons at Cadek's Conservatory of Music, having studied piano at the conservatory for several years prior. The voice teacher, a professional performer herself, told Jean, "You have a talent that can take you all the way to the top." It was a comment that was often repeated by others over the years. Jean was considered a musical prodigy, and at an early age, she was already singing arias from *Madame Butterfly*, and *Aida*.

"Her voice, of course, is a gift from God," Kit says. "And what a voice. Jean was invited to many places to sing, and I always went with her. I never tire of hearing Jean sing."

At the age of sixteen, by going to summer school, and staying on the honor roll, Jean completed high school in three years and then entered the University of Tennessee at Chattanooga. During this time Jean began to develop swelling on her vocal cords. Doctors advised that if Jean continued to sing at the high levels of performance, she would soon develop nodes on her vocal cords that would require surgery.

Jean recalls, "This was really hard for me. The doctors told me that the only way I would heal and avoid their cutting on my vocal cords was for me to go into absolute silence for several months! Can you imagine what that's like for a teenager who has just entered college? Well, knowing the consequences, I did it. I carried around a pad and pen to communicate and didn't speak a word. I look back on that time now and laugh. John says I've been making up for those months of silence ever since.

"When the time came that I could make sounds again, my family and I realized it was crucial for me to find voice teachers who could guide my voice back to strength and health, someone of the highest caliber for teaching a young voice. We wanted the best there is. And we found it at a small Methodist-affiliated college in Virginia—Emory & Henry."

Emory & Henry was noted for its exceptional music department, but the Lane family was placing its trust in Charles R. "Chick" Davis, D.M., and his wife Adrienne, to gently nurture Jean back to full vocal health. In reflection, Jeanne sees the fragile years at Emory & Henry as an important turning point in her life. Chick and Adrienne displayed amazing wisdom, talent, and foresight in mentoring Jean; and without them, Jeanne might not have been able to develop the powerful instrument of sound that she was destined to be.

In time, Jean became the featured soprano soloist for both the Concert Choir, the touring choir of the college, and the larger Oratorio Choir that gave concerts of major choral works twice a year. In casting Jean for a recording of "Concert Choir Favorites" at a 1995 reunion of former Concert Choir members, her revered professor asked Jean to sing the first movement of Giuseppe Verdi's beautiful, but difficult, *Requiem Mass* in a virtuoso solo quartet of operatic type voices.

"Of all the very fine solo voices I had during my thirty-eight years at Emory and Henry as choral director, Jean was my selection as the one soprano who could best fill this role. Indeed she did . . . in a professional manner!"

In looking back, Kit says, "Jean and I think a lot alike; in fact, I sometimes think that we have ESP. Many times we have discovered that we were thinking about the same things and each other at the same time, even though we were miles apart geographically.

"I feel that I know Jean better than anyone. She is a loving and caring person. She never misses a birthday card or a message to me on Mother's Day. Jean may have a little stubborn streak—meaning that she has a mind of her own—but I have always respected that trait."

Jean's mother may not understand the metaphysics involved in her daughter's radical life changes since 1993, but she says that it has not been difficult to accept Jean as a leader of a visionary peace movement. The strong, determined woman was evident in the child.

UP WITH PEOPLE

Jeanne's brother Tom saw a very early performance by the first Up With People cast while a student at Memphis State University, and he called his sister who had recently graduated from Emory & Henry College. He told her that he had just seen something remarkable that they should be a part of. Jeanne recalls his exact words. "I think I've found something that you've been waiting for all your life."

Jeanne and Tom traveled by bus to Aspen, Colorado to join the internationally traveling casts of Up With People. Jeanne became a member of the new Cast C, nicknamed "The Heart Cast," and Tom was placed into Cast B. Eventually, their younger sister Jill would become, at age fifteen, the youngest-ever member of an UWP cast. At one point in time Perry and Kit had their three children in separate UWP casts disbursed on performance schedules around the world. When the nighttime TV announcer spoke a common social service message of that era, Perry and Kit could only raise their eyebrows when he said, "It's 10 o'clock. Do you know where your children are?"

Up With People in 1968 was a movement whose time had come. At its peak, a budget of $30 million was needed to keep five touring performance companies on the road. Three of the casts numbered about 150 people each. In the early years, some cast members were as young as sixteen. Later, the average age of the musicians and singers was twenty-one. In addition to providing a professional-level, uplifting music performance, the young people in the casts were undergoing leadership training. In communities across the continents, Up With People company members were hosted and fed with local residents as part of the community experience. Over its active touring years, more than 20,000 students from 79 nationalities performed in 38 countries. Their appearances included the 1976 Super Bowl half-time show, the Munich Olympic Games, and the New York World's Fair. The uplifting values demonstrated in their original songs were endorsed by John Wayne, Pat Boone, Walt Disney, and world leaders at the United Nations, among others. One year, the Up With People tour was underwritten by *Reader's Digest*.

Up With People was inspired by the work of Frank Buchman and Moral Re-Armament, an organization begun as The Oxford Group in the 1930s to oppose re-militarization after WWI. Buchman asserted, "It is not military armament that the world needs but a moral re-armament." Among other accomplishments, the consciousness fostered by the Oxford Group influenced the founding of Alcoholics Anonymous in 1935. At a Moral Re-Armament Conference in 1965 on Mackinac Island, the children and grandchildren of the delegates staged a talent show, and a remarkable idea was born. Why not take the uplifting message of young people worldwide?

J. Blanton Belk, a member of Moral Re-Armament, with the organization's support, founded "Sing Out" in 1965, which became Up With People in 1967. The musical genius behind the performance groups was Herb Allen, along with musicians and songwriters Ralph, Paul, and Steve—The Colwell Brothers. Among the feature performers were The Green Glenn Singers, who included a young future Academy Award-winning actress Glenn Close. Many graduates of Up With People casts went on to significant careers, and there is today an Up With People International Alumni Association that meets for spirited reunions.

Herb Allen recalls meeting Jeanne in this way. "My first impression of Jeanne was her maturity, her command of the stage, and her performing ability. She also had that naturalness and spontaneity that was so important to our shows. I remember on occasion when Jeanne was addressing the cast before an outdoor performance. She told them to enter the stage 'with a mind of ice and a heart of fire.' Anyone who heard those words from Jeanne will never forget them."

The phrase that Jeanne used to instill confidence and passion in her cast of Up With People was taught to her by Chick and Adrienne Davis at Emory & Henry College. "I was trained by masters," Jeanne says. "They instilled the mind of ice and the heart of fire discipline in me at an early stage of my performance career. It has kept me mentally focused while allowing me to come from the heart at all times regardless of the circumstances. And this one phrase continues to support me whenever I face an audience."

Herb Allen continues. "Jeanne was obviously talented and became one of our principal vocalists. Up With People hit a chord with people in our country, and it grew dramatically. Jeanne was in the very first Cast C, our third touring company. We were riding a wave of youthful enthusiasm, and young people poured in from across the country to join us."

A Cast C member, Jeanie Barker Powell, remembers Jeanne in her expanded role as a cast vocal coach. "Jeanne was always a gal with a big heart. She wanted us to sing the best that we could. I recall her having the stage crew cut up pieces of electric cable for each of us to put in our mouths to help with enunciation. That was back in dusty Douglas, Wyoming in the summer of 1966 as we trained to be the 'cast with heart.'

"Once or twice we were in a host family together, and I recall what a difficult time we had getting the host dad of the family to come to the show. I so wanted him to hear Jeanne's beautiful voice. What a blessing to know that her voice continues to resonate.

"On my 18th birthday, we had a Taco Bell style lunch at Judy Nobles's house in Hermosa Beach, California one rainy day in January, 1967. Jeanne gave me a special little gift, some powder. It was a tender gesture that meant so much to me as a girl so far away from her home in Florida. That was typical of Jeanne's loving acts of kindness. She was even then an earth mother, a caring heart to so many. I see now that the stages of her life's work were planned long in advance. I give true thanks for the part Jeanne played in the tapestry of my life, and it is a comfort to know that her fantastic smile with dimples, her voice of clarity, and her heart for the world still shine."

It was in Up With People that Jeanne and Jim Troutner met. Jim was a very talented performer and music director for UWP. When the two were assigned to teach at Mackinac College on Mackinac Island in northern Michigan, an extension of UWP and their ideals, Jeanne and Jim fell in love. After a year teaching students from around the world in an UWP environment, Jim was called into the Army. The war in Vietnam was raging at the time. In the fall of 1969, one month before leaving for Vietnam, Jeanne and Jim were married. Their wedding took place in the small town of Humboldt, Tennessee where Jeanne's dad had grown up.

Jeanne remembers, "This was a good time in our lives, even with a war threatening us. I do remember, though, after having three short weeks of being together before being shipped out, Jim called from San Francisco, ready to board the plane leaving for "Nam." He broke into tears, one of the few times I ever heard him cry. It broke my heart. All I knew to do was to stay strong for him, write him every single day, letting him know he was loved. It was such a hard year after that—so many dying, so much pain. I lived with his parents during the time he was gone, Mom and Pop T

(Maxine and Forrest Troutner). They took such good care of me the whole time Jim was gone. And when the fateful day came that he returned, I remember the corporate office of Holiday Inn gifting us a hotel suite. Out of our marriage came two of the most glorious blessings of my life—my daughter Jenny (Jennifer Lind) and eighteen months later, my son John David. These are two old souls that have walked beside me and brought me strength and given me courage at times when I did not think I could go on.

"After an eight-year marriage with Jim, Jenny, John and I struck out on our own and had the great adventures of learning how to survive as a single-parent family, which we did with periodic and loving support of family and friends. Through it all and to this day, Jim and I have remained good friends.

"In 1983, participating in the International Conference of Laubach Literacy International in New York, I met Sven Borei. We fell in love and after a three-year relationship that brought him to Tennessee, we were married for a brief unhappy and stressful two years. I look back on the marriages and divorces of my life and realize each marriage was perfect, and each divorce was also perfect. I don't presume to understand the why and wherefores of the concept of relationship. I just know I had to stay in integrity with myself; and when the time came, it was important to me that my children not live in a tense, unhealthy environment, as my marriage to Sven had become. He was a good person. We just didn't do well together. All I know is that I was young and doing the best I could. I might do things differently now. I don't know. I do know I must have done something right, however, because both of my children have grown into these two amazing adults of whom I am deeply proud."

It was in 1989 that Jeanne and John met through the World Business Academy, an organization of business executives from around the world whose intent was to take responsibility for the direction of the planet by taking responsibility for themselves as individuals and corporations. Jeanne was Coordinator of the WBA Chapters worldwide, and John was helping the start-up of the

Washington, DC and New York Chapters. They quickly became good friends, and after three years, with John's previous marriage already coming to an end, and Jeanne's having come through divorce several years earlier, they found themselves in a relationship different from any either had previously known. It was as though all that had gone before had prepared and brought them to that point in time. On a spring day in 1993, they suddenly saw each other differently.

Jeanne says, "It was like having a veil lifted between us. Apparently each of us had been looking for someone, not realizing until that instant that the one we had been searching for was in front of us all along. We then agreed, Spirit brought us together. Spirit is now in charge."

JOHN BRADY PEHRSON

His Beginning

When a biographer with access to John Brady Pehrson's very personal journals attempts a character summation in the fewest possible words, he might well say that John was a spiritual poet trapped inside the body of a pragmatic engineer. John's father was an electrical engineer; and John, himself with an Iowa State University degree, had a more than twenty-year career as a chemical engineer with Dupont that ended on New Year's Day, 1993. The path to occupational success and then to spiritual stewardship as a Dance Chief, however, was not traveled without conflict and intense psychological pain.

John remembers his early childhood in these words.

"My mother went into the mental hospital for the first time when I was just an infant. It was a pattern that would continue throughout most of my childhood—Mom going away. My father was traveling for his job and couldn't care for my older brother or me. My brother, Russell, was sent to Iowa to be cared for by family. Good friends of my father, Bill and Mary Aspinwall, took me in. They took care of me for almost a year. I have no memory of them, but I used to get Christmas cards from them for a long time. As an infant during this initial separation, I remember feeling tremendous abandonment. But, I decided it was partly my fault. If I had just been better, if I had been bigger and stronger, my mother wouldn't have gone away. Right then, I resolved never again to be weak . . . But, I also decided that I wasn't good enough in some unfathomable way. Over the years, this was reinforced by my father's heavy hand.

"Uncle Bill and Aunt Lorena had a farm in Kentucky near McQuady. I stayed with them for a year when I was four years old, *and* Mom was again in Marlboro State Hospital (in NJ). This time, they subjected her to electric shock therapy. She came home missing half of her memory.

"While on the farm in Kentucky, I remember climbing the huge old oak tree out in front of the porch. I remember snipe hunts with older brother Russ and cousin Charlie, riding cows and falling in cow pies, getting a whipping for setting gasoline on fire, learning to fire a shotgun, drive a tractor, and getting sprayed by a skunk and having to be scrubbed with tomato juice.

"Mom read *Uncle Remus* stories to Russ and me at bedtime. We used to make Christmas cookies together. Lunches in downtown Plainfield with Mom—hamburgers and cokes, Chinese food at Leechee's.

"Dad taught me to make gravy when I was seven or eight, and I became the gravy-maker for the house.

"I was in a foster home during my kindergarten year. My foster brother beat me up on the back porch. Russ didn't defend me. It set a pattern for the future. The message was, 'Be strong. You can't rely on anyone else, not even your older brother.'

"Mom was an elementary school teacher in Iowa before she and Dad married. She taught me to read and write early. In Mrs.

Mobay's first-grade class, I was already helping other children with their penmanship.

"In second grade, the teacher had a Lassie ring. It was a reward given out once in a while to a student who'd done something noteworthy. It was given to me one weekend. I lost it in the grass in front of my house. I searched everywhere to find it with no luck. I cried for hours.

"That same year, I was a tin soldier in the school play. I remember feeling embarrassed when I had to strip to my underwear to be fitted for the costume.

"During summers, my brother Russ, the neighborhood gang and I constructed tree forts and had dirt bomb and BB gun fights. We'd also fill empty CO_2 capsules with match heads. When they were packed full, we'd stick them into a hollow pipe, light them, and shoot them off like a cannon."

John Pehrson has the classic Nordic features of a Swedish male prototype. His skin and hair are fair, his facial features are dominated by a high forehead, square jaw, noble nose, and sensitive mouth, and his body build is athletic. At age thirteen, with a "blonde bombshell" girlfriend, John temporarily lost his handsome attributes. Here are John's notes on the event.

"It was March 3, 1963. Russ drove his beautiful, two-tone 1957 Ford into a telephone pole while driving me to meet my girlfriend. The accident was the result of the hot ash of his Lucky Strike cigarette falling on the seat between his legs. It diverted his attention. The car drifted over into the telephone pole. We were only going about 25 to 30-mph, but it was enough to total the car. Russ walked away with sixty stitches in his neck just under the chin. I went through the windshield. There was blood everywhere inside the car. I must have been a mess. Dr. Ursula Weinberg, a plastic surgeon on call that day, put over 300 stitches in my forehead, nose, and eyelids (that were sliced in half without hurting my eyes). I looked like Frankenstein's monster. My girlfriend didn't want to be seen with me. She started going out with an older guy who had a car. My father and I weren't speaking at the time. But, as I lay in the hospital, he came to the room asking if I wanted to see him. So, the accident broke the ice and brought us back into a speaking relationship."

Every individual who carefully reviews their past can identify momentous forks in the pathway that directed them to the place that is today. For John, it was an event of juvenile delinquency.

"One crazy night, three of us hotwired a car right off of a used car lot and went for a joyride. As we turned right onto Route 22, a police cruiser spotted us. Suddenly, there was the wail of a siren and the flash of blue lights in the mirror. We pulled over, opened the doors, and ran for the woods. The police shot live ammo at us that went zipping by my head, and slammed into the corner of a wooden shed as I cut behind it. Two angry policemen ran after us. When we got to the woods, we hid under some leaves in a shallow gully. The cops came right up to the edge, cussing a blue streak at us. Finally, they got tired and left. It was a long walk home that night. A few days later, I was called into the principal's office in junior high school. A detective was there. As it turned out, one of us in the back seat had gotten caught that night. He'd been in trouble before and ratted us out. I had to go to court with my father. I got six months of probation. Dad and Mom had been divorced for over a year. I was living with my mother. This incident gave Dad the ammo to sue for custody and win.

"After divorcing my mother, Dad was remarried to my first step-mother, Hazel. I called her, not so affectionately, Hurricane Hazel. I didn't attend the wedding. But, after Dad won the custody case, my brother and I went to live with them. Hazel had jet-black hair, wore cats-eye glasses, smoked Salem cigarettes, and often spoke with an acerbic tone in her voice. She lived with her eighty-year-old mother and had never before been married or had children—especially kids like us. It was a bad situation. Six months later, Hazel had kicked us out of the house. To save his marriage, Dad sent us off to Bonnie Brae Farm for Boys. It was a pivotal point for me. It was

January 1965, a month before my fifteenth birthday. And I would live at Bonnie Brae until I graduated from high school in May 1968."

Bonnie Brae Farm for Boys was established in 1916 on 365 rural acres of upstate New Jersey near Bernardsville. The first Kiwanis supported cottage, a two-story Tudor brick building with basement, was occupied in 1924. Generally, the cottage housed a cottage parent and four to six boys each in four to five bedrooms. There were usually ninety boys, aged seven to eighteen in residence. They ate in a common dining hall and shared farm and domestic chores on the property while attending local public schools. If John was not a tough kid before he went to Bonnie Brae, he soon became one. Here are some of his memories.

"Pop Farrell was a relief cottage parent. He was Heavyweight Champ, Gene Tunney's sparring mate in 1926. In WWII, he was All-Hawaiian swimmer for the army. He was a tough guy that took a liking to me. When one of the boys did something wrong, instead of punishing them with 'time-out hours that had to be worked off,' he'd make them 'run for the roses.' This meant that they had to start at the door of the cottage parent's apartment, run across the living room, up the far stairs, back across the upstairs hallway, and down the near stairs. Pop would be hot on their heels, chasing them with what he called his 'bolo bat.' It was a cut down hockey stick that stung if he got you with it. Once we attempted to lock him in his apartment by setting a heavy dresser against the upstairs door. But, as we turned around, Pop came out of a hallway closet holding his bolo bat and saying with a chuckle, 'I got you now, you tricksters." He saw it as a game. We loved him.

"Mom & Pop Smith were the black cottage parents. Mom had a gospel group that was a known as *Madame Lessie Smith and her Famous Gospel Stars*. She was once a matron in a women's prison. A religious woman, she once got mad at a boy and cussed him out in no uncertain terms. She was so upset with herself that she spent the entire night on her knees in prayer.

"At Bonnie Brae I became the headwaiter in the dining room, started a newspaper, and served as a liaison between the staff and the boys. I held my own in some fist fights and was on my way to becoming 'Duke,' the toughest guy on the farm. I also learned to dance Motown-style from some of the black guys there."

In high school, John discovered his intellectual ability as well as a performing talent. He also found a partner for matrimony.

"Ridge High was in an affluent, upper middle class community. The students were, by and large, teenagers of privilege. We called them 'townies.' They thought they were better than the guys from Bonnie Brae. We knew we were tougher and more street wise. Still, the teachers assumed that the guys from Bonnie Brae were 'bad boys.' So, I had to work extra hard to earn their respect. I did it through academic and athletic excellence.

"In advanced chemistry, I conspired with the teacher to wake up a slumbering lecture class. While the teacher taught in vain, I made silver acetylide and touched some of it off with a Bunsen burner—boom! I also invented a device to precipitate particulates out of industrial smoke stacks, only to find out that my Eureka experience had been duplicated twenty years prior by a chemist named Cottrell. That was my first experience of tapping into the collective consciousness in a practical way.

"As an athlete, I played strong side tackle for Ridge High. At 175 pounds, I was quick off the line and really enjoyed banging heads as a kind of anger management activity. We had a great team but lost the championship in the mud on Thanksgiving Day to Bernardsville.

"My greatest success senior year was getting the lead in *Kiss Me Kate*, Ridge High's showcase musical event. During rehearsals, I met and danced with the choreographer, Diana Cecelia Daniels. Dee had studied dance since she was three. She had long auburn hair, hazel eyes, and a ballerina body. We fell in love. That fall, Dee went to the University of Cincinnati to study dance while I went to Iowa State, but then she tore her Achilles tendon her freshman year.

With her dance career ruined, Dee transferred to Iowa State and changed her major to elementary education. We did not live together until we married during the summer of 1971, just before our senior college year. Stepmother 'Hurricane Hazel' was sure that it would mean failure for me. She thought that Diana would get pregnant and I'd drop out of college. Actually, my grades improved until I was making Dean's List consistently."

One incident at Bonnie Brae haunted John enough to write a poem in college about it and to keep a file on Johnny Pederson his entire adult life. In John's recollection, Pederson picked a fight with him and suffered his teeth being knocked out in the fisticuffs. Later, while John was in college, the Pederson boy was killed in Vietnam. His name appears on the black marble wall at the Vietnam War Memorial in Washington, and John has touched it there.

At the same time that John was pursuing a chemical engineering degree and becoming a married student, he was already exploring his spiritual nature in Edgar Cayce meditation groups. In the early 1980s, John took the Silva Mind Control course and sat for Ross Peterson readings. Peterson, like Cayce, provided answers to questions from a trance state.

Working for Dupont meant frequent transfers for the new chemical engineer. Periods at Dacron® polyester fiber plants in Tennessee were followed by assignments in Wilmington, Delaware, at the Dupont corporate headquarters.

In Hendersonville, Tennessee, John and Dee became active in the Presbyterian Church. Dee, an elementary school teacher, managed the nursery during church service while John sang in the adult choir, directed the youth choir, played organ at the early service, and served as a church deacon. The first two of their three sons were born during these years—Ryan in 1974 and Sean in 1977. Son Alan came in 1979 after a move to Wilmington.

The equation of upward career mobility, young children, forced relocations, and social dispossession equals extreme stress in any marriage. Then, too, there is the financial corollary. As John remembers it, his style of checkbook management was a conservative pay-as-you-go, while Dee preferred a more deficit financing approach. Credit card debt was a constant negative factor in the couple's relationship.

Executive corporate life can be a jungle where survival of the fittest is practiced with extreme guile. Deceitful cunning too often wins over honest resourcefulness in the frantic competition of American business. John was a bright star with rapid advancements at Dupont. Some of his associates, however, saw his rising star as a clay pigeon on the horizon, which was an appropriate target for trapshooting. In the carpet fibers division as a business strategist, John had profit-and-loss responsibility over almost a billion dollars in sales. Before his transfer, the division netted $240 million after tax, an income record at Dupont.

In his more than twenty years at Dupont, John met mentors, friends, tyrants, and cover-your-backsides corporate politicians. One of the corporate politicians was the catalyst for his sudden departure from Dupont at the end of 1992. The dispute was over mistakes in John's expense accounts, totaling less than $120, that were turned over to an inter-company investigation board. Although exonerated of all charges of expense account fraud, John was so outraged that he demanded a separation package from Dupont, which was downsizing at the time. Although the separation package deprived John of a sizable performance bonus, there was a $5,000 education benefit which propelled him toward his destiny.

There were other events that in retrospect freed John for a life altering new direction—the deaths of his mother and brother.

"My mother died in February 1987 of heart problems. We were living in Wilmington at the time. I remember the doctor calling me on the phone from the hospital in Mason City, Iowa. They were working on Mom as he talked to me. She had lost consciousness, and they couldn't bring her back. I had to make the decision to let her go. It's not a decision that any son should have to make.

Afterward, I went into the bathroom, sat on the edge of the bathtub, and cried for a long time—something I do not do easily.

"My brother died on Thanksgiving Day in 1992—also of heart problems. He'd been living in Klemme, Iowa, a little town of about 600 people. We were living in Hockessin, DE. The local minister in Klemme found him three days later and called me. Russ died of a massive heart attack while bathing. Dad and I climbed on separate planes and met in Des Moines, Iowa to make funeral arrangements. We wound up staying a week in a little motel room in Garner, Iowa driving back and forth the six miles to Klemme in a blizzard. It turned out to be a healing time for Dad and me. I guess it was Russell's last gift to us.

"Another synchronistic event was an introduction to Magaly Rodriguez Mossman and Carol Ann Liaros by a Dupont colleague in the late eighties. Magaly and Carol Ann taught me the imaging process. Magaly called it 'light work' at the time. Later, a diverse, cross-functional group that coalesced around Magaly and Carol Ann helped change the name to 'Creative Imagery.' Carol Ann was a psychic who taught us to work with energy and to engage our psychic abilities—starting with an intensive three-day session in Minneapolis. During that period, I was also involved with the World Business Academy, an organization focused on putting spiritual values into practice to change business. The WBA is where I first met Jeanne at a New York Chapter meeting at the Open Center in Soho in 1990. We had lunch at the Spring Street Café and became friends."

By the time John left Dupont, he had formed his own learning company called Creative Change Technologies. The practical engineer part of himself was still attempting to quantify a spiritual method. With his marriage to Dee coming apart, John desperately sought answers to the eternal questions of relationship, and he used the Dupont education benefit money for a March, 1993 Community Building Workshop in Knoxville and an April ten-day

Avatar course in Tulum, Mexico. And whom should he encounter at both of these places in time but Jeanne.

What is the meaning of relationship? What is its purpose? And if relationship is the test of our philosophy, what does it mean when relationships fail, especially the intensely personal relationships of marriage? But what if relationships, all relationships, are part of the elemental process of purpose? Suppose all relationships are designed to be instructive, and that even in their complexities, they give us direction to a spiritual goal. What if we are never actually rejected by anyone, but merely redirected as spiritual purpose would have us go?

In 1993, when John and Jeanne came to realize that they had a common destiny as companions on a spiritual mission, the choice to be together was not an easy one. Jeanne was just ending a seven-year relationship, and John was married. There were five children involved—John's three sons, 19, 16, and 14, and Jeanne's daughter, 21, and son, 19. It was an intense time for everyone. For John it was particularly traumatic and emotionally painful.

"The Avatar course helped me to realize that Diana and I wanted different things out of life. We'd been on different, diverging paths for some time. I suddenly realized that the distance between us had grown so great that our marriage was at an end. I returned from Tulum to tell Diana that I no longer wanted to be married. As a result, we talked to Alan and Sean about our intention to separate but decided not to tell Ryan because it would disrupt his studies during finals. In retrospect, this was a big mistake.I began sleeping in a separate bedroom in a six-week trial separation. At the end of this period, I left.

"I picked Ryan up after the close of his freshman year at Northwestern. On the way out of Evanston, I broke the news to him about Diana and I splitting. It was a tremendous shock for him. Normally, Ryan would have loved the long drive in his favorite car—my five-speed, silver 1990 Maxima. Instead, it was a long, tense drive home that neither of us enjoyed. It took years for Ryan to forgive me.

"1993 was a year of major change and a pivotal point in my life. Ancient wisdom at some level was guiding me; but not knowing how all this change would turn out, I'm amazed that I took the leap—leaving a high-paying corporate job, leaving a 22-year-long marriage, and leaving my boys. And for what? For something totally unknown to me then. It was a cosmic leap into the void, for sure."

EGO OR DIVINE CALL

As a bright and talented child and teenager, and then as a wife and mother, Jeanne suffered an ongoing relationship dilemma. Inside, at the very heart of her beingness, she felt called to do something special, meaningful, and perhaps important with her life. That core belief in herself gave Jeanne a certain spiritual confidence that people around her misinterpreted as arrogance, as a product of an excessive ego. Over time, as her enthusiasms were put down as inappropriate to those of a proper Southern young lady, Jeanne retreated psychologically and began to doubt her own self worth. In her American generation, women were expected to cower and conform to the stereotyping of their gender and class. Women were not wanted as leaders among the religious offices of men whether they be recognized clergy or the ad hoc ministers of a New Age.

The result of these social and cultural pressures caused Jeanne to pull away from established friends and family as she gained spiritual insights. She restrained herself from talking about her spiritual path because people too familiar with her often misinterpreted her motivations. When all she wanted to do was share her discoveries, they saw her as advertising her specialness. For many, Jeanne's intensity was seen as an obsession, even a delusion. In their eyes, she had become a non-Christian spiritualist, a fanatic of the occult. They saw her as chasing an ethereal dream outside of organized religion, and thus she was to be pitied rather than taken seriously.

Who did she think that she was? Who did she think that she could become? A prophet? A healer? How dare anyone that we know so well espouse such a thing as identification with the mysterious divine. How dare those we know to raise themselves above our concepts of life and pose themselves as our instructors, let alone our models. We are offended by such posturing. We do not accept our peers to be enlightened if we have not gotten there first!

But what was Jeanne to do when throughout her life, beginning in childhood, people outside her family and peer group were recognizing a quality that radiated from her as a vibration that spiritually sensitive individuals could feel? How was she to react when strangers encountered her and told her that they perceived the finger of God on her, that they could see a divine aura around her, that she was the fulfillment of some ancient prophecy? How was she to respond? And what was she to do? How was all this identification to be fulfilled?Even Moses of the *Bible*, when spoken to directly by Jehovah, looked over his shoulder and essentially asked, "Who, me?" And soon after the "Who, me?" question comes the second obvious one. "Why me?"

Jeanne must have asked those questions in their many forms a thousand times. When great missions are presented, every leader questions their worthiness. If they did not do so, they would lack the necessary humility to deserve the role that they are destined to play. The difference between those who prevail and those who are defeated is the willingness to surrender to the assigned role, to obey intuition, and to be available wherever destiny leads. Doubts must be overcome with faith, and finally, with courage. Prophets of old were regarded as lions, not pussycats.

No one in Jeanne's family attended a ceremonial dance until the September 2005 FTOD in Graham, North Carolina.

"It is strange because I have one of the most loving and support-ive families in the world," Jeanne says. "John and I are vehicles through which the energy moves, but it is much bigger than any one or two people. Our purpose is to awaken the reality that each per-son is a master. And the ones who are coming to dance are the ones who are ready to recognize that within themselves."

There was one area where Jeanne felt totally supported—her two children. Jeanne talks about them in this way:

"Jenny and John have been the stabilizing forces in my life, par-ticularly through times when I wasn't sure I was going to make it. Even as small children, they seemed to have an understanding and wisdom about them that, to this day, continues to awe me. But I shouldn't be surprised. After all, I prayed for two old souls, a girl and a boy . . . and my prayer was answered through these two extraordi-nary beings.

"There are so many stories I can tell, but two come to mind—short ones. The first was when I was first getting divorced from their father, Jim; and at one point, the pain was too great, and I sat on the edge of my bed (at that time, in a small apartment tucked away in Lake City, Colorado) and sobbed. I cried long and hard. I then became aware that these two tiny beings—John, 2, Jenny, 4—were suddenly beside me. Jenny sat next to me and held my hand, while John stood in front of me, smiled, and said, 'We're here with you, Mommy.' My heart expanded to the size of the earth in that one precious moment.

"Another moment happened a couple of years later when I was living in West Virginia, trying to support my small family. When I received a telephone call saying that I no longer had a job, I went into sudden despair. Jenny and John asked me why I was so sad. I told them. Hours later, I got a knock on my bedroom door where I had been resting trying to get myself composed after such devastating news. These two little tykes had been scheming and had come up with what they thought was a good solution. They looked at me proudly, with sunshine glowing from their eyes, and

Jenny said, 'John and I've decided we can help. We will sell strawberries to all our neighbors and can bring in three dollars a week.'When I saw the hope in their eyes and the pride, I found myself quickly rising from the depths to embrace them both with laughter and deep, deep love."

THE WILLIS HARMAN CONNECTION

W illis Harman (1918-1997) was one of the most influential practical philosophers of his generation, and his books, and the organizations that he either founded or led, continue to be globally significant. Dr. Harman became a mentor for Jeanne when she was in her second marriage as Jeanne Borei, and much of his wisdom is reflected in her world mission of today.

Dr. Willis Harman was Emeritus Professor of Engineering-Economic Systems at Stanford University for many years. He then served as Senior Social Scientist at the Stanford Research Institute for sixteen years. In 1977, he became the President of the Institute of Noetic Sciences at the invitation of Edgar Mitchell to help in "expanding knowledge of the nature and potentials of the mind." Dr. Harman authored important books in this field of study that included *New Metaphysical Foundations of Modern Science* (1994), *Creative Work* (1990), *Global Mind Change* (1988), *Paths to Peace* (1987), and others.

Willis Harman was also a co-founder of the World Business Academy, which he introduced to Jeanne in its first year of inception. Founded in 1987, its Academy Fellows include authors Gary Zukav, Gerald Jampolsky, Gay Hendricks, Deepak Chopra, and others who contribute to the goal of "best practices within a new business paradigm through dialogues, research, publications, meetings, and networking."

Willis Harman viewed life in both its practical and spiritual aspects. "Business has become," he said, "in this last half century, the most powerful institution on the planet. The dominant institution in any society needs to take responsibility for the whole." About integrity he said, "A person with integrity is a person whose choices at a deep spiritual level are all the same, and you sense that somehow. You sense this is not a person who is divided, unsure. A person with integrity is a person that you sense there is a oneness, there is a wholeness there." When asked about the wisest thing that he knew, Dr. Harman said, quoting a Native American, "You only have to remember two things. One is, everything in the universe is alive. The other is, we are all relatives."

Jeanne talks about her experience with Willis Harman in these words.

"One day when I was in the corporate world, a flyer came across my desk that read 'Consciousness as a Causal Reality.' It was a conference that was to take place in Houston Texas. The year was 1988. I was fascinated with the title, and every fiber in me said that I was to be there. I continued on to read that a noted scientist and engineer, Willis Harman, who had just written the book *Global Mind Change*, was going to speak at the conference. I immediately went out and got the book.

"In another couple of days, I realized I wanted to meet this man. I wrote a simple letter of two sentences, asking for a meeting. In less than a week after mailing the letter, I received a phone call. It was Willis, and it was the beginning of an endearing friendship. In essence, over the next years Willis became somewhat of a mentor. It happened like this.

"I went to the conference only to find myself surrounded by some of the world's top scientists and engineers. I didn't even attempt to find Willis, as I knew he would be swamped with people and a busy schedule. As it turned out, the first day at lunch, people gathered around individual round tables (that sat six persons or more) in the dining room. I ended up at a table with two beautiful older women who were part of the Jung Institute in Houston. Suddenly one of the women looked up to see Willis coming through the main door. She threw up her hand, waved and called to him. He came over, smiling at his old friend, and quickly accepted an invitation to sit at the table with us. He sat down beside me. In that moment, I introduced myself, and we both laughed at the serendipity of our meeting.

"And so we enjoyed a conversation that included answering his many questions, particularly about my children. When he found they had an interest in space travel, he told me of the organization that he and the astronaut Edgar Mitchell had created—the Institute of Noetic Sciences. And that Noetics was presently involved in a book project that would contain photos and documented experiences of astronauts around the world who had had mystical, even spiritual, experiences that neither NASA nor any of the other world's space agencies knew what to do with. And so the Institute of Noetic Sciences decided to produce a book that contained all this wonderful information. It was called *Home Planet*. Willis said the book had not gone to print yet, but he wanted to send me the galley proofs that contained copies of all the photos so that I could give this source of inspiration to my children. In later days I found a package in the mail. It was this amazing special gift that he had promised. I will always be grateful for this kindness to my children.

"One other important thing happened at this luncheon. At one point, Willis asked if I had ever heard of the World Business Academy. When I said 'no,' he proceeded to tell me that this was an organization that he had helped to found that was new and was being made up of business executives from around the world who were concerned about the state of the planet and who were willing to take responsibility for causing change. He asked if I wanted to be part of this. When I said 'yes,' I knew then that something had just shifted for me, though I wasn't sure what.

"Over the next months and years, I had the great honor and privilege of meeting some of the world's finest and most concerned business people, as well as scholars, authors, and philosophers. One of them would become my beloved partner and husband, John Pehrson, who was a manager of a worldwide business for the Dupont Corporation in Wilmington, Delaware.

"It was also during this time that Willis and I had many conversations, often taking place over lunch, dinner, a walk along the beach, or a hike through a forest. The talks were rich with philosophy and theory. He at one point said to me, after my having shared a hypothesis with him concerning the state of perceived existence, that there were probably only eight people in the world who understood and got what I was espousing. I was humbled deeply by his praise.

"Another time, we were talking in a parking lot, when he said, 'It's as though you've prepared and are ready . . . and now, you're just waiting for the Universe to give you orders.' And then he said something that has been a theme throughout much of my later life—'keep saying yes.' I've never forgotten this. It, too, was a major teaching of Joseph Rael, Beautiful Painted Arrow.

"While I was attending a World Business Academy Conference in Ascot, England, Willis asked if I wanted to go to a luncheon where he and a handful of other scientists were meeting to discuss Crop Circles. I was flattered by the invitation and, of course, accepted, as "Crop Circles" was a subject that fascinated me. And so, sitting with these esteemed scientists around a table, listening to their ideas, I was filled with awe. It was then that Willis turned to me, with the consensus of the other scientists, and asked, 'Jeanne, what do you think the Crop Circles are?' I swallowed, took a deep breath and shared my thoughts. They listened intently and with great respect. Again, I was deeply humbled to have even been part of this gathering, much less to be asked to share my own thoughts and ideas.

In 1992 I was awarded the Willis Harman Award by the World Business Academy. This was only the second year that this prestigious award had been given. I look back in retrospect and realize that Willis Harman, just as my own parents did, empowered me to move beyond my own limitations. He believed in me and inspired me to follow a destiny that now has pulled me full force into its path."

THE CENTER FOR PEACE

I n 2005, the Center for Peace had been in Tennessee for twenty years. The genesis for the center began long before when Perry Robinson was in his second year of Presbyterian seminary.

"I got it very clearly that worship was not what this spiritual thing was all about. In fact, it was a side track and a way of avoiding engagement."

Nevertheless, Perry Robinson was ordained and served as a Presbyterian minister for eight years because, as he says, "I knew nothing else."

Frustrated with his inability to change the organized church, Perry left the pulpit for the secular world and had a fifteen-year career in automotive leasing and the management of an auto parts store. The couple had moved to California from the East Coast and had four children by then, but Perry and wife Jeanne Robinson had not given up their ministry. In California, their service took the form of foster care with three other adults. They specialized in teenagers who were considered lost to the system; and at one time in 1973, with twenty-five teens in their care, they ran the second largest foster care home in California—all the while Perry keeping his day job.

After the Vietnam War, Perry and Jeanne Robinson became one of eight sponsoring agents in California for the resettlement of refugees from Southeast Asia. They taught English and found homes and jobs for 1,500 people that included international refugee Kurds and South Americans as well as Vietnamese and Cambodians.

In 1985, Perry and Jeanne Robinson began a serious study of *A Course In Miracles*; and by the time they were through the first half of the day-by-day workbook, they knew that they were going back into a full-time spiritual ministry. They moved to Atlanta, Georgia, near their ancestral family base, and incorporated as the Society of One, which founded the Center for Peace (CFP). Perry and Jeanne would go on to teach *A Course In Miracles*, beginning in Unity churches, for sixteen years.

In Georgia, Perry Robinson began journaling as an adjunct to meditation. After a daily period of silence in a wooded setting, Perry would write what came to him as a result of stilling his mind. The process became channeled writing from a source that he recognized as beyond his mind. One message seemed clear—there is no need of a guru of any kind. And then Perry was warned with a sense of humor: Do not even apply for the job!

When earth changes became apparent to them, Perry and Jeanne Robinson looked to relocate the Center for Peace to the Southern Appalachian Mountains. A friend told them about an abandoned youth camp in the mountains east of Knoxville, Tennessee, and they were able to negotiate a lease for the 8,000-acre property. After four years, however, the remoteness of the property and the high operational expenses caused them to re-think the location. In journaling, Perry received a startling message in mid-October of 1986. The message was to move from the present site to another mountainous site and complete the move by the end of December. The short notice of the message did not reveal the new location. Their youngest daughter was seventeen at the time and in high school, so the move was complex. There were also associates of the Center for Peace to consider in the relocation.

For another four years, the Center for Peace operated its meditations and workshops from the couple's home and held gatherings at the nearby home of two associates on a beautiful rural mountain property near Seymour, Tennessee. In August of 1993, the house and property at Seymour were donated to the CFP in a newly created non-profit Tennessee corporation. By Tennessee law, the founders and board of directors cannot profit from the sale of the property; so although Perry and Jeanne moved into the headquarters house in 1995 to direct the activities of the center, they do not own anything connected with it. With a permanent center secured, board members and students of center programs relocated to homes in the vicinity, and a core group of center workers was then established.

When Perry Robinson was still in Georgia meditating at Stone Mountain in the 1980s, he had journaled that Native Americans would help the CFP in its work. Perry assumed that he would have to go in search of them. Years passed before the journal prophecy was realized; and realistically, it could not have happened before there was a place, a sacred space, for ceremony to occur that would involve a sweat lodge, an outdoor dance arbor, and a Peace-Sound Chamber.

The Native American who showed up to significantly influence the programs of the CFP was Joseph Rael, Beautiful Painted Arrow. The CFP group first learned about Joseph in October 1991, when they visited the site of a Peace-Sound Chamber at Swannanoa, North Carolina that was under construction. Chamber keeper, Zoe Bryant, had just hosted Joseph for an annual Drum Dance. Zoe told the CFP group about Joseph's visions for Peace-Sound Chambers and for vision quest ceremonial dances that were open to all people, not just Native Americans. She showed them a photo of

Joseph, and in that moment, the CFP group knew that they had to meet Joseph.

The next month Perry and Jeanne Robinson and two others associated with the CFP took off from Tennessee in a travel trailer headed for New Mexico and a personal encounter with Joseph. They met Joseph on Thanksgiving Day and did a sweat lodge ceremony with him that evening. In December, Joseph came to the CFP where he poured a sweat lodge and then dedicated a site on the property for the construction of a Peace-Sound Chamber. Joseph's visions for Peace-Sound Chambers, ceremonial sweat lodges, and vision quest dances seemed a natural extension of the spiritual practices already evolving at the CFP. With Joseph as Dance Chief, the CFP staged their first Long Dance in 1993, then a first Drum Dance in 1994, and a first Sun-Moon Dance in 1995. The experiences of the dances were life altering. Jeanne Robinson coordinated the dances and danced herself in many of them until others with experience could take over the demanding dance logistics. In a mentoring program, coordinators for the different dances were trained, and the CFP began to offer a variety of dances each year in addition to fire ceremonies, drumming, chanting and story telling, sweat lodges, and other programs designed for personal growth.

Perry Robinson says that in participating in the dances, he has had more of a visionary experience in his work with Jesus, and the presence of Jesus in his life, than he had ever had in the organized Christian church. He then realized that he was doing what he was supposed to be doing in his call to the ministry. After years of seeking, he had finally found what worked for him as a fulfilling spiritual practice, and in that, a great sense of past-life completion.

There is an anecdotal story that needs to be related about when Joseph and the CFP leaders walked the Seymour property looking for an appropriate site to build a Peace-Sound Chamber. In the woods distant from the house, the search party found an arrow sticking upright in the ground. Archery was practiced over a distant hill, but too far for an arrow to travel, much less to land and stick in a totally vertical position. The shaft of the arrow had a painted design. It was, in fact, "a beautiful painted arrow." The sign was not lost on the search party, and thus the Seymour Peace-Sound Chamber was constructed with the arrow point as its architectural center.

With the Peace-Sound Chamber completed, and the dance arbor and sweat lodge in place, this then was what Jeanne and John Pehrson found when they visited the CFP in December of 1995. What was present there would radically alter the course of their lives.

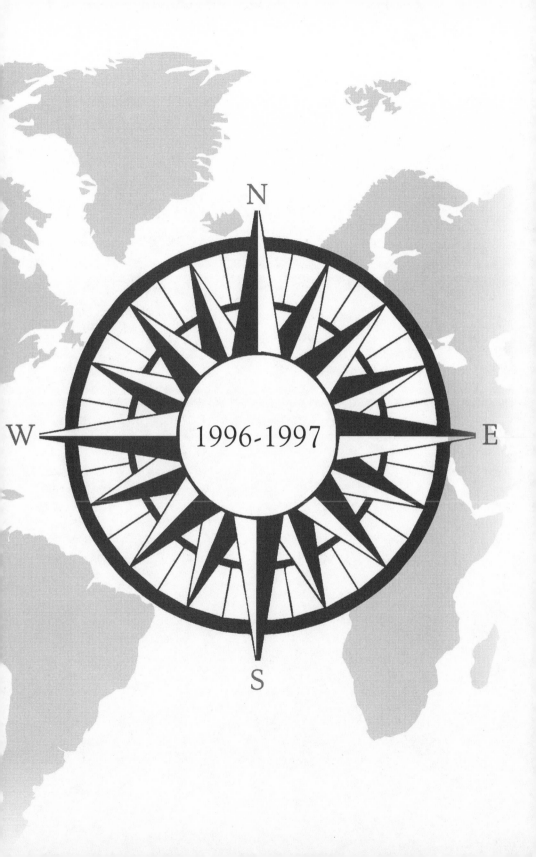

JOSEPH RAEL

Beautiful Painted Arrow

Before Joseph Rael entered their lives, Jeanne and John did not know the power of ceremonial dancing. Before Joseph, Jeanne did not have the name Jeanne White Eagle.

Joseph Rael, Beautiful Painted Arrow, is an author (seven books), artist, visionary, and master storyteller of the Ute and Picuris Pueblo American Indian traditions. He has also been called a mystic and a spiritual guru. His life and teaching has been devoted to the understanding of vibration and its role in the creation of conscious reality. In 1983, Joseph had a vision to establish Peace-Sound Chambers around the world, where people of all faiths and creeds could chant for world peace. He built the first Chamber at his home in New Mexico and then personally supervised the construction of others on distant continents.

Joseph's original Chamber was a 33 by 22-foot oval, eleven-feet high, with a flat roof. Part of the structural walls were imbedded in the ground. Many of the Chambers that came after were much larger with dome roofs. Today, there are over 70 Peace-Sound Chambers in process in such diverse places as Swannanoa and Saxapahaw, North Carolina; Sao Paulo, Brazil; St. Andria, Austria; Worcester, England; La Paz, Bolivia; Wasserkoog, Germany; Isle of Skye, Scotland; and Maldon, Australia. These Peace-Sound Chambers, as sacred places, were to become essential in the nurturing of Jeanne and John's own spiritual visions.

Another Joseph Rael vision created the Sun-Moon Dance. The Dance is not a Native American ceremony. Joseph's vision was that the Dance would be open to anyone, male or female, who sought a greater spiritual awareness and who was willing to invest the effort. The dance was thus conceived to provide "the special condition necessary for a direct experience of Spirit and of spiritual realms." In many aspects, the Sun-Moon Dance requires a physical, mental, and emotional ordeal not dissimilar to the rigorous demands of a traditional Native American vision quest. Dancers commit themselves to four days of prayerful dancing without food or water. They rest in the sheltered circle of a remote outdoor dance arbor when they are not dancing back and forth to the central tree or pole. The dance arbor is the sacred "medicine wheel" that contains and nurtures all life. The drum sounds the heartbeat. To prevent curiosity seekers and those who thought to make a gesture rather than a commitment, Joseph required dancers to commit to dance a full cycle of four dances, spread across four years.

In September of 1995, Jeanne and John were members of a six-person American team giving a Community Building Workshop in Moscow for fifty participants from former Soviet states. Jeanne had co-authored two books on community building, and John had co-authored two books on applied intuition in the workplace. They were a kind of dynamic duo as trainers and coaches in this field of conflict resolution.

One of the members of their team had a vivid dream about Jeanne that he felt compelled to tell her. The substance of the dream was that Jeanne's ancestors were calling but could not find her. The exact words were, "Bald Eagle, Bald Eagle, from the four winds, the Grandmothers and the Grandfathers are calling. The Ancestors are calling Jeanne, and they cannot find her." Jeanne considered the message significant, but she did not know how to respond to it. "I remember my eyes filled with tears, and a chill ran over me. It was a strange feeling—to know someone is looking for you, but you're not certain how to say, 'Hey, I'm over here.'"

Having just returned home from the Moscow trip, Jeanne went to the bedroom to unpack. Next to the bed was an end table full of books that she hoped to read. Unexpectedly, the books were overturned when she sat on the bed, and all but one fell to the floor. That book flipped onto the bed, and Jeanne suddenly heard the words prompted by the dream in Russia, "Your ancestors are calling." Then she read the book's title. It was *Being and Vibration* by

Joseph Rael. The book had been given to her eight months prior, but the odd occurrence of the book flipping into her awareness, coupled with hearing the dream message from Russia, caused her to begin to read it right away.

Two days later, as Jeanne was midway through the complex content of *Being and Vibration*, a friend called to catch up on their common interests. When Jeanne told her that she thought that she was being called back into work with sound, the woman told her that it was now time to meet Joseph.

Jeanne said, "Joseph who?"

Her friend answered, "Joseph Rael," at which point Jeanne sang a few bars of the *Twilight Zone* theme. Jeanne had said nothing to her friend about having just started Joseph's book nor of the colleague's prophetic dream in Russia. In Jeanne's words, "I felt something closing in on me—some huge force over which I seemed to have little control." When she told her friend she had begun to read *Being and Vibration*, they laughed about the synchronicity. Then the friend called back later that day to tell her that Joseph was going to be in Tennessee in two weeks and that Jeanne was supposed to meet him.

Jeanne and John traveled in December from their home in Chattanooga to Seymour, Tennessee to meet Joseph at the Center for Peace, founded by Perry and Jeanne Robinson. It was their first visit there, and they could not know what was in store for them. After general introductions and activities, Jeanne had her first opportunity to sit down with Joseph. She was shocked by his first words to her.

"I put the call out there. You heard. I knew you were coming."

Joseph then proceeded to tell Jeanne about his vision for the Peace-Sound Chambers, and he told her things that he had not published in his books. In his original vision, he said he had been shown that someone would appear in twelve years . . . leaving it to Jeanne to complete the thought. Their meeting took place the 12th month of the 12th year. Then he paused and asked her, "Are you beginning to remember?" Later, Joseph told her, "I am from Sirius. You are from the Pleiades. The brother and the sister have found each other."

Jeanne remembers the moment. "I had the feeling that I was waking up from a dream."

After this remarkable meeting, Jeanne felt that she would accept Joseph's invitation to go to the original Peace-Sound Chamber in Bernalillo, New Mexico for a vision quest. She made the trip in the first month of 1996. With gentle manners, Joseph prepared Jeanne for three days and nights of total fasting in the adobe Chamber.

"I'll know when you need me. You may think that you need me, but I will know when you need me."

Jeanne remembers: "The first two days and nights passed without any supernatural incidents. I had a cot to sleep on and a small wood furnace to keep from freezing. I had done a lot of praying and was aware that the lack of food and water was taking all resistance out of my body. On the third night, I was lying on the cot facing the East wall when I heard a voice. At first, I assumed that it was Joseph, but then I recognized that it was not his voice. I froze. I said to myself, Jeanne, if you have never before been still in your life, now is the time. The voice told me who I was and what I would do.

"When I opened my eyes, there was light in the Chamber. I assumed it was past dawn. I got up and began to write everything down that I had been given in the vision, including diagrams of the physics of sound and how it works through the Chamber. Then, in thanksgiving, I lit candles, said prayers, and waited for Joseph to come to end the vision quest. I waited so long that I fell asleep, and when I awoke, the Chamber was completely dark. All the candles were out. Then it hit me. The light that lit up the Chamber earlier had not been daylight. It was angelic light. Suddenly I was wide awake. Something extraordinary had taken place, something beyond my comprehension. I sat up and waited until the real dawn of morning came.

"At daylight, Joseph knocked at the door and entered with a hearty 'Congratulations.' In his hands he held a painting. It was a portrait he had painted of me receiving visions on a mountaintop. While I had been in vision, he had received my new name, a name that changed my life forever.It was Jeanne White Eagle, Seeker of Visions—Chu Pah T'ah."

The day after her vision quest, Jeanne was driving to Colorado to visit another Peace-Sound Chamber near Boulder when she ran into a blinding snowstorm. The wind-driven snow made swirling vortices on her windshield, and she prayed that the passing trucks would not run her off the road. Although the highway exits were obscure in the blizzard, Jeanne found an exit with a motel and claimed the last available room, greatly relieved to be off the road. The next morning, she opened the motel door to sunshine, blue skies, and no trace of snow on the ground. She immediately called Joseph for an explanation.

"You have been initiated," he told her. "That was eagle down, not snow."

A few days later, when Jeanne arrived at the Colorado Peace-Sound Chamber, friends were waiting to greet her. Jeanne's arrival had been heralded by the circling of an eagle over the Chamber. She was told that eagles had not been seen there for some time. Jeanne accepted the eagle fly-over as an omen that her vision quest, which began with Joseph, was complete. The fact of the eagle's presence also confirmed for Jeanne that her visionary experiences during the vision quest were real.

There is a tendency for most people to question their sanity when paranormal events occur. They wonder if the visions and voices are divine manifestations, or the hallucinations of a schizophrenic. Although Jeanne grew to accept metaphysical reality as a common occurrence in their spiritual practice and ceremonial experience, neither she nor John came to it without the doubts and fears of rational, educated adults.

"After the vision quest experience, my life took a 180-degree turn," Jeanne recalls. "The naming by Joseph prompted my mother to reveal to me the depths of my Cherokee heritage. American Indian blood ran strong in my maternal grandparents, but to avoid the stigma of an earlier age, the connection was not told to my generation. And it was not told to me until I became Jeanne White Eagle.

"During those early months, Joseph asked me, 'How fast do you want to go?'

"I answered, 'As fast as you can take me.' Perhaps it was not the smartest thing to say, but it was the wisest. I knew that I was on the fast track to somewhere; I just didn't know where.

"Joseph said he wanted me to do the dance he asks of his graduate students—the Sun-Moon Dance. The next one took place at the Center for Peace in Tennessee in July. It was now January. So prior to the Sun-Moon Dance, I was to return to New Mexico in April to participate in the walk to Chimayo.

"Chimayo is a small village in the New Mexico mountains that houses one of the oldest churches in North America. It was built atop an ancient and sacred Native American site where it is said many miracles have occurred. In Joseph's tradition, his people for many generations have made a yearly pilgrimage to Chimayo at Easter. So in April I returned to New Mexico to do this sacred walk. We began in Bernalillo outside of Albuquerque and over sixty miles from Chimayo. It was a three-day walk during which we walked twelve to fifteen miles in a day, were picked up by cars at the end of a day, returned to our homes to rest overnight, and then returned the next morning by car to the place where we left off the day before and where the new day's walk was to resume. All in all, we walked over forty miles, driving a few of the miles to meet up with an old friend of Joseph's who generously cooked breakfast for everyone on our last day.

"At one point in the walk, Joseph's knees began to bother him, as a result of an earlier injury. He stayed behind to rest, saying he would catch up. I was walking with Ben and Mary Hitchner who had flown in from New Jersey to do the trek. We had walked for some time, when I looked up to see that a couple of hundred yards down the road ahead of us was Joseph. I blinked my eyes and turned to Ben and asked, 'Isn't that Joseph?' Ben said, 'I believe it is.' No cars had passed between the time of our having left Joseph resting by the road behind us.

"Joseph had spoken more than once of bi-locating or relocating during our time with him. He said that we all know how to do this. We may not remember now, but in the event of circumstances that might demand it, we would remember. To experience this now on the Chimayo road was a powerful teaching moment . . . and fascinating.

"It was in July of 1996 that I found myself preparing to do the Sun-Moon Dance in Tennessee. And for the first time in my life, I found myself curious and interested in finding out about my own Cherokee heritage on my mother's side of the family. This happened as a result of my having chosen to go to West Tennessee to my mom's house in Martin, where I would make my ceremonial dance dresses.

"It was wonderful. My sister Jill drove down from Covington, Kentucky to help. Not wanting to be left out, my brother Tom drove up from northern Alabama to be in the middle of it all. Before long, I found myself sitting in the living room of my mom's house, looking across the room at my mom, my brother and sister, and my two aunts, Charlene and Edna. Here were my ties to my Cherokee roots.

"I had only recently learned that my great-grandfather, Grandpa Cross, had been murdered many years ago because of a home robbery. I was told that no investigation had ever been done because Grandpa Cross was Cherokee. My mom and aunts had never said anything to me, my brother, sister, or my cousins. No one knew. In these moments of that time preparing for the healing ceremonial Sun-Moon Dance, and in seeing my family's beautiful faces, I said, 'It's time to move beyond the shame. It's time to be proud of who we are and where we come from.' Since then, I've realized how much I honor my own heritage and those who are such a significant part of it.

"I had two weeks to make my dresses and my shawl. Once this was done, I left for the Center for Peace where I was to meet up with John. The four-day dance that followed, with no food, no water, dancing in my grandmother's moccasins, and wearing the shawl that carried the prayers of my ancestors, became a turning point in my life.

"Up to then, despite all my preparations, I truly didn't know where or how to begin the sacred work that I'd been shown in my January vision quest. It was here at this dance that an angel appeared in vision with the words, 'Just begin.' Joseph had said to me, 'If you wait until you're ready, you'll never be ready.'

"And so, I jumped off the cliff and found that I could fly. With the help and love of John, I found the courage to start."

During the later months of 1996, Jeanne drove the three and a half hours from Chattanooga to Seymour every other week to spend two or three days in the Peace-Sound Chamber at the Center for Peace (CFP). She refers to the time alone as a period of training by the ancestors. In effect, the days spent fasting there were a continuation of her vision quest. Jeanne's only companion during this time was a Center dog named Red Wolf. He was well recognized as a spirit-dog, and he came and went in the dance arbor and Sound Chamber as he pleased.

On the weekend of September 27th, Jeanne and John returned to the CFP for simultaneous vision quests—he in the Chamber, and she in the dance arbor. The vision quests began with a traditional hot sweat lodge of four rounds conducted by Brenda Sue Taylor as the lodge keeper. Cheryl Patterson was the fire-tender, and Wendy Patterson also served. Earlier, John had put up a tarp on the section of the arbor where Jeanne would stay, and an inflatable mattress was laid for her sleeping bag.

All that remarkable Saturday, a light rain fell, and toward evening, it turned bitter cold. Jeanne felt guided to dance sixteen paths, or spokes, honoring the four directions all day long into the early evening barefoot in the rain. Then she slept in the arbor in the sleeping bag and resumed dancing at daybreak. Mid-morning, the sun broke through the overcast. By then, Jeanne had crossed over into a visionary state.

Dancing in the arbor, Jeanne, who had fasted from food and water, at one point danced to the center tree, and she saw an old man standing next to it.

"I will never forget his face, and if I was a good artist, I could reproduce that face. His eyes were closed, which I learned later this is how the Ancient Ones appear. As I approached him, he began to sing, but the songs did not come from his lips; they came from mine. To myself, I sounded like the voice of an old man. These were songs that I had never heard before. The sounds were spontaneous, and I felt that they were ancient. When the old man stopped singing, I continued to dance and to sing my own spontaneous songs. The day passed into afternoon, and the old man was joined by some kind of a light being that might be described as an archangel. He was big and tall, and as he began to sing, the old man joined him; and to my amazement, both voices, both songs merged and began to come out of my mouth."

Up on the hill that overlooked the wide pasture where the dance arbor was constructed, two women stood on the deck of the Peace Center and heard the singing. One was Ula Rae Mynatt, a true mountain medicine woman and caretaker of a Peace-Sound Chamber in Cosby, Tennessee. The other was Wendy Patterson, daughter of Cheryl Patterson, who was a regular Peace Center ceremonial firekeeper and drum chief. Both witnesses were so drawn by the unusual singing that they came off the deck and sat closer to the arbor on a hillside. After the singing ended, Jeanne was given more intuitive information and told that she had been given the sound keys to the four directions.

A grasshopper that had attached itself to the top of the central arbor pole at the very beginning of her vision quest, and had stayed there throughout the long hours and freezing rain, was now gone. Jeanne saw it as a natural sign that her vision quest had ended. Her attention was then called to large birds circling above the arbor. Jeanne watched and counted sixteen of them. Elated, but weak from the fasting, Jeanne left the arbor and started up the hill to the Center building. Ula Rae and Wendy came running to greet her.

They called out to her, "Jeanne, are you seeing this?"

"Yeah," Jeanne answered, "sixteen buzzards."

"Those aren't buzzards," Wendy said with excitement. "Those are hawks!"

Hawks in American Indian metaphysics are considered the messengers of the Ancient Ones. The two women then led Jeanne by the hand through the house out onto the deck to see the marvelous sight. And as they watched, the sixteen hawks flew from the arbor to the house and circled above their heads.

"Then it really hit me," Jeanne recalls. "Whatever had occurred at the arbor was real. It was real!"

This seminal experience became the genesis for Jeanne's spiritual practice of spontaneous singing and ultimately for the creation of the "For the One" Dance.

During Jeanne's long hours in the arbor, John was in the Chamber having a different kind of experience. Relationship issues from his past seemed to be a black spot that went all the way through him at the heart level. Some issues extended from childhood, others related to his divorce and sons, and yet others to complicated friendships. All through the first day and night and into the morning, Red Wolf, the old German shepherd, stayed with John and gave him comfort. Brenda Sue, a gifted spiritual teacher, felt John's struggle in the Chamber and sat with him at various periods to give counsel. In the afternoon of the second day, John did a second sweat lodge alone with Brenda Sue, with Cheryl and Wendy assisting at the fire. He finally felt some of his defenses let go. He prayed intensely to receive clarity in his visions and to be instructed by the Grandmothers and Grandfathers.

Back in the Chamber, John played his cedar flute for long periods and sang the five vowel sounds as he moved ceremonially around the altar at the center of the Chamber-as-medicine wheel. Then night, perhaps the dark night of the soul, descended. John recorded what he felt in his journal.

"As it began getting dark, I sensed my death outside the Chamber. It is an experience straight out of Castaneda—the Grim Reaper waiting outside—maybe because I was totally alone. Wolf did not come to the Chamber at all on Sunday night. Brenda Sue had already gone. I felt completely alone. With death lurking outside, I also felt afraid. I'm not terribly afraid of dying. Sometimes, Lord knows, I invite it, *long* to go 'home.' But meeting Death face to face is frightening."

Although John had not eaten for forty-eight hours, and had no water for thirty-six hours, he met the challenge of death by again chanting the vowel sounds and moving around the altar in a sunwise direction. Finally, the fear of death subsided, and an exhausted John fell on his cot to sleep.

In the night, he was conscious of vivid visions. His visionary state made them seem like dreams. First, a huge brown and white eagle flew into the Chamber from the west. Eagle was one of John's spirit animals. It landed in front of him and wrapped him in its wings. Then Tiger, another animal spirit, appeared and sat down on John's left as Eagle sat on his right. Bear was also seen in the west. Feeling happy about these visitations, John tucked himself in his mummy sleeping bag and then received a further surprise. Chief Joseph of the Nez Perce appeared in full headdress and regalia carrying a peace pipe. He invited John to get up from his bed and participate in a pipe ceremony, which John did. In John's memory, his vision quest ended with the pipe ceremony. In his journal John wrote, "The aftermath (of this experience) for me is a longing for a space to be introspective."

At that time, John felt that his visions were just images appearing in his mind. He wrote, "There's the ego part of me that tends to discount these images because they didn't come draped in the fanfare that Jeanne's images do. No breakthrough. No Ancient One speaking to me or appearing before me out of the mist. Why not? Aren't I as worthy as Jeanne? I suspect that they (The Ancients) want me to deal with my ego issues first."

In spiritual work, the assignment of levels of attainment and comparisons between seekers is a mind-game to be avoided. It is the most common trap on the road to enlightenment, and yet it often makes victims of the most sincere. In the sharing of his personal story, perhaps John's greatest gift is his willingness to show the painful vulnerability of his own soul's progress.

Joseph told the members of the board at the CFP that Jeanne would teach them a new way to chant. Jeanne had sung the vowel sounds, but she had not yet evolved these sounds into spontaneous songs. As far as chants were concerned, her only exposure had been the Gregorian chants that she had heard at music college. She could sing no chants from any of the religious traditions that practiced them. Even after her magical experience in the arbor with ancient voices singing through her, Jeanne did not make the connection that she, and indeed anyone, could sing spontaneous songs of the spiritual heart. Joseph, however, felt that a new way of chanting would come through her.

Jeanne says that she did not know how to articulate the power of spontaneous singing when it came. The insights were not sequential or even tied directly to events of vision. Time, Jeanne discovered in this unfolding, is an illusion. Years sometimes passed before she understood visions that had occurred in her vision quests, but eventually the pieces came together into a wholeness that she could realize.

Looking back, it seems that life's circumstances had conspired to give Jeanne the freedom to pursue her vision. Although she and John were together by then, Jeanne had an important career as director of human resources in her father's international company, Tel-A-Train. Then in December of 1994, the company was acquired by a larger firm that already had Jeanne's position filled. She was then free to join John in the consulting company that he had started after leaving Dupont—Creative Change Technologies, Inc. Together they began to make a living giving workshops like the Community Building Workshop. This occupational change allowed the couple to make their own work schedules and thus be free to devote themselves to the long series of vision quests. Eventually, all life for them became a spiritual ceremony. Instead of setting aside hours for meditation, all acts of living became a meditation—the breathing, the walking, the shaking of hands, the hugging, everything.

"If it is honored in that way," Jeanne says, "all life is a ceremony. Then there is nothing that is mundane. Then you begin to see the purpose in everything. Even when we go through our own conflicts, our own growth edges, it is still a dance that is occurring. One moment is as sacred as any other. But it is not easy in a negative world view that asks you to your face, 'When are you going to get a real job?'"

When a son or daughter announces to a family that they have been called by God to enter the priesthood or to be a nun, and that they renounce all ambition and take a vow of poverty, the family rejoices. Yet the same dedication made outside of organized religion is considered foolhardy. If there is no organizational auspice of authority, a missionary of any stripe has no public credibility. Too often, Jeanne and John are challenged with the question, "What organization do you work for?" And when they reply that it is just the two of them, their authority is suspect in the faces of the questioners. In the worldwide atmosphere of divided religious hierarchies, it is remarkable that Jeanne and John have found so many dancers across the globe who are willing to trust their own experiences over existing dogmatic belief systems.

When Jeanne accepted the vision for the new dance, she did not know how to actualize it. First, the new dance was similar to the Sun-Moon Dance, and it would require the expensive construction of a dance arbor and a sweat lodge, as well as the full complement of a support crew. It was one thing to be a Dance Chief, but another to assemble the Moon Mothers, Sun Fathers, Elders, Drummers, Firekeepers, Dog Soldiers, and Kitchen Angels to facilitate a new dance.

Jeanne asked herself, "Who is going to show up for *me*? There were people who had been working with Joseph for years and years, and there were full-bloods in the Native American traditions who gave vision quests. Who was I to offer a new dance? For seven years, my dance vision went into gestation. I did not talk about it except one or two times with John. Then in January of 2003, I told Beautiful Painted Arrow that I had been given a vision for a new dance. I had been given every piece but the name."

Joseph said immediately, "For The One."

"And I said, 'For the One what?'

"For the One Dance."

"That April we did the first 'For The One' Dance in Graham, North Carolina near Raleigh. I was surprised so many people showed up."

Joseph once said, "If you've had a vision, and it's a true vision, once it starts to take off, all you can do is hold on for dear life."

TIME OF TERROR

October 1996

After one of the CFP dances, John had to go back to work on a consulting appointment. John went to the airport, and Jeanne was left to drive their car cross-country back to New

Mexico. She was uneasy about the circumstances and the long road trip alone.

Somewhere on I-40, between Memphis and Little Rock, crossing Arkansas on an interminable piece of highway through a seamless wooded landscape, Jeanne ran into the gully swamper of all rainstorms. The horizon on that summer day had turned black with thunder-laden clouds, and as Jeanne remembers, "Every truck that has ever been created drives all at the same time whenever I am on that road."

The rain increased in intensity from hard, to driven, to violent, and ultimately to blinding. To make the situation even worse, Jeanne was hemmed in by the specters of the behemoth speeding trucks that kept her in their convoy without the hope of seeing an exit. She, like any mortal, slowly began to panic; and then, by spiritual discipline, she began to pray. The prayer seems almost humorous, but it is pure Jeanne in its spontaneity.

"God, if you guys really exist, I really need your help now!"

Suddenly, the interior of the car imploded with a crush of angels, so many that they were contorted into comic positions like an overabundance of clowns in a miniature circus car. The vision seemed hilarious in seeing the details of the amazing beings intertwined with each other and faces pressed against the windows. But along with the comic lightness came something that took over Jeanne's hands, and a steadiness came into the steering wheel.

"I started laughing," Jeanne remembers. "I tried not to, but their images were so comical, so familiar like characters in a neighborhood café, or even truck drivers at a truck stop. They had rushed in to help me. My terror passed in the warmth of their good humor, and I did not wreck."

In retrospect, perhaps Jeanne had not been wise to leave so soon after the completion of a four-day fasting dance. Both she and John would learn that they needed time after intensive spiritual ceremonies to restore the biological equilibrium in their bodies.

There came a time at the end of her series of vision quests at the CFP that Jeanne faced what she terms "my time of terror." It occurred in October 1996.

"I told our dear friends Perry and Jeanne Robinson that I was being forced to go into the darkness and that I was afraid. I didn't know what to expect."

The Peace-Sound Chamber at the CFP is isolated in a woods beyond calling distance to the house. On this day that Jeanne felt foreboding, her usual companion Red Wolf refused to accompany her to the Chamber. The shepherd's instinct was that Jeanne needed to be alone. Jeanne was to remain alone for three days and two nights of total fasting.

Jeanne's practice in the Chamber was to ceremonially fast, sing and dance, and as she did, a wall of fire erupted to frighten her. Over a long period of hours, the fire intensified to hellfire proportions, and a face that instilled horror in Jeanne appeared. A friend had given Jeanne jars of sand for ceremonial sand painting, and Jeanne faced her fears by drawing the tormenting face with sand on the Chamber floor. There were periods of dancing followed by periods of sitting and staring at the fire in a state of complete hopelessness and defenselessness. But before nightfall, Jeanne saw another figure emerge from the fire. At first, she thought it might be an angel, but the form came complete as a white eagle, and she recognized the eagle as herself. Night came and there was total darkness in the Chamber. Jeanne did not light candles. She lay on a cot, feeling cold, but she was sweating profusely. Perhaps she fell asleep, but then she was conscious that she was frozen into a near fetal position. She could not move. She was terrified. Finally, the morning light appeared in the glass panels at the top of the Chamber dome, and Jeanne felt a kind of victory for merely surviving the night. She was able to move again; and although she did not understand the nature of her fear, she began the day with dance.

The second night began, and Jeanne went to sleep on the cot, not knowing what awaited her. Very late, something moved her to awake, and she sat up and attempted to look through the darkness, but she could see nothing. Then an intuitive voice advised her to look "at" the darkness rather than "through" it. She remembers a sense of curiosity rather than fear, and with this new point of view, she sensed an intelligence in the darkness. It was not fearful. It was rather the nature of a mother's womb; it was the kind of void from which life comes.

"I had an awakening that the dark was as much a part of us as anything else. I began to relax, and then the most beautiful songs that I had ever sung came out of me. I felt other beings around me, but it felt natural. There was nothing to be afraid of. Some kind of veil had been lifted, and I experienced darkness as I never had before. Years later, I was told by both Joseph and Don Alejandro, a Mayan priest, that I was as much a friend of the darkness as I was of the light. In 2000, Joseph would tell me that I had the ability to balance both the light and the dark, but in those first hours in the Seymour Chamber, there was more awe than practical understanding."

Nevertheless, in recent years, Jeanne has begun to question the cultural conditioning around the fear of darkness. Darkness has been demonized, but it need not be with an experience of its birthing nature. In cataclysmic times, a new teaching about the nature of darkness might remove the paralysis that precedes spiritual defeat. Jeanne sees this new teaching as a paradigm necessary for a successful human future.

On the morning of the third day, Jeanne was allowed to know the cause of her personal fear of the dark. When Jeanne's mother was at the end stages of her labor in giving birth to Jeanne, another mother needed the single doctor more, so Jeanne's mother was given a shot to delay her delivery. In essence, the infant Jeanne was trapped in the womb, perhaps with an overriding sense of being smothered in the dark as her natural birth was artificially delayed. In childhood, and even into adulthood, Jeanne had a pervasive fear of smothering in the dark. Now, finally, she was released.

At her last CFP retreat, before Jeanne and John moved to New Mexico, Jeanne went into the Chamber to give thanks to The Ancestors for her training and to say goodbye to her faithful companion Red Wolf. The old shepherd went into the Chamber with her, but when Jeanne was ready to go, the dog would not get up to leave. She tried to move him, but it seemed that he refused to see them off.

As they drove down the dirt road from the Chamber, past the dance arbor in the valley pasture, both John and Jeanne could not help from being disappointed by Red Wolf's behavior. Then when they reached the top of the hill and the paved road near the Center, Red Wolf miraculously appeared, and he began to howl—actually to sing. Jeanne rolled down the window and began to sing with him. It was a tearful parting for the humans. And although Red Wolf has now returned to the spirit world from where he came, he is missed by all whom he companioned at the CFP, and he is never forgotten.

JEANNE'S JOURNAL: 1996

This early journal is a wire bound 6 x 7 ½ inch cardboard covered book with about 100 lineless pages. Jeanne wrote on about half of these pages on both sides of the sheet in a legible hand that showed the upswings and flourishes of old school penmanship. Taped to the cover by clear tape is a bookplate that features an angel motif and the word "Journal." The entries are records of her dreams and thoughts as much as they are documentations of her experiences. Dates are usually boxed, and three penned asterisks are used to separate events or ideas. Within the pages there are a few feathers, one the striated brown feather of a hawk, and a few scattered handwritten notes to remind her to make certain entries. The journal is dog-eared and water stained on some page edges, perhaps from tears. If it were not dated, it would appear to be a hundred years old.

Jeanne records a visit to Taos Drum to select a personal hand drum for herself. The drum that she selected thrilled her with its low, deep tone, and she wrote, "The interesting thing is that the sound my drum sings is almost identical to the one John P. has." That day, the terms for renting the new house at Placitas were finalized; and when Jeanne asked if the owner would come down on the deposit due to the coming Christmas season, he cut it by half.

In the Bernalillo Chamber that week, Jeanne's Cherokee grandmother, Biggie Mama, appeared to her. "I was stunned and so surprised to see her in Bernalillo rather than in Seymour," Jeanne wrote. "She (Biggie Mama) said that she would walk right beside me for as long as I needed her because this road was not going to be an easy one. I cried!!"

As Jeanne learned to drum and to sing spontaneously, which she initially felt was a kind of channeling, she received insights that she recorded in her journal.

"Each person has his or her own unique vibration . . . song, that in effect, cannot be duplicated. Interestingly, that when I channel at present, it is primarily vowel sounds coming through. When consonants do come through, more often than not, they have effort connected to them. The vowels flow. Energy is in the vowels."

In the material world, the signs that Jeanne and John were being led continued. Needing cash, they hoped to sell their piano. It was sold to an East Indian couple who saw a photo of Sai Baba in their house and told Jeanne that they felt led to buy that particular piano. In conversation, the couple taught Jeanne a Sanskrit mantra of protection.

As Jeanne began to dance in ceremony, she thought how wonderful it would be to dance in Biggie Mama's moccasins, and that Christmas she received them as a gift from Lynn Lane, her sister-in-law. She also began to explore with Lynn's Cherokee friends the necessary steps for tribal registration.

Brenda Sue Taylor was then acting as a friend and mentor to Jeanne and John and teaching them about the dances, sweat lodge ceremonies, the sacred pipe, and other rituals associated with Joseph's spiritual practice. Brenda Sue was a highly respected Moon Mother of the Sun-Moon Dance. In early December, after Jeanne's having had a dream of the ancient Buddhist chant "Om Mani Pahdme Hum," Jeanne was guided by two Tibetan Buddhist monks to sing this chant until it taught her what she needed to learn. Brenda Sue suggested Jeanne sing the chant 109 times each day.

Jeanne had a dream soon after. "It was sometime in my future where what I'm doing and who I'm becoming gets challenged by unbelievers though it doesn't make any difference because the miracles are happening anyway, and the vibration of the earth (in part because of the Chambers) is changing anyway. My eyes are 'other worldly,' and John is walking at my side to protect and support me."

Most people do not dream about animals who take center stage in their dream consciousness. Dreams of animal spirits usually occur to native peoples, like American Indians, who have traditionally been taught the characteristics of the animals in their environment. In Jeanne's journal, she frequently reports animals who appear in her dreams, and also in visions associated with vision quest dances. This is one of the longer recorded visions that came during a Long Dance chiefed by Joseph in early December 1996.

"The Great White Eagle whom I met for the first time at the Long Dance last year, who at that time appeared out of nowhere to swoop me up in its talons to drop me into a great pack of white wolves (leaving me to the mercy of the wolves . . . my teachers, my tormentors) came once again this year. And this time to again thrust its relentless talons onto me, jerking me up from the wolves (who for one year have taught and sheltered me) to fly high into the sky over majestic mountains and lakes. It was during this flight that something wondrous happened. Being of human form, clutched in the sacred claws of the Great White Eagle, I, myself, mid-flight transformed into a white eagle almost, but not yet, fully grown.

Once fully developed, the Great White Eagle released its talons, and rather than falling (as I might have had I stayed in human form), I flew. I began to fly with my own wings, blessed with the majesty of The Great Spirit."

In the second part of the vision, Jeanne experiences another vivid animistic message.

"I found myself on the back of a giant earthworm (looked a bit like the worms out of *Dune!*) It glided along the earth's surface only to suddenly plunge into the depths. It was there that I was shown the great gashes and places of pain felt by our planet mother. Then I heard her voice crying over and over, 'Help me. Help me.' At this point I found myself in her center, and there was this amazingly beautiful glowing gold-white ember . . . a fire, though small, very much alive and waiting. And still I heard, 'Help me, help me.'"

In the third part of the vision, Jeanne returned to her eagle form.

"Suddenly, as the newly formed white eagle, I somehow appeared flying against the dome ceiling of a Sound Chamber I've not seen before. The dome itself was huge, expansive, and made of glass. I began the eagle cry, not knowing why, but driven to break through the dome. And as I flew against the dome with the vigor of newborn wings, my cry, the song of the eagle grew, became relentless, persistent, explosive . . . and then it happened."

For emphasis, Jeanne labels the climax of her vision as "Part IV."

"The huge glass dome exploded, becoming open, and where only a trickle of light had seeped through before, now great torrents of light and energy began pouring through the opening. It flooded the Chamber that then acted as a funnel, a vehicle, to send this oncoming river of light to the core of our mother earth . . . to the patiently waiting glowing ember of light, filling her once again with the fires of birth that will lead her and us back home."

Within a year of this recorded vision, Jeanne would begin to actualize it by traveling to five continents to perform Awakening

Ceremonies in domed Peace-Sound Chambers. As Jeanne White Eagle, she would burst open the limitations of any ceiling and reconnect the earth's vibration to its energy vortex. But she could not have known any of this when she wrote this prophetic vision of her own destiny in her personal journal.

Often Jeanne and John receive undeniable confirmations that their steps along the spiritual pathway are correct ones. Visiting her sister Jill two days after the White Eagle vision at the Long Dance, one of those confirmations occurred, and it became the next entry in her journal.

"Today the most amazing thing happened. Several weeks ago Jill sent an article to me about a man commissioned by Poland to paint a picture of their national bird, the White Eagle!! This creature was real several centuries ago and has since gone extinct. John Ruttner, the artist, released several prints of the original that will be presented to the Polish government in January. Today Jill and I went to get one of these prints at the Cincinnati Museum of Natural History. When they learned that my name is White Eagle, they called Mr. Ruttner, and he is making a special trip to the museum to sign the 29th print (of 300). That I'm getting this amazing painting, I, along with everyone at the museum, was deeply touched that he would do this. Jill will pick it up and bring it to me at Christmas.

"This is amazing as it has occurred within this first year of my awakening and having received this Spirit name of White Eagle from Beautiful Painted Arrow. Interestingly, the pose of Mr. Ruttner's eagle is the same as that that I received in my vision a few weeks back and put onto my banner for the Long Dance."

Jeanne was spending a lot of time in the Bernalillo Chamber by herself, and sometimes sleeping there overnight. She carried her drum and two blessed ceremonial rattles into these vision-questing sessions. One of the rattles that she had acquired on a visit to the Hopi homeland in Arizona seemed to carry male energy. The other was a Cherokee rattle made of deer hooves that carried female energy. Here is a journal entry from mid-February.

"I sang the vowel sounds in all directions and found that while facing south, my hands wanted to shake the rattles each to a separate beat. I realized that it is in the south where I may need healing; and oddly when I completed singing the circle, while turning to the south again, my hands had switched rattles, and I was holding the male rattle in my right hand. So there may be a male/female imbalance that Spirit is showing me through the Elders. I pray for balance that I may be completely healed to do this work."

Even early in her evolving, Jeanne was having insights into her later work. In February 1996, she wrote, "Each of us is a Sound Chamber, and each is to channel his or her own unique sound as well as a collective sound." On the 20th, Jeanne noted that her deceased voice teacher Adrienne Davis had come to her several times in dreams to help her vocally. Brenda Sue also advised Jeanne to start practicing as if she were to sing concerts again.

At times in the Chamber, Jeanne was amazed at her own voice. It sounded, "indigenous with a sense of also being from another world, another dimension." Jeanne found it helpful and respectful to drape a ceremonial shawl completely over her head, especially in the daylight. About the rattles, she wrote, "For a time the rattles played alone. I was being taught something . . . perhaps, in part, that their sound alone carries great power."

Jeanne began to feel powerful as her Chamber experiences intensified, but she still faced the cultural conditioning of doubt. Often she felt the oscillation of traveling back and forth between a divine centered self that communicated directly with Spirit and her self of the body with all its baggage of Jeanne, the wife, mother, and female stereotype. A journal entry gives evidence of a dichotomy that must exist for all those on the path to enlightenment. It is the ultimate question to be faced—Who am I?

"It almost felt that beings from another place were singing through me, and we were teaching the Elders. Is this presumptuous, or was this really happening? I guess I have assumed that they knew everything and were always in a teaching mode to me. Perhaps in some things we will learn from and teach each other. It's so important for me to be in no-mind when this occurs. That way this ego is a servant as it should always be!"

An interesting aspect of Jeanne's personal journal is the way in which she reports the visual presence of animal spirits. Her reaction reads like the account of a Native American or South American shaman who has dealt with such visionary creatures for a lifetime and considers them no more unusual than extra guests for tea.

"Had a long talk with Brenda Sue who helped to give me insights on what is going on with me. The fact that the Mountain Lion was pacing back and forth the whole day and night before with the White Eagle quietly watching from the upper right hand side of my head was, in part, telling me to *move*, to walk, to do something in movement to get my body strong; that I am feeling disjointed and that, in part, is because I am integrating the new gifts and info that have been given me. I'm synthesizing even down to a cellular level, letting it all come into my being and my being into it."

At the end of February, in the sweat lodge Joseph gave Jeanne a large cat claw from a mountain lion. Brenda Sue advised her to wrap the claw in red cloth wrapped within a white cloth and to sleep with it under her pillow as an aid to emotional healing. Afterwards, in the dreamtime, the large cat that Jeanne had seen pacing back and forth in the Chamber settled down and sat at her left hand while the White Eagle sat on her right.

On March 4th Owen James, the medical intuitive, told Jeanne that she had cancer cells in her blood that had not yet lodged themselves in her organs. He also identified her need for an emotional healing with regard to past and current family relationships. Although Jeanne was shocked by the sudden and unexpected cancer news, her journal entry of that day shows a remarkably insightful perspective.

"What this cancer is about, it seems, is a wakeup call for me to let go of control, become quiet, do 'nothing' and allow Spirit to work. Owen said my mind is very strong, which accounts for its being able to override those parts of me falling apart. It is now my mind that must sit down and become quiet so that the other parts of me can be empowered, leading toward a balanced me. Then, and only then, will I be able to do the sound work I'm being asked to do."

On the trip to the Yucatan the third week of March, there was an eclipse of the moon, the passing of the Hale Bopp comet, and the occurrence of a solstice. Jeanne was told by Mayan priests that she and those present—tall and blonde with blue-green eyes—were the fulfillment of ancient Mayan prophecies. Jeanne wrote, "I returned (home) with a sense of having participated in something holy and (felt) honored to be a part. What we had done had been prophesied in the Mayan calendar."

Back in New Mexico, Jeanne and others associated with Joseph took another long 48-mile walk to Chimayo. The little adobe mission church, called the Sanctuario de Chimayo shrine, is treated like the Lourdes of America. Around 1810, a local priest followed an unusual beam of light into the mountains and discovered a crucifix in a dirt hole. Although the crucifix was passed up the clergy ladder, it disappeared only to be rediscovered in the same dirt hole. In 1816, a mission church was built around the hole, and pilgrims to Chimayo found that dirt or sand from the pit had remarkable curative powers. Today 300,000 people each year visit the site, and some pilgrims crawl the last hundred yards to the church door and then to the prayer room of the sacristy where discarded crutches, braces, and thank-you plaques line the walls. The sacred sand that they remove has to be replaced each day by the dedicated priests of Sanctuario de Chimayo.

In the first stage of their Chimayo walk, Jeanne found a gold pendant with a lapis center. Joseph told her that it represented "the mother" and that something was opening up, being born. Brenda Sue said that the lapis implied communication, and the gold a controlling or focus of energy. As one of the seven semi-precious stones, the lapis also signified the coming of the Venus-Aphrodite feminine energy that portended success. Jeanne considered it a "wonderful sign."

During this period, in and out of the sweat lodge and Peace-Sound Chamber, Jeanne was confiding her dreams and visions to Joseph who commented on them. Joseph could never be characterized as being verbose. His Pueblo-Ute cultural disposition was to listen carefully and then to respond with very measured words. Although what he said was often terse, it was always concise, and if it seemed simplistic, later reflection showed that what he spoke in counseling often had several layers of meaning to be explored later.

One of the recurring images in Jeanne's visions were glyphs, symbolic figures, perhaps Mayan, that conveyed nonverbal information. In a late March vision Jeanne saw an object, triangular or pyramid shaped, lying flat on the ground. As the wind blew away the dust and sand, more and more of the glyphs were uncovered. It was the fourth time that the glyphs had appeared, and Brenda Sue assured her that it was a true sign of Divine communication. In the newspaper that day was a reported sighting of mountain lions across the street from the Placitas house. Jeanne put the news in her journal with exclamation points.

For all Jeanne's confidence in making the radical commitment to enlightenment, the specter of cancer qualified her progress. Despite the transforming experiences, which Jeanne felt were so important that she wrote, "I am not the same," her euphoria hit the wall of disease. Owen James said that the cancer was a manifestation of past life conflicts. In her journal she examined her condition with this entry.

"It's time now to release the hurtful energy, fill instead with a healing empowering energy. In effect, heal me. Not until this happens can I continue down the path to do the Chamber work.

"At present my 'life vibration' is higher than any Owen has seen except for a child. The idea now is to bring all of this body into that high vibration."

Owen taught Jeanne a method of energy focus that involved specific colors. The focus was used like radiation therapy to devour or assimilate cancer cells. The process then continued with a liquid light cleaning of the body systems and a final bathing in blue-magenta light as a kind of energy cool-down. All was done with sound and imaging, and along with diet recommendations, this energy process was Jeanne's daily self-therapy, usually begun at 3 A.M.

A common metaphor for serious spiritual work is the peeling away of the layers of one's collected fear, anger, and guilt like the peeling of an onion. At the end of this process, when the last layer is peeled away, there is nothing left except pure being, a born-again, enlightened human being. Jeanne, although blessed with great talents and personal charisma, was not spared this painful process. For her, facing the cancer, the process seemed a matter of life or death. A journal entry in mid-May reflects her struggle.

"I, in the clearing process, am dealing with anger. This morning early, I realized there is one person in my life at present that evokes anger in me. It's (she names a woman). I dealt with that in my clearing and saw two things: a demon in (*the woman*) that causes her to be cruel when I am not convinced that is her own intent, and (two), I saw Don Alejandro and how he dealt with those who meant him ill. He was *always* loving and including them in his conversations, always patient. I with the help of Spirit, will do the same with (*the woman*). My life may depend on it."

In late May, Jeanne received a "progress report" from Owen. She wrote in her journal, "that everything is going beautifully. I'm healing from cancer, and I'm stepping into a place of innocence." Owen then made some changes in her medicinal diet.

By June 14th she could write:

"These last days have been filled with healing. I have continued with my early morning ritual and have felt my body responding to it and to a midday ritual I've begun with sound (ee), crystals, and blue-magenta cloths."

At this point in her journal, there was a break, and then on October 7th Jeanne gave a brief summary of the intervening months. At the New Mexico Sun-Moon Dance, Jeanne supported several of the dancers, but she also had her own powerful vision.

"The White Eagle came and said, 'Come with me. I want to show you something.' Then he flew into a rainbow and showed me that all colors are made up of individual people. That's what creates the depth of the beauty of the rainbow. Then he showed me the human being, and he said, 'Each of you is a Sound Chamber.' At that point I felt an overwhelming sense of compassion and understanding and I got it. Each of us is a Sound Chamber, and each of us holds within us the sounds that can heal the world. I realized that I was hearing clarification of my original vision during January of 1996."

As Jeanne's personal vision emerged, she sometimes felt that she was encroaching on her mentor Joseph's territory. A July 20th entry describes how this feeling was resolved.

"After struggling with vulnerability and the need to speak with Joseph, I did indeed speak with him, saying that I felt fragile and wanted to know that what I was about to do in fulfilling my vision with the Chambers had his blessing. This was important to me as Joseph was getting ready to retire after December following his vision from the Men's Dance that he wouldn't be around. Joseph did give me his blessing, and I carry that with me now as I move into this work."

At the end of July, Jeanne danced the Sun-Moon Dance in Seymour, Tennessee, and she wrote:

"This was a powerful dance. I experienced Biggie Mama and Granpa Cross (Jeanne's Cherokee great-grandfather) dancing beside me and dancing away the pains of the Native Americans. I slept in the South gate. The White Eagle was constantly with me and the mountain lion, the eagle on my right and the lion on my left."

Although Jeanne's journals are handwritten and are erratic with regard to chronology, unlike John's, which are word-processed, voluminous, and almost academically documented, Jeanne's entries are very telling about her emotional process. The two journals thus play off of each other in both point of view and in content. For the biographer, these separate parallel documents of the couple's life together provide a depth that interviews alone cannot hope to achieve. If personal journals are anything, they are the intimate accounts of unguarded moments that provide naked truths about the individual writer.

In late November 1998, Jeanne and John attended the Gathering of the Chamber caretakers at the Peace Center in Tennessee. En route, they stopped for the night at a Cherokee motel in Oklahoma. It seemed that everywhere Jeanne went, she was undergoing spiritual process. About the motel, she wrote:

"The kundalini began to move through me. When it was done I opened my eyes to see many souls standing in front of me, mostly Cherokee. They seemed to have been waiting. Out of my mouth came loving but stern words that it is time to let go of the pain, the anger, and move into the light. After the healing, I knew why it was important to stay there."

At the Seymour gathering, Joseph, as chief, blessed and anointed Jeanne who was dressed in full white deerskin regalia. Jeanne wrote, "It was here that I truly stepped into who I am as White Eagle." The next day Jeanne sang a gift for the gathering. The group itself was then brought into the sound, and the result was "heavenly."

"It was here that the brochures were passed about and where I shared my vision. At this gathering I was launched into the mission I came to do in the first place. Brenda Sue has reminded me of what I've now given up! My life is different now."

CHERYL'S STORY

C heryl Rose Patterson did not go to the Center for Peace; the CFP came to her. Her next-door neighbor, Flora Ruth, offered the use of her home and property to Perry and Jeanne Robinson for CFP programs after they had had to give up their campground location. In 1990, Flora invited Cheryl to attend a new cycle in the study of *A Course In Miracles*. The CFP taught the *Miracles* course in annual cycles to conform to the workbook for ten years. Cheryl, at 42, had personal issues to resolve, so she joined the group. Finding a spiritual home, she began weekly meditations with CFP regulars; and within three years, she and her then husband Charles accepted roles on the CFP Board of Directors. She was thus in position to meet Joseph Rael on his initial visit to the CFP in 1992 and to take part in all dramatic growth thereafter.

At age 18, Cheryl had gone to work in a hospital and become trained as a laboratory technician. Years later, she took examinations to become federally certified and licensed. In 2005, to be available for CFP activities, Cheryl worked three part-time lab technician jobs—half-days in two doctors' offices and two nights a week job-sharing at a commercial laboratory. She is also the CFP bookkeeper. In appearance, Cheryl is a robust brunette with a welcoming smile and a gentle communicating intensity in her eyes. She is both open and articulate.

Cheryl was at the CFP when Jeanne and John came to Seymour to do their first Long Dance with Joseph. Afterwards, when Jeanne came back on the weekends to do her personal solo vision quests in the peace-sound Chamber and in the dance arbor, Cheryl and her daughter Wendy served as Jeanne's unofficial guardians and caregivers. They were there with food and water at the end of a long fast. They saw that the Chamber woodstove was lit to keep Jeanne from freezing. Cheryl was also a witness to the sixteen hawks who flew over the arbor after Jeanne had completed a three-day personal ceremony of singing and dancing the sixteen directional paths to the center pole, the genesis of the "For The One" Dance. Brenda Sue Taylor, when overseeing Jeanne's quest in the arbor and John's separate quest in the Chamber with wise counseling, stayed in Cheryl's house next door to the CFP.

When Joseph came in 1992, Cheryl says that they were all "babies" with respect to vision questing and ceremonial dancing. Perry and Jeanne Robinson had just done their first vision quest with Joseph the year before, so it was all exciting and new for associates of the CFP. "That sixteen hawks should over fly Jeanne White Eagle after dancing the sixteen paths seemed an amazing miracle at the time," Cheryl says, "but now it is ordinary to have the spirits of the land and the animals confirm what is happening here. We don't take it for granted, but we don't give it the same amount of awe now as we gave it then.

In 1998, responding to a dream where Australia aborigines came to Jeanne and pointed to glyphs on a cave wall, the Pehrsons organized a walkabout through Australia to find the glyphs. Cheryl Patterson made the trip with them, and there she found her spiritual singing voice.

"I had never had any idea of being a drummer or a singer before Australia. At that time, I was working fire, which is still one of my loves. That was my way of service—to fire tend for sweat lodges. I had no inkling that I would be given drumming to do, and to be told to go and sing for the people. When that voice came out, a voice from me that had never been there before, even people who knew me well and heard me sing, asked who was that in my direction singing. They could not believe that it was me. That voice doesn't always sing with me now, but I do call on her."

Did Cheryl and the others at the CFP have any idea that Jeanne was ramping up to become the spiritual powerhouse that she is today? "Oh God, yes," Cheryl remembers. "We didn't know how it was going to play out, but I was in awe of her at the very beginning. Her willingness to open herself to spirit and to listen to the ancestors, and to totally revamp her (and their) life, as it turned out, has been like a beacon to all of us. A lot of what has transpired in my life has not come about specifically because of Jeanne, but a lot of my confidence in being willing to take the tiny leaps has come about because of witnessing what she and John have done and participating in small ways with them in their travels. Yes, I knew it was going to be something wonderful from the beginning.

"When John first came here, I thought that he was an extremely stuffy, corporate, rigid, and tight person. We were looking at Jeanne, who has always been Jeanne with that electric personality, and we wondered how John fit in. Then I went to New Mexico to support Joseph's Sun-Moon Dance. At that time, the Sun-Moon Dance was only being given at the CFP and on Joseph's land in New Mexico. Long Dances and Drum Dances were given elsewhere, but not the Sun-Moon Dance. John and Steve Citty had just danced the Men's Sun-Moon Dance for the first time; and when I saw John in New Mexico after that dance, he was a different person. His whole posture was different. He was nothing like the Mister Stuffy that I had met before.

"I always say that John is my hero because to me he has made the greatest changes, and in some ways the greatest sacrifices, because he came from being Mr. High Corporate Muckety Muck. To give all that away to follow what originally was Jeanne's vision, not even his own, although later he has found his own, I think is amazing. John would say today that he has gained immeasurably; but at the time that he gave up his affluent lifestyle and career, he didn't know that.

"I never saw their home on Signal Mountain, but I did visit their home in Placitas, New Mexico that was an extraordinary house—absolutely gorgeous. It was on the top of a mountain with wonderful views, and its interior design was filled with wonderful objects of art. It is hard to believe that Jeanne and John gave up all of that within a year of me being there.

About the FTOD, Cheryl says: "When people go through the process of the 'For The One' Dance, and the barriers to peace are broken down, lives are changed, and peace becomes real. Maybe the vibrational energy changes DNA. I don't know, but it might be interesting for a scientist to test the DNA of the dancers before and after the dance. But the proof is only necessary for people who have never experienced the dance. The people who have had the experience don't need the scientific proof.

"My own experience of dancing the 'For The One' Dance occurred at a point in time when I was an eight year Sun-Moon dancer. I was used to taking my issues to the dance and quote 'working' on them in the process of the dance and coming out with insights. But the 'For The One' Dance worked in an entirely different way for me. I had my issues, but somehow in the process of singing and going through the dance, I never got around to 'working' on anything. And even during the course of the dance, I remember saying to myself that this was not working for me, that I miss my turkey bone whistle and the form of the Sun-Moon Dance, and that nothing was happening here. But after the dance, I became aware that what I had taken into the dance as issues were no longer issues, and I hadn't consciously done anything to change them. It was not like I got this astounding insight. It was just that the problems were no longer there in my life.

"That's why I think that the 'For The One' format takes the dancers to a different level, a level that doesn't involve the thinking mind. I think the singing is the key piece, and with the different drum beats and the participation of the elders, dog soldiers, and even the firekeepers supporting the dancers, the energy seems to come up faster than in the other dances where the dancers are more on their own."

John differentiates the Sun-Moon Dance and the "For the One" Dance in this way. The Sun-Moon Dance, a dance longer by a full day, is a "visionary" dance, whereas the "For the One" Dance is a "medicine" or healing dance. This distinction is better recognized by the dancers themselves than by observers.

THE THREAT OF DISEASE

O wen James, a well-known medical intuitive who lives in Toronto, as a student of Joseph's, was in New Mexico for ceremony. Joseph recommended that his students consult Owen for a "check-up," and Owen began to schedule appointments. John and Jeanne were last on Owen's list; and Jeanne, completing a 37-day fast of water and lemon juice, and feeling that her system was clear, said that she did not need Owen's service.

John, with his engineering background, was a self-professed medical skeptic when he met Owen James for the first time. The consultation was held in the Bernalillo Chamber, and Owen amazed John with his intuitive knowledge of John's medical history, which included everything from a recurring toothache, a previously broken left arm, to an old hernia operation.

Jeanne entered the Chamber, more in support of John, and as a courtesy to Joseph, than in anticipated need.

Owen's first words to her were, "So you're the one."

"I'm the one what?" Jeanne asked.

"You're the one with cancer."

Over the next day, Owen taught Jeanne how to support her healing process with natural herbs and food products. His intuitive knowledge of her medical history astounded her as Owen had John. Jeanne had no doubt that she was being guided correctly.

One can imagine, however, the psychological impact of being pronounced with cancer and all the negative mental mythology that the disease implies. Having been called to the self-sacrifice of full-time spiritual work, the presence of cancer must have seemed so unfair, so detrimental to Jeanne's path. Had she come this far only to have her strength sapped by disease? God is often accused of cruel jokes in the happenstances of enigmatic lives that anthropomorphize their deity. Jeanne, however, was able to see her disease as another opportunity to learn and to engage existence itself on the cellular level. If there are tests of faith, a disease like cancer tests on post-doctoral levels. It tests who and what the patients realize themselves to be.

Owen James's intensive study with Joseph Rael from 1995 to 1998 was only one set of experiences that gave him credibility with Jeanne and John. Owen had music in common with them, having a degree in music and having been a professional musician and performance coach for ten years, but, like them, Owen was driven to explore alternative ideas. In the 1970s, he studied humanistic psychotherapies at the Esalen Institute and spent four years learning Rolfing Structural Integration from the inventor herself—Dr. Ida Rolf. In an exploratory journey of more than twenty years, Owen also received certification in Transactional Analysis, Psychic Healing, Therapeutic Massage, Acupuncture, Chinese Traditional Medicine, Cranial Sacral Therapy, Visceral Therapy, Naturopathic Medicine, Homeopathy, Auricular Medicine (USA and France), and Lymph Drainage. In the 1990s, his interests evolved to studies at the Past Life Institute, Shamanic training in Peru, and his years with Joseph Rael, which led to Owen becoming a Sun-Moon Dance Chief and the builder and caretaker of the Sacred Arrow Peace-Sound Chamber, the first such Chamber dedicated in Canada.

When asked what Owen does as a medical intuitive, both Jeanne and Owen agree on the elemental importance of vibratory energy. In his consultations, Owen looks at the energy vibration states of all the major organs, the endocrine gland system, bone structures, and the patient's emotions. He says that he establishes a blueprint of the total person and then advises methods to heal the affected vibration. The methods could include projected internal color therapy, visualization or thought projection, and meditation.

Jeanne and John so trusted Owen's diagnosis of her condition that they did not feel the need to confirm it by allopathic medical means.

The house in Placitas was tucked away from other residences in a wilderness that had a view of three ranges of mountains. The house had no hard edges in design, and its kiva fireplace tied it directly to the ancestral grounds of the Pueblo Indians. It was very beautiful and very nurturing, and Jeanne felt that there was no bet-ter place for her healing from cancer. Her practice of alternative methods to healing went on for five months.

"I had come to the place where I was willing to let go of all my attachments to everyone and everything. And that included my husband, my children, my vision, and Beautiful Painted Arrow. I had to free myself from all attachments so that I could experience that there was only Spirit existing and me. Without this freedom from attachment, I was creating limitations that multiplied within me and expressed themselves as cancer cells.

"Non-attachment does not mean that we push our loved ones away. It means that all others are in a space where he or she can finally unfold without your holding anything to them, and you, in the process, are able to blossom and unfold because there is noth-ing binding you to that person or a set of circumstances. Achieving that with parents and children means that you can totally love them because you are free from past attachments, which are nothing more than mental judgments."

When people write to Jeanne about her cancer experience, she generally responds with this piece that she wrote about her healing.

"First, I've been through two experiences of cancer—one in the blood, and one in the small intestine. I learned a lot during that period. The cancer became a powerful teacher that demanded that I listen to it. What I learned was that it was a *part of me* that had forgotten that fact. It was somehow asking *me* to remember that it and I were not separate. I worked with spontaneous sounds, with colors and with imaging . . . until miracles began to happen and the cancers were transformed—both in less than five months! Their vibration literally shifted. I saw one of the cancers initially as Godzilla, who changed over a few weeks to a beautiful fluorescent lizard floating in white light, and who ultimately changed into a wondrous childlike angel to which I heard another angel say 'See, you were one of us all along.'

"*I never saw the cancer as an enemy.* Simply a teacher. I also remember sitting at the computer and hearing this small voice go through my head saying, 'How can you be about world peace if there is a war going on inside of you?' It was at that point that I saw the language I had been using, and so, rather than saying things like 'the cancer *attacking* the healthy cells' . . . *fighting* the cancer . . . my immune system *attacking* the cancer, etc., etc.—all of which is language of war and separation—I changed my language to, 'I'm going to empower my immune system to move through my body and find what is not moving at the vibration of Love and help it shift.' That took care of not only the cancer but anything else that needed clearing and healing.

"One of the things I did that was very powerful, is that everyday I went through my entire body, saying out loud, 'I thank you' to each and every part of my body—the organs (by name), the blood, the hair, the skin, the various systems (nervous system, immune system, etc.) etc. I would start with my ethereal self, moving to my astral self, and when I got to my physical body, I would go through my body step by step, piece by piece, being consciously aware of getting in touch with each part of me. It was literally like meeting old friends that I hadn't seen for years. And the odd thing was that these 'friends' are what are supporting me in this physical world, and I was clearly out of touch with that crucial element of my self.

"I changed my diet for that time to a macrobiotic one. That helped immensely.

"It's good to know, too, that cancer cells are the most active at 3:00 in the morning. Yep! And so each morning, I awoke to listen and be in 'conversation' with this radical teacher I had helped to create. This is when I was in intimate contact—conversation, if you will—with the cancer. And together we (the cancer and I) set out on a regimen that included what I talk about in the above paragraphs—primarily the sound, with exercise to bring in more oxygen into my body, bathing (lying) in water (liquid light) as I worked with the sounds, the colors, the massage, and the 'thank you' exercise.

"What I did came to me intuitively. Should you ever have to deal with a disease, what you will do will come in the same way. It is not necessarily that you should do what I did, but trust yourself enough to know you already know the path back to a body that remembers who it really is.   Of what I did, the sound provided the pathway to it all. Trust it. Trust yourself. Trust love."

MAKING THE COMMITMENT

A t the end of 1996, Jeanne felt that she had completed the phase of her spiritual training at the CFP and that she was called to relocate to New Mexico to further train in the original Peace-Sound Chamber there. During the previous year of their combined experiences at the CFP, John had earned their living as a contract resource for Ernst & Young as a sales training and executive coach in workshops around the country. Now, they agreed, it was time to sell their beautiful house on Signal Mountain in Chattanooga and follow their vision.

In the months prior to moving, Jeanne had sketched out on a marker board a picture of her ideal house. The picture of her affirmation was then posted where it could be seen every day. Jeanne had not anticipated a sudden move when she drew the picture; and when the impetus to move came, the details seemed overwhelming. How long, for example, would it take to sell the Signal Mountain house?

Within a period of less than forty-eight hours after the decision to move was made, there came a knock on their door. They opened the door to a young woman who asked the question, "You wouldn't want to sell your house, would you?" The young woman had admired their house for months and had finally taken the initiative to find out if the owners would accept an offer. Within days, the sale contract was made at a very favorable price for Jeanne and John.

As they planned the move, Jeanne and John both realized that it was time to start letting go of "stuff." There was a small garage sale, but what followed was more like a give-away in the American Indian tradition. By the end of the process, many of the accumulated treasures of their past lives had been let go—including Jeanne's prized piano. What remained fit easily into a small moving van with room for all of the household plants, too.

On the house-hunting trip to the Albuquerque area, the couple went immediately into a real estate office; and while they were waiting to talk to an agent, Jeanne found her dream house posted on the "Properties For Sale" board. The photo looked exactly like her drawing, but the couple wanted to rent, not purchase. When they explained their position, the agent seemed dumbfounded. The house in question was brand new, and it had been on the market so long that the owner had stipulated that very morning that he would now accept a lease. The house as listed included every amenity on Jeanne's wish list, except for a Jacuzzi; but when they toured the house, they found an unlisted Jacuzzi in the master suite. The do-do, do-do first notes from *The Twilight Zone* theme song is one of the ways that Jeanne and John react in humor to such events. Pure wonderment has got to make you laugh. In reflection, Jeanne says that these events of wonderment teach us about "immediate manifestation."

Jeanne ignites her explosive laugh about a spiritually seeking friend who felt called to make a similar cross-country move. Her affirmation was that Spirit provide a single room for her to stay in at the end of her journey, and so it occurred that she was miraculously provided with a cabin, a one-room cabin. The joke is that she might have affirmed for a mansion and received one.

In New Mexico, Joseph and the Peace-Sound Chamber were only fifteen minutes away from the newly leased house. Joseph opened the Chamber for their use, and Jeanne was there almost every day. Jeanne's usual practice was to be in the Chamber by four A.M. and stay until sunrise. It was another period of intense learning.

Many spiritual seekers accept the euphemism that when the student is ready, the teacher will appear. But it is difficult for some people to believe that the teacher need not be physical. In Jeanne's experience alone in the Peace-Sound Chambers, the silence of the sacred space was soon filled with many ethereal voices who taught her new songs.

In February Joseph came to bless their new home in Placitas, and he and John had a conversation. John had stayed in the background and provided support for Jeanne's work with Joseph since their meeting in December 1995. But now, with Joseph only eight miles away, John asked to become Joseph's student, too.

Joseph responded, "What are you doing tonight? We are doing a ceremony in the Chamber. Would you like to participate?"

With a simple "yes," John became Joseph's student.

"Bring your sweat clothes and a sleeping bag," Joseph instructed. "Show up around 5 P.M. We'll start with a sweat and then move into the Chamber. We'll be sleeping there. You might find it useful to have an intention for the ceremony."

In the sweat lodge with Joseph and another student, a New York City executive who had flown in for the ceremony, John prayed his written intentions: to gain the experience of enlightenment, to clear away blocks to financial well being, and to heal his anger and resentments.

In the Chamber, as the vibrations increased, John says, "the veil between this physical awareness and its much larger Source was ripped away.

"The experience was way beyond just cognitive. It was palpable and visceral in ways that are difficult or impossible to adequately describe. My whole body was involved, right down to the smallest cell or unit of conscious awareness. In this place of knowing, I also remembered why I/we came here—to seed this planet and bring it, over time, to cosmic consciousness. Joseph, Jeanne, and I (with others) all agreed to do this. It is what we do. Then we move on to other worlds and do it all over again. In fulfilling this destiny, we each have swapped roles in the tapestry of time—Adam, Avatar, priest, and disciple. Sometimes I led and sometimes I followed. No role was more important than the other. Now is the time of remembering.

"In this space beyond time, I also had the experience of knowing things immediately without an intervening process of rational or analytical thought. Throughout the night, Joseph would occasionally give me little tests. In each case, I knew the answer.

"Can you see the Being of the Chamber?" Joseph asked.

"Yes," I said. "I can see him without seeing him, in my mind's eye."

"That's the way I see, too," Joseph replied. "What does he tell you about the Chamber?"

"I responded without hesitation, "He tells me that *we* are the Chambers."

"You got it."

For the next month, John continued to have extraordinary experiences with Joseph in the sweat lodge and Chamber, and he was given visions that Jeanne was indeed an Avatar. Nevertheless, he was conscious that a full-time visionary state was not yet possible for him.

"After this all-night ceremony, I rested for several days—with the glow of being able to go back to the void, to remember and feel my Source. Since then, in the press of the everyday world, the visceral part has faded. I wish it could remain fresh forever. Maybe when one gets to the level of the fully enlightened being, he or she does so because of being able to hold this awareness of oneness in the body and the mind continuously.

"What Joseph has done for me, is to let me step briefly through the doorway and get a taste of this holy state. Now, the task is to find my way back."

———————————

In March, Jeanne and John traveled to the Yucatan in Mexico on a spiritual pilgrimage with Flordemayo and Marshall Hall. Flordemayo was born in Nicaragua but came to Brooklyn, New York at age sixteen. She is perhaps the only Mayan priestess with a Brooklyn accent, and she also has a reputation as a *curendera*, a healer. She and Marshall lived in Rio Rancho, north of Albuquerque.

The Flordemayo-led group went to Mayan sacred places for ceremonial purposes. At Dzibilchaltun, they arrived on the equinox to watch the sunrise through the eye of the pyramid. At Chitzen-Itza, in a crowd of some ten thousand people, they came to see the phenomenon of light and shadow called the "descent of the rainbow serpent." Seven triangles of light form on the side of the north stairway up the magnificent pyramid, forming the body of the serpent. The serpent's head is carved out of stone at the bottom of the stairway. The mystical light show says a great deal about Mayan culture and its capabilities as astronomers, mathematicians, and artisans.

Later, the group from New Mexico did ceremony with the Mayan Council of Elders from the Yucatan and with the Quiche Maya from Guatemala. At the end of the ceremony, each of the Maya went around the circle of participants to shake their hands and to look them in the eyes. To each they said "In Lakesh," I am you, and you are me.

If Chitzen-Itza was very solar and masculine, Uxmal was feminine. John recorded part of their Uxmal experience in these words.

"We gathered in the Temple of the Moon, where Hunbatz Men, a Mayan elder, spoke about the Mayan system of sexual education that, according to him, eliminated the need for prostitution. Inside the Temple, in the courtyard, and under a hot sun and almost cloudless sky, the women gathered in a sacred circle to do ceremony. Hunbatz Men left them to their own intuition to do a ceremony for the feminine. It was here that Jeanne had a powerful experience of channeling an old woman that came through in a chant. Her message was, '*It is now time for women to step forward and take their place!*"

John's journal entries of the Yucatan trip ends with comments on Edzna and Aké.

"Sunday, 3/23: It was at Edzna that I had my first strong visionary experience. Under the guidance of Hunbatz Men, we had just finished a ceremony integrating both feminine and masculine energies atop the pyramid there. When it was the men's turn to enter the room on top of the pyramid, I went around to a dark passageway to the left. There, I put my hand and forehead against the stones. Immediately, I saw geometric shapes. I also heard a voice say, '*So you will know beforehand, we will tell you that the old must pass away for the new to be born.*' The geometric shapes that I saw looked like the Celtic cross.

"I also saw a connection with the Great Pyramid of Giza. I saw it in a vision—glowing at the top, like it was a transmitter and receiver of some kind. According to Hunbatz Men, Edzna is the Mayan site where the Maya went to travel to anywhere they wanted. Perhaps I was picking up on this.

"At Aké the entire group did more ritual. Even before we started, I saw it as a power center—a focal point of cosmic power. I saw an energy vortex in this place that looked like a funnel, as if to step down the energy to a manageable level for this reality.

"The ritual that we performed was to snake, in a long, single line, up the steps of the sacred site to drumming and chanting of people who represented different regions of the world. There is no pyramid here. At the top of the stone stairs are large stone columns still standing to form a large structure. When we got to the top, a shaman ritually cleaned/smudged us with the smoke from some smoldering copal. Then we each knelt and prayed at an altar there. It was nice participating in the ritual but I had no strong insights."

Following the Yucatan trip to Mexico, John and Jeanne returned to the sweat lodge and Chamber in Bernalillo for further instruction from Joseph. In a ten-round sweat lodge, John continued to have visionary experiences. At one point, he saw that his hand being placed into a handprint on a rock would activate something ancient in the world or in himself. This memorable vision foreshadowed an experience that John and Jeanne would have in Australia in 1999, where they found an aboriginal handprint glyph that matched their common dream.

In John's personal visionary experiences in the sweat lodge, the Chamber, or ceremonially elsewhere, there were recurring images of encountering Joseph in previous lifetimes. Joseph was seen as the Biblical Joseph, often as Chief Joseph of the Nez Perce, and even as Jeanne's father when she appeared as an Indian princess. Early in July, John danced his first Sun-Moon Dance. The dance took place in the high New Mexico desert on the eastern side of Sandia Mountain not far from the Cibola National Forest. It was a pivotal event that would impact the rest of his life, and Joseph was at its center. John recorded it this way in his journal.

"In early July, I did the Men's Sun-Moon Dance with Joseph. It is the most difficult dance in this aspect: it doesn't have drumming and singing to accompany and energize the dancers. The men only have a hollow turkey bone whistle that they blow continually while dancing to the 'inner drummer.' There is also no outside support from dog soldiers or Moon Mothers. The men support each other, which is wonderful.

"I had a powerful experience. Imaging information prior to the dance said that the experience would have something to do with service. *A message giving insight into the primary focus for my dance: 'Success is born of the joys of service.'* And interestingly, I left the dance with an assignment from Joseph to help Steve Citty lead the Tennessee Sun-Moon dance in 1998. All of this came as a result of information Joseph received from his guides in the dance. He was told that he was to retire and give the responsibility for his dances to the dancers.

"Characteristically, Joseph acted immediately on this information. He began handing out assignments: Benito has the New Mexico Sun-Moon dances; Neal Sutton has the dance in Texas; Michael Wollard has the dance in Colorado; Steve Citty and I have the Tennessee dance, and so on.

"As dancers, we were all surprised. Shocked might be more accurate. I experienced deep grief when Joseph said he was moving back to the Southern Ute reservation by year-end (I actually cried like a baby). I even felt a little anger. After all, I had just found Joseph (again) as a teacher. How dare he leave me now! Joseph picked up on the anger by saying, 'Some of you guys are mad at me. You need to just let it go.' My grief turned into a healing experience for me that tapped back into a previous lifetime with Joseph.

"In one act (retiring), Joseph forced everyone to deal with his or her attachment to him. At the same time, he is expanding the energy behind the dances because they are no longer limited to how many he can attend each year. And, each one of us, in individual ways, is now being empowered to step into our own power, to draw upon our own spiritual guidance and inner authority. Joseph says, *'You're never ready for this work. All you can do is begin.'*

"That same month, Jeanne did a Sun-Moon Dance in Seymour. It was terribly hot and humid. We all dripped sweat. But it was a good dance, a wonderful dance. Jeanne had what she calls a 'vision of a lifetime—the most important vision she has ever had.' Joseph introduced Steve Citty and me as the new chiefs of the dance for next year. Who knows where this will lead? It's an opportunity to become all I can be, to remember all that I truly am.

"Joseph says he sees 156 dances within the next 5-10 years. Each person who is now a dancer will be leading dances in the future.

"Before we left for Tennessee, Jeanne spent about 90 minutes one-on-one with Joseph talking about the Chambers. Joseph affirmed her role, and validated her part of the vision—something that Jeanne really needed. I believe she can now move forward with greater confidence.

"Jeanne is also now 100% cured of the cancer that was in its incipient stages in her blood. She did a magnificent job of focusing on self-healing and making it work."

During the months of dealing with Jeanne's cancer, demanding and dramatic spiritual practice, and the publication of his co-authored book—*Intuitive Imagery: A Resource At Work*—John, as a father and breadwinner, had to confront what he terms "abundance issues." Here is a journal entry from August.

"I have been very busy with Ernst & Young work, flying around the country doing face-to-face coaching. Even still, we seem to continue to have a few abundance issues. We've had enough to pay the bills and pay for the Sun-Moon dances. And, we have a loan from Perry Lane, Jeanne's father to pay off. Alan needs money for a car. Ryan needs money to help support him in his new apartment. Jenny needs money for another semester of college so she can become a certified flight instructor. Money is coming in, but it goes out quickly.

"To pay our current bills, support our children when they have needs, and pay off the debt we've accumulated, we still need the next level of income. Now that Jeanne has licked the cancer, she is willing to help out. Maybe that will make the difference."

In Albuquerque one day, Jeanne and John stopped at a traffic light and observed one of those ubiquitous characters of American poverty—a man with a sign reading that he would work for food.

They looked at each other, and then John checked his wallet and counted their remaining cash—a five-dollar bill and two singles. Looking at each other a second time with knowing grins, they simultaneously said, "It's magic time" and gave the man on the roadside the five-dollar bill. Although they had half a tank of gas and food in the refrigerator at home, it was a daring extravagance given their financial status. When they got home, there was an unexpected check in the mail. They did not take the money for granted, but they did marvel at how their faith had always been rewarded with the necessities of life.

The lesson that they were learning, and one that they would ultimately teach, is that when a person gets into a place of fear, particularly around money, the thing to do is to move into a place of gratitude and give away precisely that thing that is perceived as lack. If money is the issue of insecurity, then give away money. The money is not given away as a strategy for getting more. It is rather given away in order to release whatever attachment is connected to money as the source of security and well-being.

This relationship between giving and receiving is one of life's cardinal principles. The equation is also true in the practice of forgiveness. To receive forgiveness, one must first give it. To receive compassion, one must first give it. This principal equation is also the summation of spiritual balance that is experienced in life as peace. Whatever has to be put into balance, love is the fulcrum. And everything that occurs is within the sacred circle.

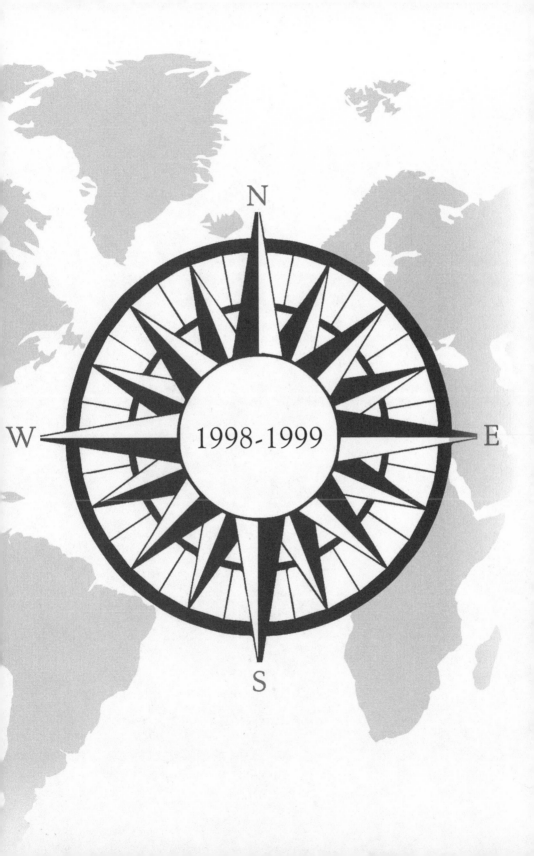

AWAKENING THE
PEACE-SOUND CHAMBERS

F or the next two years, 1998 and 1999, Jeanne and John traveled on four continents to perform Awakening (activation)
Ceremonies at sixteen Peace-Sound Chambers. If the couple
thought that frequent travel in the past had forced them to live out
of their suitcases, these next two years would set the pattern for an
almost constant travel schedule. But from where would the financial support for such travel come? The calls to go to distant places
were constant, but there were no guarantees attached to these
requests. A series of providential miracles was needed to facilitate
their mission, and in always-unexpected ways, the miracles happened. The support miracles, however, were not enough to keep the
couple out of bankruptcy, or to prevent them from homelessness at
the end of October 1998. The spiritual highs seemed compromised
by financial lows as Jeanne and John were again tested to the
extremes of their mental and physical endurance.

The ceremonial year of 1998 began in March at the place where
it all began—the Center for Peace (CFP) in Seymour, Tennessee,
where the couple had first met Joseph and first experienced the
Sun-Moon Dance. Jeanne had had many personal epiphanies in the
CFP Peace-Sound Chamber, and now gaining the maturity of her
spiritual insights, she returned to awaken and activate the Chamber
to a higher level of vibration.

The Awakening Ceremony, as it had been revealed to Jeanne,
required activity both inside and outside the Chamber. John, as the
"outside" leader, prepared very seriously for his role. He was aware
that he was to be a peace warrior, and he wore white pants and a
red ceremonial shirt that symbolized the blood of all people. One of
his responsibilities was to keep the space safe, both physically and
energy-wise. To keep what is inside, inside, and what is outside, outside. John wrote in his journal.

"Remember to use the prayer, 'only that which is from the light may enter here.' I will be protecting Jeanne and also the people by the strength of my own understanding. It has to be *me* outside. It will require great concentration and enormous energy."

To prepare for the Awakening Ceremony, all the participants first purified themselves in a sweat lodge. John made a list of what to remember as he led the lodge.

"*Sweat Lodge*:

When you pour water on the rocks in the sweat lodge, you are accepting responsibility for the souls in that lodge. Part of your responsibility is to keep people's stuff off of one another. You are responsible for the energy inside the lodge. Cornmeal circle— awareness (inside circle). Tobacco—slows energy down enough so it can be perceived (outside circle). Cornmeal trail to the fire.

Fire keeper will be responsible for energy outside of the lodge.

Part of the job is to clean up the area—energetically.

Pray for the number of rocks. The answer will come but without analyzing. Use your intuition.

Remember to use only rocks that *want* to be in ceremony.

Make tobacco and cornmeal offerings.

Use sage, cedar and sweetgrass in the lodge.

First round—7 rocks. After that, whatever you want.

Don't leave any rocks in the fire pit.

Bring in one rock first, pray, invite the Spirits in, then start.

At the end of the lodge, make sure to thank the Spirits and then release them."

John felt that it was important to have two additional people in outside Chamber support. At the Seymour Chamber awakening, it was Dennis Ogle and Steve Citty, Chief of the Tennessee Sun-Moon Dance. John was also conscious that he and Jeanne would need rest after the ceremony. He noted that water, watermelon, and watered-down juice should be provided and that Jeanne's food cravings should be honored. In the checklist, there was also an unusual caution.

"Nobody is to have physical contact with Jeanne for five (5) hours after the ceremony. Other people's touch might be painful to her, or she might hurt someone else. Her energy will be very high."

In ceremonies prior to leaving for Seymour, Jeanne had cried at the immensity of what she had been called to do. John's Guides were unequivocal in his deep visionary states as they told him, "There's no turning back now. Once committed, doors to the old life close behind you. It's like stepping through a one-way gate. You can never go back. Your life is going to change, and change rapidly now."

Those who have never extended themselves to the highest levels of human energy will find it difficult to imagine what can occur in an intensely charged ceremonial space. Jeanne and John, and spiritual practitioners across many separate cultures, accept their common experiences as dimensional shifts that transport them to a reality beyond normal sensory life. This transdimensional awareness can be both blissful as visionary learning and terrifying as an ultimate leap into vulnerability. Every traveler to this dimension is keenly aware of risks that are involved to the mind, body, and to the very soul of the exposed being. At the highest levels of intensity, there are dangers not unlike walking a wire that crosses a bottomless pit where frightful images appear as inducements to fall. The trip across the wire necessitates acquired skills and heroic courage. It is not a feat to be attempted by the unprepared or the uninitiated.

Jeanne had been guided to come into the Chamber very clean, with no lotions or oils on her skin lest the high vibrations injure her by burning. Throughout her previous visionary experiences, Jeanne felt that she was prepared for the Awakening; but after she entered the Chamber alone and the door closed behind her, she admits that she was suddenly at a loss as to how to proceed. She went to the center of the Chamber; and as she stood there, she humbly asked, "What do I do now?" A soft, gentle voice answered, "Do what you always do—sing." And so Jeanne sat down and began to sing.

She turned one by one to the four directions and sang the sounds of those directions. Beginning at just past midnight, she sang for six straight hours. The most amazing sounds came forth. Small sounds. Large sounds. And when the ceremony was over and the singing done, Jeanne discovered that she had huge blisters on the bottom of her feet. She limped from the Chamber, and John inspected her feet to see the blisters. Then Jeanne remembered. The shower water had not completely drained, and she had exited the tub after standing in the water that contained the oils from her body. It was those residue oils on the bottoms of her feet reacting to the high energy of the sounds that had caused the burns. It was a powerful lesson for Jeanne to pay strict attention to the details of ceremony and to do exactly what her intuitive guides advised.

The blistered feet caused Jeanne to recall an earlier incident where her carelessness had caused injury. It was her first visit to the Chamber at Swannanoa, one of the largest of all Chamber domes, and one that was designed and built with Joseph on site. The huge inside oval has amazing acoustics; and as soon as she, and John, and Brenda Sue Taylor entered the Chamber, Jeanne, in her enthusiasm for the sound, began to belt out a variety of loud tones. The innocence of Jeanne's powerful voice manifested a bright light that contained an angelic image. A huge being descended through the dome of the Peace-Sound Chamber and unfurled wings that easily reached twenty feet from tip to tip! Later, at supper, in sharing what each person saw, they surprised each other by independently naming the light image as the archangel Michael. By that time, Jeanne was already losing her voice, and the condition persisted until she could not speak at all. The message seemed clear. The power of the Chambers is not meant to be treated in a casual way. The high vibratory energy is to be reverently respected and used with intention.

Other physical effects of Jeanne's high vibration energy levels were experienced as violent shaking and, at times, extreme temperature changes including high fevers and incapacitating chills.

Jeanne has learned to have what she calls "body conversations" to reduce the shocks of ceremonial vibration, and John has learned how to minister to her before, during, and after elevated events to minimize her discomforts.

The second Awakening Ceremony occurred at the Hesperus, Colorado Chamber the first week of April. John's journal includes many of the preparation and ceremonial details at the Chamber named Wah Cha Chi Who.

"I was tired going into the ceremony at Hesperus. Jeanne also had experienced physical problems. Her body's temperature control was haywire. For several days prior to the ceremony, she went from freezing to burning up. When she was freezing, no amount of covers could warm her up. And when she started burning up, she felt as if her temperature was very high—103 or more. Finally, the day before the ceremony, I did energy work and massage on her for about 90 minutes. About two hours afterward, she regained control of her body temperature. That night, she had the first good sleep she'd had in days.

"Our physical condition was significant going into the ceremony for there was a lot of work to do in preparation. The Peace Chamber had become a storage facility of sorts. So to start, Keith Hagberry, Barbara Wunsch, Jeanne, and I cleared out the Chamber. We put some things into the greenhouse, the beds and tables into our tent, and the rest outside under the protection of the overhang of the house. Barbara swept out the Chamber, and Jeanne and I put up red cloth around the energy leaks, and the wood stove.

"When we were done, we dropped Jeanne off at the motel in Hesperus, and the rest of us went into Durango for lunch—Chinese food. We were late getting back to the motel.

"Keith and I hauled wood down to the sweat lodge by the river. We cleared out the rocks from the old lodge, repaired the lodge as best we could, and smudged it to clear old energy. I also put cornmeal and tobacco in the center pit, and did cornmeal and tobacco circles around the lodge and firepit. We picked out 25 rocks for the evening sweat, and built the fire. We started the fire at almost 6 P.M and had a difficult time getting the piñon pine lit. We had to start it using a pile of brush for kindling. Once it did start, it singed my hair.

"Jeanne and Barbara showed up at about 6:45 P.M. We didn't actually start the lodge until about 7:30 P.M. As it turned out, it was a very powerful lodge. Barbara even said it was *the most powerful* sweat lodge she'd ever been in. I think it was, at least in part, because of the power of our focused intent. All four of us were very focused on the upcoming ceremony, and prayers for the people. The spirits were very present. Barbara actually became Buddha for a time. And during the fifth round, the blessing round, a dimensional gate began to form right there in the lodge. I saw it happen. It was as if the work of the ceremony had already begun.

"Barbara and I returned to the Chamber at about 11:15 P.M and started a sacred fire. It was a powerful ceremony. I have been drawn to combine the cornmeal and tobacco of the American Indians with the granulated sugar from the Mayan tradition. We built it on the close of the Mayan day of 'Kej.' Interestingly, the medicine wheel with the circles in each of the four quadrants also is the symbol for the day, the sign of the deer. Earlier in the day, a deer ran across our path. Then, when we first got to the property, Jeanne saw six deer. Kej is the day of the deer. It was a fortuitous sign.

"Hesperus has a powerful, raw energy. Perhaps this is partly because of its location on the Ute reservation. Joseph says the land has a lot to do with the power of a place. And Wah Cha Chi Who is on rugged land. When the ceremony began, and after Barbara had done the cornmeal circle, and I had done the tobacco circle, all the spirits of the land began to come out. Some were positive energy. Many were not. I had my hands full keeping "dark" energies from entering the Chamber.

"For almost the first 1½-2 hours, Jeanne's chants were about clearing. Ancestors had gathered in the Chamber and were singing through her. There was a tremendous amount of grief and pain that was being released. I finally remembered that I'd gotten the insight before the ceremony to lay down a cornmeal line from the Chamber to the fire, which was directly east of the door. I'd forgotten to do it. As soon as I did, a rush of energy came from the Chamber strong enough to push a log forward. The fire fell to the east, and the energy shifted. Jeanne's chants, almost immediately, shifted into 'energy building.'

"My experience of Wah Cha Chi Who Chamber is that it was already partly, but not fully, open. The passage or gateway extended upward from the center and then to the northeast. As Jeanne continued her chanting, a vortex of energy built to the extent that the entire Chamber began to phase between this dimension in time and others. Finally, energy shot up through the 'gateway' and outward to the northeast—widening the inter-dimensional doorway. Later that day, when we returned for the celebration ceremony, we found that a wall in Joseph's bedroom, in the northeast corner of the house, had cracked. Was this a result of the ceremony? It did seem more than coincidence.

"From that experience I got a couple of insights. First, one way that the Chambers will help create world peace is through healing things from other times. Joseph's Chambers, and therefore all Chambers in principle, are multi-temporal and multi-dimensional. So, the healing and clearing work also takes place across multiple times and dimensions. Jeanne's experience on the inside was that the entire Chamber began to turn as the vortex formed, rotating counter-clockwise, sending energy outward."

It snowed, on and off, throughout the entire ceremony. Jeanne had entered the Chamber at midnight while the three others kept their vigil outside. John understood that he had to be willing to lose Jeanne physically in the ceremonial process, but at the same time, that he was her lifeline to the outside world. He noted this new understanding in his journal.

"At the end of the ceremony, she was actually gone from her body for a time. I had to go 'get' her. So, in a very real sense, I am her lifeline because I am anchored in one time, and one dimension, while she phases in and out of several times and dimensions. By extension, the purpose of the people listening outside the Chambers is to also be this kind of lifeline. As the Chambers develop in their power, people will need to pay attention to the reason that some people must be on the outside listening."

Jeanne stopped singing at 3:15 A.M. and came out of the Chamber at 3:40 A.M. The next day, in the early afternoon following Jeanne's recovery, the four ceremony participants returned to the Chamber to replace the beds and tables, take down the tent, fill in the firepit, and to celebrate. John noted the celebration experience.

"During the celebration, we honored the eight directions by taking turns singing in that direction. Jeanne started as Barbara, Keith, and I filled in the background. Then we took turns being the lead, and sending our vibrations into the Chamber, and out into the world. It was a beautiful experience for all of us.

"The ceremony seems important for several reasons. First, it is a way to say thank you to the Chamber and the being/spirits of the Chamber. Second, each of us receives a blessing from the Chamber because it is now fully activated. Third, we send our energy out to the world through the inter-dimensional gateway, thereby helping to heal the world and create peace."

The third Awakening Ceremony occurred at the Bernalillo Chamber, named Red Eagle Mountain Spirit, in New Mexico on Easter Day. Here is a partial account from John's journal.

"Bernalillo was again different than either Hesperus or Seymour. It was much gentler than Hesperus. Jeanne entered the Chamber at midnight on Easter and came out at 3:15AM. Participants included: Jeanne, myself, Barbara Wunsch, Keith

Hagberry, Melinda Campbell, John Stroupe, Almut Stamer, Marcus Clark, Gail Homan, and Karuna, a local Bernalillo woman.

"John Stroupe and I lit the sweat lodge fire around 5 P.M. It was dry and very windy. The fire took off quickly with only a little bit of paper, and then burned ferociously. As a result, the rocks were cherry red by the time we entered the lodge at almost 7:30 P.M.

"Prior to the lodge, Jeanne and I had a short, fifteen minute meeting with everybody. Jeanne briefly recounted the story of her vision, and we discussed the sweat lodge. Then, we gave an overview of the sacred ceremony that would take place in and around the Chamber starting at midnight.

"I poured water for the sweat lodge. A sacred number of ten people (including Jeanne and me) participated in the sweat, and all returned for the vigil during the Chamber ceremony.

"The sweat went very well, although it was more difficult than the small, four-person sweat at Hesperus. At Hesperus, everyone was very focused on the ceremony and prayers for the people. In Bernalillo, several of the people who participated were in personal pain and prayed mostly for personal transformation. We're all one person, so it's all good stuff, but the focus wasn't quite as clear. And I found myself working with the energy to clear the lodge of the 'pain' so we could go on. We did five rounds—four rounds for everybody, the fifth round for John Stroupe and Melinda . . . to bless them into their new roles as 'caretakers' of the Chamber.

"Two things happened as 'signs' prior to the sweat lodge and ceremony. Late morning of the 11th, we took a drive part way up the back of Sandia Mountain. An eagle hovered high above the car. And then, on the drive to the Chamber, a snake crawled across the road in front of the car. I managed to just straddle its length with the wheels. Since Jeanne is born *Kan*, on the Mayan calendar, these are significant. Kulkulkan is the rainbow-feathered serpent. So she is both serpent and eagle. Nature was recognizing this by sending her spirit animals. We took them as acknowledgments of the power of the upcoming ceremony.

"As with the Hesperus Chamber, there was some 'clearing work' that Jeanne did in the Chamber during the first hour or so. And again, I put down a cornmeal line from the Chamber to the fire. Almost immediately (within a couple of minutes) the energy shifted. Dogs that had been going crazy, calmed down, and Jeanne's song changed into 'energy building' instead of 'clearing.'

"My experience of this Chamber was that it was already completely 'open.' The ceremony was more about (a) hooking it up on an intergalactic basis, and (b) about Jeanne and I receiving our power.

"A vortex of energy did form, but it rotated in a clockwise direction and brought energy *into* the Chamber and the earth. This was opposite in direction to what occurred at Wah Cha Chi Who (Hesperus, CO).

Shortly before the ceremony ended, I 'saw' Jeanne through the wall of the Chamber being anointed by Jesus, assisted by a couple of other Masters. They put a white raiment around her, and a crown on her head. It was a blessing to do the work, an induction into the role, a receiving of her full power. Just afterwards, Jesus walked through the wall of the Chamber and did the same thing to me . . . I was in tears. The radiance of the white light that surrounded him was almost blinding. Yet it infused me with a sense of bliss so powerful as to be beyond description.

"Easter Sunday afternoon, at around 2:30 P.M, Jeanne blessed John and Melinda in the Chamber into their new roles as caretakers of the Bernalillo Chamber. John began shivering as energy rushed through him as Jeanne blew the sacred breath into his crown chakra.

"Everybody involved in the vigil returned to the Chamber at 3 P.M for a celebration. It is a time for all to receive a blessing from the Chamber, and to celebrate with the spirit beings gathered there. Jeanne began by chanting spontaneously with everyone else filling in a background. Each person took a turn in the middle of the

Chamber while the rest were gathered around in the four directions. The person in the middle chanted to add their personal sound to the Chamber. And as with Jeanne, the rest of us spontaneously created a symphony of sound in support of that person. I noted that being in the middle was very 'hot.' I began to sweat from all the energy. What I got was that the person in the middle received the energy from everyone and became a focal point to send this energy out to the world."

When John's very personal journal is quoted by the biographer, it must be realized that no one, including Jeanne, has heretofore been privy to its contents. The journal entries since 1993 were made on computer word processors; and by 2005, they comprised more than 1,200 pages of text averaging about 700 words, or a total of more than 800,000 words—the length of about eight books.

John had not only been diligent in documenting the details of his journey with Jeanne, but he had also poured onto the pages of the journal the full range of his emotions, including his dream life and his most persistent doubts and fears, in a manner that he obviously never expected to be seen by others. His release of the journal to the biographer was an act of unusual trust and courage. Who among us would expose our most intimate thoughts and experiences over a period of more than ten years to anyone for public attribution?

When the biographer reads that John saw Jesus through a Chamber wall anointing Jeanne, what is he to report? When the author reads John's confidential entries throughout his spiritual training that he has encountered ancient ancestors, medicine people, avatars, ascended Masters, angels, extra-terrestrial beings and historic and known spiritual personalities like White Buffalo Calf Woman, St. X'mon (Mayan), Buddha, Sai Baba, Chief Joseph of the Nez Perce, archangel Michael, and others, how is the rational mind to respond? And what about the journal entries of unusual natural phenomena—the flight of sixteen hawks over Jeanne as she completes a significant vision quest, the appearance of eagles, and snakes, and deer as propitious animal signs, and changes in weather that seem to respond to the spiritual states of human beings? How should the biographer relate these paranormal events to intelligent readers and expect scholarly credibility? But then, how can the biographer not include this testimonial material when the subjects have been so nakedly forthcoming? How can we deny them the expression of what they have so courageously earned?

THE GERMANY CHAMBER AWAKENING

Extensive travel can be both tedious and tiring. The abrupt shifts of time zones, temperature, and humidity confuse the biological clock and make any bed a welcome retreat. The fatigue of travel, however, is more than physical. It is mentally disassociative as in, "If this is Saturday, it must be Grossropperhausen, Germany."

John awoke the first few days in the small rural German town feeling that he had been drugged. The crisp dry air of the high Colorado mountains had been replaced by the high humidity of early June in the German countryside. Their hosts, Alex and Shania Racky, were Sun-Moon Dancers who lived in Grossropperhausen, which is about two hours northwest of Frankfurt. Both hosts were vegetarians, so the meals in their home were mainly from the garden. John babysat their brown-eyed little pixie two-year-old daughter Muriel one morning so that the parents could attend Jeanne's workshop on spontaneous sound.

John recorded these location details in his journal.

"The Peace-Sound Chamber here is about a quarter of a mile away. It stands on 0.8 acres of land that Shania and Alex own. They have a garden on the land, and two tiny guesthouses. The Peace-Sound Chamber and sweat lodge are on one corner of the land, the garden and guesthouses directly across. The land seems enchanted, with fairies and little people around. Almost immediately upon entering the land on Wednesday to greet the Spirit of the Chamber, Jeanne found a large four-leaf clover. She returned and gave two pieces of rose quartz as an offering for the find. And blam! She found a second four-leaf clover. It was as if the 'little people' were giving back one for one.

"The Peace-Sound Chamber itself is quite small, although Joseph once squeezed 40 people inside! It was built in 1993-1994. Its walls are almost totally below ground on all sides excepting the entrance. The roof is above ground and shaped like a pyramid.

"I am impressed with the relative simplicity yet abundance in which Alex and Shania live. The household generates less garbage than we do. The refrigerator is about half the size of an American one. Most items are bought fresh and consumed almost immediately. The garden supplements what is purchased—especially with lettuce, tomatoes, zucchini squash and peppers. There are other interesting differences. Mayonnaise comes in a tube! There are vegetable spreads that are used like jelly, and juices that combine both fruits and vegetables—items we don't see in the USA.

"For all the warm hospitality, I still get a little homesick now and again. Maybe, as Jeanne says, home is wherever we lay our heads."

In these early years of their Peace-Sound Chamber work, John took a back seat to Jeanne who was perceived by many as the heir to Joseph Rael's vision for the Peace-Sound Chambers. John was periodically asked to babysit while the others engaged in program activities. Jeanne was the focus of attention, and perhaps she felt some obligation to meet audience expectations, both on stage and off. John records this example from his perspective.

"Alex picked us up. On the way to his house we picked up his trailer. He is very proud of it. While we were doing this, Jeanne looked around and found thirteen four-leaf clovers. She has this incredible knack for it. As hard as we tried, Alex and I only found one apiece. Later, I teased Jeanne that she was indulging her ego by showing off. But the simple truth is that she's been able to find four-leaf clovers ever since she was a young girl. She can pick out the difference in the pattern."

In the beginning, the line between their roles in spiritual work was a sensitive issue that continued to surface during these years of the couple's mission. John recorded one of the flare-ups on the Grossropperhausen trip.

"When Jeanne and I were alone in the kitchen after dinner, she told me that I'd stepped on her toes. She was describing the power of spontaneous chanting to a friend while we were in his garage. We'd started chanting by sounding the directional vowel sounds and then doing a spontaneous song. I'd seen a pyramid with energy streaming into the center. I connected the pyramid with chanting the vowel sounds. So, after Jeanne related some information about spontaneous chanting, I related my experience with the vowel sounds. Perhaps I could have been more sensitive to Jeanne and what she was sharing with our friend. But I was excited that I was having a powerful vision! Yet, at this stage of our work we are both a little bit fragile."

Thirteen people, including Jeanne and John, participated in Awakening Ceremony #4. During the day, there was a sweat lodge and a pipe ceremony in the Chamber performed by Jeanne. John briefed the participants on what to expect and the ritual aspects of the event that included the tobacco and cornmeal circles. He asked them to help him build an energy field of light around the Chamber area for protection. Jeanne began chanting in the Chamber at 10:30 P.M. and continued almost without pause until 3:00 A.M.—four and a half hours later. John noted in his journal that "nobody can sing continuously for that long without the help of Spirit." Jeanne's voice was weak after the ceremony but perfectly fine the next day when they awoke about noon.

As the German Chamber began to "open" during Jeanne's singing, John recorded the presence of Joseph, Jesus, and Mary. He also saw angelic guardians at the four directional posts. John's personal guides were there, too—four very tall kings dressed in white robes of light. Both John and Jeanne saw Hitler during the first hour of the clearing phase of the ceremony.

A Pleiadian Grandmother appeared to John later and told him, "After the eighth Chamber Awakening Ceremony in Australia, go to Jerusalem. You have important work there." John had no idea what the work might be, but he did feel that there was a connection between the Grossropperhausen Chamber and Jews in Israel.

During the celebration after the ceremony, Jeanne blessed the four caretakers. Ramona, a participant, sang at the center of the Chamber later and had a powerful experience as the energy caused her whole body to shake. Another elder participant was able to sleep through the night for the first time in years. All those familiar with the Chamber agreed that the energy was different and resonated more light. Even the elements agreed. A light rain came as Jeanne sang the awakening. The wind in the trees circled the Chamber 360° as if it were a sentient being. There was sheet lightning that ringed the night sky around the Chamber, but, amazingly, there was no sound of thunder.

FACING WHAT IS, 1998

B ack home in Vallecito on June 22, there was little recovery time before the scheduled Men's Sun-Moon Dance on the July 4th weekend. Instead of a blissful contemplative week in the Colorado Mountains, however, Jeanne and John had to deal with news of a family illness and the kind of turmoil in the lives of the children that threatened to push them off center. John confided the details to his journal.

"Although it has been wonderful being back home in the Colorado Mountains, family and financial issues are impinging on the reverie. Jeanne's step-dad, Jack, a retired army vet and a large man, has continued to lose weight. He's down to 143 pounds, and the allopathic medical establishment does not know why. In my family, Ryan and Sean and Alan are all going through turmoil. Ryan and Sean, especially, seem to be at gateways in their lives.

"It's difficult not getting wrapped up in these issues on top of my own financial worries—Amex bills, whether our computer can be fixed, and so on. So, I've prayed to Great Spirit and the Grandmothers & Grandfathers for help with my children's problems as well as my own. Diana (John's ex-wife) has shown up in my dreams two nights in a row. In the dreams, she's unhappy, thinks she's been mistreated, and is bitching at me. Something here is still in need of healing."

Although most parents of twenty-something children can empathize firsthand with John's frustrations at his inability to help his sons through life's start-up turmoils, perhaps they cannot know the depth of stress placed on John's identity as a spiritual leader. What was the mind to do with the slap-in-the-face reality of family needs and a financial crisis? Peace Sound Chamber missions to Bolivia and Australia were scheduled for August and September that would require a large dollar influx before they could depart. Where was that support to come from? How is the appearance of chaos and lack to be endured by the spiritual person? John and Jeanne found recourse in their spiritual practice, and John recorded the result only three days later.

"I've been in love with life these past few days. The land seems so beautiful to me. The lake is a deep navy blue. The wind in the tall Ponderosa pines speaks to me. The hummingbirds come to our window and porch door. The neighbor dogs come to visit, and even the timid female has made friends with us. Even with lots to do to get ready for our trip to Albuquerque and the Men's Dance, I feel a real flow to life. Maybe this is part of becoming more trusting and surrendering to Spirit. There's a richness to life that I've experienced only a few times in my 48 years. My relationship and prayers with Spirit have taken on a more personal quality. I feel the arms of God around me."

Jeanne expresses their spiritual practice in this way.

"We had been living several years in learning how to be totally in the moment, learning to listen at a level that provides deep inner guidance. Whatever you call it—God, Holy Spirit—there is wisdom in being quiet and becoming aware of intuitive guidance. When you learn to live deeply within yourself and you receive a directive, you don't question it; you just do it. If there are attachments regarding fears of insecurity, they quickly surface. The rational mind may be saying *no*. To say *yes* to the inner voice, these attachments have to be released. There has to be a willingness to come to the edge of a mental precipice and leap into the unknown. You have to be willing to fall before you can learn how to fly."

At the Men's Sun-Moon Dance in 1998, John asked Joseph's younger brother, Benito Rael, the translation of the Tiwa spirit name, Wah-Chi-Who, that Joseph had given him. Joseph had written "Is Alive" as a translation on the spirit painting that he had given John with his name. Benito offered the additional translations "Walks with Life," "Walks with Light," and "He Whose Path Is Spirit."

Before the sweat lodge on Thursday, there was a double rainbow at the north end of Sandia Mountain. John saw it as a sign of blessing from Joseph since the double rainbow, one for the bow and the other for the arrow, is the symbol for Beautiful Painted Arrow.

Among the details of his experience in the dance, John recorded these.

"The Sun-Moon Dance pole was the same tree as we used last year. We dressed the top with willow branches. We also put tobacco ties of the directional colors onto the tree, each containing an entire pouch of tobacco. There was red in the North, yellow in the East, white in the South, and black in the West. During the dance, several men reported seeing the tree glow with energy that radiated outward along the dance paths of each dancer, and a column of light extending upward from the tree to the sky.

"I danced to let go of old emotional attachments and pains, including mother, father, brother, Diana, and even my children. I danced for forgiveness. I danced for my heart to be open. So when I hit the pole on Sunday, I was ready for a full release. I hit the pole, when it called to me, and it split me wide open. I sobbed and released a lot of stuff.

"I also danced a dance of surrender. I danced to be a Warrior for Spirit. I danced to be a voice for Spirit.

"I danced for my children and for my ancestors, and for Jeanne. I danced for World Peace and the Beautiful Painted Arrow Center. I danced for knowledge as a Chief of the Tennessee Dance."

NORWAY CHAMBER AWAKENING

Travel Woes

Wherever they go to perform sacred ceremony, Jeanne and John do a great deal of spiritual preparation. They use a variety of methods that include Intuitive Imaging, prayer, and meditation. They ask basic questions with regard to the place and time. What is needed to prepare for this specific Awakening Ceremony? What do these people need from us? What does the Spirit of this Chamber want us to know? What do we need to be ready? What does Jeanne (John) need from me? Often this preparation extends over a period of three days or more, and they consider it essential to their process. They pay special attention to their dreams, and they are keenly aware of natural signs in their environment that might also provide guidance or direction. In a fashion, they are tuning their spiritual instruments prior to the concert of energies to come.

In Oslo, Norway for the fifth Chamber awakening, John did personal Imaging sessions for some of the participants, and Jeanne conducted a workshop on Spontaneous Chanting. Jeanne began the Awakening Ceremony on June 9th just after midnight. During the hours of her singing chant, participants outside the Chamber reported seeing a "ball of light" in the Chamber, or they saw the Chamber "vibrating and breathing." In addition to Christian holy spirits who appeared to John, he also saw ancient Viking spirits. A mature white-haired lady, who told John that she "never sees anything, never gets images" was awed to see Eagle-Men Kachina Spirits facing outward around the Chamber in the four directions. In a report similar to one that occurred in Germany, the very ill sister of a participant who could not sleep, slept through the night during the ceremony. A young man, who admitted to being a skeptic, said that he and another participant (a woman) had experienced light coming into their bodies and the sensation of their hearts opening.

The Chamber caretakers— Gerd Bjorke, Anne Klanderud, Ole Bjorn, and Anne Haraldsen—who hosted the Chamber ceremony, also had organized the Norwegian Sun-Moon Dances. Anne Klanderud, who John and Jeanne call Anne Whale's Tooth because of her 1998 gift to them, later went to South Africa (2004) to participate in two "For the One" Dances—first as a dancer, and then as a Dog Soldier. In 2005, Anne would be instrumental in bringing the FTOD to Norway.

As a reporter of the dance testimonials, one is struck by the similarity of visionary experiences regardless of the participant's cultural background. One might expect visionary fireworks at the Peace-Sound Chamber in Bernalillo, New Mexico, where American Indians have practiced vision quests for more than a thousand years, but not in a stoical culture like Norway. And yet, despite language and cultural differences across four continents, participants in Peace-Sound Chamber ceremonies and dancers of the demanding ceremonial dances are having similar visionary experiences.

They report visual and auditory events that seem paranormal to the rational mind. Many report that they entered the ceremonial environment with skepticisms, only to have the reality of the experienced phenomena overwhelm their doubts. After crossing the threshold to the new dimension, they cannot return to their former beliefs. Perhaps enlightenment as a spiritual experience is nothing more than seeing the light of divine energy and being returned to Source.

Lest we get caught up in the wonderment of the spiritual life that Jeanne and John were experiencing, it should be recorded that they were not immune to the ordeals of travel. Here from John's journal is the account of their journey from Germany to Norway to England that makes them both wince and laugh when they retell it today.

"We had difficulty traveling both into and out of Norway. I don't know why. Maybe it was all about letting go. Maybe the Old Norse God, Loki, played with us a bit. Maybe we (I) didn't protect ourselves enough. For whatever reason, we experienced difficulties.

"As we left Germany for Oslo on Thursday, June 4, British Air forced us to check two of our carry-on bags. This was unanticipated since the airlines in the States allow us two carry-on bags each. So, we had to consolidate some items. I put the portable computer in Jeanne's new, large carry-on bag. I forgot that this had a bottle of vegetable juice in it, given to Jeanne by Shania Racky. And when we got to Oslo, two things happened. First, the bag that the computer would have been in didn't come through on the flight. And second, the bottle of vegetable juice broke when Jeanne set her bag on the hard-surfaced floor. Beet-carrot juice got all over everything—including *on and in* the computer. I was mortified. I was sure that the computer was ruined. And, I thought, a $2500 bottle of juice! That was our welcome to Oslo. For me, it was an experience—no, a test—about letting go. I had to get to a place beyond judgment and into a state of mind where it was OK if the computer was ruined.

"What happened *leaving* Oslo was even more traumatic. The day that we left, the air traffic controllers went on strike in Oslo. Gerd Bjorke, our hostess, had arranged for tickets by train to Stockholm, and seats on a flight from Stockholm to London. What transpired on the trip was traumatizing, and had to do with carrying so many bags—eight (8) bags plus Jeanne's drum—nine altogether. Too many bags! We've got to get better at this traveling stuff!

"We awoke late on Friday, 6/12 and wound up rushing to the train station. This set the stage for the rest of the trip. We arrived at the train station in Oslo at 9:10 for a 9:30 A.M. departure. Gerd and Jeanne rushed to purchase tickets, and then we struggled with all of our bags to get onto the train. If we'd had less baggage, all of our travels that day would have been relatively simple. But with the number of bags and their bulkiness and weight, it was difficult for the two of us (Jeanne and me) to manage the bags during the various transportation changes we made.

"Once on the train out of Oslo, we relaxed for a bit. It was 2-½ hours to Karlstad where we changed trains to Stockholm. Fortunately, the train to Stockholm was directly across the platform, and our car was only 50 feet down the track. So Jeanne and I lugged the baggage in shifts down to the train car. Then, again, we relaxed for a little over two hours. We ate a small lunch and dozed. As we pulled into Stockholm, we positioned ourselves at the baggage and prepared to exit the train. The train stopped, and Jeanne and I took off the luggage. So far, so good.

"Getting from the platform to street level meant putting the bags on a luggage cart and going up an escalator. This had worked well in Germany. But the Swedish carts and escalators weren't engineered as well. So, our first trauma was about to occur suddenly and unexpectedly. I led the way up the escalator with the baggage cart. Jeanne followed. At the top of the escalator, the cart stopped. The wheel would not negotiate the lip of the escalator where the moving stairs disappear under a plate of metal. It stuck. Meanwhile, the escalator was pushing Jeanne and me into the cart. Jeanne was treading the escalator while being forced into my back. She wore a long dress that was beginning to get in her way, throwing her off balance. She yelled for 'help.' If her dress had caught under the escalator, it would have been terrible! As it was, a woman nearby began pulling off luggage and I was able to 'man-handle' the luggage cart over the lip of the metal plate. We finally were free. It all happened within 30 seconds.

"Afterward, I was a bit shaken. We didn't know where to go for the bus, and we needed to get to the plane. I didn't even have Swedish kronars to pay for anything. Jeanne asked for directions, and it turned out that the bus station was right across the street. In retrospect, it would have been much better to take a cab. But we didn't.

"Following Jeanne, who had her large purse, the drum, and my overnight bag, I pushed the baggage cart across the street and into the bus terminal. We eventually bought tickets and got onto the right bus. And as I was loading luggage, a gruff, young Swedish man said, 'Get on the bus! I will take care of your luggage.' So I got on the bus. That was the first step in becoming disconnected with the luggage. I didn't see where it all went. So, when I took it off of the bus, I had to look around for it. And I didn't get it all. In fact, I left the most important bag on the bus—the ceremonial bag!

"Jeanne and I realized we'd left the bag only after the bus had gone, and we'd put our bags on a baggage cart and were moving to the check-in line of British Air. Jeanne's face went white. My heart sunk. Why had this happened? Jeanne's ceremonial dress, her embroidered shawl, all the crystals, the rattles, and the whale's tooth and crystal eagle were all gone! It was crushing for Jeanne, who felt like she'd lost her children. I also felt (and still feel) a strong sense of having completely blown one of my responsibilities. It was the most terrible time of the trip, the most terrible time in the past year. Jeanne cried and talked to the people at the bus company, and to the airline. British Air was amazing. In empathy with our distress, they stretched their own rules and assured us that they would locate the missing bag and ship it to London. They urged us to leave on our scheduled flight, and very reluctantly, we did.

"We stayed overnight at Heathrow—at the Marriott on Bath Lane. In the morning, we went to British Air Baggage service. There, we found a true angel—a man named Hardev Birdi, an East Indian. He listened, asked many clarifying questions, and went out of his way to help. Hardev then encouraged us to continue our event schedule in Western England, took our contact information, and promised to call us when the bag was found. Meanwhile, Jeanne was on the phone to British Air in Stockholm and to Gerd in Norway who would also reach out to the bus company.

"One week later, after Jeanne and I had napped and Jeanne had completely turned the issue of the misplaced bag over to God, we found that the ceremonial bag was back in the hands of British Airways at Heathrow Airport. We were gathering with a meditation group at just before 8:00 P.M. when Heather, our English host, told Jeanne that there had been a message from Hardev Birdi at 2:00 P.M. on the answering machine. He said he had the bag physically in his hands, and would store it for us until we came for it. What a relief! I told Jeanne that I had felt the bag coming back to us/her. Perhaps the crystals had work to do in Stockholm."

After faithfully recording their travel woes, the next paragraph in John's personal journal reflects a return to centeredness. It is a wonderfully sincere expression of his dedication in spite of the recent hardships.

"To open to our fullest potential, to bring balance to our world, we must think not only with our heads but also with our hearts. We must use both our intellect <u>and</u> our intuition. Then we will be able to see our reality in an expanded way. We will be better able to open to our Dance Visions, and see Spirit beings that come to assist us. We will be able to live by Inspiration—which means to live freer, and to increase our faith and our trust."

Jeanne and John had a relaxing two and a half days with William and Heather Elmhirst in Porlock, although they facilitated a group meditation on Sunday, and Jeanne taught a group about spontaneous chanting on Monday morning. Additional friends were made in this way for the potential of future activities in England. There were also drives through the English countryside, a stop at Dunster Castle, and Heather's gourmet vegetarian meals to enjoy. On Tuesday morning, Jeanne and John took off on their own by car to Avebury and Stonehenge. At their leaving, Heather had handed them an envelope which contained a note of gratitude and a check for $1000. John almost drove off the road later when Jeanne showed it to him. The totally unexpected gift moved them to deep emotions.

At Avebury, the couple touched two 5,000-year old megaliths honoring the Feminine and the Masculine, the Mother-Father God. At Stonehenge, they marveled that ancient people here had constructed a sacred circle that honored the four directions and the Mother-Father concept. The religion of these people was aware of the directional energies. John wrote, "These 'pagans' may have known secrets that we are only now rediscovering—as our genetic code is activated again."

On June 19th they arrived back in Albuquerque from London via New York and St. Louis. It had been another very long day— twenty-four hours of planes, airports, and shuttle buses to arrive two hours late at midnight. Faithful friends John and Melinda Stroupe, however, were there to greet them with Geordi, their also faithful Nissan Pathfinder.

Throughout their travels, when security people searched the ceremonial bag and were curious about the garments, the crystals, and the collection of rattles, Jeanne seized the opportunity to explain their use in ceremonies for world peace. Then she would further amaze them by giving each one a small piece of rose quartz that had been blessed in the Peace-Sound Chambers. Jeanne involves people like that wherever she goes. Even fatigue does not diminish the light of opportunity for sharing their mission. In this regard, Jeanne is recognized by all who work with her as a self-generating dynamo. For John (or anyone) keeping Jeanne on schedule, they are always subject to Jeanne's meeting someone en route and engaging in conversation. Jeanne has never met a stranger that she couldn't talk to. The strangers, fascinated by her, are of course, completely unaware that she has a plane to catch or an appointment to keep.

THE SIXTH & SEVENTH CHAMBER AWAKENINGS

Swannanoa and Bolivia

The sixth Chamber to be awakened by Jeanne and John was, in 1990, the 18th to be constructed. The site is a hallowed ground of the American Civil Rights movement. Braxton Bryant, a white Methodist minister, ran a secret multi-racial summer camp there during the dangerous segregation years in North Carolina. He said that he wanted white and black families to interact and give their children the experience of playing together.

Braxton Bryant often traveled with Dr. Martin Luther King, and he was with King in Memphis in March 1968 to aid striking sanitation workers in a peaceful protest march that met with violent racial attack. On April 3rd, Braxton asked his friend not to speak at the Memphis Masonic Temple rally that night, not only because of the danger to his life, but also because Dr. King was weary to the point of illness. King, however, went to the rally and spoke these prophetic words: "I may not get there with you, but I want you to know tonight that we as a people will get to the promised land." The next day, on the balcony of the Lorraine Hotel, Dr. King was assassinated.

Braxton Bryant had also known President John Kennedy well enough to personally greet him on the tarmac at the Dallas Airport in 1963, and he was still at the airport when his sixteen-year-old daughter Zoe heard the news that the President had been shot on the car radio and called out the alarming news to her father.

In retirement, Braxton allowed his campground to be a way station for hippies on their east-west migrations. Some stayed for months, and the wise old grandfather, who looked like Moses in his long, white beard, put them to work in his woods or in the communal gardens. It was Braxton Bryant who donated the site for the Swannanoa Peace-Sound Chamber, and he was present with Joseph Rael during its construction.

Zoe Bryant, Braxton's daughter and Chamber caretaker, began her spiritual quest as a young adult, and from a Mystery School orientation, she came to Native American metaphysics as a primary source of inspiration and guidance. Joseph Rael was one of Zoe's chief mentors, but she has also been recognized as a kindred soul by many important Native American tribal elders. On this path, Zoe has also become a gifted maker of ceremonial artifacts. Her ceremonial pipes, the *Chanunpa*, are considered *lela wakan* "very sacred." Today, the Peace-Sound Chamber at Swannanoa functions as a center for education, ceremony, chanting, drumming, and dance as part of each year's agenda.

When John and Jeanne arrived in Swannanoa early in August of 1998, there was much to do prior to the Awakening Ceremony. On Saturday, John had to split firewood for two sweat lodges. The labor left his arms, legs, and hands sore, and the back-to-back lodges left him drained. Meanwhile, Jeanne had agreed to do a sound workshop, and although she did not like to do workshops on ceremonial days, the sound work did serve to prepare the Chamber. One of the firekeepers, David Stephenson, had just returned from dancing (and piercing) in the Lakota Sun Dance.

After Jeanne had entered the Chamber at midnight, John reported that, "the vortex of energy, as it began to spiral upward, called in the wind spirit. Even the smoke from the fire began spiraling upward in the same direction as the energy in the Chamber." Many of the participants saw spiritual manifestations. John again saw his guides, The Four Kings. Sammye Jo Harvey saw the Ancient Ones assemble as a Council of Elders. For the first time in performing the Awakening Ceremony, Jeanne did not visibly shake afterwards. In the celebration that followed the ceremony, John sensed that the lives of the people connected with this Chamber would never be the same.

Traveling to Bolivia to bring the Awakening Ceremony to a small Peace-Sound Chamber in a very remote place is illustrative of a dedication that overcomes all difficulty. Living the way that they were—out of suitcases, largely dependent on the generosity of supporters for accommodations and meals—John and Jeanne had to manage all the details of their travel, plus pay bills, communicate with family, and find a private space for their own personal relationship. When appearing at workshops and ceremonies, as well as in encounters with supporters who they depended on, the couple was expected to be spiritually centered and extraordinary in all the expressions of their mission. In a car ride from the airport, at meals, sitting in an apartment living room, or being introduced to strangers—in all the wakeful activities of normal living—they had the onus of being perceived as always wise, and always profoundly interesting. Wherever they went, the spotlight of great expectations was always on them. In his journal, after examining their travel schedule for the remainder of the year, John lamented that their only private time at the cabin in Colorado would be a couple of days in September and maybe a couple of weeks before the next major trip.

The Bolivia trip began at the Atlanta Airport. John's son Sean, wearing overalls and his Sun-Moon Dance T-shirt, had a brief visit before the ever-faithful Ula Rae Mynatt drove them there. The first leg was a long flight to Lima, Peru. Jeanne had brought small blow-up neck pillows, and so both of them slept through the six-hour overnight flight. The Lima airport was small—six gates, three shops, one restaurant, and a transit lounge where the couple spent an uncomfortable eight hours before their flight to La Paz, Bolivia, the highest elevation airport in the world at 12,850 feet above sea level.

John recorded their arrival and impressions in his journal. The journal is remarkable for its historic and geographical detail. The precise engineering aspect of John is a huge bonus in this regard.

"Upon arrival last night, we were met by Esteban Ryan Taylor, an American who has worked in Bolivia for six years and in La Paz for two years. He is an Associate Director of the Peace Corps here. Interestingly, the airport is named John F. Kennedy airport. It is Kennedy who began the Peace Corps (Cuerpo de Paz).

"I felt light-headed and short of breath at the airport just after arriving. But, the city of La Paz is at a lower elevation—around 12,000 feet. Esteban lives in the hub of the residential area of the city with banks and restaurants right up the street. It's even lower in elevation, maybe 11,500 feet. Whatever the altitude, after some traditional "mate de coca" and not so traditional miso soup I slept well, glad for the time that Jeanne and I have spent living at 8100 feet in Vallecito, Colorado.

"Esteban is a tall, slender man with close-clipped hair, a soft voice and a dry sense of humor. He gave us his room for the week. The hotel Calocoto conveniently 'lost' our reservations made over two weeks ago. It is a National Holiday here, the celebration of Bolivian independence from Spain some 173 years ago. Simon Bolivar started the revolutions in South and Central America that led to countries breaking away from Spain one by one. Anyway, Esteban has taken the guestroom and graciously given us his room.

"Mountains ring the city, some with sheer walls and striated layers with colors that remind me of the New Mexico topography driving NW out of Bernalillo on Highway 44. There is a sacred mountain near here that must be 20,000 feet high. It is called 'Ilimani' (pronounced ee-lee-mah-nee). To the left of it is another, flatter one called 'Mururatu.' When we visit the Peace-Sound Chamber today, we will be as close as any civilization is to these mountains."

Preparation for the Awakening Ceremony began on Saturday, August 8th. Again, John's journal provides the details.

"Don Policarpio did a burnt offering ceremony. He is an Ayumari priest from Teohuanaco. His title is 'Tata,' similar to 'Taita' as we addressed the shaman from Columbia. I assume that it also means 'Father.' After the burnt offering ceremony, Jeanne did a workshop. Then, we built a sweat lodge fire—no easy feat at 13,800 feet due to the lack of oxygen at this altitude. Miguel Kavlin poured water for the sweat lodge as Esteban carried stones.

"The day at high altitude sapped almost all of my energy, and we still had the Awakening Ceremony to do. After the sweat lodge and an uncomfortable ride down the mountain in the back of Miguel's Toyota jeep, I was as exhausted as I can ever remember being. So, I showered, rested for an hour, and got ready for the second trip up the mountain over bumpy cobblestone roads and even bumpier dirt roads. I was still very tired as we began the ceremony.

"The night ride was clear and crisp as we began. I had taken the precaution of wearing long underwear and two pairs of socks. Even so, I was a bit chilly as I entered the kiva with Jeanne to do the Pipe Ceremony.

"While we were doing the Pipe Ceremony inside the Chamber, Ron Smith and Miguel built the ceremonial fire, and drew a corn-meal star on top of the Peace-Sound Chamber. Actually, it looked more like sunrays emerging from a ball of light. A little 'sacred alcohol' bought on the way up the mountain had a stately fire going before I came out of the kiva. Ron had also built a beautiful Lakota

altar for his pipe behind the fire. Ron added a lot to the ceremony.
I gained a deep respect for the strength and depth of his beliefs. He
felt like a brother from another time. (He has also seen the 4 Guides
that I met in ceremony in March!) We are truly a family coming
back together.

"Charro (a native Bolivian friend of Esteban) and Esteban laid
the cornmeal circle around the kiva, and Miguel and Raul Tapia
laid the tobacco circle. I added the cornmeal line to the fire from
the kiva. Then, we were ready to go. About ten minutes later,
Jeanne began to sing.

The skies were clear as Jeanne started the spontaneous chanting that began the Awakening Ceremony in earnest. Ilimani and
Mururatu were clearly visible under the golden light of the full
moon. Although not as dramatic as some, the ceremony was gently
powerful. Interestingly, preparations for this seventh (7th)
Awakening Ceremony were made on 7 Batz (of the Mayan calendar,) and had 7 participants!

"As the ceremony continued, clouds first came in from the valley to the east and then from all over. The Grandfather Mountains
were obscured. Designs began to show up in the clouds. Ron and
Charro both saw an arrow, a sign of Joseph's presence. When the
Chamber *opened* fully, the clouds above moved away. They actually
parted and revealed the full moon's splendor once again.

"Tata Policarpio explained at some length on the ride up the
mountain that his ceremony was one of unification—of all peoples,
of all faiths. He shares a belief that all of humanity is one people.
Don Policarpio is an Amauta—the highest level or wisest of
Medicine Men or indigenous priests. His people are Ayumari. He
has 23 villages under his care. He is 76 years old. He is the eldest of
the Teohuanaco community, and also the most open, according to
Esteban.

"Most really wise 'medicine people' that Jeanne and I have met
are like that. They share a belief in the basic spiritual oneness of
humanity. And, perhaps, they also see that we don't have the time

for factionalism and war and cutthroat competition. It is time to remember who we really are, to remember our Source. The Awakening Ceremony is a step in that direction for all people. I feel good about that. At the same time, I hunger for more stories and signs of the momentum of the shift that we are helping to create and its physical effects."

A few days following the Chamber Awakening Ceremony, Jeanne and John, with Miguel and Ron, accepted an invitation to have a meal with Tata Policarpio at his humble high-mountain home outside Teohuanaco close to Lake Titicaca. Tata's wife and daughters greeted the visitors and welcomed them into their dirt floor home where the beds served as couches. Outside, chickens and pigs roamed freely in the courtyard. Despite the humblest of surroundings, Jeanne and John remember the meal of the boiled blue potatoes dug from the garden and fresh made cheese as one of their finest dinners. Tata then shared some of the wisdom of the Ayumari people. At the end of his discourse, he asked Jeanne to kneel for a special blessing. He told her that she would need a great measure of energy to undertake what she was being asked to do in the world, and that he wanted to give her a blessing to help her and remind her that he was near if she ever needed him. Placing his hands on Jeanne's head, the blessing was pronounced in Tata's native language. Jeanne felt the energy surge through her, and she was brought to tears. Tata's unexpected gift proved its power by becoming a source of strength to Jeanne throughout the ensuing years.

The flight from Lima to Albuquerque gave Jeanne and John less than twenty-four hours to prepare for their flight to Melbourne, Australia. They spent the night in Bernalillo where they paid their respects to the Peace-Sound Chamber that had started it all. John did not get to bed until 2 A.M., and he was up at 7 A.M., still exhausted. Jeanne was on the phone all morning taking care of trip details, and John had been demanding to get her to the car on time for the trip to the airport. Everywhere he turned, someone was there to push his emotional buttons.

At LAX, the United Airlines terminal was torn up for renovation, and John felt that the turmoil was a fit metaphor for his thoughts. During the flight into LAX, a kid in front of him had fully reclined his seat back and left it there, unchallenged by the stewardess, even during landing. John was already uncomfortable with sensitive feet and general body ache. Ahead was a twelve-hour flight to Auckland followed by another three and a half hour hop to Melbourne—all the way in economy seats!

In LAX, the beautiful people hurried past, postured in their images of wealth and success. All around, there was too much noise, too much traffic, and too many people chasing the illusions of fashion. John observed the public obsession with the social game, and he wondered how he and Jeanne could change it. Sometimes, in his exhaustion, the moving tide of an unconscious humanity seemed overwhelming. And yet, later, when he recorded these feelings in his journal, John could write, "Sometimes I forget how wonderful the human experience really is, struggles and all. To experience taste, touch, and smell. To eat huevos rancheros with green chile. To see the stars on a clear, dark Colorado night—like diamonds against black velvet. These and a thousand other sensations make each day an adventure." If there was an internal struggle between the practical chemical engineer side of John, and the intuitive poetic side, the poet often showed himself.

Jeanne does not remember this period of intense and difficult travel in the same way that John recorded it in his journal. Althoumany others, are in the flux of very powerful energies. Missteps are not only painful but actually dangerous. The center line of perfect peace and absolute harmony is never guaranteed. It is, as measured in relationship, a high-wire walk across a chasm of burning discontents that has to be mastered step by step.

AUSTRALIA CHAMBER AWAKENING

August '98

J eanne and John left Bolivia on the 11th and arrived in
Melbourne on the 15th, having lost a full day over the international dateline in four days of constant travel. They slept, ate, and
bathed in sinks in a state of aerial suspension. Their host at the
Casurina Peace-Sound Chamber north of Melbourne was Junitta
Vallek. John's journal gives a great sense of Junitta and the landscape.

"Stepping outside at Junitta's place this morning to do my
tobacco prayers, a large eagle came and circled over the Chamber!
What a wonderful omen! Upon later reflection as we walked the
property with Junitta, it could have been a hawk that circled the
kiva, but it would have had to be a very large one. There are hawks
nesting on this land in a large tree. Some of the trees here are 800
to1000 years old.

"Junitta is an old student of Joseph's. The Peace-Sound
Chamber here dates from 1984 and is the fourth one ever built.
Junitta, herself, is one of those high-energy, type 'A' personalities
who is in constant motion. She's in her early 60s, maybe. Her once
dark hair is now salt and pepper. Her face is leathery and wrinkled
from time in the sun. Indeed, she built her house mostly with her
own hands. She was once a silversmith and ruined her lungs from
the fumes of hot metals and solvents. As a result, her breathing is a
bit raspy, but it doesn't seem to hold her back much. She seems to
compensate by her ability to network, and get things in motion—
especially around the Chamber. She's a sparkplug. She is also a compulsive photo-historian. She has photo albums from past years that
cover an entire bookshelf.

"We awoke this morning to the loud chuck notes of an
Australian magpie. The magpies here are larger birds than in
Colorado, with great swatches of white down their backs and on

their wings, outlined by black. Their tails are not as long either. But their songs are magnificent, like listening to an accomplished flute player.

"The Australian countryside is beautiful. The first thing that strikes you as a native of North America is how different the trees are here. There are magnificent eucalyptus trees and 'wattles,' which are acacia trees. The wattles have brilliant yellow flowers like little balls of flame with sage-colored leaves that look like miniature palms. There are several types—four on Junitta's property alone. All are quite beautiful with the combination of various depths of sage green and brilliant, flaming yellow.

"Junitta has 100 acres of land with a pond, several groves of old-growth trees, and three labyrinths. The women's grove is the largest and has the labyrinth of the oldest design—from 5800 years ago. Many women have come here to do full-moon celebrations and walk or dance the labyrinth. Women seem to be leading the way for the spiritual re-awakening of the planet. Many more men seem to be still caught in form, caught in the identity of their jobs. I can certainly relate since I am still having difficulty breaking that form for myself, wondering what my part is in bringing in the money we need to continue this work, and meet our commitments.

"The men's grove has a 1000 year-old eucalyptus tree where an ancient aboriginal spirit dwells. Its massive trunk has been hollowed out by a fire at some time long past. Drawing close to it, you can feel a tremendous energy, an electromagnetic force that is emanating from the tree. We introduced ourselves, and the spirit in the tree seemed to smile and welcome us closer. Nearby is a second labyrinth of a 1000 year-old design.

"Further along the property as we followed the fence line is the couple's grove, so named because one couple went there to work out their problems—successfully. The kangaroos seem to also enjoy this spot. They dig shallow holes here to sit in or lie down in. We saw a group of a dozen or so kangaroos hopping off into the distance as we walked toward the couple's grove."

John's journal also intimately reflects what it means to enter the space of total spiritual devotion.

"Much has happened in my life since we started this work in March of this year, and I was told that my life would change dramatically. The Four Tall Kings that appeared to me, and blessed me into this work, knew what they were talking about. My life has turned upside down. It is filled with joy much of the time but also uncertainty.

"We are in a place of financial uncertainty due to empty reserves. I have no idea where the money to send Alan for September will come from—to say nothing of paying our own rent, or Amex, or our other bills. Yet, all the readings we have had, all the guidance we've gotten has said, 'All will be well. You will be supported.' Now is the time of fire that will burn away the doubts we have. Perhaps we have reached step #8 with this 8th Chamber Ceremony—being willing to fall, to fail. Everything is on the line now. And as we move through this step, the next will bring a harvesting of great rewards. Who knows? We may have to lose everything we consider dear to us. I hope not, but it *is* possible. I am reminding myself that the power comes *through me—but I am not in control.*

"The next question is this. If I'm not in control of my life and what happens to me, what use is the process of manifestation? Where's the balance between passively allowing life to *happen* to me, and shaping my own reality? Do I create it all through my thoughts? Or, does Spirit control those thoughts? How much of the New Age metaphysics is true? How much is bunk? I get all balled up and confused. The harder I try to make things happen, the more information I receive that I am not in control. What seems to work are things that just *show up*—things beyond my ability to plan.

"So, I've been learning to just *show up, shut up, and do what I'm told* (by Spirit). Perhaps the most I can do is to hold a picture in my mind and an awareness of the ideal outcome, and leave the rest to Spirit. That's where it is important to rid myself of doubt. It is difficult to do sometimes when what I really feel like doing is to roll up into fetal position and cry.

"Right now, Jeanne is also afraid. We are walking the high wire without a perceived 'safety net.' She needs me to be strong for her. She needs me to be the one who says, 'Don't worry. Everything will be alright.' And to do this even if I have doubts myself. I can see Tata Policarpio's eyes looking at me and saying with a smile—'Don't doubt! All will be well!' So, I must find this reservoir of belief and courage within my being."

In the headlines those mid-August days was the news that the United States military had launched seventy cruise missiles from ships at sea in an attempt to destroy a pharmaceutical plant suspected of manufacturing chemical weapons in Sudan and also a terrorist training camp in Afghanistan. The Saudi terrorist leader that they hoped to undermine in these attacks was Osama bin Laden, a name that would become infamous.

John reacted to the news in his journal, and in retrospect, his comments seem prophetic.

"Whatever the motivation, I can't see how we are closer to preserving peace through making a military strike. Like begets like. Violence begets violence that, in turn, leads to more violence. It's a self-reinforcing, expanding cycle. The terrorists will pull back for a while, perhaps, and then strike again. More polarization will occur. More terrorists will be the result. And maybe it will bring more terrorist acts to our home soil in the United States."

The bombing news was heard while Jeanne and John were visiting Michael and Jenny Coles on their fifty-five acre farm in Malden. Michael is part Australian and part Chinese, and Jenny is East Indian. Both have very expressive, creative, and enthusiastic personalities. John noted, "Being with Michael and Jenny is like taking an energy bath." The first morning of their visit, the guests awoke to a barnyard chorus of animals, and the sounds of roosters, ducks, pigs, cows, and dogs reminded John of the Kentucky farm where he had stayed as a young boy with his Uncle Bill and Aunt Lorena.

That Monday night was the regular gathering of a spiritual study group that rotates from house to house. Jeanne and John shared their spiritual journey with fifteen members of the group. Jeanne sang a spontaneous chant, but John was too congested with a cold or allergy to join her.

Jeanne and John were then invited by Graeme and Lucy Reed to spend a few days at their Kiama Sanctuary. Kiama is an aboriginal name for the Great Spirit. The land had been declared "covenanted land," which meant that it was a protected place for bio-diversity for both plants and animals. Graeme and Lucy were environmental activists, and they had organized a grass roots effort to prevent a gold mining company from cutting down trees to make a new power line right-of-way.

The host couple had a beautiful five-bedroom, ranch-style country home with the kind of décor that reminded Jeanne and John of their own previous homes on Signal Mountain and Placitas. John and Jeanne also related to Graeme on a business level. Graeme had recently left a lucrative twenty-five year career in financial consulting that included offices in London and Chicago in response to a spiritual call.

In all their travels, the focus had been on Jeanne White Eagle, her visions, and her experiences in working with the Peace-Sound Chambers. Jeanne's story-telling ability was both captivating and entertaining, and audiences looked to her as the enlightened one, the spiritual master. But where did that leave John, who was a dance chief and also blessed by Joseph, the original visionary master of the Chambers? John did not seek the limelight that Jeanne was so suited for, but he did want his role, and his partnership with Jeanne, to be acknowledged. Jeanne, in her natural enthusiasm and innate drive to share her experiences, was often unaware that John was pushed to the sideline as the attendant to her featured star.

When Jeanne was aware of John's feelings of being sidelined, she tended to pull back and not exercise her full power.

Anyone who has worked full-time with a spouse knows that too much togetherness is stressful. There is often very little to share outside of the daily experience. Gone is the opportunity to ask the all-encompassing marital question, "And what did you do today, honey?" Then, too, the spiritual partnership aspect of Jeanne and John's relationship seemed, at least to the program observer, unequal and unbalanced. Jeanne was obviously perceived as the senior, most important partner. And yet, in practice, they equally shared the struggle and the sacrifices required of their mission. John sought acknowledgment of this fact from Jeanne during the Australian trip. He also wanted her to be more aware of his own spiritual role in the performance of their work. Jeanne tried to reassure John by saying, "Without you, none of this works."

An example of the type of event that depressed John is the visit to Melville Caves with Graeme and Lucy. John was losing his voice completely due to congestion, which only added to his feeling of being an outsider. Here is his journal entry.

"Near the top is the largest of the caves. It has both a front and back entrance. I hesitated before entering. I didn't feel welcome. So, I said a prayer to the Spirits there asking permission to enter. Finally, and rather tentatively, I entered the cave. At the front, there is an opening in the roof where, looking up, I saw a large and weathered eucalyptus tree glowing in the afternoon sunlight. Turning around, I could see that Graeme had already come into the cave from the other entrance and was sitting in the semi-darkness upon a ledge at the level of the back entryway tunnel. Lucy followed me in, and finally Jeanne. I was uncomfortable in the energy of the cave. I left after about five minutes, preferring to sit outside on the boulder across from the cave that overlooked the valley below. Again, it felt good to be in a solitary space with myself for a brief time.

"Inside the cave, Jeanne began one of her spontaneous chants. This one was slow, deep, and sonorous. Graeme and Lucy chimed in on a second chant. It was clear, as they came out, that they'd had a spiritual experience. Jeanne saw the spirit ancestors of that place. They appeared with their eyes closed, like the elders of the Peace-Sound Chamber in Seymour, TN first did. And, after Jeanne's chanting, the wind blew through the cave—to the amazement of both Graeme and Lucy. For all of their exuberance, I felt separate and distant.

"Later, at the overlook at the top, Jeanne and Graeme said prayers, and we all did a chant together, asking for blessings on the mountain and the forests, that they would be protected. Once again, my ego felt frustrated because my voice seemed to be getting worse and not better. I guess that it is nearly impossible to feel included when I feel so separated by not being able to talk."

John recovered his voice to lead an Intuitive Imagery Workshop two days later, and then he was the pourer (leader) for a sweat lodge the following day. Half a dozen people, including Jeanne, complimented him on the power of the lodge ceremony.

The 8th Awakening Ceremony occurred at the Casurina Chamber with a total of twenty-two participants. John's journal entry is extensive and gives a detailed insight into his personal experience.

"During the first hour of the ceremony, I saw the aboriginal ancestors appear in the kiva. They began singing through Jeanne's voice. Her voice was very low and melodious at this point, almost like the didgeridoo. Several of the ancestors were dancing in the Chamber.

"Unlike the other ceremonies that we've done in Peace-Sound Chambers around the world, there was no period where *negative* or *dark* energies needed to be cleared. The energy at Casurina was already clear, and the people who came to support the ceremony held a very positive space.

"Joseph, Beautiful Painted Arrow, was present in the astral—as he has been for all of the Awakening Ceremonies that we have done. I saw him walk through the Chamber wall and out to the fire. He was smiling and pleased that the 8th ceremony was under way.

"The Chambers are very connected with the *Christ energy*. In fact, in a vision in February of 1997, I saw Joseph Rael not only as Chief Joseph the Nez Perce peace chief, but also as the Biblical Joseph. So, I've come to believe that the soul who is Beautiful Painted Arrow in this life was also the father of Jesus in a previous incarnation. His vision of building Peace-Sound Chambers around the world is very much like being the father of the Christ since it is through the Chambers that we may again help the world reach a new level of consciousness, and the often prophesied thousand years of peace.

"It is also not surprising that Jesus is one of the masters that frequently shows up during the Awakening Ceremonies in the kivas. In Norway, for instance, when Jesus showed up, there was a brilliant white light that radiated from the Chamber. Others besides me saw the light clearly and reported on it afterwards. This time, when Jesus showed up in the Casurina Chamber, two things happened. First, there was a replay of the entire nativity scene inside the kiva. Joseph was there, as was Mary, the baby Jesus, and *four* wise men. In the Biblical account, one of the wise men stayed behind and came later. All four were present this time as large light beings dressed in white robes. They had long white beards and were wearing crowns. Then, after the nativity scene, Jesus then appeared as an adult. He blessed the Chamber, and blessed Jeanne in her work, and blessed the people who were gathered outside.

"I saw the energy above the Chamber grow during the ceremony. At first, there was a dome of energy that surrounded the kiva and extended perhaps two feet above the roof. During the ceremony, as Jeanne chanted inside, the dome of energy grew larger until it extended upwards for 10-15 feet or more. At the same time, I saw a *corridor* or *portal* that extended above the Chamber, coming off the center and bending towards the N-NE. Joseph's Chamber at Hesperus, CO has a similar portal. The portal was apparent from the beginning of the ceremony and is separate from the energy gateway that formed as Jeanne chanted in the Chamber.

"As Jeanne continued to sing, and particularly during the final hour when she was chanting *Wah-Mah-Chi*, the Tiwa name of God, an energy gateway began to form above the Chamber. An energy vortex formed in the Chamber that, curiously to me, began rotating clockwise at first. Most of the time, in ceremonies in the Northern Hemisphere, the vortex forms anti-clockwise at first. As the vortex gained strength, I saw the energy above the kiva take on different shapes and colors. Primarily, it appeared to me like an iridescent blue, although it also turned green at some stages. I saw it form a huge 'Y,' like the Sun-Moon Dance pole, a symbol of transformation. Then, it changed into the interlocking circles of the *vesica piscus*, the figure 8. Perhaps this is not surprising since this is the 8th ceremony, but it's the first time I've seen this happen. Mostly, I see the energy gateway opening and new energy pouring into the Chamber and the earth while, simultaneously, energy flows upward into the heavens. This time, in addition to forming this gateway, it also formed the symbols that I've described.

"At one point during the last hour of the ceremony, the Chamber became almost translucent. I had the odd sensation of feeling very connected to the Chamber and its energy but being in a different dimension, a different time. I could see the molecules of the kiva vibrating. And I could feel the Earth hurtling through space like a huge spaceship. It was a very strange feeling. This may have been the time when others saw the Chamber disappear, and saw lights around me."

After the Awakening Ceremony, Jeanne and John took an overnight bumpy bus trip to Queensland. Their hosts were Anne (Patient Wolf) and Graham (Gray Buffalo) Kiellerup. Anne was a student of Grandmother Twila and thus the Indian names. The Wolf Clan couple introduced their guests to Auntie Pearl King, an aboriginal elder. Auntie is a title of respect in the same way that female American Indian elders are called grandmother. Jeanne and John did private sessions for friends of Anne and Gray, and then Jeanne did a mini-sound workshop that was inspiring and well received. Auntie Pearl told Jeanne before they parted that Jeanne would be back in Australia sooner than she expected. A year later, Jeanne and John did return for an extensive walkabout arranged by Anne.

Clearing Customs was always a challenge for Jeanne and John. Of special concern were the eagle and condor feathers that they carried, which required a documented proof of origin that they did not carry. This trip into LAX, Jeanne concealed the feathers under her leggings after seeking advice from Intuitive Imagery. Sure enough, the ceremonial bag that usually contained the feathers was selected for random inspection. Had the feathers been inside, they might have been confiscated by an overzealous Customs agent.

The couple finally arrived at their little log cabin at 8100 feet in the San Juan Mountains on the 10th of September. Within two days, they were back on the road for another two weeks.

JOSEPH CHANGES THE FORM

J oseph, like so many master teachers, did not want his students to get stuck in form. To correct this tendency, the master requires his students to make radical changes in direction. He disrupts their spiritual comfort zones and dispels their dependency on expectations.

At one time, Jeanne and John expected to be the caretakers of the original Chamber on Joseph's property in Bernalillo. John had even set up the legal structure of The Beautiful Painted Arrow Center, where they planned to do seminars, workshops, sweat lodges, Peace-Sound Chamber ceremonies, and dances. Joseph had already retired to Hesperus, Colorado, and was no longer chiefing the ceremonial dances that he had introduced to the world.

Jeanne and John were at the little farmhouse in Corryton, Tennessee, in mid-November when they got the 5 A.M. telephone call that Joseph had been taken to the hospital in Durango unconscious and barely breathing. At the time, Joseph was not responding to treatment although the doctors had ruled out heart attack and stroke. The couple reacted with prayer and then drove an hour to the Seymour Chamber where they prayed and chanted with Perry Robinson and Cheryl Patterson until they felt a shift in energy. Other Chamber caretakers around the world were doing the same.

The next day, Joseph was fully recovered and released from the hospital. Later, he related that he had had a vision, that he had died to the old Joseph and become a new Joseph. He said that this kind of rebirth had happened to him about every fifteen years and that his energy was renewed and that his body was getting stronger.

In a ceremony following his near-death experience, Joseph was told that the Spirit of the First Chamber wanted to travel and teach. Joseph is famous for acting immediately on his visions, and so he prepared a Medicine Bundle and transferred the Spirit of the First Chamber into a stone that could be carried worldwide to the other Chambers. With the removal of the Spirit Being from the Chamber, the original reason for The Beautiful Painted Arrow Center no longer existed. Joseph then announced that he would sell the Bernalillo property.

Jeanne and John were already en route to New Mexico to begin residency in Bernalillo as the new caretakers of the Chamber when they got the news. Suddenly their plan for developing a spiritual center at Bernalillo was useless. Confusion and hurt was like a heavy fog within the car as they drove the two remaining days. In council with Joseph that week, however, Jeanne and John ceremonially became the "godparents" of the First Chamber Spirit Child, and in that responsibility, Joseph told them that they were his equals. In releasing form and expectations, the couple had traveled from the depths of despair to the mountaintops of their own spiritual destinies. Joseph had released his students from a specific and limited place of service to one that was universal in scope.

Within months, the new owner of the Bernalillo property removed the house trailer where Joseph had lived and bulldozed the empty Chamber that had stood 22 by 33 by 11 feet tall. Gone was the special place where Jeanne and John had been spiritually initiated and named by Joseph. Gone were all the material landmarks that had played such an important part in their personal spiritual development. All now that was left was what they held in their hearts, and the continuing, often painful lesson of non-attachment as taught by a master.

FIRE AT THE CABIN AT VALLECITO AND BANKRUPTCY

We based out of the cabin at Vallecito for about a year while we were still in transition. It was a difficult year because this is when the constant traveling started. This was also the year that we went from financial security, as we had known it, to a very different way of living. For example, we might fly into Europe with a total of $40 in our pockets. We learned to have faith that we would always be taken care of."

Perry Robinson of the CFP encouraged Jeanne and John during those frightening days by saying, "God has called you, and you have shown up and said *yes*. Shame on God if He will not now take care of you."

The cabin in the San Juan Mountains of Colorado was a treasured retreat. There was a deep blue lake amid stands of tall Ponderosa pines and summer hummingbirds who visited the colorful hanging plants on the porch. John was 48 years old that year; and although his sons, aged 24, 21, and 18, struggled in a culture of profit and loss, winners and losers, their father could find some relief in partial solitude. Their problems, however, were not far from his awareness, and John experienced some level of torment when he realized how financially incapable he had become to help them. In his personal journals of the day, John noted every detail of his sons' struggles, from employment disappointments, to lost girlfriends, to auto crashes, to apartment evictions, to crises of faith. Every parent knows the place where helplessness is the primary parental emotion regardless of personal finances. Sometimes conflicting circumstances simply overwhelm the parental senses, and all imagined solutions get swamped in tears. Not even a beautiful mountain environment can save parents from those emotions and the heart pangs of disappointment.

Jeanne was in her fifties when the shift in inner and outer lifestyle began. She uses the analogy of a lifeline extended to a novice swimmer that is played out foot by foot by an unseen hand. The learner gets deeper and deeper into the water, and farther and farther from the security of shore in a gradual process. Eventually, the lifeline becomes superfluous as the learner realizes that he or she can swim with a faith and confidence that is apart from the reassurance of any former safety device. The process, however, is not without the fears of deep water and the imagined presence of vision-eating sharks.

In the swimmer analogy, the deep water is not theoretical. It is substantially real, and its shore extends across months of time into years, where treading water for Jeanne and John had to be raised to an art form of endurance.

"I was raised never to consider bankruptcy. Whatever you create, you take full responsibility for it. Even as a single parent with two children, I may have prayed over my debts and done ceremony to determine what would be paid and what postponed, but our obligations were always met. John and I both had this philosophy as part of our social and cultural conditioning, so when our lives took a 180° turn, bringing with it debts from another 'lifetime,' our minds told us that bankruptcy was not an option. Even in our imaging over a two-year period, the subconscious taboo of bankruptcy was so strong that the answer was always *no*."

When John and Jeanne look back at the period of debt accumulation, they see no reckless or frivolous expenditures. Had there been no past debt, the income from their workshops and concerts would have supported their reduced lifestyle and enabled them to contribute to the needs of their children. But ultimately, debt was strangling them and threatening their mission itself.

How could Jeanne and John explain their bankruptcy to their respective families? In the old conditioning, bankruptcy equaled failure. But there was no sense of failure in their new work of awakening the Peace-Sound Chambers. Throughout 1998, their reception in countries on four continents had celebrated fulfillment, not defeat.

In mid-September, John confided in his journal, "Financially, we are at the point of desperation—almost no cash to our name and credit cards on suspension. We are totally in the hands of God at this point. Our journey has reached truly Biblical proportions."

And so, one morning they looked at each other, and with very few words, did prayers and an imaging whose results produced an answer they already intuitively knew. It was time—time to file for bankruptcy. Remembering two old friends in Denver who were lawyers, and hoping they might give some guidance, Jeanne called Micki and Christopher. John and Jeanne had already decided to file papers on this and simply needed some help to get started. When Micki answered the phone, and Jeanne told her that she and John were thinking about filing for bankruptcy, Micki's response was a surprised, "What? You mean you haven't done that yet?" And then she related how she and Christopher had done this a long time ago when they saw their lives taking a strong spiritual turn.

Micki and Christopher guided John and Jeanne through the process, with John's printing out forms from the computer, filling them out, and sending them off with a blessing. The bankruptcy ball had been put into motion, and the day of reckoning was to come several weeks later in the Denver Federal Courthouse.

In the meantime, in early October, Jeanne's Power of Sound workshop went well, but the income covered only their travel expenses and a single car payment, nothing more. Another workshop in Sedona netted about the same hand-to-mouth result. Then John Troutner, Jeanne's son, broke his leg in five places as the result of an accident. The seriousness of the injury compelled the couple to cancel any income work plans and drive 1700 miles to Chattanooga, where they stayed with Perry Lane (Jeanne's father) and Peggy (her stepmother). Generous, observant Perry slipped John $100 and then another $75 before their return to Vallecito. At the same time, Jeanne's mom in Martin, Tennessee sent $100. Both parents, though not always understanding their decisions, always lovingly supported Jeanne and John whenever they could.

Trying to avoid the expense of motel nights, Jeanne and John drove 670 miles the first day from Martin, Tennessee to Clinton, Oklahoma (west of Oklahoma City). Another long, long day on the road, and they arrived at the cabin in Vallecito, completely exhausted. John's journal records what happened about three that morning.

"Loud noises woke us up this morning. I was still half-asleep. Jeanne said, 'What is that?' I considered the noise in the fog of near dream-state and replied, 'Someone's in the shed out back.' I thought Michael Elkins, our landlord, must have been rummaging around in the large tool shed east of our house.

"A short time later, the sound of breaking glass and voices woke us again. This time, Jeanne bounded out of bed and looked out of the west window because of an orange glow casting eerie shadows in our room. In shock, she said, 'It's on fire!' The cabin next door had flames shooting out of the upstairs window and out of the roof on the far side!

"I quickly put on my pants as a persistent knock came at the door downstairs. It was a neighbor telling us we'd better get out of our house. Flames were about to engulf the tall spruce trees next to the cabin on fire. In the midst of these trees was the propane gas tank. If the trees went up, the propane tank would blow, and our cabin would burn for sure.

"Jeanne, still in the buff, jumped into action mode, calling 911 and grabbing essentials. Our suitcases, still packed, went into the car. Jeanne's ceremonial dress was next. Then, the tent, my ceremonial things, Joseph's paintings, our briefcases, passports, the harp, my didgeridoo.

"Fire engines began arriving at the point that I was almost certain that the trees would catch on fire, and that our things were a 'goner.' How easily we left behind our attachment to this place! We were ready to walk away from it all.

"It was a miracle that, in the end, the blue spruce trees didn't catch on fire even though flames literally licked the needles. It was also a miracle that we had heavy rains last night and this morning. It was a miracle that the firemen and women arrived in time and were able to contain the fire. It was a miracle that we woke as quickly as we did (Jeanne first), and that we were able to act quickly, and be ready to just walk away from it all.

"How quickly life changes! How suddenly we were tested! And, we've been tested a *lot* since our return from Australia.

"Nothing happens by chance. What are we being told—to walk away from this cabin? We may have to do it. We have almost no money. Maybe the fire was a way of showing us that we could easily let go of it all."

Jeanne notes that every fall for three consecutive years, she and John had received unavoidable signs to move. First, from Signal Mountain in Tennessee, then from Placitas in New Mexico, and now from Vallecito. And in each move, they stripped away more and more of their possessions until there were only the basics. The couple stood down the road watching the fire threaten what remained in the cabin—their desktop computer with all their scheduling and contact information, and a collection of favorite movies on tape that was their only entertainment luxury.

Jeanne remembers the moment: "As we watched the flames engulf our neighbor's cabin, realizing ours could go at any second, an astounding realization came to both of us. It was time to move again . . . now . . . by the end of the week, when the monthly lease was up. I felt a flip in my stomach, then I turned to John and said, 'Well, we know what it is to do this in fear. Let's make a conscious decision to come from *joy*, and treat this as an adventure.' In retrospect, we realize that this moment was a crucial turning point for us in how we were living, then and now. It gave us the guideline that would lead us through the years that would follow."

When the day dawned, and the fall gold of the aspens emerged from the fog of the structure fire, it appeared that the firemen had saved their cabin from destruction. Jeanne retreated upstairs to their bedroom, and John could hear her crying softly. Jeanne recalls, "I was crying, in part, to release the tension of the morning, but most were tears of gratitude. I could feel there were miracles on the way." Their cash resources were about $50, and now they had decided to move out of the cabin, store what they could not carry, and live like turtles with their home on their backs. But where would they go?

In the full light of day, calls had to be made to the network of family and friends. They could not just disappear from their Vallecito address. As the word went out, miracles began to happen. Within twenty-four hours, Jeanne and John received four offers of housing. Ula Rae Mynatt, an old friend from the CFP and moon mother at Sun-Moon Dances, offered the free use of a furnished farmhouse in Corryton, Tennessee. Another friend sent an immediate $150.

Then there was an amazing commitment that came from very dear friends in England—William and Heather Elmhirst. The synchronicity of their call still leaves Jeanne and John in awe. Jeanne recalls, "William and Heather had called to ask how we were doing, and so we told them what had just happened. William asked, do you need any money? We both became silent, and we said yes. William asked, how much? I reluctantly said, '$3000 would be ample to help us get on our feet.' At that, William said, we will send you $5,000. John and I were speechless." The decision we'd made only a few hours earlier to face change with joyous wonder was being confirmed with immediate manifestation. Life was different from this point on."

In making a total commitment to their Peace-Sound Chamber mission, John dissolved Creative Change Technologies, Inc., their last connection to income as consultants to the corporate business world. All the vestiges of their former careers were now gone.

With the bankruptcy papers in process, Jeanne and John set out across country toward their next Chamber Awakening in Pennsylvania. Along the route, they stayed with friends and family. At a stopover to visit Jeanne's family, there were many awkward moments. Although certainly not true of Jeanne's son John, and her daughter Jenny, who wholeheartedly supported their mother, other family members seemed threatened by Jeanne's new identity and were not open to hearing Jeanne talk about Peace Concerts and Chamber Awakenings. This was a common theme of reactions from both family groups. Among family members, there was a barrier to accepting who and what Jeanne and John had become. The families wanted to relate to the familiar characters that they felt they once knew. The vagabond spiritual adventurers who now occupied the bodies of Jeanne and John were alien strangers to them. The breakdown of some relationships was emotionally painful on both sides.

***

The final Chamber Awakening Ceremony of 1998, the ninth, occurred in the second week of November at Knauertown, Pennsylvania. The caretakers of the Birdsong Peace Sound Chamber were Tom and Kristen Bissinger who were long-time students of Joseph. Tom had been an active stageplay director but was then mostly teaching and writing. Kristen was a dancer who also taught dance.

John sensed that the Birdsong Chamber was more grounded than others he had experienced, and that may have accounted for a reduction in the psychic pyrotechnics that usually accompanied Chamber awakenings. Many of the eleven participants reported physical sensations in their bodies and elevated flows of energy. John reports his experience.

"My own experience was not at all ethereal. I did sense the energy building in the Chamber. I saw White Buffalo Calf Woman in the Chamber and later, Krishna. I saw the quality of light on the roof of the Chamber shimmer an almost unearthly white in the moonlight of an overcast night. And I saw the energy column form over the roof of the Chamber, shooting energy up into the sky and down into the earth. Also, the ceremony lasted 3 hours from start to finish, which means that Jeanne sang the spontaneous chants for only 2-½ hours—the shortest of all the ceremonies so far!

"Even without the spiritual pyrotechnics, the energy in the kiva afterwards was cooking. The proof of the experience is in the results. The outpouring of support from the people was amazing. Following the Awakening Ceremony and Celebration, Jeanne and I had two days of almost non-stop work in private sessions.

Jeanne and John began their relationship without the consideration of marriage. John was going through a divorce, and Jeanne was convinced psychologically that she would never marry again. But then the question came up. John was approached by a corporate headhunter for a very lucrative executive position, and he accepted a preliminary interview because of the couple's financial concerns and because the spiritual direction of their life together had not yet been established. Back from the job interview, with formal application in hand, the couple read that one of the criteria for the position was that the manager had to be married, as if marriage equaled corporate executive stability.

Jeanne surprised herself by her response. "Well, maybe we should get married."

John replied, "Well, maybe we should."

The first day dealing with the question, they practiced Intuitive Imagery three times, and each time the answer was, "yes, get married." Then next day, they asked when they should get married, and the answer came back, "this month." It was February 1995, not exactly the romantic month of May. They were both shocked, so they tested the marriage question ten times, and every time the intuitive mechanism responded "yes."

Jeanne and John were married that month on the sands of Virginia Beach while attending a conference. The romantic, shoreline ceremony from a distance might have resembled two former hippies with flowers in their hair re-tying the marriage knot. The ceremony was performed by a spiritually aligned friend, Ty Clements, but it was not sanctioned by Virginia law because no marriage license was obtained. That small detail did not prevent Jeanne and John from considering themselves married and going on a honeymoon to Disney World.

No one challenged their spousal relationship until it came to filing documents for their bankruptcy in 1998. In Denver, at the service counter of the Clerk of Court, the couple realized that they had to be legally married to file for joint bankruptcy. Off the top of her head, in Jeanne's usual spontaneous style, she asked the clerk, "Do you have to be married by a minister in Colorado? We are both ministers. Could we marry ourselves?"

"Honey," the clerk replied, "you don't even have to be a minister to marry yourself in Colorado."

"Really?" Jeanne asked. "Is there a waiting period?"

"No."

"You mean we can do it right here, right now?"

"Yes."

Jeanne turned to John and said, "Well, I do, do you?"

John smiled and said, "I do, too."

"There—you're married," the clerk said. "I'll send you the certificate tomorrow, and I'll sign as your witness."

There came a day when John and Jeanne had to appear in a Denver courthouse to work through the bankruptcy process with a trustee. They were nervous and practiced imagery in the hallway outside the court. The surprising image that came up was that of a comforting teddy bear. Inside the courtroom there were litigants, about twenty-five people with their attorneys. Jeanne and John appeared before the trustee without an attorney. As other couples appeared before the judge-like authority with stories of spending excesses, the court trustee dealt with them in a stern manner. And then it was Jeanne and John at the bar. The heavy-set trustee examined their filing papers and then, with compassion, counseled them to the best financial outcome they could hope to achieve. He could not have been more helpful, more comforting, more like a teddy bear.

Three months later, Jeanne and John, along with about fifteen others, gathered before a judge in the 10th Circuit Court in Denver for final bankruptcy proceedings. The judge was a woman, and she began the proceedings with a speech that moved Jeanne to tears. The speech was not about guilt and failure. It was an uplifting—even patriotic—talk about how the founding fathers of the United States were all debtors. They had come to the new world for "a fresh start." The judge described bankruptcy as a sacred American right that enabled everyone in debt in this country to get a fresh start. In America, we do not send debtors to prison. The judge's speech turned the bankruptcy court from a place of shame into a place of possibility.

When the judge dismissed the rest of the assembled group, declaring them released from their debts, she directed Jeanne and John to remain behind. In that moment, their hearts skipped a beat, not knowing what to expect. The judge called them to the bench. In a motherly voice, she said, "You've submitted a document that recommits you to the debt for your Nissan Pathfinder. In your best interests, I cannot authorize this and will not sign it. What this means to you is this. You can keep the car for as long as you make the payments. But should you find that you cannot afford them, you can turn the car back in to any dealership and owe nothing. In my opinion, this is your wisest move. You can do better."

It was an important moment. The judge was protecting Jeanne and John just as the trustee had done earlier in the process. Indeed, six weeks later, they did turn in the Pathfinder when another car was unexpectedly given to them—another miracle along the path.

When the judge's ruling was completed, Jeanne asked a parting question.

"May I have a copy of your speech?"

The surprised judge responded, "Why would you want that?"

Jeanne answered, "To show to our children."

The judge then smiled and said that she had never had such a request before. Then she handed down her copy of the speech to Jeanne.

END DAYS OF 1998

After the bankruptcy court appearance on December 21st in Denver, Jeanne and John had a difficult journey to the little donated farmhouse in Tennessee. There was heavy snow and ice through Colorado and Kansas, and then sleet and freezing rain in Kentucky that forced them to travel at moderate speeds in four-wheel drive. Much of the trip was very hazardous, even at speeds of 30 to 40 mph, and there were 1330 miles of it!

Jenny and John, Jeanne's children, 26 and 24 respectively, came for a Christmas celebration with a decorated tree and an exchange of presents on Christmas morning. The visit was "delightful," but John missed being with his sons Ryan (24), Sean (21), and Alan (19) at that traditional time for families. A few days later, the 29th, the couple quietly celebrated Jeanne's 55th birthday.

The year 1998 ended in an antiquated remote rural Tennessee homestead for the couple who had traveled the world. Their experiences had been extraordinary by any measure, and their acceptance by diverse cultures in the United States, Germany, Norway, Bolivia and Peru, and Australia was a high honoring of their spiritual gifts. And yet, there they were at the end of that remarkable year, bankrupt and living without the promise of relief, like homeless refugees. If ever trust and faith in their calling was tested, these were the bitter days where even the elements, expressed in the flat brown farm fields folded in frost, bespoke of a winter frozen with discontent. Somehow, Jeanne and John, who had experienced the highs of spiritual enlightenment, had to find the courage of their convictions if they were to continue.

The farmhouse at Corryton is small and wood-built probably in the 1920s. The front porch, now enclosed to give the house a second bedroom, faces a narrow road and a railroad tracks where trains still rumble by late at night and again before sunrise. There is a weather-beaten shed and a barn-like structure behind the house to indicate that the adjacent property was once farmed, but the aspect is that the old farmstead has passed its usefulness and is an antique of a past age when subsistence family farms dotted the Tennessee landscapes.

Inside, the kitchen, the bathroom addition, a dark, heavy sideboard, and other antiquated furnishings might remind senior citizens of long ago visits to rural grandparents. There is electricity and indoor plumbing, but there is no air-conditioning or any other elements that would elevate this retreat to anything above functional.

Corryton, although only about thirteen miles from I-40 east of Knoxville, is not easily accessible. Directions from the interstate highway take the visitor through a maze of two-lane rural roads. If Jeanne and John had wanted a hideout instead of a retreat, the little old house at Corryton would have served that purpose well. No one would expect to find world travelers in residence there.

Jeanne talks about this retreat place. "This little house and the land on which it stands, in its simplicity, has nurtured us with kindness and beauty and fed our souls in times when we most needed it. This precious farm is very like our friend, Ula Rae Mynatt, who grew up here and now owns it—generous, kind, wise, and comforting. It indeed has been an oasis for us, time and time again."

THE POWER OF SOUND

In an article for the web titled *The Power of Sound*, Jeanne summarizes her visionary experiences with vibration and puts her mission with John in perspective. This piece was written before the "For The One" Dance evolved.

"Consider that everything we perceive to exist is vibration . . . the simplest thought, the wind, a laugh, a table, a chair, a speck of dust . . . that all we perceive to have existence is vibration.

Consider that vibration is sound . . . that sound is music.

Think of it, then . . . the possibility that everything we perceive to exist is fundamentally a song . . . the leaf of a tree, the tree itself. Even you. You are a song! A living, breathing, moving, speaking, singing song! Everything about you is a song!

Sound strange? Let me continue . . . When I met Joseph Rael, Beautiful Painted Arrow, in 1995 I was reminded of what I had long forgotten . . . that I, that we, come from "between the slices of light." Each of us has been sung into existence. Joseph's people of the Ute and Picuris tribes teach this, those of my own Cherokee heritage teach this, the Australian Aborigine teach this, the Mayan elders teach this, as do so many other of our indigenous relatives . . . "We sing our world into existence."

In 1983, Joseph was told in vision to create Peace-Sound Chambers around the world, sacred kiva-like structures into which people might go to sing for world peace. It was in these Chambers that I learned the power of singing the ancient sounds of the directions. In an extraordinary vision, in 1996, I was shown that when we sing the sounds of the directions, allowing them to flow spontaneously, we create vibrations that change us all, that help us all remember who we really are and where we come from.

The idea is that when we sing spontaneous songs with the ancient sounds of the directions – ah, eh, ee, oh, oo – we are able to ride the sounds like a magic carpet "back" to the point of creation

. . . back to the original vibration from which all comes . . . And from this place we can create anything . . . new worlds, a healthy body . . . even a planet of peace.

In 1998, living in the San Juan Mountains of Colorado, in one week, I had three dreams . . . With the first, I was standing before some 40,000 people in a stadium, teaching them to sing spontaneously, each person singing who he or she was. You would think the sound would be chaos. It was! But, what happens when you leave something in chaos long enough? The law of physics says it will find its way to order . . . and in this case, to harmony. In the dream, I could hear what would happen. The mass of voices did find their way to harmony. It was the sound of the heavens opening up. It was indescribably beautiful!

The second dream was similar. I was standing on a stage in an auditorium seated with hundreds of people . . . again, teaching them to sing in this sacred way. The impact was overwhelming in its power and beauty.

Then came the third dream. I was standing in the United Nations. I had asked each of the delegates, representing countries from all over the world, to stand and sing who they were. Note: when one sings the sounds of the directions, allowing the self to go into "no mind" or "between the slices of light," the ego is not involved. Thus, when the UN delegates began to create spontaneously, from an ego-less state, I heard a miracle. I heard the sound of Peace. I heard the sound of an entire planet that was remembering who it was. It was the vibration of absolute truth . . . the remembrance that there is only one person here and that all there is, is love.

If this whole concept sounds impractical or unbelievable, try it yourself. Create your own songs. Above all, don't think! Start with the building blocks of "ah, eh, ee, oh, oo," in whatever order they naturally want to come. Then, observe. None of this is complicated. It simply takes the willingness to let go and allow.

My husband, John Pehrson, and I have traveled the world giving Peace Concerts, teaching workshops and seminars, encouraging people to sing who they are . . . moving beyond ego into a state of pure spontaneity. We have watched miracles unfold before our eyes. We have been in war zones and seen, firsthand, the impact of the power of spontaneous sound . . . the singing of Peace into the land.

Indigenous peoples have done this for centuries. It is in all of us to sing in this sacred way. It's just that most of us have forgotten. It's time now to remember.

I leave you with two pieces of homework. First: Create a song everyday. Do this, even if it is just for a few seconds. What this does is place you in a space of total awareness, in an ego less state . . . where you remember that you are the sacred "hollow bone" through which Spirit blows the breath of life. In those few seconds you will experience direct communion between you and Spirit. The more you do this, the easier it is to live and operate from this state of awareness.

Second: Love what is in front of you in this given moment. Everything else will take care of itself. Love what is in front of you just this moment, then move to the next moment doing the same, then onto the next and so on and so on. This is really so simple . . . though may not always be easy. Do it, though. Trust your ability to love in the present moment.

Consider the possibility that there is only one person here. Consider the possibility that all there is, is love. Perhaps it is this that we have forgotten. Perhaps this is what we are to remember. And so it is here . . . It is to this sacred remembering place that the singing takes us . . . bringing us home. Bringing us to the place from which we all come . . . from "between the slices of light."

T he new year began on the road again, staying with spiritually
like-minded friends and doing workshops and personal consultations when asked. On January 8th, they were in Shiro, Texas at
Neil and Beth Sutton's place, where they were greeted by two large
mahogany-colored mules with their chin whiskers billowing over
the corral fence. Three horses, a cat, and an Australian sheepdog
named Shadow also lived there.

At Charles and Donna Court's place, Jeanne and John attended
a fire ceremony and sweat lodge, and then Jeanne led a group of
twenty-two people in chanting. The powerful experience for the
participants led to a workshop request and a few private sessions for
the both of them.

Moving on to Placitas, New Mexico, the couple said farewell to
Joseph's old place at Bernalillo, did a sweat lodge, and then workshops that produced only limited income. There were old friends
associated with Joseph to visit, but generally their association with
the area around Albuquerque was over, and with it went some
measure of security and safety. Also came the realization that as a
couple moving continually from one accommodation to another
that there was little privacy to be had for marital intimacy. This was
one of the personal challenges that nobody in spiritual work tells
you about.

There were aspects of their staying in people's homes, and the
observations that come from those close encounters, that were
important. Tom Bissinger of the Birdsong Chamber in Pennsylvania,
who with his wife Kristen had hosted Jeanne and John several
times, observed that the couple lived "lightly" as houseguests. By
this he meant that they carried their own weight by pitching in on
the dishwashing, clean-up chores and meals, as well as washing
their own bed linens and re-making the bed before leaving. When
the Pehrsons moved on, Tom said that he actually missed their not

being in the house. The old adage that both fish and guests begin to smell in three days did not apply to Jeanne and John.

Tom Bissinger also confided to John another important observation. He said that he had carefully watched how the couple worked together, especially how John supported Jeanne in her visionary work. He made John realize that other men in their travels were also watching him support Jeanne in the expression of her Goddess energy. This recognition of Jeanne as a spiritual leader was significant to women along their journey, but it was also mind-altering to many men who had been trapped by tradition into stereotyping the role of women in spiritual practice.

Before the Pehrsons continued their schedule of Chamber Awakenings, Jeanne accepted an invitation to participate in a conference in Hawaii called the "Whale Quest Conference." Here is her account of the unique experience.

"I arrived late into the airport in Maui and was quickly driven to the Conference site. The first meeting had already begun, and upon entering the conference hall, I was quickly whisked onto the stage and asked to teach the participants how to sing the spontaneous songs in the way I do.

"The next morning the entire conference of people, several hundred, went by bus to meet a ship owned by the 'Save the Whales Foundation,' where we were to be taken out into a part of the ocean where the humpback whales give birth to their babies. This was in an area of the water under which a crater existed, causing the immediate water to be warmer and more conducive to birthing. The ship we were on went to the edge of the crater, careful not to go further so as not to disturb the whales.

"At one point, the leader of the conference, Maitreya Rogers, asked over the paging system for the group to begin creating songs in the way I had taught them the night before. I began to sing . . . and one by one, people began to create their own spontaneous songs. The overall effect was a massive symphony of sound that began to move out over the ocean. What happened then was something I will never forget. At first, a whale here and there began to come to the surface, and then another began to surface and another, until there were whole pods of whales surfacing. It was when we got toward the end of our song that something happened that even Disney couldn't have choreographed better.

"Three giant humpbacks surfaced side by side, jumped up out of the water, and as the song ended, the last thing you saw were the three tails simultaneously disappearing under the water . . . along with all the other whales. At that moment, there wasn't a sound on the ship . . . and I found tears running down my cheeks, trying to understand what had just happened.

"It wasn't until later that John and I had a discussion and surmised that maybe what had happened was this. The whales are said to be the 'record keepers.' I actually never knew what that meant. What may have happened in this experience I just described is that the whales were celebrating because finally we 'two-leggeds' were getting it . . . we were remembering. Singing spontaneously in the way we had took us to a place beyond the ego and literally took us 'home to the original vibration from which we all come. It is in this place that we remember we are not separated from each other, but are all part of each other. That's worth celebration.

"The last full day of the conference I was asked to do a private session for one of the conference participants. In our one-hour session, I was guided to teach her how to sing her fear, and then to let the higher or wiser part of her sing a song back to the part of her that experienced fear. In this way, it would change the vibration and help her to transform the fear. (Basically the same method I used with the cancer).

"Later that day I received a call from her asking me to come to her room. When I arrived, there were other people standing around. The first thing she said to me was, 'If I had not done the session with you earlier, I am convinced I would be dead.' What had happened was that she and several others had gone into the ocean to practice some new skills they were learning. There apparently was an ebb tide they were not aware of, and four women began to be pulled out into the deeper water. Two of the women got back with help from some more experienced swimmers. One woman was rescued by two surfers and taken immediately to the hospital. The fourth woman, the one I had done the session with, was being pulled out so far so quickly that no one could get to her. She began to panic. Suddenly, an angel appeared and said, 'Remember what you just learned.'

"At that point, she began to spontaneously sing her panic. I have no idea how she did this as she was being pulled under water the whole time. Nonetheless, she sang and sang until there was no more song. And then, from what seemed like a distant place, she heard another voice . . . calm, soothing . . . and realized that sound was actually coming from her. This was the voice of the higher self singing back to the part of her that panicked . . . transforming the fear. In those few moments, her adrenaline began to flow, and she found clear focus and strength and was able to pull herself all the way back to the shore.

"An amazing story, I think."

The 10th Awakening Ceremony occurred in Gold Hill, near Boulder, Colorado, at the end of February. It was a clear, cold night with an occasional high wind. While Jeanne sang inside the dirt-insulated kiva, fifteen others outside kept the vigil with John. Although the ceremony was the shortest yet, with Jeanne singing only two hours, the participants felt an energy shift. Perhaps the shift was not so dramatic because of Jeanne's earlier visit to the

Thunder Song Chamber the previous October. Nevertheless, something miraculous occurred. John noted what happened in his journal.

"Perhaps the most powerful insight came from Jeff Combelic during the celebration ceremony. Jeanne had laid out stones for each person to take after they had been blessed. Some of the stones were rose quartz and some were malachite. With wide eyes, Jeff said he'd received a message a number of years ago that 'the Chamber would not have power until the stones come.' And now the stones had come! I got chills all over when he shared this with the group. It was a confirmation of the power of the Awakening Ceremony!"

Participant Michael Woolard told John that when Joseph first began teaching people to chant in the Sound Chambers, he said that there would one day be a seer inside and a group listening on the outside. The Awakening Ceremony appeared to be the fulfillment of that prophecy, too.

The 11th Awakening Ceremony was held on Serpent Mountain in Cosby, Tennessee. It was late March, the Spring equinox, and the anniversary of their first Awakening Ceremony at the Center for Peace in Seymour, Tennessee. Faithful friend and Moon Mother Ula Rae Mynatt provided the site and would be its caretaker, but first the roof had to be put on the Chamber. Jeanne and John, with the help of seven other volunteers, accomplished the task in four muscle-challenging days.

Jeanne says that John petitioned the Rain Spirits for a dry window over the Chamber on that rainy and overcast night, but it rained anyway. "The Spirits reminded John that 'everything is part of you. You don't have to ask us to stop the rain. You can do it yourself!' It took some time to digest that thought. But finally, in the presence of the Thunder Beings who announced their presence in great claps of energy, John was able to stop the rain."

Inside, Jeanne sat at the center of the Chamber under an open (unfinished) skylight. Unseen by those outside the Chamber, she took off her ceremonial dress and allowed the rain to fall on her naked body. It was the first time that she had done the ceremony naked, or in an "unfinished" Chamber. As the vortex of energy formed in the kiva, John sensed the Star People helping to open the energy gateway. Karl Gruen, keeping the vigil outside, saw the energy vortex form in what he described as a "barber pole" spiraling upward. Inside, the aboriginal sounds were coming through Jeanne as if the elders from Australia were calling. It was a magical night.

By April of 1999, with more Chamber Awakenings scheduled in Europe, Jeanne and John realized that they could not make further car payments and that they would have to turn in the Pathfinder. But how could they pursue their mission without a car? It was in these circumstances that they attended a send-off dinner given for them by a couple of friends, Cheryl Patterson and Marcus Ambrester, who had participated in their work. In the course of the evening, Jeanne and John confided their transportation predicament. Without a pause, Marcus said, "I've got your car. It's sitting in the driveway. It's a BMW. It's yours. We can do the title and registration tomorrow."

The story behind the unqualified generosity was that Marcus, at age six, was in the house of his church minister when he witnessed something that he could never forget. The minister had just acquired a brand new car, probably the first new car that he had ever owned. It was talked about. It was admired. And then a young couple in crisis came to the minister's door, and he counseled them, and then young Marcus saw his pastor hand over the keys to his new car to the destitute young couple. Marcus ended the story by saying, "I have waited my whole life to do something like that."

Jeanne says that she realized at that moment that it was as important for Marcus to give the car as it was for them to receive it. A humble receiving is necessary to the act of giving. A *Course In Miracles* teaches that giving is receiving.

When Jeanne and John took possession of the 1986 BMW325E and were talking about a name for the car, another vehicle pulled in front of them with a bumper sticker that read "Grace Happens." And so the small BMW became Gracie, and she served them well for the next four years.

The Chamber at Grafton, Ontario, Canada was the 48th to be built. Owen James, its principal caretaker, purchased the forty-acre site and Joseph blessed it in 1997. It is called the Sacred Arrow Peace-Sound Chamber, and its grounds see Long Dances, Sun-Moon Dances, and Owen's inspired Spring Renewal Dance, as well as sweat lodges and other programs on an annual basis. Jeanne and John arrived in Grafton in mid-April to perform their twelfth Awakening Ceremony. It was to prove one of their most powerful experiences largely due to the work that Owen and an "awake" group of participants had done previously on the site.

John poured a five-round sweat lodge with the last blessing round for the Chamber caretakers being especially powerful as the caretakers blessed each other with water. After a sacred pipe ritual inside the kiva, Jeanne began singing and chanting about 12:45 a.m. as snow fell. Laila, a student of Grandmother Guadalupe Rios (a Huichol Indian from Mexico) began sensing the energy immediately. Her hands began shaking, like Jeanne's often did, as the Spirits appeared.

At the height of the energy level, John and others outside the Chamber said that they experienced ecstatic states of bliss as the Masters and the Ancient Ones were manifested. A ball of brilliant white light radiated outward from the center, filling the entire Peace-Sound Chamber and extending to the people keeping the vigil and beyond into the trees. Afterward, participants acknowledged that it was a blessing beyond description.

John was again visited by the Four Kings who had initiated him the previous year, and this time they knighted him with robes and a tall miter-style hat. Later in the morning, Pamela Friendly told John that at one point during the Awakening Ceremony, he appeared to be much taller than his usual self, and that he was wearing a hat. John accepted her observation as a validation of his experience with the Four Kings. As the participants celebrated the events of the awakening, the snow stopped, the overcast cleared, and the entire early morning sky was full of bright stars. The unpredicted change, in marked contrast to the weather forecast, reinforced the idea that significant ceremony created its own patterns in the natural world.

Sue Mehrtens had been very important to Jeanne in recognizing and confirming her persistent call into spiritual work. It was Sue who had rushed to Jeanne with the amazing portents clearly evident to her in working Jeanne's astrological chart. Now with a schedule break near the end of April, Jeanne and John went to visit Sue at her home in Long Island, New York.

Jeanne says about Sue, "It's helpful to know, for those who have a more pragmatic and practical approach to reality, that Sue's background borders on that of genius. She is a brilliant writer and analyst, speaks five languages, and can read up to a thousand pages in a day. To experience her as a psychic and a seer, without prejudice or limitation, is to know the possibilities of unlimitedness and expansion that lie within each of us."

John recorded in his journal Sue's insights for both Jeanne and himself during their visit.

"*For Jeanne:*

Jeanne has been undergoing an enormous expansion of horizons and energy field.

She has reached about 1/3 of her full development. She will reach a plateau in roughly 3 years (2002) where there will be a consolidation and a feeling of solidity.

Then, another spiraling will occur—a widening—that will result in even greater effectiveness. She will walk into a room and shift the energy of the entire room. This will occur in about 5 years (2004).

Then, still another spiraling will take place. Jeanne will have the ability to achieve a global mind link and communicate with others around the world via telepathy. This will characterize her fullest development."

For himself, John recorded:

"My overall orientation is different than Jeanne's. My expansion and growth is inner, deeper, which is what allows me to go out and go higher—a paradox.

I am transmuting the inner darkness into outer light.

This has been a journey that has been underway for many decades. Now it is more conscious and intentional.

As I allow visioning time, and allow certain insights to play against my mind screen, this will intensify my journey.

Mine is a set of descents into deeper levels of my core being. I am now starting on the second of six descents.

My Spirit Guides are very carefully guiding me.

The energies become more and more intense as I go deeper. Each step peels away a new layer. Each peeling away helps me to become a more transparent transmitter of energy, the energy of the very *being-ness of my presence.*

As Jeanne will find her presence to expand to fill the space, I will have the effect of reaching someone from within. They will feel that they've been *filled up.* This is not something to "effort" about. Simply allow images to come to my mind screen; allow myself to relax and get higher insights.

"An exciting *coming around* will occur for us. Relationships and things that we have given up will come back to us."

NORWAY 1999

As a result of their Chamber Awakening Ceremony in Norway the previous June, Jeanne and John were urged to return, which they did in early May. Gerd Bjorke was again their host, and she made the introductions and announcements at a Peace Concert on Sunday, the 2nd. The site of the concert was an old factory building with cement floors. A group called the Taranoids opened with Bernt Balchen's five didgeridoo players sounding low "D" notes that correspond with the second chakra. A trio of singers (Celia, Kolbjorn, and Mia) then sang unusual melodies accompanied by Mudras or movements to enhance the sounds. There were about 160 people in attendance when Jeanne stepped into the center of the audience ellipse to sing. John and the organizers had set a sacred space around the entire audience area using cornmeal, and they had smudged the participants and the audience with sage smoke.

John notes Jeanne's performance and the audience reaction.

"For the next hour or so, Jeanne sang and taught. At times, she sang to the accompaniment of the didgeridoo, or the flute, or with my voice or Mia's voice. She wove this together with teaching the audience about spontaneous singing using the vowel sounds. She pulled the audience in, little by little, until the entire audience was singing. At the end, there was tremendous applause and a standing ovation that kept going until Jeanne agreed to sing one more song—*Amazing Grace*."

In concerts, John was Jeanne's principal back-up singer, Native American cedar flute player, rattle percussionist, and didgeridoo player. His musical background included four years of serious piano lessons, church and school choir membership from the age of nine, and the playing of the clarinet in his high school band. He was self-taught on the dij, but on this trip to Norway he received formal dij training from a master.

"Today, Jeanne has been busy with private teaching sessions while I spent over 4 hours with Bernt Balchen. Bernt picked me up just after 9:00 A.M. and drove me to his house, which was very cold inside! Even before we finished a cup of coffee, Bernt took my didgeridoo and me into the basement where he has a small work-shop. There he doctored my dij. He reamed and smoothed the inside of the end of it, put a harder wax on the mouthpiece, and varnished the inside—patching a few places with plastic wood to boot!

"Once the didgeridoo was doctored, he taught me a lot about making it sing in different ways—tongue movements to create over-tones, incorporating vocal sounds, and using rhythms. It helped to watch a video on dij playing by a guy named Allan Shockley from Arizona. We practiced a bit. And Bernt taught me about *microleptic energy shells* that are formed as the dij is played—some so powerful at various distances that they made my body vibrate! I learned quite a bit that will take practice to master. The Aborigines teach that the didgeridoo is an extension of the respiratory system. It takes diaphragmatic breathing to play it, and all the sounds come from *inside* the body. I am already a better dij player just in the couple of hours I spent with Bernt. But I have much to practice."

During this visit to Oslo, John gave an Intuitive Imagery Workshop. Part I dealt with using the imagery to get guidance. Part

II concerned the use of intuitive imagery to promote healing and transformation. Jeanne had been suffering a sore throat, so as a demonstration to the group, John worked with Jeanne to seek energy symbols that would promote her healing. In a six-step process, it was indicated that blueberries were the key to her recovery. John reports the result in his journal.

"I believe that healing took place with the imagery work. But it also provided insight: (1) Jeanne has been eating foods on her 'avoid' list. This is contributing to the health issue. (2) She began 'singing' her prayers last night. She says that she has known for a month that a change was coming in the way she was praying but didn't know what it was. The imaging provided the answer. (3) Although blueberries were not available, Anne Haraldsen had some blackberry concentrate syrup. Jeanne has been taking a small amount diluted with water to form a delicious juice.

"Today, about 16 hours later, Jeanne reports that her sore throat is almost gone! The other important insight here is that it is important to allow the issue (sore throat) to speak and be heard—just like in Jeanne's sound healing process. That paves the way for healing and transformation to occur."

That same week, Jeanne and John had another opportunity to learn more about the magical sound generation of the didgeridoo. John records.

"Last night, Jeanne and I spent several hours with Bernt Balchen and his wife, Martha (Marta) at their home. Their home is Bernt's boyhood home where he lived from the time he was six, excepting for a few years in the U.S. Bernt took Jeanne and me deeper into the techniques of overtone chanting—and overtones created with the dij. With a couple of the didgeridoos, we also experienced the power of the *silent sounds* that occurred for us after the dij stopped sounding. With the G-dij, the 'after-sounds' were much like the humming of a refrigerator! The other, lower, very special Australian D-dij turned on a whole chorus of silent overtones a brief moment after it stopped. There was just a brief, silent delay followed by a chorus of 'silent sounds.' It affirmed the importance of what Joseph teaches about listening to the silent sounds."

On a side trip to western Norway, the couple visited Gerd Bjorke's family and friends in a rural region of fjords and glaciers and lakes where dairy farms dotted the landscape and fishing boats docked at the farmer's landing. There were narrow, winding country roads, short ferry rides, little villages with slate-roofed houses, and small factories making woolen socks, sweaters, and underwear. Breakfasts were made from bread and cheese, cherries, pickled beets, cucumbers and fruit. Days were ended singing Norwegian songs with neighbors and folk dancing late into the night. Facing the granite-faced cliffs, where only moss and mountain grasses grow with a few accents of white wildflowers, Jeanne and John and Gerd saw a high mountain waterfall with its accompanying rainbow, and they sang a spontaneous song to acknowledge its majesty. This was the Norway that Gerd wanted to share with Jeanne and John.

THE SCOTLAND AND ENGLAND CHAMBER AWAKENINGS

The Isle of Skye in Scotland was the location for the 13th Chamber Awakening. The mountains and the glens there overlook the North Atlantic to small offshore islands in the mist. The coast is rocky, but there is green growth everywhere and sheep dotting the landscape. It is the land of fairy people and the ancient Celtic spirits.

To facilitate the Awakening Ceremony, John had to construct a sweat lodge. The weather in mid-May might have been stormy with gale force winds, but generally the weather held with warm temperatures and only brief periods of light rain or misting. The sweat lodge was built with local willow branches gathered by Ocean

Graham and Jeanne. Scotty, Ocean's husband, helped secure the lodge by tying the willows fast with twine.

Ocean and Scotty Graham were the caretakers of the Isle of Skye Chamber. John describes Ocean as very English and Scotty, a homeland history buff, as very Scottish. The couple met on a kibbutz in Israel in the 1980s, and when Ocean was pregnant, they returned to Scotland. Later in the year, Ocean and Scotty would join Jeanne and John for the Australian walkabout.

The sweat lodge was a snug fit for eleven participants. On the fifth round, the Blessing Round, five people stayed in the lodge with Ocean and Scotty to accept responsibility for the caretaking of the Chamber. It was a miracle of support as far as Ocean was concerned.

The Medicine Bundle containing the Spirit Child from Joseph's First Chamber arrived in time for the Isle of Skye Ceremony. During the ceremony the Spirit Child-Warrior danced inside the Chamber, occasionally jumping into the vortex of spiraling energy that formed as Jeanne sang. As Joseph had directed, it was teaching the Spirit of the Isle of Skye Chamber. At the end of the ceremony, the young Spirit Warrior from the First Chamber said to Jeanne, "You can leave now, Mother." It was the first time that the Spirit had called her "Mother," and Jeanne was moved to tears when she related the experience to John.

In every national environment where Peace-Sound Chambers are built, the usual local suspects who have experienced the conflict of war and peace there make an appearance. John records what he saw at the Isle of Skye.

"The Spirits of ancient Scottish warriors appeared around the Chamber, including one who seemed to be William Wallace. He was a big (tall) Spirit—as tall or taller than I. He wasn't so happy or excited about what we were doing—creating energy for peace—since Scotland didn't really have its independence from England. After a time of mental dialogue, he changed his mind. The kind of peace we were working for was raising the vibration of everyone and everything that will ultimately lead to the greatest level of self-determination. At this point, Wallace himself became a sentry at the door to the East, and three other Highland Warrior Spirits replaced the angels in the other three directions."

On the 18th of May, Jeanne and John, with Stella Longland, a student of Joseph's and a "sparkplug" of organization, were on the Scottish mainland en route to Lancaster, England, a 400-mile trip that took twelve hours. After an overnight with Stella and her partner Bob, Jeanne and John rented a car and continued on to Felindre, Wales, where the 14th Chamber Awakening was scheduled.

Although John had a great deal of back pain, and a headache too, a walk in the Welch hills to a waterfall, where Jeanne waded in the cool water, made him feel better. John and Paul Benham built a sweat lodge frame in about two hours out of long and flexible hazel saplings. Paul and his partner, Jan Elliott, operated the Primrose Organic Farm and were caretakers of the Chamber. Later, in September 2004, Jeanne and John, as licensed clergy, would join the couple in marriage. Again, as at the Isle of Skye, eleven people entered the sweat lodge, and five remained for the blessing round for those called as caretakers for the Peace-Sound Chamber. This commitment was followed by a water blessing where caretakers blessed each other to help remind them that they are Masters in their own right.

During the Sound Workshop on Saturday, Jeanne got a very strong insight that this Chamber, and the people associated with it, were about "clearing the land." Later, Peter Terry, a mountain of a man from Hereford, said that the name of the Chamber was Song of the Clearing. John felt that all concerned were in sync about the purpose of the place. The Awakening Ceremony, the

14th, beginning at midnight, Sunday the 23rd on Primrose Farm, attracted a multitude of spirits including the First Chamber Spirit-Child Warrior, and Eagle-men who stood sentry in the four directions. Jeanne felt that the Spirit of the Wales Chamber pulled her hair at one point. She also felt that she was processing something very ancient in the land, and she was aware of traveling. Later, she said that she got it more strongly than in any other ceremony just how important the people are on the outside of the Chamber who act as beacons.

"The witnessing made all that was happening real," Jeanne said. "As Joseph taught us . . . the chair exists because the table is listening and vice versa."

CHALLENGED

Although Jeanne and John go only where they are invited to perform ceremony, crossing cultural and religious boundaries can sometimes lead to confrontation. There was a five-story pyramid in Kelowna, British Columbia that was constructed to the exact proportions of the great Giza pyramid in Egypt. This sounding space did not follow the guidelines of the Chambers as envisioned by Joseph, but it was nevertheless a powerful place for ceremony. Stephen Cipes, its owner, requested that Jeanne and John come and perform an Awakening Ceremony there. It would be their fifteenth such ceremony. Weeks before their trip, Jeanne asked if permission had been granted from the indigenous people for them to perform the ceremony, and they arrived under the assumption that this courtesy and show of respect had been done.

The area was the homeland of the First Nations People, the West Bank Okenagan tribe, and the first indication of local resistance came when a native man refused to construct a sweat lodge for the ceremony because of his traditions against whites doing sweats.

The resistance compounded when an Okenagan structure called a *kacoolie* was provided by the white hosts as the site of the sweat lodge. The structure was round with a conical roof built of pine, fire pit at its center, and a smoke hole in its ceiling. The exterior walls were packed with earth. The kacoolie was considered the traditional winter home of a bygone era, and the event sponsors seemed unaware of any ceremonial significance associated with it.

John and Sean Pegg thus went about constructing a large square, non-traditional frame inside the large kacoolie, and covering it for use as a sweat lodge. Roughly forty-five people came for the lodge ceremony, and John and Sean built the sweat fire in a sacred way using cornmeal and tobacco, and heating sixty stones until they were cherry red. Outside the lodge, a cornmeal and tobacco circle was ceremonially laid around the entire structure, and a cornmeal energy line was laid from the rock pit at the center of the lodge to the fire. All these serious, prayerful rituals conformed to what John had been taught in his initiation by Joseph.

Since there were so many who had come to sweat, half the people entered the lodge for the first two, East and South rounds, and the other half for the West and North rounds. The fifth round was the water blessing round, and it lasted a long time since each participant receives a blessing and then blesses someone else in recognition that as One, they are all Masters. The intent of the lodge experience to "feed the people" was done with spiritual integrity, and the participants responded in kind. For some it had been "wonderful," and for others "life-changing." John, who poured the sweat, had explained in advance the sacredness and the metaphors inherent in the lodge experience, and he had used the focus in the lodge itself for gentle teaching.

The Awakening Ceremony itself that followed that night around the pyramidal Peace-Sound Chamber was a very wet happening for the over forty people who stood vigil with John outside.

Inside, Jeanne sang and experienced a whole line of Masters entering the pyramid. Both John and Jeanne reported bi-locating in the British Columbia pyramid as they felt the energy connection to the Giza pyramid in Egypt. Throughout the ceremony, the steady rain soaked the observers, who took their turns at the fire that stayed strong and warm all night. Despite this test of endurance, the same vortex of energy spiraling upwards from the Chamber and then returning as a shaft of light descending into it was observed as the same phenomena that had occurred at other Chamber Awakenings.

The next day, however, a challenge arose concerning the sweat lodge ceremony that Jeanne and John had performed. Two native women called for an appointment to see Jeanne. One of them was thought to be the sister of the native man who had refused to build the sweat lodge. She appeared at the door of host Stephen Cipes's home to confront Jeanne. The two native women had arrived fifteen minutes early for their appointment, and Jeanne was meditating, perhaps in preparation for their onslaught. They were not pleased to be kept waiting. John was not present, as he was involved in teaching an Imaging Workshop elsewhere.

The moment Jeanne sat down with the Okenagan women, the leader immediately expressed her anger.

"What you have done is wrong. It will take a very long time to heal the land."

What the women were deeply offended about was the sweat lodge ceremony that had been done in the kacoolie.

"You don't come onto 'my' land and do ceremony without asking 'my' permission. Who are you? Who are your elders? They didn't train you very well. You have ruined the first-time sweaters."

Jeanne responded in love, but she stood her ground. She named Joseph as one of her elders, and also the "Tall Ones" in the Spirit World.

The two women seemed nonplused by Jeanne's statement, and they got up abruptly to leave. Jeanne had already told them that she never intended to offend the Okenagan people, and that she was deeply sorry that they "felt" offended. As the women were leaving, they told Jeanne that she should be glad that they had come and not a delegation of the male tribal elders. Jeanne responded by giving the angry women an honor gift of tobacco wrapped in red cloth; and as they departed, she said, "Thank you for being my teachers."

How this story is told around the council fires of the Okenagan is unknown.

The lesson for Jeanne and John was to make sure wherever they traveled that they personally would obtain official permission from indigenous people prior to any ceremonies being held on native lands. This permission would never be assumed again.

WATERSONG 1999

The 16th Chamber Awakening occurred during mid-August at the Watersong Peace-Sound Chamber in Graham, North Carolina. The Chamber was new, built in 1999, on the land of caretakers David Stephenson and Cheryl Braswell and their daughter Robin, known to friends and family as BZ. The event attracted a gathering of many people who had played key roles in Jeanne and John's spiritual growth. Perry Robinson and Brenda Sue Taylor, for example, and others had come to participate from the Center for Peace in Seymour, Tennessee. Those who had made the Watersong Chamber construction possible also came to witness the Awakening. R. J. Dobmier (called Dobs), a master firekeeper, and ardent supporter Lance Davis were there as were several others who would later travel the world as members of the "For the One" Dance crew. The Watersong Chamber community would prove to be a key resource for many Moon Mothers, Firekeepers, Drummers, Dog Soldiers, and Kitchen Angels who were willing to serve dances as far away as Israel and South Africa.

The Awakening weekend began significantly when Brenda Sue arrived on Friday night carrying the medicine bundle that had been the traveling residence of the Spirit of Joseph's first Peace-Sound Chamber—He Who Sings, Chaa Tah Meh Eh. The original Chamber had been dismantled when Joseph left Bernalillo, but its Spirit was still alive and active. Saturday morning, the bundle was taken into the large kiva-like Watersong Chamber for a ceremony honoring the young chief. Each participant took their turn in holding the bundle and connecting to its Spirit. It was a powerful experience, and many tears were shed. When the group then chanted the vowel sounds, a healing vibration was created that directly affected some of its members who later reported the cessation of their physical or emotional distresses.

An hour after the three-hour Medicine Bundle Ceremony, thunder and lightning appeared followed by a hard rain. Visitation by the Thunder Beings after a ceremony has been considered spiritual applause by Native Americans for eons. The weather brought smiles to the faces of the participants, but as the rain continued, there was concern about maintaining the sweat lodge fire. Then the rain stopped for the duration of the late afternoon lodge ceremony, only to start up again about 9 P.M. The rain then became a constant downpour, and John talked to Jeanne about the beginning of the midnight Awakening Ceremony. Would he and those who kept the outside vigil get soaked again, as they had in British Columbia? The answer came around 11:30 P.M. when the rain ceased, and John was able to escort Jeanne to the Watersong Chamber without water falling from the night sky. Nevertheless, the Watersong Chamber seemed appropriately named.

As Jeanne sang the Awakening Ceremony inside the Watersong Chamber, the outside vigil keepers were having mystical experiences similar to those experienced by participants at previous Chamber awakenings. David Stephenson, a student of Grandfather Dubray—the Ceremonial Chief of the Lakota people and Sun Dance Leader on the Pine Ridge Reservation in South Dakota, the person who had inherited the medicine bundle of the legendary spiritual leader Fools Crow—saw Fools Crow in the shimmering energy of the kiva as it seemed to change shape and breathe. Kevin Schriver, attending the ceremony from Texas, saw another Chamber, an inverted energetic mirror image below the physical one. A woman who had found three feathers between the time of the sweat lodge and the Awakening Ceremony, perceived a spirit guide named Three Feathers. She also felt the presence of her great grandmother, named Amanda. Later, in the Sunday sharing, Jeanne would misname an eight-year-old child named Amber, whom she knew well, and call her Amanda, to the woman's amazement.

John recorded in his journal that several people shared his experience of travel and a changing landscape accompanied by a sense of being out of time. "My belief, supported by these intense, empirical experiences, is that these Peace-Sound Chambers do energetically reach beyond time and space and into other dimensions. So, the healing that takes place, the energy that is created, flows outward around the physical planet, but also flows outward in time, creating wrinkles in time-space from the nexus point of the kiva, and outward into other dimensional or parallel realities as well. It is a fantastic thought to contemplate!"

In the same journal entry, John further explores the primary thesis of his and Jeanne's mission in working with the Peace-Sound Chambers.

"The sound work being done in the Peace-Sound Chambers, which includes the Activation Ceremonies as well as the regular chanting, is important and healing because it takes us back to the *original sound* of Creation. This awakens our genetic memories of who we are and where we came from.

"I also believe that this work seeds *pure* consciousness into the collective much like putting a pure crystal into a super-saturated solution. What precipitates out are pure crystals, free of the impurities. Although that is not an exact metaphor, it *does* approximate my meaning. The net effect is a seed of pure, uncontaminated consciousness that has a purifying, awakening, decontaminating effect. Much like what Buddha, Krishna, Christ, White Buffalo Calf Woman, and others did in seeding a memory of pure being that is in right relationship with God, the work with the Chambers does the same thing. Only it does it (hopefully) in a way that won't get caught up in dogma and eventual religiosity. The difference is in promoting individual awakenings and a direct experience that is unmediated by gurus or priests. It awakens the inner Master by awakening this primordial memory of our connection with the Creator and Creation . . . .It's hard to distill this realization into words."

John, of course, was not alone in attempting to articulate what he was experiencing as a spiritual reality. Perry Robinson remarked during the sharing time on Sunday that "our experience of ceremony is not so much about what is happening 'out there.' Rather, what is happening 'out there' is really about what is happening *in here, inside of us*."

Also during the sharing there was what John termed "a neat connection to Australia." The previous August in Australia, Aviv, an eight-year-old boy, had presented his just lost "baby tooth" to Jeanne. At Watersong, Amber also offered her just released baby tooth to Jeanne. Amber's tooth was then added to the little medicine bag where Jeanne carried Aviv's tooth. This anecdote would be retold in the coming weeks as Jeanne and John headed back to Australia for an extensive walkabout of the aboriginal spiritual landscape. The year, 1999, would climax with the fulfillment of more amazing prophetic dreams.

WALKABOUT

I n 1998, during their first trip to Australia, on a bus trip from
Queensland in the North to Victoria in the South, Jeanne, at
one point, slept. In her sleep, she dreamed. She was visited by a
tribe of Aborigine who told her she was to return to Australia the
following year to do the same ceremony she and John did for the
Peace-Sound Chambers in other countries. She was shown a cave
wall with ancient glyphs and told the ceremony was to activate
something agreed upon millennia ago.In the process, she was told
to sing on their journey to find the glyphs, re-establishing old "song-
lines" disrupted by the imposition of roads and human development, to help the people find their way.

Jeanne was unaware that at the time she was having this powerful dream, a friend in the North, Anne Patient Wolf, was also
being given a dream. She was being asked to prepare the logistics of
a trip that Jeanne and John would eventually take. Jeanne says,
"When Anne and I talked, and she first shared her dream, I felt
chills. I knew something extraordinary was happening . . . something beyond my comprehension. "

And so, one year later, in 1999, Jeanne and John returned to
Australia, walking into an adventure they would remember for the
rest of their lives. Anne had fulfilled her part of the dream contract
and had arranged, in detail, all logistics necessary for a safe and successful fifteen-day journey into the outback, including assembling a
crew of 7 and 4 desert-capable vehicles. In addition to the 7-mem-
ber crew, 14 other brave souls from around the world came to support Jeanne in the vision she had been given. This journey would
take them from one aboriginal sacred site to another, with Jeanne,
John and everyone singing all along the way . . . creating new song-
lines as well as re-establishing ancient ones.

The walkabout party included Perry and Jeanne Robinson from
the Center for Peace in Seymour, Tennessee, Vicky Jones, and

Cheryl Patterson. It was while Jeanne was experiencing the original summons to Australia, that Cheryl dreamed she saw Jeanne, wearing red shorts and a T-shirt and carrying an Olympic-type torch, leading a group of people through the Australian outback. When Jeanne and Cheryl later compared their dreams, Cheryl became excited and immediately began preparing for the trip. When Vicky heard about the trip, she hesitated in committing to participate, until one night after a meeting, heading home in her car, an Aborigine spirit appeared on her front windshield. When she shared this with Jeanne, they laughed, agreeing this was a pretty strong sign. Perry Robinson had known for some time that he was to go to Australia to reconnect to the spirit of the land and the ancient peoples there.

On a beautiful clear September morning, the entourage of 21 set out on a journey to find a cave wall of glyphs, without any idea of where it might be. All Jeanne, John, Anne and the others knew was that they would be guided from day to day. Their job was simply to pay attention and move in the direction that the signs of the day would give them—eagles, wind, budding flowers, lizards, all playing a part.

One important message that guided Jeanne and the others throughout the journey was something Auntie Pearl had told Jeanne just before making the trek into the outback. Auntie Pearl was a beautiful, old and highly respected Aborigine grandmother, who, when Jeanne asked if there was any last-minute guidance she could give, said this, "Go gently." This has become a mantra for both Jeanne and John over the years.

Going gently into the desert, the group became attentive to the subtle messages guiding them. During the first leg of their trip, one of their vehicles broke down. To fully repair the car, a part had to be flown in from a town many miles away. Because their schedule was a spontaneous one, other than a rough outline of a journey planned by Anne and her crew, everyone was able to relax in the small town where there was only a camper park, a couple of stores and a pub.

The group passed its time by sharing stories and simply being together.

During the car repair stopover, the group was visited by two Aborigine "Aunties" and their grandson. It was in the sharing of stories during dinner that night that very quietly one of the Aunties said, "You might want to visit the Harts Mountains." That's all she said. It was quietly spoken and almost missed. The next day, after the car had been repaired, and the group was on its way again, Jeanne read something about the Harts Mountains in a guide book. The Harts range included a mountain site where both ancient and modern peoples had once mined crystals. The mines themselves had been abandoned and their entrances blocked, but the center of the mountain was thought to be a giant crystal which served as a vibrating beacon to intuitive peoples.

The Harts Mountains were then added to the trip itinerary, and Jeanne felt inspired to perform an Awakening Ceremony there as a means of awakening the memory of the crystals.

With permission of the local Aborigine, the walkabout group followed a dusty track, in 105-degree temperatures, that ended at a trail to the top of the mountain. It was to be the first Awakening Ceremony to be done outside of a Peace-Sound Chamber. With help from John and her friends, Jeanne found a ceremonial center and began to sing for almost two hours in the blazing sun of the mountaintop.

Everyone participating in the ceremony began to sing and have their own visions and powerful experiences. Cheryl Patterson later shared that she saw the female spirit of a nearby mountain who came to her and gave her a singing voice that she could carry away and use in ceremony. This gift made it possible for Cheryl to eventually begin her role as a lead drummer and singer at future ceremonial dances.

Throughout the Australian journey, songs were sung, ceremony created, ancestors honored . . . all the way to Uluru (Ayer's Rock) and back. As for the group itself, in the words of Barbara Wunsch from Boulder Colorado, "We turned out to be a good group, each of us picking a job we liked, setting up tents, cooking food, or unloading supplies. Each morning we began with Jeanne and John leading the spontaneous chanting, and then we were off on the day's adventure. The trip across the desert was a time of listening to Spirit with Jeanne and John orchestrating the movement."

On the return part of the journey, having camped across the desert in the outback, Anne Patient Wolf, quietly said to Jeanne that she had a feeling of where the cave wall glyphs that Jeanne had seen in the original dream were located.

Headed in the intuitive direction, singing at each rest stop along the way, the group met the caretaker of a large parcel of land where there were a number of ancient sites.Since the land was private, few people knew of these sites, and thus their antiquities remained in pristine condition. Perhaps sensing a spiritual purpose, the caretaker led the group to a giant cave that had endured decades of erosions so that only a wall, several hundred yards in length, remained. When Jeanne first saw the wall, she had an instant recognition that this was the same wall that the Aborigines had shown to her in her dream. And here on the wall were the glyphs that she had seen, the ancient drawings of some lost tribe.

Standing nearby, John remembered a vision that had occurred several years before of a hand on a wall. He was told that if he placed his hand within the painted hand, something powerful would happen. John then found such a hand. Following John's example, each member of the group found a similar painted hand and placed their own hands into the ancient imprints. Everyone lined along the wall then began to sing. The singing itself turned the event into an Awakening Ceremony. Jeanne recalls, "It was obvious that within each person something was awakening, something that had been asleep for centuries."

Perry Robinson shared his insight that if they looked carefully at the glyphs, what they were seeing was a star map looking not from the earth into the cosmos, but just the opposite. It was a view from another system looking at the Milky Way, specifically Earth, from an outside perspective. He suggested that those who were there in that moment were the beings who actually had come from far away, put these glyphs onto the wall as a "map", leaving a message. In the very ceremony that had just taken place, Perry said, they had activated something that would help the world survive through the transformative times to come.

The trip to Australia, for both Jeanne and John, had validated their visions. What they had searched for from an intuitive revelation actually existed, and they had been guided to its fulfillment. They were also conscious of the faith and courage required of those who traveled with them. Their shared experience on this spiritual trek was the stuff of stories to be told by them as elders to young people gathered around a campfire.

Before leaving Australia, there were two additional events of significance. Jeanne and John, with many members of the walkabout crew, participated in a ceremonial Sun-Moon Dance at the worldwide gathering of the Peace-Sound Chamber caretakers. Joseph Rael, Beautiful Painted Arrow, whose vision had created both the dance and the building of the Chambers on five continents, was on hand as the hosts' most honored and cherished guest.

After the caretakers gathering, Jeanne and John were invited to participate in the erecting of a Peace Pole outside of Brisbane, initiated by James Twyman, known as the Peace Troubadour. In front of a group of around 150 people, they and several members of the walkabout crew demonstrated the spontaneous chanting that had carried them across Australia.Barbara Wunsch remembers, "As Jeanne and John invited the audience to begin singing with us, the first sounds were a bit tremulous. But as each person let go of the fear and just opened to the potential, the sound became the beauty of a choir, with each voice contributing to the vibration of oneness."

Anne Patient Wolf and Graham Kielerup had arranged a bonus trip for Jeanne and John, Barbara Wunsch, and Kevin Schriver to visit New Zealand. Anne had grown up among the indigenous

Maori people, and she had arranged a down-river trip to meet the Owl Tribe of the Maori.

Arriving in New Zealand exhausted but excited, the group of six was greeted by some fifty Maori. As is their tradition, the tribal members greeted Jeanne and John and the others with a song. One of the Maori grandmothers stepped forward from the large circle and said they wanted to say a prayer for their guests. You can imagine how surprised the "guests" were when they heard the prayer to be a simple singing of the vowel sounds, "ah, eh, ee, oh, oo." Jeanne and John were learning first hand that the singing of the vowels, even the spontaneous singing, is an ancient way to pray and connect with the Divine. They had also been told this by the Rabbis in Israel. Vowel singing has been done for centuries by indigenous peoples across the planet.

Barbara Wunsch recalls her own unique experience. "We were introduced to a family of the Maori people who took us to sacred sites of their culture where we were invited to share in their heritage.One of the traditions of the Maori is for everyone to share a bit of themselves by offering a poem, story or a song. For me this was terrifying because I had no idea what I was going to do. Then it struck me. What had I been doing with Jeanne and John everywhere through Australia and, now, New Zealand? We had sung on mountains, in concerts, even a special time in a Cathedral Chamber in a cave in New Zealand, but this was to be my own song in the moment. This was my moment of trust for all the love that Jeanne and John had given me in opening up to the Divine. As I opened my heart, I heard for the first time who I was, and the love, joy, compassion, and openness came through me, and I knew what it meant to be the open channel and fill the space with that love. After the stillness of the song dissipated, I was a new person and my life had changed."

Despite the wonderful experiences that took place in New Zealand, something was occurring with Jeanne that no one knew about at the time, not even Jeanne. A cancer was beginning to grow in her body. Jeanne was exhausted, but she chalked up her physical distress to the travel and the horrendous schedule that she and John had been following for months. Although Jeanne had contracted walking pneumonia at the end of the Australian trip, and had come into New Zealand barely able to speak, and with little energy to sustain herself, the years of training in the performance area enabled her to be present and participate in the events so lovingly gifted by Anne, Graham, and the Maori people. After five days on the Wanganui River, in the wet and cold, however, the pneumonia had become deeply embedded in Jeanne's lungs.

On the final day of their river journey, Jeanne, John and the rest of the group were honored in a memorable way with food, song, and celebration. Jeanne says, "I wouldn't have missed this for anything. The Maori are such a beautiful and kind people. It was hard, however, for me to function because I was so sick. I found myself withdrawing." The last few days in New Zealand were hard ones. Jeanne, with pneumonia and a cancer that was yet undisclosed, chose with John to leave New Zealand early.

In retrospect Jeanne and John realized their time in New Zealand was an unusual and special one. They had been privileged to participate in the customs and ceremony of the Owl Tribe. They had seen into the hearts of an ancient people and been nurtured by their wisdom and songs. At some point, Jeanne and John would return to New Zealand, and this time, hopefully, with the gift of the dance, "For the One."

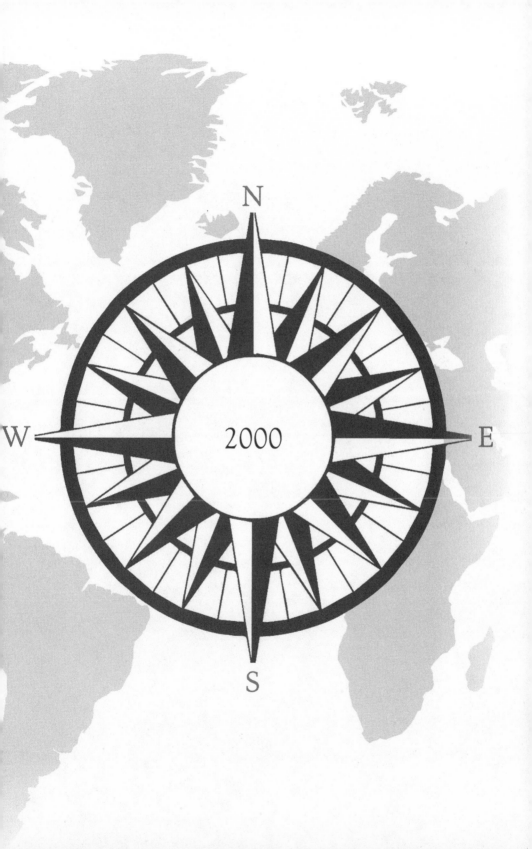

MILES TO GO

T he first days of 2000 began for Jeanne and John back at Ula Rae's farmhouse in remote Corryton, Tennessee. The Y2K predictions of a catastrophic beginning to the New Millennium passed over them and slid into the chronicles of human fears that have periodically enslaved doomsday minds. The breadth of this 21st century technological fear was greatly enhanced by the already ubiquitous computer, which like a restless, vengeful, man-invented god both gives and takes away.

If the little farmhouse was supposed to be a retreat after months of continuous travel, the couple's repose was not long lasting. There was, of course, the renewed responsibility to support themselves and to care for the needs of their children. Too often, Jeanne and John returned from their foreign missions without bankable profits. Going where they were guided was spiritually rewarding; but frankly, support income barely covered the expenses of foreign travel, and the deficits accumulated. There was little time to settle in Corryton for a long winter's nap of contemplation and physical recovery. They would soon have to go on the road again.

Jeanne's daughter Jenny was in her last semester en route to becoming an airline pilot, but the necessary flight time needed to obtain her multi-engine rating required an immediate $1500. Since the couple couldn't supply it, Jeanne wrote letters to family members to explain both Jenny's and their financial circumstances. Money then flowed to Jenny, and with an unexpected loan from a commercial source, her needs were met.

Needs such as Jenny's were constantly cropping up as they do for any family. In Jeanne and John's case, however, the parents did not have the regular income sources to either plan for or respond to the needs. Faith and creative initiatives carried them through these challenges, but emotionally it was very difficult to accept the condition of material lack. And practically no one who knew of their extensive foreign travels realized that they always traveled on a wing and a prayer. They were definitely not living the adventuresome high-life that some people imagined.

Jeanne would say that she never considered their condition as one of financial poverty or lack. The weeks at Corryton and other donated retreats were viewed as times of "inhalation" that were training grounds in themselves. The lesson was faith, and the test was to respond in grace that what appeared to be empty would soon be filled again as their mission required.

At the end of the first week in January, John went to the Center for Peace to do Intuitive Imagery sessions with clients. The sessions were designed as a therapy tool to help people get "clear" of the "stuff" that was blocking them from moving forward in their lives with confidence. As a group and individual trainer of this method, John had a good reputation, and he had also written a book on the subject. Perhaps if John had an established home base, he might have built a lucrative practice in Intuitive Imagery consulting. As it was, friends and clients availed themselves of his service on a catch-as-catch-can basis.

In reading Castaneda's last book *The Active Side of Infinity*, John explored the role of "inner silence" in his spiritual practice. He felt that he had experienced the totality of it when he "hit the pole" at his most recent Sun-Moon Dance. Although the experience that Castaneda termed a "state in which perception doesn't depend on the senses" did not last more than five minutes, John felt like he had crossed a threshold that he could now more easily access.

Don Juan also described the need for a "breaking point" as a pre-condition for surrendering to inner silence. John felt that he had experienced several breaking points. One was his commitment to Jeanne and their mission. Another was their bankruptcy. Since 1997, he had let go of nearly everything that had been a reference point in his life—mother, brother, father, a marriage, children, career, and home. Jeanne had done the same.

A contemporary American Indian Wisdom Keeper, Cherokee Grandmother Red Leaf, has people approach her for training and initiation into the perceived secrets of spiritual life. She asks them three qualifying questions. Why do you want to learn these things? There is only one acceptable answer—*to serve the people*. And how long are you willing to stay in this practice? The right answer is *for the rest of my life*. The final question Grandmother asks is, what are you willing to sacrifice to enter into this service? The one-word answer must be *everything*.

Many people gesture at a commitment to spiritual life, to a life dedicated to service, but they cannot meet Grandmother's basic criteria. They cannot truthfully or correctly answer her three questions. Who in this modern age is willing to sacrifice everything in the service of peace? Who will serve the desperate needs of the One humanity without title and without recognition or reward?

While John was at the Center for Peace, Jeanne was praying for two seniors in her family who were seriously ill. Jack Newman, who had married her mother Kit, was emaciated by cancer and was not given long to live. Perry Lane, Jeanne's father, was also declining from a degenerative nerve disease akin to Parkinson's. He required constant care due to loss of his motor abilities, and he was also losing his ability to communicate. Cash reserves were down to $40, and Jeanne wondered how they would manage a trip to Chattanooga to see her father, have food for the week, and enough leftover for the supplies needed for a scheduled workshop. An unexpected invitation to speak to a mid-week CFP group provided just enough income to cover their expenses, and thus they were able to go to Chattanooga and aid in the care of Jeanne's father.

Back at Corryton, John gave an Intuitive Imagery workshop, and Jeanne gave her first full-day Sound Healing workshop; then near the middle of the month they traveled to the Watersong Chamber in Graham, North Carolina to do a few private sessions with group members. The one-way drive through light snow in the mountains around Asheville took five hours, but the income was a great relief.

Their next destination was Albuquerque, and with heavy snow forecast for the North Carolina mountains, they hurried back home to Corryton ahead of the storm. Then looking at the bad-weather forecast across their path west, they practiced their intuitive imaging, washed clothes, repacked, and left for New Mexico by noon of the same day. They drove 700 miles before stopping in Fort Smith, Arkansas for the night. The next day, old faithful Gracie, their gifted BMW, covered another 760 miles. Considering the trip from North Carolina, the couple had driven 1800 miles cross-country in three days and avoided all the bad winter snowstorms that had hit in their wake.

While out West, the couple scheduled time with Joseph at his new home near Durango, Colorado. They discussed the content of their dreams with him for interpretation, told him about their experiences in Australia, and laid out their plans for the new year. In counseling them, there was a subtle difference in the way Joseph responded to them. At times, he spoke to them as fellow elders, not as students. In summary, he told them that the litmus test about where to direct their efforts resided in the question, "Will it benefit others?" In other words, service to the people is the litmus test. This service, he told them, also activates the universal forces that bring the most return. Yet the return is a by-product and not the focus.

Two days of ceremony included a medicine ceremony with lodge sweats before and after, and the ceremonial releasing of the Spirit Child of the Peace-Sound Chambers. The medicine bundle that contained the Spirit Child was opened to be released into the La Plata River where he would spread as a generator for world peace. The waters of the La Plata merge with the San Juan River, which flows into the Colorado at Glen Canyon. The Colorado then reaches the Pacific Ocean below Baja, California and thus becomes the water of the wide world. The Spirit Child of the Peace-Sound Chambers came from Joseph's original Chamber in Bernalillo. When Joseph moved to Colorado, he had another Chamber in Hesperus, but it was decided to release the original Chamber Spirit to its global mission.

On Super Bowl Sunday, Jeanne and John were in Aspen with friends, some of whom had been on the Australian walkabout, when they got the news that Jeanne's stepfather Jack Newman had died. They completed a Sound Workshop with the Aspen group and then drove straight through to Tennessee. Since leaving Watersong in North Carolina just over two weeks before, they would drive 4400 miles. The trip from Aspen began in snow after the full-day workshop, and it was a white-knuckle ride the first 200 miles to Denver. Due to fatigue, the couple pulled off the long 1300-mile road to sleep twice for an hour. They arrived at Jeanne's mother's home after twenty-six travel hours.

There were two funeral services for Jack Newman—one a memorial service in Martin, and a second graveside service the following day in Chattanooga. As a military veteran, Jack received full honors from a nine-man uniformed contingent and a rapid-fire rifle salute.

Exhausted, Jeanne and John returned to the Corryton farmhouse on a Friday. The next day they were scheduled to begin a three-day Community Building workshop for the board members of the Center for Peace. There was barely time to wash clothes, repack, and organize the materials for the workshop. Thankfully, the CFP was only 38 miles away, and only 50 minutes of drive time. And yet it seemed that they always had miles to go.

TESTS AND REWARDS

The Community Building weekend program at the Center for Peace began on the first Saturday in February. This workshop format was perhaps the most potentially commercial counseling activity that Jeanne and John offered. The process had broad applications to business, non-profit organizations, and even to government agencies that they had demonstrated in past years, but their spiritual path did not lead them in a commercial direction. Rather, the workshop was directed to small, dedicated groups of people, like those associated with Peace-Sound Chambers, as a powerful method to communicate and connect.

The process was not an easy one. In some ways it resembled a group vision quest. Interpersonal conflicts would be exposed and individual vulnerabilities confessed. Social armor would have to be taken off for the revelation of true selves to emerge. The purpose was to learn a more deeply authentic way of relating to each other while enhancing the ability of the group to accomplish meaningful goals. Because the process was often emotional, and sometimes painful, John and Jeanne asked each participant to commit to being present for the entire three-day process. They knew that frustration, anxiety, doubt, and even depression were steps along the path to healing. Jumping ship in midstream would thus deprive the deserter of the sweet, happy destination ahead.

The weekend following the Community Building Workshop, Joseph arrived at the CFP to lead a Medicine Ceremony. There was a question pending about whether to continue the Awakening Ceremonies now that the Spirit of the original Peace-Sound Chamber had been released into the rivers. In the lodge, Jeanne and John independently were given the clear direction to continue what they were doing. Jeanne was also told that the couple were supposed to go to Israel that year. Eighteen months before, John's guides, The

Tall Ones, had told him that he and Jeanne had important work to do in Israel. Now they had both received the same guidance.

When the couple talked about Israel to Joseph, he told them of his Spanish ancestry and pointed out that his surname had been shortened to Rael, from the Hebrew meaning "bearer of light." Joseph suggested to the couple that they were being asked to go as bearers of light to Israel.

Back at Corryton on Valentine's Day, John awoke and padded to the bathroom to find that Jeanne had decorated the room with red, heart-shaped messages that read "kiss me," "hot stuff," and like romantic enticements. John got the gist and went back to bed.

That week, Gracie went to the shop, and the auto doctor's news was not good. Gracie required multiple repair operations, and BMW fixes were not cheap. Without the funds, Gracie—dented and moaning from her wheel bearings—was taken home.

On February 19th the couple celebrated their fifth wedding anniversary, their seventh year as lovers, and their ninth year as friends. Each of them had composed a love letter to the other which they were to ceremonially share. Jeanne's "letter" turned out to be twenty heart-shaped Valentine helium balloons that she had somehow managed to hide from John. Each balloon trailed a floor-length red ribbon, and on each ribbon there was a note that gave a reason why Jeanne loved John. Although John's letter was more traditional, it gave him the opportunity to say the important things that husbands should remember to say to their beloved wives.

Later in the week, John and Jeanne were back at Cheryl Patterson's house at the CFP to help facilitate a vision quest for Eric Butcher. John functioned as Eric's primary support person for the three-day process and guided him through the sweat lodge initiation and the long nights alone in the Peace-Sound Chamber. John enjoyed the role of teacher and mentor, but Eric's process also brought up John's own "stuff" that yet needed resolution. In his journal, he wrote:

"I am feeling love for my children. I am getting in touch with a part of me that wants desperately to progress spiritually so I can, in that way, give something greater to them by being a 'way shower.' And that is the *me* that is afraid of screwing it up."

In another contemplative moment, John realized that he was receiving spiritual insight apart from medicine ceremonies, and that the "medicine" helped him trust what he received in the process of daily living. In the gentle knowing, John realized that he should not beat himself up when magnificent visions appeared to others but not to him.

After the Sunday sweat lodge, John, as the rock carrier, was one of the last persons to reach the house for the traditional feast. As he walked through the house door with Steve Citty, thirty people yelled "Surprise." It was John's 50th birthday, and Jeanne had gotten him again! Her smile was nothing short of delicious as she placed a gold paper crown on John's head and led the singing of the happy birthday song. Several people presented John with gifts, including needed cash, and he was a very short emotion away from being overwhelmed by love, if such a thing is possible.

At the end of February, Jeanne took some days to visit her mother in Martin, and John remained at the farmhouse doing necessary chores and battling his allergies. His sinuses were running, his eyes itching, and he was sneezing. Most hours of the day he had tissues at his nose, and he was as miserable as spring pollen was plentiful. The antihistamines that he was taking to subdue his runny nose only reduced his energy to work.

The second day in April, the reunited couple made the 330-mile trek to Graham for a planned Community Building weekend with the Watersong Chamber group at Jo Fisher's house. En Route, Gracie's brake lining alarm light came on, and the next day the car was covered with tree pollen. John's allergies were exacerbated with constant sneezing and maddeningly itching eyes. His use of Kleenex alone should have raised the manufacturer's stock price. Nevertheless, the workshop was both successful and powerful, and

Georgia Stone, the octogenarian patron saint of the Watersong Chamber, told her black church congregation that Jeanne and John were the ministers of her peace group.

At the end of the workshop, John recorded in his journal some of the things that the participants shared. Although the words were spoken, John realized their poetic nature, and thus he wrote them down as stanzas. Here are unattributed poetic samples that demonstrate the depth of what occurred in the personal process of community building.

"I am offering you
the strength I've gained
although I don't know how
to give it.
I've lost the path
that leads to my heart.

Once,
in a vision quest
up on Bear Butte
with sunny days
and freezing nights,
my fear surrounded me
like the rattlesnakes gathered
outside the sacred circle,

Suddenly,
a marsh wren perched,
full of joy,
unconcerned with all the stuff
that made me scared.
Its heart song
sang to my heart:
'You have everything!'
Life has never been the same."

"My father was a rage-aholic.
And everything I ever loved
was taken away.
Even my dog,
who one day wandered
down to the creek
and fell in.
She had an epileptic fit
and died—drowned,
only her head under water.
It was my final exam
to see if I
would still love God
if everything else
was taken away.

Scatter my ashes
on a field of wild flowers."

"When you speak
from your heart,
your face softens,
your eyes widen,
I can see deeper
into your soul."

"Don't be sorry.
This is just how I'm feeling.
If you can't say
'I love you,'
just say,
'I care.'"

During this period, Jeanne was experiencing pain in her back under her shoulder blades, as well as in her solar plexus and stomach. She had suffered in silence for almost two months, but now the pain was affecting her sleep and could not be ignored. Finally, she called Owen James, and he put her back on the cancer medication and diet regime that he had prescribed for her in 1997. John privately admitted to fears of losing Jeanne. He could not believe, however, that God would put them on a spiritual path only for Jeanne to die prematurely.

To compound the contemplation of death and dying, Jeanne and John went to Chattanooga to care for Perry Lane while his wife Peggy went to Florida for five days. Her trip was a necessary therapeutic break from the constant invalid care that she was providing. Perry, who two years before had been vibrant, was now totally dependent on caregivers.

Perhaps it was the poetry he had heard at Watersong that prompted John to express his experience with Jeanne's father in a poem. The free verse, titled "Trapped," certainly told the story.

"The gentle old man
of seventy seven,
bald-headed except
for a few white wisps
of hair near the ears,
sits much of the day
in the big, blue chair,
TV on, but eyes fixed
on some other more distant place.

He now sees things
that we cannot;
gets lost mid-sentence,
his soft voice
trailing off into whispers,

leaving only the echoes
of thoughts behind
a painful gaze that says,
"Help me, I'm trapped!
Here – inside!
There's a brain-body disconnect,
and the 'I' that is 'me'
can no longer leap
(through thoughts)
across the synapse gap
to spur this freezing shell to act.
With each new sunrise,
my mind sinks deeper,
deeper into ice."

In truth,
with each new sunset
the old man's body
forgets how to do
another simple, basic, thing:
get up, sit down,
eat, drink, get dressed,
talk, shave, pee.
These days,
the gentle old man wears a diaper
under trousers that fasten with Velcro;
steps over invisible hurdles
at the seam in the carpet;
takes ten minutes,
sometimes,
to shuffle from kitchen to den;
and needs a helping hand
to eat even
the simplest of meals.

Funny how life works.
As a younger, self-made man
his biggest fear was this:
being unable to care for himself.
From that younger place in time,
twenty years ago now,
did a part of him,
even then,
know how it would all end?"

The month progressed, and the couple spent a day with John Troutner, Jeanne's son, and at about the same time, Jenny called to say that she had gotten a $1500 scholarship from Federal Express as a result of her attendance at the Women In Aviation Conference. The money would go to more multi-engine aircraft hours that she needed for certification.

Jeanne, still in pain from her disease, went to Serpent Mountain in Cosby, Tennessee to spend two nights in Ula Rae's Peace-Sound Chamber. There she received healing massages, Reiki treatments, and was fed a very cleansing diet. A few days later, John went to the CFP to participate in a sweat lodge poured by Perry Robinson where he prayed for Jeanne's healing. In the lodge, John was shown that he needed to remove two aborigine spears that were sticking out of Jeanne's back. The image harkened back to their time in Australia and may have been related to an aborigine shaman who had energetically attacked Jeanne, for some reason still unknown to them.

On the 28th, the couple headed for Toronto, Canada and the home of Owen and Heather James. They drove the 825 miles door-to-door in fourteen hours. After Owen examined Jeanne, he told them that bottom line, Jeanne was just burned out . . . exhausted. There were also issues with her blood and lymphatic systems that needed cleansing and purification. In addition, he felt that there was cancer in her small intestines. As Owen worked daily with

Jeanne, he also suspected that both Jeanne and John had picked up parasites in Australia.

On Sunday, the couple traveled with Owen and Heather ninety minutes east of Toronto to their farm in Grafton where the Peace-Sound Chamber was located. Owen's purpose was to perform a Santo Daime Ceremony there in his role as a minister of the Christian Mystic movement. While John was experiencing anger and emotional turbulence that went back to childhood and his feelings of failure that were exacerbated by Jeanne's illness, Jeanne had a death experience during the Santo Daime Ceremony. Her blood pressure dropped to zero before she returned to her body.

In retrospect, John saw the month's events as signs of a metamorphosis. He felt that he and Jeanne were both in a process of change. He believed that they were being asked to move up to a higher level on the spiritual spiral. Jeanne's cancer, he felt, was a teacher. The last time it came into their lives—1997—was a year of tremendous growth for both of them. This year was to prove no different. The effect of Jeanne's death and rebirth in the Santo Daime Ceremony, John observed, was that she had gained a Buddhist-like detachment from issues, people, things, and events. And in this way, perhaps Jeanne had also gained detachment from disease.

After the Canada trip, the couple did not share the same bed so that Jeanne could focus on her healing and get up at 3 A.M. each morning to meet her cancer with a regimen of visualization and sound vibrations. John battled his emotions and a succession of bad news. Workshops that they had depended on for income were cancelled; the friend of a close friend committed suicide; and John was having nicotine withdrawal in an attempt to stop smoking cigarettes. When their financial situation again seemed desperate, the Watersong group provided another miracle with a gift of $1500. But there were more obligations than funds and yet unresolved financial issues with John's former wife. While Jeanne cocooned for her metamorphosis, John felt the emotional weight of their material circumstances and judged himself unrighteous because he could not seem to rise spiritually above them.

Gracie was back in the shop. As long suffering as she was, the 1986 BMW was not to be trusted for the long haul without an estimated $1,000 in repairs. Well, what was there to do but return to faith? Spirit had provided before when there was $5 and half-a-tank of gas left to their names, so John surrendered. Within days, four $500 checks of support arrived, and Gracie was made serviceable again. As an observer, most people would say that you'd have to be "out of your mind" to live the way Jeanne and John did. But that was exactly the couple's spiritual goal—to be out of their minds.

As Jeanne began to respond to treatment and became pain free, she scheduled a Sound Healing Workshop at Watersong for the end of April. The couple's major supporters attended. At the very end of the workshop, the group put John in the center of its circle and sang his name. John sensed pain around his heart, and he felt it was more physical than emotional. As it turned out, the stress of the recent months would manifest itself in July, and this event would be remembered as a precursor to John's heart attack.

But for now, into May, with Jeanne feeling well, there were workshops to give that produced income enough to meet their needs. Perry Lane had his 79th birthday, and Jenny graduated. As ordained ministers, John and Jeanne officiated at their first wedding ceremony. The groom was David Stephenson's son Scott. David and Cheryl had been the source of so much support during the past year that performing the wedding ceremony seemed like a very small payback. And yet, their gift was returned with another incredible flow of abundance.

The Watersong Chamber caretakers presented Jeanne and John with a powerful IBM laptop computer loaded with software. The computer provided an essential record keeping and communication tool for their work. All they could do was weep in appreciation and awe. But Jeanne and John have a reputation as gift givers, too.

Jeanne gave Cheryl a beautiful long dress for her drum dance, and John gave David his most special eagle talon ceremonial necklace.

After so many experiences of such diverse natures, the year was barely half over.

HEART ATTACK

In early June, Jeanne and John visited Tom and Kristen Bissinger, caretakers of the Birdsong Peace-Sound Chamber, in Pennsylvania and did a concert, workshop, and private sessions in the Chamber. Over the years, Tom and Kristen had become close friends; and in their private times together, the couples were mutually supportive in acknowledging with empathy the sacrifices of the spiritual path. Also during the visit, Jeanne and John made a connection with Jeff Romanowski who invited them to Croatia to help with a Sun-Moon Dance. The couple saw this invitation as another example of how Spirit was acting in their lives.

On to Brooklyn, New York, the couple stayed in the apartment of Maitreya Rogers in a multi-cultural neighborhood. On the busy streets they heard Yiddish, Russian, Spanish, and Chinese being spoken. John exchanged an Intuitive Imagery session with Maitreya for one of his trance channel sessions. In recorded question-and-answer sessions with both Jeanne and John, the channeled identity confirmed that the couple should go to both Israel and India. John did other Imagery sessions for private clients, and Jeanne was able to rest and then reconnect with an old friend in the area for dinner.

On Thursday, Jeanne and John drove to Kent, Connecticut to visit new friend Jeff Romanowski and his partner Ulli at a small rented house on ten acres of land. Jeff surprised them by asking them to do a sweat lodge that night. Ulli left the next day to go to Germany, and so Jeanne and John stayed extra days to keep company with Jeff and to enjoy the Connecticut countryside. John, still anxious about Jeanne's condition, got some relief when Jeff did energy work on his body. The session provided a powerful release that produced a flood of tears for John.

In Imaging work with Jeanne, the couple explored the nature of her cancer and what was needed for her healing. They also inquired into whether or not she should serve as a Moon Mother in the scheduled Sun-Moon Dance in Canada, and whether, in her condition, she should participate in the retreat following the dance. The guided answers were "yes" on the Moon Mothering and "no" on the retreat.

Their next stop was the site of the Sun-Moon Dance at the Owen James farm in Grafton, Ontario. They would be there for ten days. The large dance arbor was newly built with 3,000 square feet of plywood covering the dancers' shelter. The arbor had two architectural features that gave it a magical appearance. First, all the poles that connected the uprights were angled 30º and extended into the arbor toward the center pole, and secondly, the East gate was covered so as to provide a tunnel effect into the large dance oval. But before the dancers arrived, there were three days of hard labor to prepare for the event. Copious amounts of firewood had to be cut and stacked for the sweat lodge and ceremonial fires; caulking of the roof seams had to be completed; grass had to be cut; outside toilets made ready; and a general clean-up performed. Then on the Friday morning of the dance, the dance pole—a tall poplar tree—had to be cut down, trimmed into a 26-foot pole, and then erected at the center of the arbor and decorated with greenery and the color flags of the directions. While this was being done, a kitchen was being prepared and stocked to serve the Dance Chief and the support crew. All of this was done to provide the thirteen dancers an opportunity to slip into timelessness.

In a short article for the Tennessee Center for Peace Newsletter, John wrote about what he and others felt about the Sun-Moon Dance.

"The Sun-Moon Dance takes place on many levels. Those who are called to the dance come to participate at a personal, planetary and cosmic level. It is, as Grandfather Joseph used to say, truly a dance for 'graduate students,' who desire to make a step change in their own lives, and assist in the grand work of planetary healing.

"On a personal level, the Sun-Moon Dance will bring deep healing, transformation, vision, and acceleration to your spiritual progress that lasts throughout the year. The commitment to dance at least a full cycle of four dances brings about healing on mental, emotional, physical and spiritual levels. And since each of us is a microcosm of the planet, the healing we bring to ourselves also heals the planet. For these reasons alone, the dance is a powerful gift that you give to yourself and those you love.

"On a planetary level, the dance works with the energy and spirits of the land. The dance arbor is the sacred Medicine Wheel, and represents the planet and all the people, as well as the entire cosmos. In the dance, we work to bring in the directional energies of the east, south, west, north, up above, and down below. The web of energy created by the dancers energizes the land, and spreads out around the planet to bring healing. At a deeper level, the dance and the drum unlocks crystalline structures deep within the earth, releases energy, and brings new spiritual energy up to the surface to be used for peace. The Sun-Moon Dance works at all of these levels. So, in bringing your energy to the dance, you are not only healing yourself, but you are healing the planet and making peace possible."

After serving the Canadian Sun-Moon Dance, Jeanne and John drove the 795 miles to the Watersong Chamber in North Carolina straight through. Operating a motor vehicle between the physical and spirit world that Joseph calls "between the slices of light" can be an amazing experience. The driver, who is in a meditative state, functions expertly in all traffic situations, but especially on interstate highways, there are time lapses that rationally seem alarming. The driver "snaps out of it" to discover that perhaps a hundred miles have been traversed without a trace of memory of its land-marks or its passing. An hour of clock time has evaporated. What happened? Perhaps science has an explanation as to why this com-mon experience of deeply centered individuals poses no threat to the driving public. And if you have ever achieved a transcendental state close to thoughtlessness, you know the power of true aware-ness. You see and hear and sense everything on an acute level that allows not only for perfect peace, but for perfect safety as well. Jeanne and John have reported driving hours like that. How else could they survive?

At Watersong, David and Dobs completed the building of a new, large sweat lodge. David had a non-specific urgency about get-ting the job done. When Jeanne and John arrived, David offered them a traditional Lakota lodge. He told them that as the lodge pourer, he was going to get out of the way and allow the Grandfathers to guide his words and actions. As the round for the West began, Jeanne went immediately into an altered space and began speaking a trance language that later she could only describe as "the language of White Eagle." Throughout the four rounds of the lodge, Jeanne prayed ardently in the trance language and shed tears. Then in the fifth round, she screamed, cried, and vomited. Something inside of her was let go. Owen James had told Jeanne the night before the couple left Canada that Jeanne had both a fascina-tion for, and a fear of death that was different from a fear of dying. He forecast that she would be going into a cave where she would confront this fear, a fear he felt came from another lifetime. After what happened at Watersong, perhaps the cave that Owen saw was actually the dark, closed environment of a sweat lodge.

With intermediate stops at the Center for Peace in Seymour and then Chattanooga to see Jeanne's dad Perry, the couple finally got back to the farm. They had been on the road for six weeks, and they looked forward to both rest and healing; but when they parked their car in the gravel driveway, they noticed a pile of rubble at the back corner of the house. A local plumber hired to install the drain to the old-fashioned, stand-alone ceramic bathtub and a toilet had run into problems. The tub was unusable, and the toilet wouldn't flush without being plunged. Plumbing supplies, tools, and junk littered the dirty floor of the back entryway and the bathroom. To add to their discomfort, the house was like an oven in the July heat. Jeanne, emotionally exhausted, and wet from sweat, broke down and cried. To add to the plumbing dilemma, Jeanne's mother was scheduled to visit within days.

Although they cleared the entryway, swept and mopped the floors, the bathroom remained mostly unusable. Then, too, whenever the plumber worked, the water was shut off, sometimes for most of the day. In desperation, John dug a latrine hole in the woods away from the house for business that would not flush. Ula Rae, of course, was not to blame. She had contracted to fix the bathroom, but in rural Tennessee, time and repairs move at the pace of a three-legged dog who often pauses to scratch himself for fleas.

After only two days at the farm, John went to the CFP for a Sun-Moon Dance preparation workday. The four men separated into two teams. Steve Citty and Dennis Ogle, who brought his chainsaw, drew the wood-cutting detail, while John and Perry Robinson set out to build the composting toilets. The hard labor drained John. Back at the farm, Jeanne felt dizzy and disoriented for a time, but the vertigo passed as mysteriously as it had come by the time John returned. As he pulled into the driveway, he recognized Kit's maroon Lincoln Continental. His dear mother-in-law had arrived bearing indispensable gifts—two large circulating fans.

During her visit to the farm, Kit, a 77-year-old widow, got an invitation for an outing from Tom Haynes. Tom was an old friend of Kit's deceased husband Jack, whose wife had died of cancer the same month that Jack had passed. Kit, a bit shy about the relationship, was not sure that she should be "dating." Nevertheless, she went with Tom for breakfast and a day trip to Helen, Georgia. The driving time allowed for lots of talking. Two days later, they had a dinner "date." Jeanne and John thought that they detected the spark of romance between the senior couple, but Kit was not about to admit it.

John stayed busy with trips back and forth to the CFP, and he did an Intuitive Imagery workshop at Medicine Ridge in Newport, Tennessee. In the group discussion, it was noted that the protocols for Remote Viewing and Intuitive Imagery were quite similar. That week, Jeanne went to Chattanooga to spend time with her dad.

In another workday at the CFP, John finished building the last composing toilet, mowed grass in the dance arbor meadow, and split and stacked firewood. The hard labor left him with a day-after energy drain and grogginess.

Two days before the Saturday of the Sun-Moon Dance at the CFP, with Ula Rae visiting the farm, they saw an ambulance enter the driveway of the next-door property. John and Ula Rae followed the ambulance to see if they could be of help to their neighbor, a truck driver. When they got to the house, the paramedics were already performing CPR on an elderly workman, a truck driver, who was lying on the ground. As John and Ula Rae watched, John whispered to her, "I don't think he's going to make it. His spirit just left. I saw it." The rescue squad employed their most desperate measures, but the man could not be revived.

Back inside the farmhouse, Jeanne called from Chattanooga to say that Perry, her dad, had been taken to the emergency room. His body had locked up to the point that he could not function. Tom, Jeanne's brother, was there from Alabama. Perry's prognosis was very grim.

Before leaving on Thursday with Jeanne for the Sun-Moon Dance, John made a prophecy fan with a wedge-tail eagle feather and a condor feather. An ancient prophecy known to tribal nations on both American continents says that when the eagle of the North and the condor of the South come together like the fingers on a hand, then peace will prevail on the planet.In John's fan, the two feathers came together in a carved walnut handle that was wrapped in tan leather and sewed with sinew. During the carving,

John accidentally cut his left thumb deeply enough for it to bleed profusely and require bandaging. He considered the hurt a blood offering to the dance.

Friday night John and Steve Citty poured the sweat lodge for the dancers. For some reason, he did not build the ceremonial fire or tend it, and the fire did not cooperate with the people who did. It was difficult to light, and it burned unevenly and had a "funky" energy. John gave an offering of his hair to appease the fire, and after the lodge, another feeding of chocolate. These acts were his gestures of apology for not honoring the nature of the fire as a fire holder should.

John got to bed about midnight that Friday. With the dancers, who had danced hard, put to bed, Steve and John, as co-Dance Chiefs, were looking forward to Saturday. In retrospect, there were already signs of trouble. Coming up from the arbor meadow, up the steep gravel drive to the house, John had felt more winded than usual, and his throat was irritated. Very unusual for him, the intense heat of the sweat lodge had driven him out after only the second round. Some intuitive guide had told him, "Get out of the lodge! Now!"

In bed, John was having chest pain and feeling the irritation in his windpipe. The throat pain then radiated outward to his neck and jaw, and then out to his shoulders and down his arms. John tossed and turned from midnight to 5 A.M. when he got up, too uncomfortable to remain in bed. When he went up a flight of stairs to the bathroom to shave, the pain increased and ran down the inside of his left arm. John recalls thinking, "What they say about heart attacks is true."

Steve Citty was up and came to John's aid. While they waited for Jeanne and Brenda Sue to arrive from another house, Steve did energy work on John; but as soon as Jeanne arrived, he insisted that they go immediately to the St. Mary's Hospital emergency room in Knoxville. Jeanne drove, and Steve alerted the hospital to expect a heart attack patient who was en route. On arrival, John was examined, given a nitroglycerin pill, and put on a blood thinner intravenous drip. Later he was removed to the Cardiac Care Unit for further treatment.

With John stable, Jeanne called Owen early Saturday morning in Canada. Owen told her where the vascular blockage had occurred and that John had suffered heart muscle damage. On Monday, with all the laboratory reports in hand, the hospital doctor confirmed everything that Owen had said. Indeed, John had had a damaging heart attack, a probable four on a scale where a ten is a massive attack that kills you. On Tuesday, the cardiologist wanted John to take an exercise stress test in lieu of a heart catheterization and angiogram. The test did not go well, but John was not about to agree to any surgery. He had more faith in Owen's recommended treatment, and during those days, there were frequent telephone consultations.

As intuitive friends came to support John, the focus of their attention was not on the disease itself but on the conditions that caused it. Every individual has life shocks that have physical consequences. Psychologists sometimes rate the most common of these shocks and assign them a numerical value. When the shocks are listed and the numbers totaled, a stress value can be assigned as a diagnostic tool. One number prompts the doctor to advise "take a vacation." Another higher number may indicate a career change. Anything near the top of the scale necessitates serious, immediate therapy.

Sue Mehrtens listed John's life shocks and assigned values on a ten-point scale that she felt contributed to his heart attack.

- John's separation from his wife and three sons in 1993. Rated at a high 9 or 10.

- Abandonment issues from his childhood. Rated at 9.

- His brother's death in 1992. Rated 4 for one aspect, and 8 for another.

- The betrayal in leaving DuPont. Rated 7 in its lasting effects.

- Personal bankruptcy and the loss of material security. Rated at 6

- His father's death in 1995. Rated 5 to 6.

To these might be added:

- The stress of constant travel. Rated by the author at an average 7, with many 10s in the overall scoring.

- Jeanne's serious illness and the possibility of her loss. Rated by the author at 10.

- The everyday uncertainty of their lifestyle. Author rated at 7.

- The degenerative disease of Jeanne's father. Author rated for John's stress at 8.

Whatever the total score for John, it would be fair to say that his life shocks generally exceed the statistical norm, albeit that tens of thousands of Americans die from internalizing their stress everyday. For John, however, yet another life shock should be added.

- John's judgment of his own spiritual growth. Author rated at 10.

This weight of self-judgment is the most damaging of all because the mind says that if I only had full enlightenment, none of the fears and failures of my past would come into play. The fact that I am still weighted down by my past tells me that I am not yet spiritual enough. I am not yet free. Why am I not yet free? Why am I not yet in perfect union with God? Whatever the biographies of the Saints record, these questions must have been in their consciousness. If not, then why did so many of them die of cancer and heart disease?

There is another interpretation of John's heart attack that was noted by Joseph. After John got out of the hospital, Joseph told him, "You were doing what Dance Chiefs do. You were carrying something for the dancers." It was true that three Sun-Moon dancers that year had heart conditions. The traditional Native American teaching was that anyone who accepted the role of ceremonial chief had to be prepared to take on the pain of the spiritual awakening process of the people that he served. This was not a commitment to be taken lightly or unaware. Taking on the people's pain could cost the Dance Chief his own life. There were precautions that Chiefs practiced to protect themselves within the crucible of ceremony, but a certain vulnerability always existed. As the number and intensity of their dances increased, both John and Jeanne would suffer physically from their exertions in the metaphysical dimensions of the sweat lodge and dance arbor.

GERMANY, CROATIA, AND NORWAY 2000

By mid-August, Jeanne was feeling cancer free, and John surprised his cardiologist by the progress of his recovery from the heart infarction. John had quit smoking, was honoring a heart-smart diet, and was walking two miles a day in under 35 minutes. Although it was less than a month since John had been rushed to the emergency room, the couple decided to resume their travel schedule, beginning in Germany.

The Croatian Sun-Moon Dance was on their calendar near the end of the month. John's strength was tested right away as he loaded their heavy luggage into the car for the trip to the Atlanta airport. His heart hurt. Then in the unloading, he experienced mild pain and some light-headedness. He thus concluded that he had to avoid heavy lifting, and he also began to be concerned about fulfilling his physical role in Croatia. The trip to Frankfurt via Amsterdam took 23 hours door-to-door to reach the familiar Grossropperhausen home of Alex and Shania Racky where Jeanne and John were considered grandparents to the young Racky children, Muriel and Noah. After some lunch, John went to bed and slept more than 18 hours.

Jeanne kept the household atmosphere happy and upbeat, but John was not feeling well enough to be a social guest. There was a return of the irritation around his windpipe and periodic chest pain. With months of travel ahead, John felt isolated by his condition and sometimes wished that he had stayed in Tennessee. John was also ruminating about the barriers that he felt were the legacy of his father's instructions and judgments. In the summing up, he chided himself for still being at their effect. Emotionally, John still felt "bottled up." Why, he wondered, was he not able to "cry it out?"

After only five days in Germany, the Pehrsons responded to an invitation from Jeff Romanowski who had come from Connecticut to stage a Sun-Moon Dance in Croatia. Jeff had a worldwide client base for a new system of energy massage; and as a longtime student of Joseph and a Sun-Moon Dance Chief, he urged his clients to dance. In a dream, Jeff had seen a woman in the distance singing over the dance arbor. He believed that the woman was Jeanne, and so he invited both Jeanne and John to come to Buzet, Croatia via Frankfurt, Nuremberg, Munich, and Salzburg to fulfill his dream.

They arrived just before dark to be greeted by Jeff and then placed in the arbor with the support crew to spend the night under the stars. The next day, the couple set their tent at the support crew campsite. The landscape was very rocky and dry although it was only about 30 km from the Adriatic Sea. The climate reminded John of Southern California except that the nights cooled quickly from the north winds off the Alps.

Four Sun-Moon Dance Chiefs had come to support Jeff. In addition to John, there was Lukas Weber from Kassel, Germany; Rick Cotroneo from Albany, New York; and Keith Hagberry who had come directly from chiefing his own dance in West Virginia. In an amazing animal sign the previous week, eleven eagles had circled the arbor. Eagles are not known to flock so Jeff, who witnessed it, accepted the eagle blessing as a very positive omen.

The dance indeed was powerful. There were fifteen dancers including Alex Racky and Ulli. John believed that the dance energy made him stronger every day and that it was, in fact, healing him. In serving as a Dog Soldier, he worked long hours in the hot sun and even stood the early morning, 3 to 6 A.M. watch at the Dance arbor fire. With his didgeridoo and flute, he and Jeanne sang to wake the dancers in the morning and to put them to bed at night, thus fulfilling Jeff's dream. John felt so good, he even did some of the drumming. He had also put 200 handmade tobacco prayer ties into the sacred dance fire. Each carefully tied cloth package contained John's most ardent prayers for Jeanne, for the Dance Chief and crew, for the dancers, for all the individuals he knew with special needs, for family, for The People, and finally, for himself. In traditional practice, the tobacco burns, and the prayers rise in its pungent smoke and spread on the winds to be recognized by the Spirits of all the directions. The ritual is a metaphor, but the intention is that the prayers are both real and answered.

At the conclusion of the dance, the American and German participants took a two-day holiday to Rovinj, a resort on the Adriatic. The coastline was rocky with no sand beach, but there were sunbathers, swimmers, snorklers, scuba divers, and boats everywhere in the tourist area. After days of camping out in primitive conditions, Jeanne and John welcomed the hotel bed, shower, and flush toilet. They both were feeling tired and withdrawn after the intensity of the dance, and they had little pocket money to spend on extravagances such as hotel lunches or touring. They did, however, see ancient Roman sites, near the coliseum in Pula, where scenes from the Academy-Award-winning movie, *Gladiator*, were filmed, as well as the village of Hum that had been in existence since 400 A.D. On the final night, Jeff led the dance crew on a long trek to a seaside restaurant for a celebratory meal of Adriatic Sea bass with spaghetti and shrimp. Keith, realizing that John and Jeanne had walked four miles to the restaurant, sent them back to the hotel by taxi.

When they returned to Germany, Jeanne and John began an active schedule of workshops and private consultations. A Peace Concert on September 3rd attracted a good audience that was generous with its donations. Individuals touched in a personal way by the concert requested private sessions with both Jeanne and John, and they stayed busy in Grossropperhausen. Their only break was weekend visits to friends Lukas and Jutta Weber in Kassel.

In a workshop facilitated by Iris Wunsch one Saturday, Jeanne worked with the deep pain and fear of German women who had, as children in WWII, suffered the bombings of the war and the terrible aftermath of an angry world's retribution. In John's Intuitive Imagery sessions with clients, he was also encountering post-war angst that resembled a dark entity that vigorously resisted spiritual growth. Some of these cases, unfortunately, were beyond their reach as short-term counselors. In some, the anger and the rage were self-sabotaging, and the pathway to potential healing was blocked. How many millions of people lived in this condition as the result of war, Jeanne and John had asked? The seriousness of their peace mission came clearly into focus after these and similar encounters.

On their last day with the Racky family, Jeanne and John went to the apple, plum, and pear orchards to pick fruit. Alex told them that the fruit here had kept people alive during WWII when there was no other food. John and Alex took a ladder from tree to tree, and Jeanne, Shania, and the two children collected the fruit into boxes. The best fruit would be stored in a cool cellar while the bruised fruit would be pressed into juice.

The financial resources were building from their series of workshops and private sessions, and there were yet venues in northern Germany, and Oslo, Norway to help support the trip to Israel. As they traveled up the German peninsula to Husum on the North Sea, John was reminded of his maternal ancestors, the Harms, from this region. In Kiel there was a *Harms Strasse*, and even a large freighter named the *E. H. Harms* in the harbor. There was no time, however, for John to trace his genealogy and locate his distant cousins.

Their host in Wasserkoog on the peninsula was Sophia Peters, caretaker of the Peace-Sound Chamber there. It was Sophia who facilitated Joseph's travels around Europe when he first went abroad. Her Neule Schule (New School) was a center of activity in the area. Jeanne and John were in high demand, and they worked for four days non-stop in concert, workshops, ceremonies, and private sessions. The intensity of their encounters was also very high. People in deep pain with serious problems sought them out. Some of the pain was WWII war-related, and Sophia and others had a personal empathy for their healing. One person's own father, who was killed in an accidental laboratory explosion, had been a V-2 rocket scientist for Hitler. The stigmata of this wartime association was something which that person had healed in her spiritual work.

The major ceremony at Wasserkoog was the Awakening of the Peace-Sound Chamber of the Wind. The Chamber had been built in 1994, and it was the 18th time that Jeanne and John had done this ceremony. John cleaned the lodge fire pit and prepared the sacred ceremonial fire himself. The lodge lasted about an hour, with a fifth round water blessing for Sophia, its caretaker. John kept the sweat heat gentle, both for his heart, and for the first-time sweaters. Jeanne came to the Chamber just before midnight in her deerskin dress and white moccasins, and even without makeup, she looked radiant. Inside, she sang for nearly an hour and a half. The weather was mild throughout the ceremony.

People who experience the Awakening Ceremony are important mirrors to Jeanne and John, and the couple is always interested in feedback from those participants. At Wasserkoog, women especially wanted to talk to them about the male-female balance and equality that they witnessed. They said that they appreciated John for his confidence in fully supporting Jeanne in her leadership role and standing vigil for her. They also witnessed Jeanne's total support for John in the sweat lodge. This balance they saw as a powerful energy of love radiating from the two of them as they stood together. For some of the women, and men, too, Jeanne and John were redefining male-female relationships. Early in their process of coming together, the couple had aspired to a way of living that eliminated fear and jealousy and the sense of having to "possess" one another. They dreamed out loud of a relationship of equal portion, total openness, and complete communications. Their spiritual dimension had allowed them to demonstrate this goal in their ceremonial work and in their concerts and workshops together. They only fell short of the ideal when the focus shifted off service to the doubts of the small self. In this regard, they could sometimes be like any married couple on the planet. This earthbound experience was obviously paradoxical to their spiritual work, and there was only one remedy when they realized that a marital argument was occurring—laughter.

Jeanne and John took the overnight ferry from Kiel to Oslo. It was a calm sea crossing, and after much needed sleep, the couple awoke to a warm late-September morning as the ship navigated the islands of the Oslo fjord. Good friend Gerd Bjorke greeted them and took them to her Oslo flat. When Gerd went off to her job, there was an undemanding, luxurious quiet that was further enjoyed by a long soak in a hot bath. Frequent travelers know this sensation after weeks on the road. "Please, show me no more sights. Just show me a quiet room and a hot bath." And privacy, too, can be the rarest of moments when you lead a public life that is always dependent on the considerations of your hosts.

The events in Oslo included the fifth anniversary celebration for the Norwegian Spirit Quest Chamber. About 25 supporters gathered to share their experiences in the Chamber and to honor its Spirit. The event ended with drumming and singing led by Jeanne. The couple also performed a concert and did several workshops. In private imaging sessions by John and sound work sessions by Jeanne, most of their clients as usual were women. It seemed to both of them that women were taking the lead in healing the 21st century world. Women were showing more courage generally than men in seeking healing for themselves. It seemed like they were pregnant with hope and also willing to suffer the necessary labor that would birth humanity the new enlightenment of peace.

In telephone consultations with Owen in Canada, both Jeanne and John were able to work through their physical and emotional limitations. Norwegian women who had met John on his previous visit told him that he looked younger. When John attributed the compliment to his weight loss, a friend said, "I know what it is! You've gotten your innocence back. It's in your eyes!"

John would not have felt complete in Norway without a visit to his didgeridoo guru Bernt Balchen. Jeanne wrapped gifts of sage picked from Joseph's land in Colorado and a stone from Ayers Rock in Australia, but she allowed the men their space. After travel stories, the men "played some dij" and then Bernt gave John a sound massage for his heart on the F-note dij. Later Bernt and Marta Balchen came to Gerd's flat to visit Jeanne. Bernt had fashioned a small eagle feather and a crystal for Jeanne to wear in her hair during her stay in Israel.

Friday night, there was dinner with old friends Ole Bjorn and Anne Haraldson at their flat. The meal was macrobiotic with Norwegian cloudberries for dessert. The cloudberries look like yellow raspberries and only grow in the Arctic—one berry to a plant. After the unique dessert, Ole and John entertained on the C-note and D-note didgeridoos.

On the final weekend, Jeanne did a Saturday sound healing workshop for sixteen people in a large teepee with a floor of birch branches covered by reindeer skins. On Sunday, the couple combined for a sound and visioning workshop for about the same number. Jeanne was especially in demand for private sessions, and her available hours were soon filled.

On October 3rd, after ten event-filled days in Norway, Jeanne and John were on an Airbus to Tel-Aviv via Frankfurt. The news from Israel was not good. Forty-four people had died, and more than 1000 had been injured in five days of West Bank and Gaza Strip violence. A renewed intifada had begun. Jeanne and John felt spiritually called to Israel as peacemakers. Their first trip to the Middle East was to be a baptism of fire.

FIRST TRIP TO ISRAEL

J eanne has the habit of acting on her visions without regard to what might be viewed as practical obstacles. So the day after a vision called her to Israel, she was on the phone to the only Israeli that she knew. It was Maitreya Rogers' partner Ortalia. Maitreya was the person who had organized Jeanne's Whale Quest trip to Hawaii, and he and Ortalia had been their friends for several years. After eight months of planning, others joined to make a party of thirteen intent on exploring the spiritual aspects of the "land of the prophets." Traveling with a group on a set itinerary felt odd to them after making so many trips on their own. The Tel-Aviv airport was very busy and very tense. The group had to pass through two check-points before entering the terminal. Security officers grilled them with questions and inspected their passports and tickets with minute care. Jeanne did not act on her usual tendency to engage security screeners and talk about their peace mission as she felt it would not be welcomed by the stern-face inspectors.

Jeanne describes her experiences in this way.

"We arrived in Israel three days after the Intifada began in October of 2000. I will never forget the awe and wonder I felt in stepping off the plane onto the land that Abraham and Jesus had walked. It was overpowering. But it didn't take long for me to move into the 21st century where I was pulled into the present day drama of what was beginning to occur on this ancient soil now, in this moment. We arrived at the beginning of Yom Kippur. There was an odd sense of quiet in the city considering that a war had just begun. At one point I stood on the balcony of the hotel we stayed in, in Jerusalem, and wondered at the lack of traffic and the fact that most of the people were fasting that particular day. It made me think of something Beautiful Painted Arrow said to me once: 'If somebody asked me how to create world peace, I would say to put all the world leaders into a room for 24 hours with no food and no water, and then ask them to make decisions.' Who knows? It might just work.

"I remember we had planned to go to the Wailing Wall inside the Old City (Old Jerusalem) on a Friday. Ortalia woke up one morning earlier in the week with a clear thought that we were not to go on Friday, but were to go Thursday or earlier. It was a good thing. On Friday there was violence at the Wall, which included the throwing of stones. After this occurred, we learned to listen intently and moved throughout Israel in safety . . . threading the needle. Often violent situations occurred just before we arrived or right after we left a place, but never while we were in a place. We truly felt we were being watched over by angels.

"One afternoon, under the guidance of Ortalia and Hagit Ra'anan, we went to one of the border crossings between Gaza and Israel at the Erez Checkpoint to plant a Peace Pole. There were around 16 of us in our vanbus, along with other friends who participated in the ceremony, including the press. It was a sweet ceremony, with John playing his didgeridoo into the hole in the earth just before the pole was planted. Several of us then placed sacred items into the hole. As the pole itself was being placed, we sang and danced in a circle. The pole said 'Peace on Earth' in four languages: Hebrew, Arabic, English, and Japanese. Immediately after the ceremony, on the Palestinian side of the fence that divided Gaza and Israel, two young Palestinian men walked toward us. They saw the pole, read it, and smiled. Being Arabic, they said to all of us 'Shalom, Shalom,' which is a Hebrew greeting for peace. Interesting that they said it in Hebrew rather than in their own language, which is 'Salaam.' We smiled. The pole was already working.

"It was on this trip to Gaza that we first met our dear rabbi friend, Eliyahu McLean, an extraordinary young man who has taken many risks in his effort to bring peace to that land. There are so many . . . Dvorah Brous, a young Jewish woman who works closely now with the Bedouin (nomadic Arabs); Ibrahim El-Hawa, a Palestinian who with Eliyahu has traveled the world with a message of peace; Jeff Goldstein who bravely facilitates and supports peace activities that touch thousands inside Israel; Anael Harpaz who works with teenage Palestinian and Israeli Jewish girls bridging differences with love. There are thousands of people working diligently at the grassroots level to bring peace. We have long been convinced that it is at this level that the changes will be made . . . not in the political arena.

"Walking with Eliyahu to the Peace Pole site, across a vast deserted plot of land situated next to the fence, I looked down to see a single white feather. I was awed when I saw it, so I picked it up, and together Eliyahu and I did a blessing on the land with this feather that now is part of John's and my sacred altar.

"Before leaving the States, Owen James had an insight that it might be important for me to create a song in the 'cave' underneath the Dome of the Rock in old Jerusalem, that this somehow would help to bring back together what had been separated so long ago. This was easier said than done. The Dome of the Rock is Muslim, and neither John nor I were allowed to go in. I knew that what Owen said had some truth in it, but I didn't know what to do other than trust that Spirit would work it all out. I mentioned to Hagit Ra'anan that I wanted to get beneath the Dome of the Rock, and she actually pulled off a minor miracle. Underneath the wall of the old city there are ancient tunnels, most of which have only recently been unearthed. Not everyone knows of their existence. They are very sacred to the Jews, particularly the Orthodox Jews. And because it was Yom Kippur, one could only go into the tunnels with special permission. Somehow, Hagit arranged that we might go. And so, even though we weren't able to enter the Dome of the Rock, we were able to go into the tunnels underneath the surrounding area of the Dome. When we were deep within the tunnels, we came into a space where there was a large rock that had been specially marked. It was the backside of the corner stone of the Dome! I was astounded! I placed my head against the stone and began to sing the song that was forming. As I sang, I experienced an explosion of light that seemed to be two shafts of light coming together into a single powerful beam.

"Once the song was done, and having left the tunnels, I learned two extraordinary things. The first was that John experienced something similar, which confirmed that at some point in time, a split had occurred on this historic Mount Mariah, where Mohammed is said to have ascended, where Abraham is said to have offered up his son Isaac, and where Solomon built the first temple. In these precious moments, an energy had reunited with itself. I had no idea what effect that would have, if any, on the mass consciousness. I only knew that something beautiful had just happened. The second piece was not made evident until two weeks later when I finally got around to reading some printed material on the tunnels. It turns out that the enclosed space in which I sang had, a long time ago, been named 'the Cave' by the Jews. Owen had told me to go sing in the 'cave' underneath the Dome of the Rock. Without knowing it, that is exactly what I had done. Strange how Spirit works.

"In the Judean Desert next to the Dead Sea we had the privilege of meeting one of our now closest friends in Israel—Victor Barr. Victor had a talent for helping one to feel safe while imparting teachings that touch the deep part of our souls. One of the most memorable moments happened on a hike to one of the caves near Qumran, the home of the ancient Essenes, where the Dead Sea Scrolls were found. We had been driven to this spot by a beautiful Arab man named Wasaam. He and all the rest of us climbed a steep hill of dirt, sand, and rock up the side of a mountain to access the cave. It was not easy for me, and I was in total awe of Victor, Wasaam, and other natives who seemed to move on this terrain like mountain goats.

"We arrived to the cave via a thin ledge that curved around the mountainside and tilted outward from a stone ledge. It was truly unnerving. We went into the cave and had a beautiful meditation. When it came time to leave the cave, I was acutely aware that the cave floor itself also tilted down and outward so that I felt as though I were being poured from the cave, much like tea from a teapot. When it was my time to go, Victor gave me his hand to hold onto for as long as I could as I ascended precariously onto the ledge outside the cave. I walked oh so carefully, clutching my toes to the ledge, grasping Victor's hand, until little by little I had to let go of his hand. I almost panicked. Just when I had to let go of his hand, he said to someone around the corner, 'Do you have her?' At this point, I heard the soothing voice of Wasaam, saying 'yes,' and just as I let go of Victor with my left hand, Wasaam grabbed my right hand. I simply cannot find the words to tell you what this felt like. With their help, singing all the way, I made it to the bottom safely and unharmed. Once down, I instantly got an amazing insight. On the ledge, I was held in safety on one side by a Jew and held in the same way on the other side by an Arab. I could not have done what I did without both of them. There seems to be a powerful teaching in this. Particularly at a time when a new war had just begun."

The nine-week journey completed, the couple returned to the Corryton farmhouse. John took to re-reading the *Bible* and a book on Islam in an attempt to reconcile the jealous, ruthless, judgmental God of the Middle East, and his own religious conditioning, with his current beliefs. He felt that the patriarchal voices and their dogmatic views were very limiting and still very troubling.

The financial dog barked again, and the couple had to remind themselves that they had been in the same circumstances a hundred times, and always, always, they have been shown God's grace. It was not that they waited for angels to descend with fistfuls of dollars. They were working full-time to give concerts and workshops and dances, but the income from these events was then required to get to the next place, perhaps a continent away, when they were invited.

November turned cold in Eastern Tennessee, and John fed the woodstove in the farmhouse to keep the chill out of the four inhabited rooms. The presidential election was in chaos with no declared winner between George W. Bush and Al Gore. After a protracted court battle, the Supreme Court of the United States would vote along political party lines and make George Bush the president; but until then, the television watching public would manifest the mental, emotional, and physical gridlock of a divided country.

Isolated on the farm, John became very introspective; and with Jeanne in Chattanooga visiting her dying father, John wrote a poem to his deceased father Vernon. The poem conveyed everything that he needed to release from his childhood.

TO VERNON

This is a poem to my father, Vernon,
whom I have loved and hated a thousand times
whose stern voice and hard hand
still shapes and limits the life I lead
though he's been dead these past five years.
You died too soon for us to be friends
or give my childhood memories an end:
divorce at eleven, sent away at thirteen
never, really, to come home again
never time for us to make amends
except for the grown up hugs I gave
your stoic coolness melting at last
in the fire and tears of the cancer
that hid your eyes with morphined pain
and finally took your life.
You thought I knew you loved me
even though I was never told
but that's a thing that no one knows
until it's told and felt and shown
before, in growing old, time takes us all away
so I write this now for you and for me,
for forgiving and forgiveness,
for healing hearts across place and space and time,
for hearts breaking down and breaking free,
for living and loving beyond all limits,
for you my father, Vernon,
now dead these past five years
dear Dad, please set me free.

After a Friday evening Peace Concert in Johnson City,
Tennessee, Jeanne and John with Teresa Hutson drove to the

Swannanoa Peace-Sound Chamber near Asheville, North Carolina on Saturday. On a visit with Zoe Bryant, the Chamber caretaker two years before, Jeanne told Zoe that she had been called to have a ceremonial pipe. Zoe was not only a pipe carrier trained in the Lakota tradition, but she was also a maker of Native American traditional pipes. Jeanne admitted that she had no experience with the sacred ceremonial pipe, but that she knew that she was supposed to learn about it. Zoe says that she felt guided to lend her personal pipe, a Snake pipe, to Jeanne although it was the first sacred pipe she had made. Part of her did not want to release the pipe, but after a "short argument with Spirit," Zoe took the pipe down from her home altar and presented it to Jeanne. They then walked up the mountain trail to the Chamber where Zoe did a Pipe Ceremony as a basic instruction in its use. She told Jeanne that the Snake would teach her the rest, and that when Jeanne was ready for her own pipe, she would know and make a pipe especially for Jeanne. Brenda Sue Taylor was also very helpful in providing initial instruction and information. After Zoe and Brenda Sue, the ancestors seemed to take over. Jeanne then carried the Snake pipe for almost two years as she initiated Chambers with sound in many countries.

In the meantime, Zoe received a vision for Jeanne's personal pipe, and she crafted an Eagle's Head pipe out of the same piece of African soapstone that she had used to carve the Snake pipe. Zoe then informed Jeanne that her pipe was ready and that she was "lonesome for her Snake." Since Jeanne and John were still abroad, Jeanne asked Zoe to bury the new pipe in the sand at the center of the altar in the Swannanoa Chamber. Now Jeanne had returned to Swannanoa to claim her pipe. After the Eagle pipe was recovered from the sand, Zoe loaded it with tobacco while Jeanne loaded the Snake pipe. They then performed the ritual offering of the smoke to the directions and switched pipes. Thus, Zoe completed the ceremony with her treasured Snake pipe, and Jeanne finished with her new and personal Eagle pipe. Another year would go by before Jeanne and Zoe would come together in an even more significant exchange of sacred pipes, but it was an event that neither one of them could have predicted in 2000.

On the last day of November, Jeanne and John drove to Graham to visit Cheryl and David. Gracie, the Beemer, was running rough, their finances were critically low; and to make matters worse, they had gotten a $115 speeding ticket for doing 75 mph in a 60-mph zone. Cheryl and David cheered them up with a surprise restaurant dinner party with friends. In talking about her Eagle pipe, Jeanne asked David to create a ceremony that would help her step into her new role as a pipe carrier. David himself was a pipe carrier steeped in the Lakota tradition. It was the Lakota who were given the original Pipe Ceremony by White Buffalo Calf Woman, so the pipe is very sacred to David. The pipe carrier agrees to carry the burdens of the people, and the "chanupahs" themselves are seen as prayer instruments to higher consciousness. Jeanne's request required David to pray for an answer and for a vision of what should be done in ceremony. In saying yes, David told Jeanne and John his vision insight. In their transition from the corporate world toward enlightenment, they were carrying the world. As they grew, so did the planetary consciousness. John remarked in his journal that David's words rocked him back on his feet and made him feel awed and humbled. And yet, at the same time, it confirmed for Jeanne and himself that despite their struggles, they were on the right spiritual path.

The ceremony that David brought to them in the Watersong Chamber combined form and no-form. The Chamber was prepared with candles around the central pit, or *sipapu*, which represents the womb of the Earth Mother. Blankets were then spread in the four directions, and an altar was created in the West for the chanupahs. Dobs, a ceremonial participant, placed crow wings in the North, and he and David heated seven rocks and placed them in the central pit for a purification sweat. David poured the water and led the prayers. David then presented Jeanne her Eagle pipe, and she loaded it with red willow bark, lit it, and offered smoke to the Great

Spirit and to the six directions. John records that the party of five that included Cheryl were very aware of the presence of Spirits in the Chamber throughout the ceremony.

On the weekend of the ninth, the couple returned to the Center for Peace to do another Community Building Workshop. They renamed the workshop to better reflect its metaphysical dimensions. It was now titled "Pathway To the Open Heart: An Experience in Community." By mid-month, they were back at Watersong to record a 17-song CD album to be titled *Between Slices of Light*. The album had been in the planning stages for months, but they had had to wait for all the support elements to come into place.

Saturday, the 16th of December, was a cold, rainy day as the sound engineer set up the microphones in the Chamber. Dobs furnished his Dobs-mobile as an operations center so that the sound equipment would not litter the interior space. Jeanne sang and played a native drum and traditional rattles; John did harmony vocals and played the flute and didgeridoo; Cheryl and David added vocals; and Blaze Kielar enriched the session on the violin and viola. The first 16 cuts were spontaneous songs like those Jeanne had sung in concerts and ceremonies around the world. The longest, *Creation*, was five minutes and forty seconds. The shortest, at just under two minutes, was *Prayer for the Children*. The album ends with a song that Jeanne often sings to conclude her concerts— *Amazing Grace*. The second verse is sung in Cherokee to honor her ancestors, and as she sings, a hard rain can be heard as background on the album. Then as she ends the song, the sound of thunder can be faintly heard as applause.

Financial underwriting for the album was provided by Cheryl, David, Dobs, and Jo Fisher, and through advance orders. The cover painting for the CD album cover was done by Joseph Rael. His participation was uniquely appropriate, because it was Beautiful Painted Arrow's vision for the sacred Chambers in the 1980s that had brought these individuals together to sing for world peace.

The touring year ended for Jeanne and John with two late December concerts. The first was generated from their experiences in Israel, and it took place at the Laurel Theatre in Knoxville. The event was facilitated by Deborah Oleshansky, and its sponsors included the Ramallah Palestinian Organization, the Alliance for Mideast Peace, and the Children's Villages Organization. Even the Buddhist community got involved. Kevin Schriver played a magical flute and Teresa Hutson a spirited djimbe drum in accompaniment. On the following evening, December 21st, Jeanne and John went to the Ancient Wisdom Center in Boone, North Carolina to give a winter solstice Peace Concert. Ancient Wisdom was a center of New Age activity with a bookstore, gift shop, and a functions room for workshops and seminars. The author's wife, Pat, wanted to attend the concert, but her husband, having worked all day on a book manuscript, was reluctant to go. He was well known to be hermit-like when he had a book in progress, which generally was most of the time. Nevertheless, he respected Pat's intuitive talents, and when she gently insisted, he agreed to go into town.

The concert itself was intimate and engaging for the thirty or so in attendance. Jeanne sang spontaneous songs using the five vowel sounds, with John adding harmony vocals, and sometimes playing an accompaniment on a flute or a didgeridoo. Teresa Hutson joined them on the djimbe drum. The Joynes couple recognized Jeanne's amazing vocal virtuosity, but they also recognized the resonate vibrations that felt like the peace and healing of a profound meditation. As in every concert, Jeanne taught the audience to sing their own vowel vocable songs. People who had never sung in public, like Pat, were encouraged to find their inner voice and express it. The results were amazing. With each audience member singing the personal song of him or her self, the rational mind might predict that there would be cacophony, a chaos of discordant sounds. But miraculously, each voice finds its level, and the blend then seeks unity, and unique harmonies appear. In hundreds of venues in multicultural environments where languages, cultures, and religions would seem to clash, the communal singing at the end of a Jeanne and John concert achieves harmony and even transcendent beauty. Often, when the song ends, there is a moment of awe expressed as silence, and then there is laughter as the wonder of what the collection of former strangers has created is realized. It was the same in Boone that night.

After the concert there was a potluck supper for those who brought a dish to share. Pat had brought a dish, so the couple got to meet Jeanne and John on a more personal basis. When the author returned home, he did something that he had done only once before. He sent Jeanne and John his Booker Series novels in acknowledgment that their work was also his work. He and Pat also included an invitation for them to be houseguests on future visits to Boone. Thus began a relationship that resulted a few years later in the writing of this biography, a two-year effort that became the hardest writing job the author had ever loved.

Christmas at the Corryton farm was low budget for Jeanne and John that year. Jeanne had done her gift shopping at discount stores, and there was very little cash to add to the presents. Nevertheless, there were two Christmas week traditional dinners—one for John's sons Sean and Alan, who had traveled by bus from Chicago after Christmas with their brother Ryan and mother Diana, and another for Jenny and John Troutner, Jeanne's children.

Although there were workshops and concerts scheduled into the new year, what must it have been like for Jeanne and John after the children were gone, to ponder their faith-based future? On cold winter days, feeding the farmhouse stove from woodpile scraps, wondering if a sick Gracie would carry them to the next venue, and praying for relief from their serious health issues, what future could they anticipate? Far-flung destinations had again called out to them—Germany, Croatia, Israel. How were they to respond? And if India had been mentioned? Well, they might have laughed.

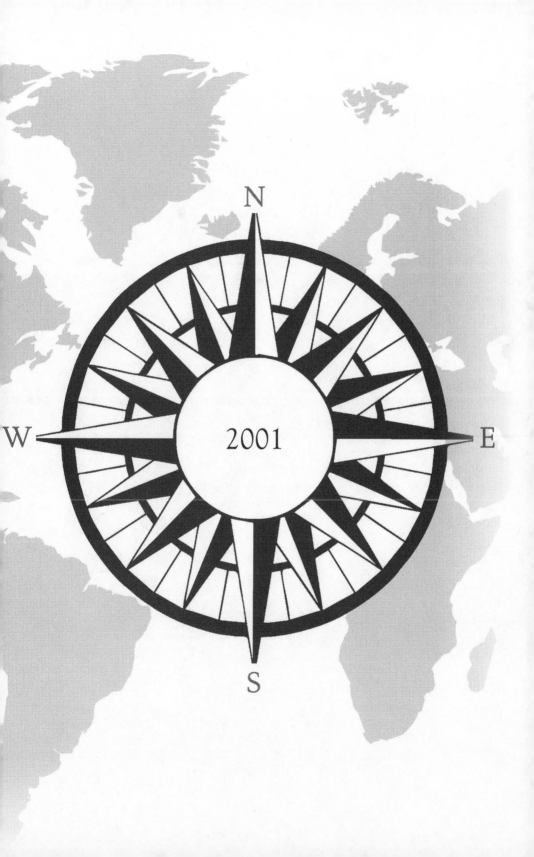

EACH YEAR A BEGINNING

To open their 2001 concert, workshop, and ceremonial season, Jeanne and John traveled 1530 miles to Santa Fe. The events were scheduled for Sandy Misage's new Hydration Café, and although Sandy did the usual promotions, she was embarrassed by the poor turnouts. John and Jeanne cut their losses by sleeping on a futon in Sandy's small one-bedroom apartment.

During the cross-country transit, the couple had stayed overnight with supportive friends and family members who usually treated them to their best meals of their trip. While in the Southwest, they drove to Durango to see Joseph who took them to Christina's, Jeanne and John's favorite restaurant in Durango. The couple had finally come to a place of relaxation in the presence of their spiritual mentor.

In a Medicine Ceremony, John got a strong message to stop smoking cigarettes, even the few that he had indulged himself since his heart attack. Joseph also gave John a new slant on the death of the man next door whom John had seen expire and spiritually leave his body in Corryton. Joseph speculated that the man had died for John. If God was going to call someone, perhaps the man had volunteered to go instead of John.

After returning to Corryton, the couple went to Pennsylvania for five days with Tom and Kristen Bissinger. They presented a new two-day workshop: "Living in the Moment, A Journey of Faith" in the Birdsong Chamber. The participation was a financial success, and there was a great deal of positive feedback. Later in the month, Jeanne and John drove 560 miles to Gulf Shores, Alabama to attend the funeral of her father's younger brother. En route, they stopped briefly to console Perry Lane who was sad over his sibling's sudden death. Being very ill himself, he had expected to pass first.

The next working trip was scheduled for the Boston area, a journey east into a cold Massachusetts February. In Lexington, they did a Peace Concert, a Sound Healing Workshop, and several private sessions. Their host was Selena Britton-Woolf. In Concord, Jeanne and John celebrated their 6th wedding anniversary at the home of Tom and Anne Rarich. After the Lexington Peace Concert, people kept calling for information on the two scheduled workshops and for private consultations. Anne Rarich joked about her secretarial activity in answering the phone for them. On his 51st birthday, John gave a three-hour Imaging Workshop at the Illuminations Bookstore owned by Ariana Butz. All in all, the two-week Boston area tour was very productive, and they had established a base of interest for future returns.

In March they were back at Watersong in Graham, North Carolina. Cheryl had important news. In a meeting with Grandfather Joseph at the Center for Peace, Cheryl was told to dance the Sun-Moon Dance. When she speculated that she might dance there in Tennessee, Joseph said, "No, dance on your land, this year, with John Pehrson as Chief." The appointment to chief a new North Carolina Sun-Moon Dance came as a total surprise to John; and while he felt like Joseph had just kicked him off another cliff, Cheryl and David were elated. Since John was already co-chiefing the Tennessee Sun-Moon Dance with Steve Citty, a four-year obligation, the chiefing of another dance would require another four-year annual commitment. John could only laugh at the irony of the unexpected prospect. The man with leadership doubts had once again been called to lead.

In his journal, John speculated about cause and effect as it creates the future. "In the broad sweep of time," he wrote, "where all our lives are simultaneous, we plant seeds of the probable future with each action we take. Moreover, the future manifests immediately, so seeds of conflict instantly create their own probable futures. There is something important about this fact that has the power to heal the planet, but it is not a fully formed thought yet."

The wear and tear on Gracie finally resulted in violent shaking as Jeanne was en route to see her dad in Chattanooga. She had no other option than to pull off the road and find a repair shop. Gracie continued on her way with new front-end calipers and rotors while the Pehrsons were out something over $500.

That mid-April John completed reading the four novels in the author's Booker Series, and he quoted a passage from *Dead Water Rites* in his journal about the difference between the English language and Native American languages of the Southwest. He noted, "Monty talks about language in much the same way as Joseph, Jeanne, and I did in the Medicine Ceremony this past January." The reading of this literature played a key role in John's later willingness to trust the author with his extensive journals.

On a Wednesday, April 11, Jeanne and John began a pilgrimage to the ashram of Sai Baba in India. The genesis of this odyssey had begun seven years prior, and Sai Baba had repeatedly appeared to Jeanne in visions over the years. Finally, the coming to Sai Baba was to be realized in another impractical leap of faith. When Jeanne felt called to a place, she accepted no obstacles in the process of going there. Her energy was spontaneous, and so was her behavior. On the day that they left for India, the couple had no idea where Sai Baba was physically in residence. They would find him, Jeanne assured John. Or, Sai Baba would find them. Anyway, since Baba had spiritually called them to India, he would take care of the travel arrangements. That was Jeanne's irrepressible attitude and conviction. Rational observers could only shake their heads in wonder.

COMING TO SAI BABA

I n the South India village of Puttaparthi around 1940, a fourteen-year-old boy declared himself as Sai Baba, an Avatar who had come again for the redemption of mankind. Three years later, he pointed to a hillock south of the village and said that he would transform the region into a place of the highest peace. Today, the mandir (temple) and ashram complex in that place and in Brindavan welcome tens of thousands of spiritual pilgrims each year who travel from around the world to experience darshan or sight of Bhagavan Sri Sathya Sai Baba. His biographer, Sri Kasturi, wrote, "It has been the scene of countless transformations of character, revolutions in belief, confirmation of faith, curing of disease, calming of temper, discarding of hatred, salvaging of souls, and reunions of hearts."

It is believed that Sai Baba appears to individuals in visions and dreams to give them strength on their spiritual paths. Jeanne had such experiences even before she knew his name or saw his photograph. The road to India and their personal experiences with Sai Baba began in May 1994. Jeanne begins the story.

"I think it was a regular workday, and I slept through the night, and John was already up and out of the bed. It was early morning, and I was just staying in the bed getting a little extra sleep; and all of a sudden, boing! I hear this voice: 'It's Time.' And I remember sitting up in the bed. In Signal Mountain our bed faced out to Chattanooga, faced out into the woods, which I used to love, and I was sitting up looking around the room and out into the woods, and I said out loud, 'It's time for what?' And the voice said, 'It's time to begin your work with sound.' It was very clear. It was a voice, and you know, psychologists can say whatever they want to, but this is what I was hearing. I remember saying, 'How do I begin?' And these are the exact words. 'You'll begin with Sanskrit.' I just kind of laughed inside myself.

"Sanskrit? I knew nothing about Sanskrit. I'm sitting in the bed, and John walked in, so I told him what had just happened. Rather than thinking that this is crazy, I thought, this is exciting. I didn't say it like that, but I could feel it inside. Something was happening, and I needed to pay attention. Immediately my brain kicks in, and I'm thinking, ok, Sanskrit, Sanskrit. Call the university library, so bam! I called the university library, and I was told immediately that there was a woman there from India, and that she might be able to help me. She was in the reference department of the university library. I got right straight through to this woman, and I said, 'Dr. Murgahi, this is going to sound a little strange,' and I told her what had happened. I said, 'I'm being told to learn Sanskrit. Do you know anybody that can help me?' She then said, 'I learned Sanskrit for nine years growing up, and I've been waiting for a time to hone my skill. Come see me now.'

"I remember walking into the library and seeing this beautiful woman behind the desk. When I saw her, my eyes just filled with tears. I remember saying to John, 'When the student is ready, the teacher will appear.' I walked up to her and told her a little more about what had happened that morning and said, 'I really would appreciate it if you would consider teaching me Sanskrit, and I'll pay you whatever you think it is worth.' She said, 'I don't want any money. I've been waiting for someone like you.'

"And so that began my lessons in Sanskrit. I didn't have many of them. I didn't need them because the insight came very quickly. She worked with me in the beginning a couple of times a week. I learned all the symbols and was taught something very significant.Sanskrit was never meant to be written down. It was always meant to be sung.She said that gods came and taught her people how to write it down. She said there is a legend that if you can make the sounds of Sanskrit exactly, then it alerts the gods.

"Very soon I got the insight that I didn't have to go into academic levels of Sanskrit. Sanskrit was a doorway to the divine nature of sound and vibration. The mother languages of us all, from Sanskrit to Tiwa, the native language of Beautiful Painted Arrow, are based on sacred vibrations.

"From our meeting with Dr. Murgahi, we went immediately to a new-age bookstore in search of a Sanskrit primer. When I told the store manager what I was looking for, she got a strange expression on her face. The previous day, while re-shelving her inventory, she came across a Sanskrit primer and an audiotape of Sanskrit chants that were completely out of sequence with everything else. She considered them odd pieces of inventory that would probably never sell. John and I looked at each other with the same thought—when you are headed in the right direction, there will be signs. Here was definitely a sign.

"Within days of beginning Sanskrit, I had a dream about my old music professor, Chick Davis. I was being told to go to him. It seemed a further indication that I was being pulled back into my work with vocal sound. Since we had a trip planned through Washington, DC, we thought that we could stop on the way back in Emory, Virginia to look up Chick at Emory and Henry College.

"A friend advised us that Deepak Chopra was giving a workshop on vibration in Washington during the dates we were to pass through. I saw the information as another sign, so I called to see if I could attend. I was told that the workshop was full and that only a limited number of people can register because Deepak Chopra sees each participant individually at some point. I responded, 'It is really important. I can't explain other than to tell you that this call was prompted by a dream.' There was a silence on the other end of the phone, and then the person suggested that I show up at the workshop hotel a day prior to the event and see if there have been any cancellations.

"Standing in the registration line, I heard an East Indian woman reject many latecomers in front of me; but when I started to walk away, I felt an invisible hand on my shoulder guiding me back in line. All I could say when I faced the workshop registrar was, 'It's really important. I don't understand why. All I know is that I've just come up from Chattanooga, we're on our way through Washington, I had a dream, I'm supposed to be here.'

"The woman looked deep into my eyes, and then she told me to come back in the morning to a specific meeting room. When I saw her the next day, she was politely telling two women that there was no room left in the workshop. Then she turned to me and

invited me in. I was astounded and very excitedly said 'thank you.'
She replied, 'Oh, you don't have to thank me. It is your karma that
you are to be here.'

"I attended the workshop, and Deepak Chopra personally
worked with my vibration, but I have no memory of what occurred.
Whatever happened, I was convinced of one thing—I was where I
was supposed to be.

"On our trip back to Chattanooga, I called ahead for a meeting
with Chick. We had not seen each other for thirty years, but
because he is one of the special souls in my life, I wept at the sight
of him. We embraced, and he said, 'I've been looking everywhere for
you.' I said, 'I thought that I was looking for you!'

"Chick had been looking for me to sing in his dream concert.
He was very near retirement, and he wanted to re-assemble the
prime voices of his elite concert choir over the years for a recorded
concert. He wanted me as his soprano in the Verdi Requiem. The
other soloists—baritone, tenor, and contralto—would be professional opera singers. I had not sung in this way in thirty years.
Frankly, knowing Chick's high performance standards, I doubted
that I could sing the demanding *Verdi*. He asked me to sing something for him, and the only thing that came to mind was *Amazing
Grace*. He seemed pleased. Then to settle my doubts, he said,
'You've got a year to train.'

"As the concert date approached, I tried to work with Chick
once a month. He told me that something had happened to my
voice that moved him. My singing was no longer just based on talent and great vocal range. My soul was now coming through the
sound, and Chick said, in front of John, that my voice was one of
the five most powerful female voices on the planet. I practiced
when I was guided to do it. Sometimes in the car. Sometimes rever-
berating a house with very high pitches from the Verdi. John—bless
his sweet heart—supported me the whole time.

"A month before the concert, we were attending a Stephen
Halpern musical workshop. There was a very elderly man there—a

tiny, short, beautiful precious man, with white hair and deep ocean-blue eyes who needed support, so I volunteered. His name was Harry, and as we talked quietly in the background of the workshop activity, I noticed an amulet that he wore around his neck. When I asked about it, Harry told me that the amulet had been manifested out of the air by Sai Baba. 'Who?' I asked. Harry then told me his experiences with Sai Baba, and he said that anyone who held the amulet would see Baba. Then he took the amulet off his neck and put it into my hands, and I will never, never forget this: I saw his eyes change from ocean blue to deep, dark, almost black, and I began to weep.

"Harry put his hands over mine, and I felt compelled to confess my fears about the upcoming concert. I told him that I did not know if I could do it. 'I'm scared,' I told him. He looked deep into my eyes and said simply with a reassuring smile, 'You just forget who you are; that's all.'

"A month later, we were in dress rehearsal for the concert—four soloists backed by 250 highly trained and gifted voices. I struggled with the music to the point of tears. Everyone must have been thinking, she's lost it. Chick comforted me by saying, 'You'll find it again.'

"The next day, I had one of those experiences of absolute surrender. Something in me said, 'You've been working at this all your life. You're ready. Just let it go. Just surrender.'

"And then as I stood on stage waiting for my solo cue, a beautiful face with big Afro-looking hair appeared as an apparition before me. I had never seen the face before, and then there were hordes of angels. This was my experience while I was singing, and the sound coming out of me was beyond description. Something in me had shifted. The music flowed out of me, out of all of us. And for the first time, I saw the vortex being created inside the auditorium by the vocal vibrations. I saw the angels, and I saw pure energy working in a way that I had never seen it before.

"Months later, when I shared this experience with a friend and described the face that had appeared to inspire me to impossible heights, a photo was produced of Sai Baba. I was stunned. Yes, this was the man! As Harry had promised when I held the amulet, I did indeed see Baba. It was shortly after this experience that I realized the voice I had heard one year before, telling me to begin my work with sound, was Sai Baba.

"For the next seven years, he came to me in dreams or visions. It was finally in mid-March of 2001 that he came in a dream and simply said, 'I am waiting.' I remember saying to Joseph, 'It looks like I'm being called to India to meet Sai Baba.' His reply was, 'Yes, you will go one time . . . so that you will remember you can do all that he does.' I took that comment into my heart and realized that this is true of anyone. All any of us has to do is listen, surrender, and remember."

Jeanne had serious concerns about the long journey to India. Their only practical information on transportation and accommodations had come from the friend of a friend. There were also concerns about John's recent heart attack. If Sai Baba wanted them in India, Jeanne and John prayed that he would provide for them. Leaving Knoxville on stand-by tickets, the first sign was a miraculous upgrade to business class at every stage of their forty-hour journey. Jeanne had dreamed Baba saying, "Don't be afraid. I am here with you," but the comforts of business class, with its reclining bedlike seats and excellent food service, seemed like Baba was making their way easy. Realizing the virtual impossibility of the stand-by ticket upgrades, Jeanne and John could only say, "Thank you, Baba."

India is usually a shock for American travelers. The hot, humid air envelops like a steam bath, and too often it carries the smell of urine and sweat and the buzzing of flying insects. There are beggars and thieves and the crush of crowds. The short drive from Bangalore to Brindavan reveals a third-world standard of living where cows wander in village streets and water buffalo pull wagons.

Time, especially in rural India, has a non-western dimension. If the western mind makes demands of time, it will always be transported to the peaks of frustration.

When the couple arrived at the Bangalore Airport, they had no idea where they would find the 74-year-old holy man. Sai Baba had three ashrams, and generally in April he was at the Kodai Kanal location, ten hours away, but because of the Tamil New Year celebration, he was still in Brindavan, only forty-five minutes away. Jeanne saw this as another sign of Baba's plan, and she was grateful that after the long trip, John would not be subjected to more travel stress.

John and Jeanne got a room in the Sai Towers, a new hotel in Brindavan, a short distance from Baba's ashram. Their room had two very firm beds fitted with a bottom sheet and a coarse woolen blanket—no top sheet. The room was clean, but the water in the toilet and sink was brown. The shower water ran into a drain behind the toilet. It was no Holiday Inn, but it only cost $15 per night. The first day in India, the couple could do little more than flop on their beds and recover sleep.

Both Jeanne and John wanted Indian clothing for their ashram encounters with Baba, and so an Indian contact, Yousuff, took them shopping. John purchased two white pajama outfits for under $22, but Jeanne was troubled at having to pay $25 for a sari. There was a great deal of sales pressure, and Jeanne cried when she left the upscale shop without a garment. Jeanne recalls the experience.

"I was very tired from the trip and feeling vulnerable in the newness of India. Baba appreciates that women wear saris to his ashram, and I was told that a beautiful one could be purchased for no more than $10. Crying over $25 was reacting to the fact that we had less than $500 to sustain us for our two weeks in India. Spending that money so early in our visit seemed to rob us of the financial flexibility that we would need later. I was afraid while still trying to be brave and trusting."

John's drama of the day was the theft of his new $10 American thrift store sandals inside the gates of Baba's ashram. He had removed his sandals to move closer to hear Baba's translated morning discourse. Baba said that anyone who still had anger would never find peace. Afterwards, John found his sandals stolen, and he got an abject lesson about his own anger. Although he missed the sandals, he justified the loss as part of Baba's message, an event perhaps meant just for him.

The daily schedule at Baba's ashram begins at 5 A.M. with the temple bell ringing nine times. By 5:40, devotees are chanting Veda around the area. At 6:45, Baba appears for his morning darshan. Hundreds of pilgrims who wish to see Baba have sat in lines for hours—men and women separately. Then there is a lottery to decide which lines go first to the best positions inside the open-air temple or mandir where Baba walks. As Baba passes the wide rows of seated pilgrims, he collects letters offered from those in prime positions who reach out to him. He gives blessings, and occasionally he manifests objects like amulets and vibhuti, an ash-like substance, and gives them away. To some he may grant private interviews. A temple devotee follows Baba to aid him in the details of his progress. Later in the day, devotional groups sing Bhajans (hymns).

Vibrations created by the human voice are very important to spiritual exercise at Baba's ashrams. Aspirants start the day by chanting the Pranava, the primordial sound which creates powerful vibrations. This practice is followed by the Suprabatham, verses sung in praise of the Lord to awaken the divinity within. Finally, bhajans or hymns are sung by men and women separately to purify the environmental atmosphere with divine vibrations. In India, the vital importance of spiritual vibrations has been known for thousands of years. Considering where Jeanne and John were being led in their spiritual destiny, it is little wonder that India was a necessary experience.

John's journal reflects that he was working very hard to let go of his traditional fears. Each day in the darshan, as Baba walked among the rows of serious men and women pleading for a spiritual blessing, John prayed, "Please help my unbelief. Open my heart and mind. Take away the veils that cloud my sight and hold back my progress. Equip me to be a willing worker for the light that you bring to the world. Come to my aid, Baba. Hurry to my rescue. I want to believe, and in believing, I will follow. Only lead me to God and through that, to my own mastery."

Jeanne was perhaps more relaxed in her days at Brindavan. Before the trip, she had naively called their friends, Hedva and Shimshon Stahl, who ran the Sai Baba Center in Jerusalem and asked if she should call ahead to tell Sai Baba that she and John were coming. They had lovingly laughed at the idea and assured Jeanne that Baba was already aware of their coming.

Jeanne has that childlike quality of suspended time that allows her to be carefree in seemingly difficult circumstances. For example, she had been warned to avoid the hordes of beggar children who sold flowers at the ashram gate. She had been told to ignore them, or she would become a daily target of their merciless beseeching. Jeanne's reaction to seeing the children was to greet them and look into their eyes. She told them that she could not buy flowers from all of them at the same time but that she would choose three each day by name and buy from them the following day. The children came to accept the bargain, and each day they enthusiastically greeted her as "auntee" as she bought flowers from three and named three others for the next day. On her last day, she told them that she would buy flowers from them all, and she carried a pocketful of rupees to fill a bag with small flowers from nearly fifty children. Later, as she lined up with the women for the morning darshan, she gave the flowers away to the women who would accept them. It was an unusual gesture, and some of the Indian women seemed fearful of the gift.

In discussing their relationship to Baba, Jeanne suggested to John that maybe he needed to ask what it means to follow Baba.

Perhaps it is just a matter of semantics. Still much of what divides the world's religions is just such semantics, she reminded him.

After the morning darshan in mid-week, John and Jeanne made a side pilgrimage to Mysore to visit the orphanage where Sai Baba performed a series of miracles. In a shrine devoted to Shirdi Sai Baba, the previous incarnation, and Sathya Sai Baba, a portrait of the current master was seen continuously producing ash-like vibhuti so that it could be collected. The glass-covered picture was covered in ash except for the face. A nearby silver ceremonial bowl was filled with a clean, amber-colored liquid called Amrit. Seashells from the bowl with the images of the Babas were placed in their hands by a priest, and the shells then exuded surprising amounts of Amrit. Encouraged to taste it, the divine nectar tasted like a light honey. Both John and Jeanne found the production of vibhuti and Amrit miraculous, and they were gifted small bottles of each for their personal use.

In John's journal, he reviewed their path to India. Perhaps it was Baba who told Jeanne to learn about Sanskrit. Perhaps Harry of the Baba amulet, was Baba, too. Then at the Verdi concert, there was no mistaking Baba's face. And even Joseph had led them to Baba, or vice versa. And then there was the night in Colorado when Jeanne went to sleep after no one could remember the name Arjuna from the Bhavagad Gita, and a Krishna-like figure appeared at the end of the bed to give her the name. The forest of Brinda, Brindavan is where Lord Krishna played as a child. Maybe Baba as Krishna was calling them to Brindavan years before.

One day that first week at Brindavan, John's prayers were answered, and he recorded the experience in his journal.

"When Baba entered the mandir, I looked around, and all I saw were many Sai Babas. Every face was Baba's face. I thought, oh, that's how he knows what's going on with everyone. They are all a part of him—like an arm or leg. Then I heard Baba's voice inside me say, 'Yes, and what else?' So, I looked around and saw that everything was part of Baba, and Baba was part of everything—the marble of the floor, the steel of the mandir structure, the trees and plants, everything. 'Yes, and what else?' Baba asked. And I saw that the whole planet was part of Baba. The entire universe, too.

"Again the voice said, 'Yes, and what else?' So I went inside and realized that all time—past, present and future—is Baba, too. And all dimensions and realities are part of Baba, are Baba, and Baba is all—All-That-Is. And still the voice that was teaching me ever so gently said, 'Yes, and what else?' I had to respond, 'I don't know.' It was Jeanne who later added, 'The one last piece is that Baba is All-That-Is, but so are *you*."

That first week Jeanne had written Baba a long letter that she hoped to gift him with a copy of their CD, *Between Slices of Light*, recorded in the Watersong Peace Sound Chamber in Saxapahaw, North Carolina to say thank you. As the week went by, the revised letter got shorter and shorter until it was only one page. Every day, as they passed through the ashram's security screening, Jeanne expected the CD to be confiscated, but it wasn't. Still, the odds of the line lottery putting Jeanne on an aisle where she could reach out to Baba were long. Then, too, Baba did not, could not, accept all the letters extended to him. Yet, Jeanne had hope because when she and John practiced their imaging, and asked if they would meet Baba, the answer was always "yes."

Lining up for the positioning lottery separated Jeanne and John so when they were admitted to the mandir courtyard, they could not always locate each other in the ranks of devotees who were similarly dressed. One morning as Jeanne entered the mandir, she saw vacant places on the coveted aisle, and women rushing to claim them. Jeanne would not run, however, because she believed that Baba would provide the place where she should sit. Her discipline, she felt, was to stay relaxed and calm. At that moment, one of the sevidals, or ushers, motioned for her to take a place on the aisle. As Jeanne moved to take the indicated place, a woman rushed in to claim it, but the sevidal removed her. Then she smiled at Jeanne and said in English, "This space is for you."

John also got an aisle position, so he was given a front row seat to witness Jeanne's encounter with Baba. Here is the scene from his journal.

"As Baba walked by, and I turned to watch him walk further to the rear of the mandir, I noticed that Jeanne was also sitting on the aisle! As Baba got nearer to her, she said that the voice inside told her, 'Just be peace.' For a moment, Baba turned away and walked over to the men. My heart sank because I thought that Baba might pass Jeanne without accepting her letter/CD. But he didn't. He turned back towards the women and walked straight over to where Jeanne was holding the letter out. She was holding it calmly, demurely, not thrusting it out in a needy way as some of the people do. He accepted it and spoke to her. [Part of the letter was a P.S. asking if an interview was possible.]

"Baba said to Jeanne, 'Where are you from?'

"She responded, 'From the U.S.'

"He then asked, 'When are you leaving?'

"Jeanne said, 'Friday.'

"Next Friday?' asked Baba.

"Yes,' said Jeanne, 'next Friday.'

"Then Baba smiled and said, 'Today is only Saturday,' as if to answer the question about the interview.

"What happened next was quite special. Jeanne had been told that if Baba takes her letter, she should ask one question."

Jeanne, in a later interview, recalled the moment. "Asking a question was actually a suggestion from our friend Owen James who had visited Baba several times over the years. For more than six months, I had pondered what such a question might be. Suppose you were given the opportunity to ask Jesus one question. What would you ask? But when the moment came with Baba, with my heart racing, no question came to mind. Then I heard a gentle voice within me say, 'Ask to kiss my feet.' And so I did."

John's journal observation continues.

"Jeanne would be one of the last people I know of who would kiss someone's feet. But, when Baba accepted the letter, Jeanne asked, 'May I kiss your feet?' And, to the amazement of all the women around her, Baba said, 'Yes.'

"So Jeanne kissed his feet. This is apparently very rare. It caused quite a stir among the women. I cried tears of joy."

Jeanne's account of the next day is significant.

"The following morning, after the magical event of the previous day, I discovered something that has to this day remained one of the most powerful revelations in my life. As I was sitting outside the mandir, in a meditative position, eyes closed, I heard this thought. 'Love what is in front of you in this moment. I will take care of everything else.'

"Again, the same thought repeated itself. And again. And yet again. Over and over. Until it became a quiet chant. After a few minutes, I opened my eyes. I noticed that the colors of everything around me were deeper and more defined than I had ever experienced. And the song of the nearby birds was richer and more beautiful than any I had heard. And then it dawned on me. There was no need for an interview. What I had been brought to India to remember was simple, and it was freeing. 'Love what is in front of you in this moment. God will take care of everything else.' Simple. Beautiful. Powerful."

John was also having his own memorable experience as recounted in his journal.

"This morning in darshan I worked on praying love, feeling love, becoming love. As I did, I became Baba, became Jesus of the compassionate heart, and everyone around me became Baba. too. This is the second morning that this has happened. But this morning, I felt myself radiating love—helping Baba in a way. Later, I found out that Jeanne was doing exactly the same thing! It's Sunday, so there are lots of people in darshan today. Jeanne and I felt as though we were assisting Baba as people were sucking at his energy—by filling the temple with love."

Despite the rapture of identification with Baba, John, too, wanted his letter accepted. After Jeanne's glorious encounter, John expected them to be called for a private interview, but day after day, no invitation was forthcoming. John's letter asked Baba to heal his heart (from disease), to enable him to love fully, to remember fully who he is, and to serve fully. He also thanked Baba for his teachings.

An interesting physical phenomenon was occurring in John. He had been constipated ever since their arrival ten days prior. Now, surprisingly, he was starting to let go bowel-wise. He considered the body parallels to his spiritual growth as another lesson from Baba.

The nature of John's internal struggle is very evident in his journal as he deals with his focus on Baba accepting his letter.

"Baba made his normal walk down the center aisle and down the aisle that splits the two groups of men and women. He walked as close as he could get to me. Several men around me became aggressive in holding up their letters for Sai Baba to take. I felt pushed and off-balance. I found myself caught up in the emotion, and offering my letter in a needy way, as in 'Oh, Baba, take mine too—please!' Of course, he didn't take it. He didn't take any of the letters offered in this way.

"After he passed, an entire range of emotions ran through me: frustration, a touch of rejection, even some irritation and anger over not having my letter taken. I felt irritation with Baba (You told me it was time for me to write it!), and anger with myself for getting caught up in the drama of neediness. After all, hadn't I just been saying the prayer, 'I will that Thy will be my will. Thy will be done!' Even so, I wasn't entirely happy that Baba's will wasn't my will. I may have also been soaking up some of the feelings around me—with my own neediness as the seed crystal.

"All I could do is to witness my own drama being played out on my inner stage, noting that I am not yet the master of the play. I am not yet in command of my emotions. And even as the emotions played like flickering lights of variable intensity on the veil of illusion inside of me, I thanked Baba for the light show. Indeed, I was thankful for the lesson and the opportunity to work through yet another challenge."

The next day, John wrote another letter to Baba, but he did not take it to the darshan. He figured that Baba knew everything in it anyway. Nevertheless, the body of the letter, which John recorded in his journal, gives a clear indication that he fully recognized his spiritual mission, while at the same time having self-doubts about his worthiness to lead. One suspects that every spiritual worker and saint, in their most private confessions, also had these feelings.

"Beloved Baba,

There have been many lessons so far in the 11 days here with my wife. And so I begin this simple letter with a thank you for the teachings that I have already received. My stay here has made me aware of the inner link that I have with you. You have come to teach me often. Indeed, almost right from the start you told me that you come to some on the inner planes as your primary way of teaching them. Others you teach face to face. My loving thanks for being with me. As you have said, 'Before you ask, I will answer.' I have felt that to be true.

"I am also thankful for you revealing me to myself. At times this has been a means for surfacing what still blocks my spiritual progress. At other times, it has given me a strong sense of unity and oneness with you—you are in me, and I am in you, and there is no difference. Indeed, I am beginning to see you in all the faces at your darshan. Thank you for helping me to remember.

"My wife, Jeanne White Eagle, and I were 'called' out of Russia by a Native American mystic, Beautiful Painted Arrow, Joseph Rael. That was in September '95. Since then, we've given away or sold most of what we have. Now we work for World Peace via sacred sound and dance. We do ceremonial work to raise the energy of specific points on the earth (Peace-Sound Chambers), give Peace Concerts, Chief or help in Sun-Moon Dances, and teach what we are given to teach. This trip has made us both aware that this 'calling' really came from you—and earlier than Joseph. But, you already know all of this. We're really working for you. The difference is that we've come to realize it during our stay here.

"Both Jeanne and I have felt since childhood that we've come here, in this incarnation, to do something important—to serve the people, and serve God in the transformation that is gathering momentum all around us. And while we have both gotten glimpses of 'who we are,' the ego still cries out for confirmation. So, it would be a major blessing on our path to have an interview with you before we leave on this coming Friday, 4/27 (after lunch).

"Aside from this, I know that you understand my *real* needs better than I do myself. So, I ask you for those blessings that you know I have need of, and that will accelerate my spiritual progress. I have a strong desire to gain/regain a God-consciousness so that I may be an instrument of Your Love and Peace. The Native Americans call it being a 'hollow bone' through which the Great Spirit blows the breath of life.

"In keeping with this goal, my specific requests are:

Grant me the strength and courage to *love fully*. Heal my heart on a physical level (if it is not already healed – heart attack 7/22/00). Fill it with love and compassion for all.

Help me to *remember fully*. Lift the veils that cloud my remembering who I am and what I am here to do. If possible, open my energy channels so that I may use my previous attainments for the people.

Allow me to *serve fully*. Let me be an instrument for Your Love and Peace in the world.

"These are my requests. I have a sense that you have already begun to grant them. In fact, I've heard your voice in my mind say to me, 'You already have them!' Yet, at my level of faith, it would be a boon (and a great joy) to receive the confirmation that comes with your accepting my letter.

"Still, Thy Will be done. I may not be ready for that which I ask."

A few days before their departure, Jeanne experienced very severe pain in her chest for about an hour. The pain radiated in her neck and arm like a heart attack. Jeanne rubbed vibhuti and Amrit (divine nectar) on her chest and paced the floor. She forced herself to vomit, and then she sat on the floor and sang the vowel sounds. After a while, the pain was transmuted, but Jeanne felt exhausted as if she had given birth to a spiritual something.

Three monkeys were seen climbing on the building across from the hotel. They then sat on the roof and provided entertainment. Jeanne, sleeping on the bed nearest the window, had suffered numerous mosquito bites. Their diet had been a mix of Indian rice and dal and lunches at the Western Canteen where Diet Pepsi was served. Meals were generally under a dollar a day. Wearing a sari or a white pajama with a saffron scarf, John's taking malaria medicine, and the schedule of ashram protocol, discipline, and patience all contributed to the sense of a surreal adventure. But in addition to the moments of bliss, there was also an exhaustion from so much emotional intensity.

The night prior to their departure (Friday, April 27th), John had serious diarrhea. At one point, he doubted that he could attend a final darshan or even be strong enough to travel. The bathroom trots ended, however, before dawn; and although he was late to the lines, his line of men was chosen #1. Baba then walked quite close to John and acknowledged him with a glance and a smile. John felt that he had been given a graduate-level course in listening and faith, and that he had been cleansed both metaphysically and literally in body, too.

On their last day at the Brindavan ashram, Jeanne had an encounter that fulfilled all her expectations of communicating with Baba. John recounted it, as related by Jeanne, in his journal.

"One of Sai Baba's students did search Jeanne out today, running up to her. His name was Sudevan. He said that he'd been looking for Jeanne everywhere. Then he said, 'I've been praying for you to get an interview. When are you leaving?' Jeanne had noticed him on our way to breakfast. He was tall with long dark hair pulled back, a very good-looking East Indian. Jeanne said that there was something strangely familiar about him—as if she knew him but didn't know him.

"When he asked Jeanne when we were leaving, she replied, 'In an hour and a half.' Sudevan looked confused for an instant as if our leaving didn't compute. Then he said, 'That means that Baba will interview you in the dream time. And that will be more real!'

"At this point, Sudevan looked into Jeanne's eyes and said, 'Many changes are getting ready to happen. Dangerous times are coming. They will be filled with much struggle and pain for the world. I am to tell you that you are not to be afraid.' It was a confirmation of what Don Alejandro revealed in the Mayan Prophecies, and what Cyrus has told us about the 'times of terror.'

"As Jeanne describes it, there was a transfer of information at that point that was non-verbal, almost surreal. Her response to him was, 'I know. I know what is coming.' Indeed, we have felt for some years now that our role is to help others not to be afraid. What Sudevan was telling us is that God will be with us, taking care. It's a message that I hear in my head a lot now—'I am taking care.' I am so grateful.

"Then he proceeded to give Jeanne some special vibhuti from Sai Baba's interviews. He said that she was to sprinkle a little of it onto all the other vibhuti that we had. He also gave her two pictures blessed by Sai Baba and three small books of Baba's writings.

"In return, Jeanne felt moved to give Sudevan her golden medallion with the tree of life superimposed over the flower of life. She told him that it had been gifted to her and there were only two like it in the world. Tears welled up in his eyes as he resisted taking it, saying, 'But this was gifted to you.'

"Jeanne smiled and responded, 'There is no difference.' At this, he accepted the medallion. He said, 'Oh, wait right here. I'll be right back!' He disappeared down the path, returning a couple of minutes later with two additional gifts. One was for me because

Jeanne had told him that I was sick. It was a special seed that grows naturally with sacred symbols. He rubbed vibhuti on it and said it would help me feel better. The second gift was also a seed, which appeared to show the Sanskrit symbol of Om as well as the head of a cobra. Sacred serpents in Mayan teachings are the messengers of God to the people, as are eagles to Native Americans, and whales to the Zulus in Africa. All three animal messengers represent Jeanne's birth sign. Sudevan told Jeanne to put the seeds into small silver boxes and carry them close to us.

"Jeanne came back to the room full of awe. She still had the feeling that Sudevan was strangely familiar somehow. She also said to me, 'He carries Krishna energy!' This unexpected meeting with one of Baba's students felt like a miracle! It was a final confirmation for Jeanne (and me) from Baba—as if he'd personally sent this student our way with his messages of love. To me, it said, 'Be of good cheer. I (Baba) will be with you on your trip. We will have plenty of time for an interview."

Although the Mumbai airport is a major hub in India, the bathrooms are filthy, and there is very limited seating. For more than four hours, John and Jeanne occupied one free seat and the top of their luggage on a baggage cart. To complicate matters, John's diarrhea was back, and the patented medicine he was taking was not relieving the uproar in his intestinal tract. Then, an angel appeared.

The angel's American name was Marge, but she introduced herself as Ananda Sai—a name given her by Sai Baba. She had been in Brindavan during the time of their visit. She had been a Baba devotee since 1978 and had apartments in both Puttaparthi and Brindavan. John guessed that she was in her mid-to-late sixties. Most of Marge's year was spent in India as a volunteer in one of Baba's medical clinics. Baba also was responsible for a university, many schools, a clean-water program, and other charities throughout southern India.

When John confided his bowel distress, Marge produced a homeopathic remedy that John took for almost immediate relief.

For the remainder of their long wait, he was spared the need to visit the depressing airport toilet.

When John told her his darshan experience of seeing all the faces in the mandir courtyard as Baba, Ananda Sai told him that his vision was "very advanced." And when Jeanne told her about her encounter with Sudevan, Ananda Sai reacted with a wide grin.

"Don't you know who that was?"

Jeanne and John were puzzled. "Who?"

"That was Baba," she laughed. "He likes to do that . . . come to you at the last moment and in a different form."

Jeanne remembers, "At that, we all laughed at the wonderful, joyous prank that had been played on us."

John concludes the India trip with this entry.

"To be quite honest, I'm not so sure that Ananda Sai was not also Baba—giving me an opportunity for my own interview. I talked to her more than Jeanne did. And, strange for me, I felt more animated than normal, more forward in the conversation. Really, just look at the name. Ananda means bliss. Sai means mother or perfect being. I'm betting that we met Sai Baba twice today—both getting our interviews! Thank you, Baba!"

In Germany, three weeks after the India trip, Jeanne had a vivid dream. The aide to Baba, who had accompanied him in the mandir when she was in Brindavan, came to her and bid her to follow him. She followed him, running along a path, and came to a huge door where he immediately went down on his knees and prostrated his upper body to the ground. Jeanne stood dumbfounded until the man pulled her to her knees, and she understood that she should also prostrate herself. Then the door began to open outward, slowly, and a blinding white light emanated from inside. Jeanne felt a gentle tugging at the top of her head so as to raise her head to see.

The first thing that she saw was the tiny feet, the familiar childlike feet of the Master. Immediately she thought, I know these feet. I've kissed these feet. Then her eyes came up to see Sai Baba, resplendent in bright shining ruby and emerald robes. There were no words, but Jeanne felt as if she were an empty vessel being filled with love.

It is believed that Sai Baba does not appear in dreams unless it is his wish. Jeanne came to believe that this wonderful dream was the fulfillment of Sudevan's promise that Baba would visit her and bless her in this way.

On awakening, Jeanne rushed down to the kitchen to share her vision. Her hosts and their five-year-old child were there, but John was still asleep. Jeanne told her miraculous dream in English to the adults, but it was the non-English-speaking child who reacted most. She stood up in her high chair and wildly applauded and cheered as if she fully understood the revelation of miracles.

MARKING TIME

A fter their return from India, Jeanne had her hair cut short. Her new look had both a practical and a symbolic purpose. As a constant traveler, her short hair was easier to manage, and with her long tresses gone, there was a sense of a new direction. Jeanne also called her many women friends and invited them to a show-and-tell party. Back in India, low on cash reserves and wondering how they would make do when they returned to the States, Jeanne got an inspiration. She would spend everything that they could spare, about $150, on saris and resell them at a profit. Her friends were glad to get the beautiful bargain saris direct from India, and Jeanne took in about $1000 on her investment, exactly what was needed to pay for an upcoming trip to Berlin.

On May 10 the couple was in Chattanooga for Perry Lane's 80th birthday. Jeanne's father was very weak, and not totally present at times, but there was a family gathering to honor him nevertheless. Perry's prognosis was bad, and he required constant care as an invalid, but at least he was home.

In Richmond, Virginia, on a Saturday, John and Jeanne attended Alan's graduation ceremonies on May 19th. Alan had earned a degree in psychology from Virginia Commonwealth University. John's ex-wife Diana and his two other sons Sean and Ryan also attended, but there was not much interaction. The tensions of the divorce, and John's chosen life of spirituality over practicality, were still at issue.

Moving on to Minneola on New York's Long Island, the couple stayed again overnight with Sue Mehrtens, and she gave them a Cyrus channeled session. The next day they went to JFK to board their flight to Berlin, Germany via Amsterdam. This time, on discount tickets, the ticket agent gave them no chance for an upgrade to business class. Ahead on the first leg of the journey were nearly seven hours in the cramped seats of tourist class. Before the flight, Jeanne checked in with Peggy and learned that her father was in the hospital. Perry Lane had shifted into a new phase of his disease, and the family feared that home care would no longer be possible. Jeanne wrote a loving note in a beautiful card to her dad and mailed it from the Amsterdam airport post office.

Jeanne, of course, was tormented that she was headed for Europe while her father lay dying in Tennessee. John felt deep emotions, too. His own father had died of cancer two days before his return from Russia in 1995. Although the father and son had reached a rapprochement before Vernon's death, John felt an inability to express or even to feel love for his father. They had never been able to say "I love you" to each other. And although Jeanne's dad, Perry Lane, had been a mentor to John, John had never said "I love you" to Perry either.

In Berlin Jeanne and John were the six-day guests of Enrico Hilbert and Elke Baumgarten. The accommodation was a loft, five stories up the staircase of a big city apartment complex. As an artist,

Enrico had decorated the large space with his paintings and colorful constructions. He was a student of Sai Baba, he had danced the Long Dance and the Drum Dance, and he practiced Buddhist meditation. His home thus had a very peaceful and nurturing energy.

Elke Baumgarten, Enrico's girlfriend, organized a Peace Concert at the Church of the Holy Cross in South Berlin not far from where the Cold War Berlin Wall had once stood. Although Elke had had a vision that Jeanne and John's concert would take place in this historic Protestant church that had been built in the new Gothic style in 1885-1888, and then rebuilt in a more updated architecture after the destruction of WWII, the church first told her "no." After searching for other venues that proved to be too expensive, Elke appealed to the church administrator again, and they agreed to set the concert for Ascension Day, the fortieth day after Easter that Christians celebrate Christ's ascension into heaven. The day was also John's birthday.

The concert itself was a success with about a seventy-person audience. Elke and Enrico were elated that their intention to produce the concert had resulted in such a wondrous event. And again a concert had galvanized enthusiastic participants for workshops and private sessions in the days immediately following.

In their travels around Berlin, Jeanne and John were aware of the many dramas going on in the society around them. Young people in radical styles of dress and with strange-colored hair seemed more prevalent than the couple had observed in New York or Los Angeles. Spray-painted graffiti defaced many buildings. Paint-ball guns had splattered colored paint on buildings as high as the third floor. Some of the graffiti messages spoke of revolution or expressed hatred toward a religious or ethnic group. Neo-Nazi swastikas were also evident. As Jeanne and John had learned from their private consultations with Germans, there was a great need for healing in this diverse 21st century society. Despite its dynamic leadership in the European economy, Germany was not a country at peace with itself.

The Inter-City Express from Berlin to Kassel reached speeds of 160 mph and sped them out of the capital city into the German countryside. Jeanne and John were returning to the village of Grossropperhausen to stay with Alex and Shania Racky. The parents looked the same; but after nine months, the two young children Noah and Muriel had grown, of course, to the delight of Jeanne and John as their adopted grandparents. The primary focus of the trip was to perform an Awakening Ceremony at caretaker Hilde Kopesko's new Peace-Sound Chamber. The site for the Chamber had been blessed by Joseph himself in May 1994 and blessed again by Jeanne and John three years prior, but the actual construction was not completed until 2001. Initially, there were no workshops or private sessions scheduled, although from previous trips, there were many friends in the area who wanted to see them.

The first order of business in Grossropperhausen, however, was a new ceremonial dress for Jeanne. In a moment of shock on the flight to Europe, Jeanne remembered that she had left her ceremonial bag containing her deerskin dress, her large crystals, her red ceremonial shawl, and her Eagle pipe back at Sue's on Long Island. In asking "why," the insight came that the items were left behind to teach Jeanne (and John) that the power is within Jeanne (and John) and not resident in the crystals or the pipe themselves. Upon arriving in Germany, Jeanne told Shania what had happened. The Awakening Ceremony was a day away, so Jeanne needed a new ceremonial dress fast. There was a possible solution. Shania's mother, Eva, was an expert seamstress, and so the two women rushed from a fabric store with yards of white linen and a caftan to use as a pattern to the dressmaker. Within two hours of their pleas, the "darling" Eva had fashioned a beautiful ceremonial dress that Jeanne continues to use as a Chief's dress.

The Awakening Ceremony was different at Hildegard's Chamber because the power objects that Jeanne usually carried were not present. Instead, the participants were invited, one by one, to give a cornmeal blessing to the Chamber. Then Jeanne and John held hands and said individual prayers. Jeanne was then left alone to sing the Awakening as John spread the cornmeal and tobacco circles around the Chamber exterior. Jeanne sang for almost two hours, from just after 10 P.M. to just after midnight. During the sweat lodge that day and the vigil of the Awakening Ceremony, there had been forecasts of rain, and it had, in fact, rained but not in the windows needed for the sweat lodge and Chamber fires. John had even purchased a pair of rubber boots to keep his moccasins from getting soaked, but the weather miracle made them redundant.

The next night in a celebration of the Chamber attended by more than thirty people, Hilde gave each person a piece of amber from the vigil, and Jeanne handed out small crystals that had been on the altar during her singing. During the sharing when everyone is invited to speak, a German woman addressed Jeanne and said, "You are a precious gift from the universe, a gift from far away."

It was here in Germany at the home of Shania and Alex Rachy in Grossropperhausen that Jeanne had her vivid dream of Sai Baba appearing to her as had been promised by Baba's devotee Sudevan in India. Little Muriel, at age five, got the full feeling of Jeanne's passion and excitement as she listened with dark beaming eyes.

As a houseguest, Jeanne is a daily wonder. She brings worlds with her wherever she goes. Some of these worlds have names like the United States, or Israel, or South Africa, or India. Other worlds that she brings have names in their own dimensions that are not so well known in ours. Glimpses of both worlds are often recounted at the breakfast table after Jeanne has made her nighttime dreams and vision journeys. Every host has their own recollections of Jeanne's morning enthusiasms. Then, too, hosts can awaken to hear Jeanne, and John as well, singing the day into fullness on their deck, balcony, porch, or patio. Afterwards, the least intrusive question will prompt Jeanne to share her revelations.

Iris Wunsch hosted a Peace Concert in Grossropperhausen that was standing-room only. The local newspaper even sent a reporter and a photographer. The next day Sophia Peters arrived to transport the couple to Northern Germany where they would get a day off with some privacy in a little house that Sophia provided. The peninsula on the North Sea was flat and windy. The landscape was filled with grazing cattle and sheep and with high-tech windmills that clustered around the towns to generate electricity. In Wasserkoog there was an afternoon with Sophia and others of singing in the Chamber of the Wind, but John was not feeling well. He had cold symptoms and felt feverish.

Traveling the way they did in enclosed aircraft, trains, and busses, and then encountering more people at events along the way and hugging them by the score, it is a wonder that Jeanne and John were not constantly catching anything and everything of the cold and flu variety that is inherent in constant contact with the public. The physical stress of travel and the inconsistencies in their diets also made them more vulnerable to sickness. Then, too, John had his allergies to deal with. For prevention, the couple carried a supply of vitamins, herbs, and teas that they took on a regular basis, and they also carried health foods like oatmeal and dried fruit to prepare when they were provided a private space. Nevertheless, when colds or flu reached their zenith, there was no other option than to stop wherever they were, hunker down, and nurse each other back to health. They had done this for each other through cancer and heart disease. Compared to those life-threatening conditions, colds and flu were merely an inconvenience and possibly a demonstrable sign to slow down and rest.

En route back to the United States, their KLM flight from Berlin to Amsterdam was late and missed connecting to their flight to New York. KLM was thus obliged to put the couple up for the night in a first-class, museum quarter hotel, and then upgrade them to business class the next day. All this luxury on website discount tickets. Baba again got the credit as far as Jeanne and John were concerned.

A few days after their stateside return, Jeanne and John were back at Owen's farm near Grafton, Ontario to serve a Sun-Moon Dance. Jeanne served as a Moon Mother and John drummed. There was an accident the last day of the dance. Owen's dog, a small white dog named Sammy, was crushed by a car that backed over him. The driver, who loved the dog, was devastated, and the little animal was brought to the dance pole for its final moments in life. Later, there was a ceremonial funeral where Sammy, wrapped in a carpet, was put in the ground with sage, cornmeal, cedar, and a few crystals. The dance crew then sang their little dog soldier into another spiritual dimension, and although they accepted his death, they wept.

There were concert and workshop events scheduled for July, but back in Tennessee there were family needs that would take precedence. Perry Lane was back in the hospital, and the family was gathering at the home of Henry Franklin, Perry's stepson, in Chattanooga to be present when Perry passed.

PERRY LANE'S PASSING

At the end of 2000, Perry Lane, Jeanne's father, was very ill with a nerve degenerative disease similar to Parkinson's. He had been ill for many months, and Jeanne was especially concerned whenever she had to be out of the country because she wanted to be at his side when he passed. She often prayed that her father and Spirit would allow this to be so. And so it was that between trips, in a window of time reserved for them, Perry waited for his daughter before passing.

Jeanne took the night duty in Perry's hospital room. She recalls, "I had wanted to spend more time with Dad, and my sister-in-law,

Lynn, suggested that I might want to consider staying the nights with Dad in the hospital. It would give me some private time with him and give him company at the same time. My stepmother Peggy and everyone else spent their time with Dad during the day." The hours afforded her precious last moments with her dad.

The Sunday morning before his death the next day, July 9th, Jeanne went to her car in the hospital parking lot to discover that the vehicle's driver's side windshield was covered with dozens of dragonflies. Dragonflies were not evident on any nearby cars. Jeanne stood for a few moments in disbelief, and then she says she "got it." The dragonfly is a common metaphysical symbol for the transitions of life.

"I grinned," Jeanne says. "The dragonflies were a reminder that all of this (the loved one at death's door) is just an illusion."

Jeanne carefully drove her car out of the hospital parking lot, and the mass of dragonflies gradually peeled away, allowing her to see the road ahead.

Jeanne recounts the last hour. "On the day of his passing, moments before, the doctor visited the hospital room at 8:30 A.M. and gave us a brief report. Peggy talked about the possibility of moving Dad to a Hospice Care Room. I remember hearing the fragility in her voice, and in Dad's presence, I said as softly as I could, 'Peggy, I don't think the doctor is talking days here. I think that he is talking hours.' After the doctor left, I told her gently, 'Peg, I think Dad is waiting for you to tell him that you are going to be all right, and that it is okay for him to go.' After that, Peggy climbed onto the bed with him, wrapped her body around him and spoke endearing words of love into his ear. I was on the other side of the bed holding Dad's beautiful hands. In a few minutes, he was gone. I'll never forget the instant that his soul left the body. I looked at his face and saw something I had never seen before. In his last breath, as stillness came, an amazing rush of rainbow colors—red, yellow, green, blue, magenta—passed over his face. I was stunned. Then the flood of tears came. My greatest teacher was gone."

Jeanne was given almost no time for a grieving process because she and John had a commitment to do a Sun-Moon Dance—he as a co-Chief, and she as a Moon Mother, in Seymour, Tennessee. Again, Jeanne asked for a sign that her father was okay now that he had gone to the other side, and she did so in prayer at the Tennessee Peace-Sound Chamber. While she was praying for the sign, a Sun-Moon dancer entered to give her an honor gift for moon mothering the dance. The gift was a stained glass candleholder in the design of a dragonfly. A dragonfly! Jeanne wept in recognition that her prayer had been answered.

Another sign came days later as Jeanne drove along a rural road a day after the memorial service for her father. In her family, a colorful bouquet of tall gladiolas was the most common flower gift that her father gave her mother. Perry would find the perennials available inexpensively and bring them home for Kit to decorate the dining room table. The gladiolus, as their favorite flower, was thus strongly identified with her parents. So what should Jeanne happen upon with her father so prevalent in her awareness but gladiolas in profusion in a passing front yard? The homeowners were displaying an obvious passion for gladiolas, because their large beds of flowers contained nothing else. It was a gladiolas showcase! A gladiolas extravaganza! It was a sign for Jeanne not to be missed.

The blessings from Perry Lane continued as Jeanne, far away from her grieving family, asked for confirmation that her father was doing all right. After her prayers one morning in Israel a few months after Perry's passing, their Zur Hadassa (outside Jerusalem) hosts, Victor and Sharon Barr, took Jeanne and John for a ride in a hilly countryside that was covered in green grasses, yellow mustard flowers, blue lupines, and red poppies.

When Jeanne was growing up, her dad often went through the house singing one of two songs. One of the songs was commonly used to wake up the house. It was the rousing opening song from *Oklahoma—Oh, What A Beautiful Morning*. Perry Lane's version was generally belted in a loud enthusiastic voice.

Victor Barr is an Egyptian Jew who has spent much of his life in Israel. With a background in physics, he is considered an intellectual, although one who actively explores metaphysics, the point being that Victor is a very serious fellow not given to sudden outbursts of Broadway show tunes. And yet, in a lull in the conversation in the car that morning, Victor burst forth with a rousing rendition of the song that Jeanne most identified with her father when Victor sang, "Oh, what a beautiful morning. Oh, what a beautiful day."

Jeanne grabbed John's leg and said grinning, "Dad's alive and doing well." Victor unknowingly had given the sign that answered Jeanne's prayer.

Jeanne received an inheritance from Perry Lane's estate, finalized one year later. It couldn't have come at a more opportune time because Gracie, the little BMW they had been given after choosing to return their payment-heavy Pathfinder to the bank, was showing 288,000 miles on the odometer and mechanical signs of imminent demise. When the couple went shopping for a car at a local used car dealership, Jeanne said a quick prayer that it if was all the same, let another Pathfinder present itself and preferably the same color as their previous one. When they arrived, not only was there a Pathfinder, there were four late-model ones, all the same color as their original one. Jeanne, as usual, asked for one more sign, one that neither she nor John would miss that one of these cars was the one they were looking for. She found it—a big picture of Mickey

Mouse on the showroom wall. For Jeanne, Mickey Mouse has always been a symbol of joy. In this case, Mickey was saying, "right time, right place."

Jeanne and John's attitude about the inheritance was that it came from the Universal Source and thus was not separate from their spiritual mission. So after buying the essential transportation vehicle, and providing needed support for their children, the money went into their work. It was not saved as a safety net. It went to support the vision quest dancers, to build dance arbors, and to carry their peace message onto new grounds.

DANGEROUS TIMES

Although her father's death had been anticipated for months, the loss of Jeanne's anchor in life left her psychologically adrift. In the process of her grief, Jeanne's mind raised deeply emotional questions about how she was to fulfill her spiritual visions. She struggled with the paradox of how to step into her own power while simultaneously stepping back to allow John the full expression of his own. These thoughts basically questioned the role of her relationship and partnership with John as it pertained to the mission.

John was no stranger to these emotions. In the beginning of their travels in 1998, it seemed to John that he was embarked on the Jeanne White Eagle show and that his function was to tend to the luggage. He felt lost. It took months, if not years, for him to come into balance and gain an independent sense of his own purpose and power. Jeanne, he felt, was now engaged in a similar exploration although the nature of the exploration was distinctly her own. John witnessed the sometimes tearful, and often confusing, introspection that Jeanne was facing. He recognized the questions. "What compromises am I making? How am I making concessions that keep me from fulfilling my vision? And how do I balance stepping into my full power with stepping back and surrendering more fully to Spirit?"

One of the results of Jeanne's introspection was guidance that she should not go to Germany and Croatia. For the first time, John would lead the workshops in Germany without Jeanne, and he would be supporting Jeff Romanowski in the Croatian Sun-Moon Dance without her. John's own guidance was to do a private Hollow-Bone Dance at the CFP in Seymour. Marcus Ambrester agreed to support him in the three-day ordeal. John entered the sweat lodge on Tuesday, the last day of July, and that night he began his sole dance in the arbor. All day Wednesday he danced back and forth to the pole without food or water. Solo dances require the most discipline of all dances because there are no other dancers and no drum to provide energy. Only the two CFP spirit dogs, Daiska and Wolf, entered the arbor, and by licking the fallen man, reminded him to rise up and dance again. Finally, on Thursday, John hit the pole and fell to the ground. He felt filled with light, and he kept hearing the phrase, "They are all my children."

On that Sunday, John went into the CFP Chamber with his close friend and Tennessee Sun-Moon Dance co-chief, Steve Citty, to do Heart Awakening work. Men who practiced ceremonies in the Peace-Sound Chambers often supported each other in this way. The sacred environment of the Chamber and the dedicated intention of healing made each man (and woman) ministers to each other. These communities of mutual support provided not only therapy for its members but also leaps forward in spiritual growth and maturity. Both Jeanne and John had been nurtured in this way by Chamber communities spread across the planet.

Before John left for Germany, he visited Cheryl and David at the Watersong Chamber to discuss the October Sun-Moon Dance in North Carolina. The scheduled dance would require the construction of a dance arbor as well as a large sweat lodge.

John's trip to Europe would be the longest separation from Jeanne since they became a couple in 1993. The schedule called for sixteen days apart. Jeanne's intuition about not making the trip was confirmed in a telephone consultation with Owen James. Jeanne had evidently picked up a fungus infection in her lungs during the nighttime hospital vigils with her dad. Owen advised her to rest and avoid overseas travel lest the infection become serious.

It was John's fifth trip to Germany; and as he had the year before, he based with the Racky family in Grossropperhausen, and then drove with Alex to the site of the Croatian Sun-Moon Dance, about 600 miles away. Every day that he was away from Jeanne he wrote her a long, detailed letter. The letters were both travelogs and romantic valentines. He never failed to tell her how much the dance organizers missed her. Previous dancers also wanted John to tell her how much they missed her Moon Mothering and the wonderful memories of her voice as she sang them awake each morning and sang them to sleep each night. John, as Alpha Dog, took on the extra responsibility of providing the same wake-up and tuck-in service by playing his flute.

The Croatian dance was large, with 31 dancers, including 21 who had danced before. Two Croatian plainclothes police officers came to inspect the dance while it was underway. The officers asked a few questions, stayed for two dance rounds, and then went away satisfied that they had witnessed a Native American sacred dance without political overtones. John camped in a hot tent for the six days that he was on the dance site. He bathed with wet-wipes and shaved without shaving cream. His daily letters to Jeanne were written catch-as-catch can, but they always contained a romantic intensity. In reading the e-mail letters that survive in his laptop journal, one wonders what John must have written in courtship if the intensity of his passion was still so evident after eight years of constant togetherness. Old married men should learn to write to their wives in this way.

"I am counting the days until I can wrap my arms around you again. I miss having you near. I miss the little caresses that happen casually during the day. Being apart helps me to realize how important that it is to me." Monday, 8/20

"My darling, how wonderful it was to hear your voice and connect with you in that way. Your smile comes through the words you speak and lifts my heart. I miss you more than I can say. I'm counting the moments until you are in my arms." Wednesday, 8/22

"So, my precious darling, I love you more than I can express. I only know that when we're apart, part of me is missing. Maybe that's because my heart is always with you." Saturday, 8/25

On the flight back to the States, John did some amazing romantic calculating.

"I've been reflecting on the time that I've been away from you. By the time I see you, we will have been apart for 15 days, 7 hours. This is 3715 hours, which is just a hair over 22,000 minutes. It's close to 4.25% of an entire year! No wonder I miss you so much. I've also spent 15 sunsets and 15 sunrises away from you that will never come again. I've taken 264,000 breaths since I have seen you last. My heart has beat 1,350,000 times away from you. It's too many sunrises, sunsets, in and out breaths, and heartbeats apart from your arms and lips. I've missed too many of your smiles, too many of your caresses and touches." Monday, 8/27

In Croatia, Jeff had presented John with a buffalo skull for the dance in North Carolina. John did not want the bleached-bone horned artifact to be damaged in his luggage, so he bagged it to carry by hand. The sacred ceremonial object became a wonder for every airport security agent who inspected it. And for once, John wished that Jeanne were on hand to provide the explanations with her usual flare. All in all, with some financial support gifts and income from a few private sessions in Germany, John returned home with almost enough money to cover the airfare. Nevertheless, when he considered the buffalo skull, he thought that he'd come out ahead for the trip.

The day John returned to Knoxville, Jeanne was at the CFP getting turkey bones cut for the Sun-Moon Dance whistles. Their reunion at the Corryton farm must have been sweet, but they could not linger long in their retreat because they had appointments to keep in Lexington, MA. After a two-day drive of 980 miles, they arrived on September 5th. John was experiencing a great deal of fatigue that sleep did not seem to alleviate. He wondered if it was a form of depression.

On that Friday, the 8th, Jeanne and John gave a Peace Concert in the home of Selena Britton-Woolf in Lexington. John had consulted Owen James about his fatigue, and Jeanne was thus feeding John vitamin B-12, spirulina mixed with grape juice, and recommended trace minerals. Their next stop was at the home of Rob Iodice and Cheryl O'Donnell in Brookline, NH, a far suburb 45 minutes north-northwest of Boston. Cheryl is both a fine artist and a decorative painter of home interiors. Rob is in the flooring business. His chiseled Italian features reminded John of old Roman statues. Jeanne and John were having a fun time with the good-humored couple. John began teaching Cheryl the Intuitive Image process, and on Monday night, the 10th, the two couples played the card game "hearts" until midnight after Jeanne and John had sung a Peace Concert. They then went to bed like most Americans, completely unaware of the sinister events that awaited them in the morning, events that would begin 45 minutes away at the Boston airport.

Cheryl and Rob had already gone to work and left the television on in the living room. Jeanne walked into the room on that morning of Nine-Eleven just as the news channel was reporting that a commercial airliner had struck one of the two World Trade Towers in New York City. The television pictures seemed surreal to Jeanne, but she felt the importance of the event and immediately urged John to get up and witness what was happening in New York. As they stared at the television, a second jumbo jet came into view, and they watched in horror as the unthinkable happened. The huge airliner purposely flew into the second World Trade Tower. The country had been attacked. As the shocking day unfolded, a third hijacked suicide plane crashed into the Pentagon in Washington, D.C., and a fourth plane en route to Washington crashed in the Pennsylvania countryside, presumably the result of a heroic effort by its passengers to save the U.S. Capitol or other primary terrorist targets. Both Jeanne and John recognized the magnitude of these events.

In his journal John wrote, "A significant shift has taken place in the world on this day. Today is *this* generation's loss of innocence akin to what the assassination of President Kennedy was to mine, or what the attack on Pearl Harbor was to our fathers."

The Nine-Eleven attack on the financial capital of the United States seemed to validate what Jeanne and John had been told in their spiritual travels, and it obviously brought back Sai Baba's words to Jeanne as spoken through Sudevan: "Dangerous times are coming. You are not to be afraid." Jeanne talked to Perry Robinson at the CFP the same day. "Now our work begins in earnest," she said, and they both agreed that all their preparations involving the Peace-Sound Chambers and the Sun-Moon Dances would now serve them in responding to a world in chaos. It was so clear to them that all their efforts directed toward creating peace had just become more important, and even urgent.

On the 14th, the couple were guests of Tom and Anne Rarich in Concord, and the next night they did a Peace Concert at Illuminations Bookstore in Westford with the proceeds going to the recovery effort in New York City.

Jeanne felt strongly that she should respond to the destruction of the World Trade Towers, its devastating loss of life, and the feelings of revenge that the event had generated. The closest that they could drive to the World Trade Center site that week after the disaster was Brooklyn. Jeanne recounts the emotional journey by ferry to Battery Park at the tip of Manhattan where they could see the smoke and even smell the consequences of the collapsed towers two blocks away.

"Looking across the water at Manhattan, watching the ominous cloud of smoke hang over the island, we waited in line for one of the first ferries to go from Brooklyn to the city since September 11th. The young woman behind us was obviously nervous and unsettled. I turned to smile at her, giving a few words of greeting, at which point she broke anxiously into her story.

"Her name was Rosemary. She was one of those standing on the sidewalk underneath the first tower as it began to fall. She told us how everyone started to run in near panic from the billowing cloud of smoke and debris that so many of us watched, with shock and disbelief, as the scenes played on TV again and again. As people frantically were running to escape the chasing cloud, some fell . . . and others, just as she did, quickly reached for the arms of those who had fallen, each carrying the other to safety.

"It was now Tuesday morning exactly one week after the bombing of the World Trade Center. Rosemary had attempted to return the day before, to her office, less than three blocks from Ground Zero. She had traveled on the subway, thinking it was a safe way to return . . . only to find armed policemen running into Manhattan's subway tunnel, yelling for everyone to evacuate! Evacuate! There's a bomb on board! As Rosemary shared this experience, I found my heart breaking open. She was so frightened! She said she was riding the ferry this day because she thought that if there was a bomb scare here, at least she might escape by jumping into the water.

"When she finished her story, she asked why we were going to this area of Manhattan, populated now only by army trucks and personnel, armed police, and a few office workers. I told her we had been in Boston doing Peace Concerts when the attacks occurred. The night of September 11th we did a sacred Pipe Ceremony for world peace, inviting our friends there to participate, one of whom had a brother to die on the 105th floor of the North Tower. A

Jeanne is a college-trained performance singer with an amazing four-octave vocal range.

Jeanne's parents Perry and Catherine (Kit) Lane during WWII years where he served in the Pacific as a bombardier in B-25s.

A University of Tennessee graduate, Perry Lane was a successful Chattanooga based entrepreneur.

Jeanne was a performer and vocal coach for ten years with Up With People.

Jeanne's mother Kit and her daughter Jenny and son John.

John earned an engineering degree from Iowa State University and had a 21-year career at Dupont, the chemical manufacturing giant.

Top to bottom: John's sons, Sean, Alan, and Ryan pile on Dad circa 1982.

International dancers and dance crewmembers (l. to r.)
Anael Harpaz (Israel), Rhonda Factor (Canada), Alexander Racky
(Germany), Sonja Munz (England), and Monica Dantus (Mexico).

Dance activity at Rustlers Valley in South Africa.

Jeanne and John in Egypt for the 2006 FTOD in the Sinai Desert.

An accommodation hut at Rustlers Valley in South Africa.

*Sammye Jo Harvey, Elder, Teacher, and Chief on the
International FTOD crew with photographer Pat Joynes.*

*Sue Spies and daughter Danette, dance
participants in South Africa.*

*Candy Barbee (USA) and Brett
Almond (England), Chiefs of the
2007 FTOD in Germany.*

*Georgia Stone, the 97-year old FTOD
Elder at Watersong.*

*Feiruz, Hazar, and Adi celebrate the World
Youth Dance in South Africa.*

Photo by Pat Joynes

couple of nights later I was given a dream that we were to come to Manhattan, and then move onto Washington D.C., to again do the sacred Pipe Ceremony and sing the vibrations of peace into the land. On this particular Tuesday morning, one week later, at exactly 8:48 A.M., the moment at which the first tower was attacked, the ceremony would begin. At the same time others around the world would support this sacred event in their own way. As I shared this, Rosemary's eyes filled with tears. 'Thank you! Thank you!' she whispered as she cried, 'You give me hope! You help me not to be afraid!'

"I found myself humbled and full of my own tears. I had the immediate thought that if we had been brought to this place at this time, for no other reason than to give one person hope, then everything John and I do and have done is worth this journey we're on. After all, it only takes one person to change a universe. There's only one person here. Maybe her name is Rosemary."

Rescue efforts were still going on as they found a bit of privacy in the park and laid out the ground cloth and the ceremonial objects for a Pipe Ceremony. Then, without media attention or even the interest of passersby, the sacred peace pipe was lit, and Jeanne and John offered their most sincere prayers for this place, these people, this country, and this world to be healed so that there might be peace. At the end of the ceremony, they packed up their sacred objects, went back to the ferry, and continued their journey. The detour had been very private, but for them, very necessary. This, too, was a test of spiritual work. True spiritual work is mostly done when no one is watching.

The schedule for the remainder of September and October was full. First there was the extensive preparation for the initial Sun-Moon Dance in North Carolina, then the annual international gathering of the Peace-Sound Chamber caretakers—this year in Shiro, Texas—and soon after, a Peace Concert in Asheville. Jeanne and John hoped for a couple of weeks of rest before their scheduled departure for Israel in mid-November.

For the next two weeks as the media dramatized every detail of the Nine-Eleven attacks and speculated on a U.S. retaliation, John labored with David and Dobs on the permanent construction of a large dance arbor and sweat lodge. Jeanne supported by organizing the dance support crew from the Corryton farmhouse. During the building of the arbor in a meadow adjacent to the Watersong Chamber, many hawks visited, and hawk feathers were found inside the arbor enclosure and surprisingly inside the new sweat lodge. Even more significant was the fly-over of a rare bald eagle that came by during the dance at a height of only fifty feet. On the Sunday afternoon ending of the dance, there was a torrential rain followed by a double rainbow.

The powerful signs saluted a powerful event. The drum group alone represented two generations of dedicated spiritual experience. Cheryl Patterson served as the drum chief with an all-star ensemble that included Troy Amaster, Jeff Kilgore, Sammye Jo Harvey, and Jeanne Robinson. John asked the drummers to sleep in the Peace-Sound Chamber so as to allow Spirit to teach them at night. Steve Citty, John's co-chief in Tennessee, served as the Alpha Dog, and did so with selfless dedication. Dobs, who had been an assistant firekeeper at the Lakota Sun Dances in South Dakota for the previous two years, served as firekeeper. Jeanne served as Moon Mother with the assistance of Ula Rae; and to add to the family feeling of the support crew, John's sons Sean and Alan served as Dog Soldiers. Sean had danced a Drum Dance and a Hollow-Bone Dance before with his father, but this was Alan's first exposure to John and Jeanne's work in the dance arbor.

The period before their departure for Israel, when they should have been resting and "integrating," was marred by the world news. Jeanne seemed especially attuned to the sorrows of the war in Afghanistan and the emotional landscape of where they would be going in the Middle East. The grief that she hoped to relieve sometimes oppressed her and depressed her personality. Their trip to Tel Aviv included an overnight stopover in Toronto. Owen picked them up at the airport, and they had a pleasant supper together with friends at a vegetarian Vietnamese restaurant. At midnight, the next day, they were on their way to Israel for the second time, an eleven-hour trip in economy seats.

Victor Barr and his partner Sharon met the couple in the airport terminal with hugs and drove them to their home in Zur Hadassa about thirty minutes southwest of Jerusalem. After a day of rest and some introductions to the area, Jeanne and John gave a mini-concert at the home of Robin and Sonia Twite, and interest was expressed in their giving a later sound workshop.

One of the things that Jeanne was intent on doing was to go to Mount Nebo in Jordan to do a pipe ceremony. The previous New Year's Day in their Medicine Ceremony with Joseph in Colorado, Jeanne had a vision of going to Mount Nebo. In the *Bible* account, God tells Moses that he can climb Mount Nebo and look into The Promised Land before he dies, but he cannot go there. Going the opposite way, from Israel to Jordan, in modern times is not a trip to be taken lightly either. First, the couple had to find a taxi near the Damascus gate in Jerusalem's old city willing to take them to the Jordanian border. Rabbi Eliyahu McLean, who speaks English, Hebrew, and Arabic, met them at the gate and negotiated the taxi arrangements for them, and then blessed them as they began their journey. At the Allenby Crossing and the King Hussein Bridge an hour later, they had to process through both Israeli and Jordanian military checkpoints. By 10 A.M. they had hired a Jordanian taxi to drive to Mount Nebo, wait for them, and then take them back to the border bridge. The round trip cost about $50.

At the top of Mount Nebo there is a Christian church built to memorialize the spot where Moses looked out on The Promised Land. The view is impressive as Mount Nebo is higher than the mountains in Israel. Since Jeanne and John had given themselves only an hour to perform the Pipe Ceremony, they quickly searched and found a private place illuminated like a spotlight by the sun. Jeanne laid down a Guatemalan prayer cloth, set out the buffalo and moose rattles, and prepared the pipe while John laid the corn-meal and tobacco circles to enclose the ceremonial space. Their activity attracted the attention of a Franciscan priest and a uni-formed Jordanian police captain, and Jeanne explained to them what she and John were doing. The Christian priest then gave them his blessing, and the two men walked away. Later, the police captain returned to observe the entire ceremony. He was a Muslim. In this way, four spiritual traditions were represented. The event had been blessed that day by a Jewish rabbi and a Christian priest, and a Muslim had stood vigil while Jeanne performed the ceremony.

As Jeanne sang the blessing, John saw a vortex of light energy around her. Jeanne had been faithful to her vision, and on Mount Nebo she felt herself radiate energy in all directions. But what did this single act mean in the grand design of hope? A woman and a man travel thousands of miles to stand on a remote mountaintop for the purpose of ceremony to fulfill a personal vision . . . what did it all mean? John did not have a specific answer, so he quoted two pieces of spiritual wisdom. From the Jewish tradition: "Do and *then* understand." And from Joseph: "Just show up and do what you are told."

Their twelve days in Israel continued to be eventful. One morning they attended a prayer vigil in Old Jerusalem overlooking the Wailing Wall and the Al Aqsa Mosque. There were many intro-ductions and long conversations over meals with emerging friends who would later support their work. Jeanne's sound workshop attracted a record forty people. At another event, after a pipe cere-mony, a very intense spontaneous song went on and on for more than fifteen minutes. It seemed like the people did not want to stop singing. Israelis were proving their love of singing as an emotional expression. They would also prove to be great ceremonial dancers and drummers.

One day the couple went to Qumran and performed a Pipe Ceremony in the chamber of the old ruins. Then they sat for a long meditation. On another day, they did a final Pipe Ceremony at the southern wall of the Old Temple right outside the Al Aqsa Mosque. In their hearts, Jeanne and John were linking the pipe ceremonies on Mount Nebo, and Qumran, and the old Temple as a continuous spiritual event. And although they could not know what energetic shifts had taken place as a result of these private peace events, they did find hope in the people who they were meeting. There was a non-political peace movement going on in Israel that the media world was not showing. There were dedicated people from diverse religious traditions coming together in spiritual unity and harmony to work for peace through forgiveness. Yes, conflict could be healed, and Jeanne and John were seeing the individual human evidence of it in encounter after encounter in Israel.

In one encounter that would prove to be very significant, Shelley Ostroff talked to Jeanne and John about going to South Africa. There were also conversations with Victor Barr about having Israelis come to the U.S. for the North Carolina Sun-Moon Dance and about bringing the Dance to Israel. A great deal was set in motion on this second trip to Israel that would have prolific future results.

John had suffered a bad cold most of his time in Israel, and when they got back to the farm, Jeanne developed a chesty cough, runny nose, and fever. In the news on television, two suicide bombers had struck the Jerusalem Mall. The second bomb was delayed to kill rescuers. Ten people died and 180 more were injured. Jeanne and John had been in that same mall just a few days before.

The way nationalistic governments operated, it did not appear that government leaders were going to be the instruments of peace. And what about church leaders? Religions seemed to offer peace conditional on the dominance of their belief systems. John noted that an American Indian elder had once said, "We never wanted to form a church because we didn't want to argue about what we believe." How many wars had been waged over differences in the concepts of God?

In December, Jeanne was scheduling concerts and workshops in Oklahoma and New Mexico, and they again planned to see Joseph in January. Christmas Eve was spent at the Center for Peace in a kind of old-fashioned family gathering. With so many singers and musicians present, the group sang Christmas carols and old standards. For the final song, *Silent Night*, candles were lit, and Perry Robinson offered the Christmas prayer for peace, and then the group took their candles outside on the porch as a metaphor for taking their spiritual lights out into the world. The gathering ended with a late-night supper and a give-away blanket where everyone brought a gift so that everyone would receive one.

Jeanne had been ignoring tooth pain, but now she was in dire need of dental care. One tooth had to be pulled, and another would require a root canal and crown that the couple could not afford. The stop-gap measure was to treat the infection.

Their Christmas present to each other that year was an R & R trip to Disney World in Orlando, Florida. Jeanne's genius in securing low cost accommodations and theme park tickets kept expenses to a minimum, and the trip was fun despite Jeanne being on antibiotics for her infected tooth. On Jeanne's birthday, they celebrated at The Crystal Palace restaurant in the Magic Kingdom where they considered that the "best French toast in the world" is served. In checking their e-mail, they learned that New Leaf Distributors had accepted their CD, *Between the Slices of Light*, for national distribution to "new age" bookstores. The year had come to an end on a high note of expectation. What a wonderful day: a major release for their CD and the best French toast, too!!

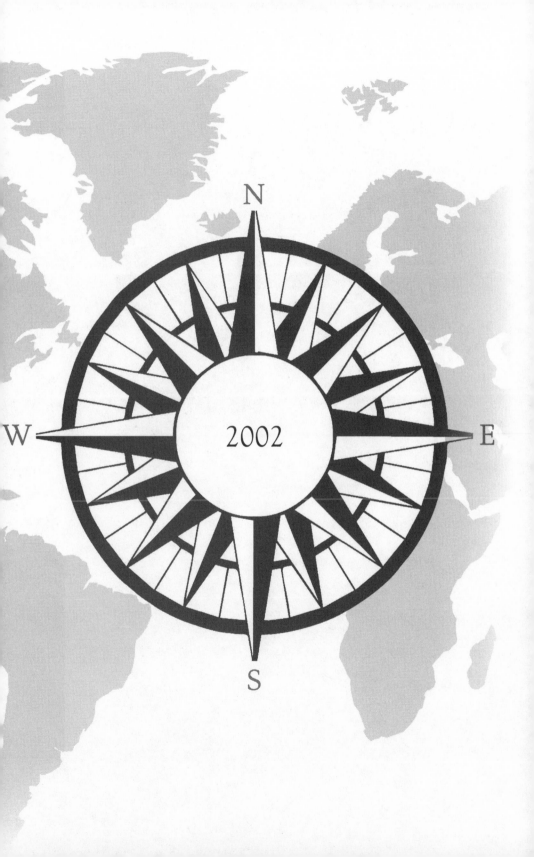

INHERIT THE EARTH

T he year 2002 began as the two previous ones had—on the long interstate highway I-40 West. There was their almost standing appointment with Joseph in January, but there was also work to be done in Tulsa, Oklahoma; Albuquerque, Taos, and Rio Rancho, New Mexico; and Crestone, Colorado. In Tulsa, the couple stayed with children's book author Krishnabai (KB) Austin. They had done previous workshops in her home. On a visit to Spirit Horse Ranch, they spent the day with Minisa Crumbo Halsey and her husband Jim, caretakers of one of the Tulsa area Peace-Sound Chambers.

Minisa (Creek and Pottawatomi) is the daughter of Woody Crumbo, a gifted full-blood American Indian artist. Jim Halsey is a very successful music impresario who has presented acts like Roy Orbison, Johnny Cash, James Brown, the Oak Ridge Boys, and many others. Jeanne and John blessed the open-air Moon Lake Chamber, saw the Long Dance arbor, and walked to the spot chosen for the construction of a Peace-Sound Chamber. When snow began to fall, the two couples retired to the main house for a vegetarian feast. Minisa gifted Jeanne with a vegetarian cookbook, and John with a beaded bracelet, and then presented them both with one of her father's paintings of the Spirit Deer. Later, Minisa and Jim would attend Jeanne and John's Peace Concert and give them an additional cash gift.

There was also a visit to Keith and Merlene Owen's place where Jeanne poured a women's sweat lodge. Everywhere that they went in the Tulsa area, the couple was treated with great respect, courtesy, and generosity. Most of their events there were impromptu; and although they had made the stopover with no real expectations of income, donations and sales of their CD had relieved them momentarily of expense stress.

Gracie had not yet been replaced, and she coughed her way through a dust storm en route to Albuquerque and needed an oil change and air filter by the time she got Jeanne and John there—another 657 miles on the odometer. The overnight stopover was at the home of Gail and Marcus Clarke, who had a 22-month-old son, Christopher, who had been sick for the previous week. The two couples enjoyed a simple Southwestern supper of tamales and Gail's chicken noodle soup (to which John added hot green chiles) and after Christopher went to bed, there was meaningful conversation. Marcus reminded John that there was nothing quite so compelling as a crazy innovative idea.

The next stop was their appointment with Joseph in Colorado. The Medicine Ceremony again was a powerful reinforcement of the life Jeanne and John had chosen. Joseph told them that the Grandmothers and Grandfathers were pleased. The couple stayed overnight with Joseph and Carolyn; and after a morning sweat lodge, the foursome went to Christina's in Durango for a hearty mid-morning breakfast. Meals at Christina's had become a tradition on their visits since 1998. Jeanne and John were "regular" customers if only once a year.

En route to Taos, the couple took a detour to Santa Fe to say hello to Sandy Misage; but when they got to what had been the Hydration Café, they discovered that Sandy had sold the business. It was now called the Dam Coffee Shop that catered to the twenty-something crowd. The drive to Taos was spectacular beyond Santa Fe as the highway snaked along the Rio Grande River Gorge. John noted, "When we crested the last rise before the city of Taos, the sun was setting, shooting hues of orange, pink and purple through the sky, and turning Taos mountains lavender." Their host in Taos was Elizabeth Eden. Elizabeth facilitated introductions to Taos residents who expressed interest in Jeanne and John's workshops.

On to Crestone, Woodora-Rose Eisenhauer hosted them and over dinners introduced them to her many friends with interest in metaphysics. Woodora-Rose was then inspired to organize a Peace

Concert that attracted about thirty people in this small town that is an hour away from the nearest supermarket. Marcia Huested, a medical intuitive, told the couple that the San Luis Valley that stretches out from Crestone between the Sangre de Cristo Mountains and the San Juan Mountains was known as the *Bloodless Valley*. Native American tribes in the area considered the valley sacred, and history records no individuals killed there as a result of tribal or ethnic conflict. Joseph's daughter, Teresa Rael, had told them that the valley represented the womb of the earth, and in local American Indian creation myths, it was considered the place of emergence. The land around Crestone also contained one of the largest aquifers in North America. For people relocating to Crestone, it was viewed as the new Sedona for spiritual pathway seekers.

The last leg of the Southwestern trip was Rio Rancho, New Mexico, 260 miles from Crestone. Judy and Maris Cardoza were their hosts, and a potluck supper awaited Jeanne and John when they arrived after an extra two hours on the road due to accumulated snow. A Peace Concert and an Intuitive Imagery Workshop in the days that followed attracted limited numbers, but in their philosophy, Jeanne and John were prepared to do the same work if even only one individual attended. Their mantra was to "show up, do the work, and leave the rest to God." And as for "prosperity," they had had many lessons on that score. Prosperity didn't always come at the time or in the way that they expected it.

Virginia Beach, Virginia was next on their itinerary, and they left the Corryton farm on February 19th. It was Jeanne and John's seventh wedding anniversary of the day that they had exchanged vows on the sands of Virginia Beach. They celebrated the beginning of their new seven-year marriage cycle at an oceanfront restaurant where they dined on she-crab soup and dinner salads. Being the beach's off-season, the restaurant was uncrowded and quiet, and they could hear the sound of the surf beyond the plate glass windows.

Virginia Beach was the place that Edgar Cayce, the famous "sleeping prophet," chose for the establishment of his Association for Research and Enlightenment (A.R.E.) in 1931. His presence there and the work of A.R.E. over the years attracted many psychics, clairvoyants, and students of mysticism to the Virginia Beach area. A sophisticated Virginia Beach party was not considered successful if it did not attract at least one nationally famous psychic.

Chandler Dennis, caretaker of the Sandbridge Peace-Sound Chamber, hosted a potluck dinner for Jeanne and John at her beach house where they would do workshops on Saturday and Sunday. A Friday night concert was scheduled for the Sandbridge Chamber at the far south end of the Virginia Beach area. Chandler's family had owned much of the Sandbridge oceanfront before it was developed into a community of hundreds of vacation homes.

Their hosts in Virginia Beach were Mary DiMartino, a fifth grade teacher of special education kids, and Leigh Carraher, a jewelry store goldsmith. Routinely, Jeanne and John stripped their guestroom bedclothes and laundered them along with their towels as a way of helping their hosts, but John often provided another consideration. He sharpened the kitchen knives. It was a skill that he practiced in host kitchens around the world.

One night Sally Perry, a new friend, invited Jeanne and John and Leigh to supper at Gus's at the Ramada oceanfront restaurant. Sally and Jeanne had a great deal in common. Both had Cherokee ancestry, and both had taken spiritual training from Joseph Rael. Sally had begun with Joseph in 1981; and by 1988, he had blessed her as a Dance Chief for the Sun-Moon Dance and the Long Dance, a dance done throughout the night without stopping. In these dances, Sally was allied with Zoe Bryant at the Swannanoa, North Carolina Peace-Sound Chamber. From 1996 to 2000, Sally spent six months a year in India living with its saints. She then began to travel extensively with Yug Purush Swami Paramanandji and facilitated his United States tours which included darshan at the Swannanoa Chamber. Sally had also written books about her spiritual path, and she gave workshops. Sally was so supportive during their Virginia Beach visit that in preparing thank-you gifts for Mary and Leigh and Chandler, Jeanne also included their new friend.

At the end of February, the couple drove to the Washington, DC area to prepare for their flight to Israel. Gracie had developed a bad oil leak that turned out to be a stripped oil drain plug, so instead of a major engine repair, a helpful mechanic diagnosed the problem and fixed it cheaply. John and Jeanne considered the event a "miracle car repair."

The author's daughter, Annalisa, and her husband Nacir Assaadi, had invited Jeanne and John to stay overnight at their home in McLean, Virginia. They could leave Gracie there, and Annalisa would provide transportation to Dulles Airport. The couple had two children—Myriam, 8, and Faris, 5. Nacir is a Moroccan from the seacoast city of Agadir. After a university education in France, he came to the United States to go to medical school, but the death of his father removed his financial underpinning. He met Annalisa, who was near her degree from George Mason University, while they were both working in an upscale restaurant. They married in 1988, and Nacir became a U.S. citizen in 1999. Both are well known in Capitol district circles. Annalisa is the National Events Coordinator for the Orphans Foundation of America and often works with members of Congress. Nacir, the general manager of an automobile dealership, was on President Clinton's advisory committee for American-Moroccan affairs, and the couple was included in White House and other functions on the State Visit of King Mohammed VI of Morocco in 1999.

In talking about the next day's trip to Israel with Nacir, John asked his host to talk about Islam. The two basic tenets of Islam are: "There is no God but God," and "Mohammed is His prophet." For Islamists, Mohammed is the *last* prophet of God. John said that he hoped that Mohammed was not the last. In the face of political cynicism, John was pleased to hear Nacir's assessment of the United

States. Nacir felt that although the government often falls short of the ideal, the "idea" of the U.S. and its cultural and religious freedom and tolerance is better than anywhere else in the world.

When John shared this conversation with the author, the author told him that he sees his grandchildren—Myriam and Faris—in the faces of all the children pictured from the Middle East, and that the only way to heal that pain is to work for peace in whatever way that presents itself . . . this biography, for example. In that regard, all grandparents must take responsibility for the earth that their grandchildren will inherit.

BROKEN PIPE, BROKEN PEACE

Tensions and violence had definitely increased since their last trip to Israel the previous November. On this third visit, everyone was on edge, even their hosts Victor and Sharon. The night that Jeanne and John arrived at Victor's apartment, machine gun fire could be heard. In the debate between spiritual wisdom and intellectual positions, the only winner seemed to be conflict. Despite the night sky being filled with the roar of military jets, Jeanne and John continued their process of networking with the better angels of peace.

On a day trip organized by Eliyahu McLean to visit the Biblical Samuel's Tomb, a prophet revered by both Judaism and Islam, the couple met Sheik Abdul Aziz Bukhari whose family has lived in Jerusalem for over 400 years. The tomb is one of the few places in Israel where a synagogue and a mosque co-exist. Prayers were spoken in both Hebrew and Arabic. Sheik Bukhari led the tour group of 25 in the Sufi prayer form called *zikar* that involves chanting and movement. For her part, Jeanne led the group in spontaneous song. Beyond the tomb, armed soldiers manned an observation post and distant machine gun fire could be heard from Ramallah in the distance.

At En Kerem near Jerusalem, the couple was hosted by Sonia and Robin Twite for a friends-and-neighbors get together. Robin was a retired diplomat, and Sonia taught Reiki. This exposure led to interest in a Community Building Workshop.

Another generous supporter in Jerusalem was Hedva Stahl, a French Jew, who with her husband Shimshon ran the Sai Baba Center there. Shimshon had died the previous month, but he had communicated the three most important attributes for living in Israel—"patience, courage, and fearlessness." Over a gourmet vegetarian dinner prepared by Hedva, she thanked her guests for coming to Israel for the hope that they brought to the people.

Before there were larger venues for concerts, workshops, and eventually dances, there were small gatherings in the homes of people where an intimate sharing of spiritual aspirations could occur. Jeanne and John were like seeds seeking fallow ground where they could grow with others to produce a harvest of peace. There was a longing for peace evident everywhere they traveled. The peace the people so desperately wanted, however, was not the short-term conditional peace of treaties and accords. It was the peace of the heart and the soul, the lasting peace that radiated from within. No form of government had ever imposed that kind of peace. The peace that a common humanity yearned for was a peace without boundaries, a peace without dogmas, a peace not imposed by bayonets. This personal peace was transforming, but it was also so individual that it could not be mass induced by any propaganda means. It had to occur in small, private groups where mutual support and loving dedication superseded any taint of exploitation. If peace were possible for the historically violent and predatory human species, it would have to rise up from a new breed of teachers. It would have to arise from the heartlands and not from the capitals of the mind.

At the end of a Power of Sound Workshop in En Kerem at the home of Sonia and Robin, Jeanne and John were asked to sing "the song of Israel" as a spontaneous vocable. John accompanied Jeanne on the dij as she sang from a place that recognized the pain, the sorrow, the fear, and the hope that they both had experienced in Israel. The musical duet soared with deep emotion, and the witnesses of it were moved in unexpected ways. Who were these American goyim who felt the Israeli struggle so profoundly?

After an evening gathering in Jerusalem at the home of Isaac Eliyahu Holly, Isaac gave Jeanne and John one of their most memorable testimonials. "This has definitely been one of the most wonderful nights of my life," he said. "Wow!" Isaac Eliyahu, who became a paraplegic in adulthood via accident, turned to spirituality and opened his home to almost every notable spiritual teacher who came to Jerusalem. Jeanne and John had given workshops there.

Marcia Barak, who provided transportation during their visit, was originally from Capetown, South Africa, and offered to connect the couple with friends there. It was not the first time that a new friend had pointed them to South Africa.

At some events, especially the workshops, the entire content of their program had to be translated from English into the language of the audience. Not only did this situation require a willing translator, but also the time allocated for the workshop was almost doubled. A day after such a session, one of the participants reached Jeanne by phone. The young woman was studying the Kabbalah at the university, and she was very excited to tell Jeanne that everything that Jeanne was teaching about spontaneous sound was consistent with the Kabbalah. "You are helping us to remember!" Elisa said.

John recorded a very interesting speculation in his journal about the connection between what Joseph had taught them and the Kabbalah.

"Of course, it didn't slip by me that the basic teachings are from Joseph Rael, whose last name is a shortened version of *Israel*. One of his ancestors was a Spanish Jew at the time of the Inquisition who came to the Americas with an explorer by the name of Vargas. This ancestor, named Rael, married a woman of the Ute Tribe. Maybe the teachings came from Israel to the Americas through this ancestor, were passed down through the years to Joseph, then to us to be brought back to Israel. Maybe things are coming full circle again."

The home of Anael Harpaz in Rosh Pina in Galilee, down the mountain from Tsfat (also written as Safed) where Rabbi David Baruch lived, was another place where touring spiritual teachers were welcomed and hosted. Anael, for many people, is a most unforgettable character because of her great humor and warmth. She would later prove to be one of the mainstays of the international "For the One" Dance crew. Significant events often happened around Anael, and Jeanne and John's visit would be no exception. The date was March 11th, the six-month anniversary of the infamous attack on the World Trade Center on Nine-Eleven. An Intuitive Imagery Workshop was in progress when Anael received an urgent phone call from Sonia Twite. A friend of Sonia's had a vision that a dark energy was entering the space where the twin towers had once stood. She was told in a vision that only the Americans could do something to clear or transform the dark energy. Sonia appealed to Jeanne and John for help as they were the only Americans she knew who were in Israel at the time. Jeanne's response was to do an immediate Pipe Ceremony.

The ceremony went according to tradition, but at the end, when Jeanne went to separate the stem (masculine) from the bowl (feminine), the stem broke off inside the bowl! At that moment, Jeanne says, she felt as if a bolt of lightning had passed through her. Both she and John knew that something very significant had just taken place, but they were unsure of its meaning. They would have to wait for an explanation until they saw Joseph in Texas at the end of April. And there was much more in store for them in Texas with regard to the pipe that would bring Zoe Bryant, the Eagle pipe maker, and Sally Perry, their new friend met at Virginia Beach, into a remarkable life-altering synchronicity.

The day following the breaking of the pipe stem, Anael took Jeanne and John to a cave overlooking the Sea of Galilee where Jesus went to meditate. The couple sat in the cave for their own meditation and then sang a vocable song together. The hillside around the cave was bursting with the spring colors of yellow buttercups, daisies, and mustard flowers, Queen Anne's lace, purple thistle blooms, blue lupines, red poppies, and tall green grasses. Across the Sea to the east, the Golan Heights was visible through the morning mist. The couple walked down the hill to visit other Christian shrines, and then they waded into the Galilee and baptized (blessed) each other with its waters.

The next two nights the couple did Peace Concerts at the home of Daniel Mark. The first night packed the house with 45 people. Many people stayed for an hour or more after the concert on both nights to talk to Jeanne and John about their work. The day after the concerts, Jeanne and John took time off to relax in the mineral baths at the Dead Sea. Then on Saturday, Daniel drove them to Jerusalem to attend a Peace Vigil with Jews, Palestinians, and Arabs. The event was marred by three young Jewish boys who heckled the vigil keepers with slogans of hatred in Hebrew. Their invective was aimed at the Palestinians and Arabs. It was a reminder that hatred is still carefully taught across many cultural lines. The ugliness was transformed, however, when the group broke out into spontaneous song that both engulfed the shouting boys and totally altered the negative into a sound bubble of love. When the song was done, the boys had disappeared.

This trip to Israel had been very affirming for their work, but the war zone energy was also very depleting. Nevertheless, Jeanne and John felt a strong guidance to return to Israel in June. There were many invitations to bring back their messages of hope.

From Israel, there was a short five-day trip to Germany to perform a return Peace Concert at the Church of the Holy Cross in Berlin. There were hours reserved for private sessions, but the primary focus was the concert, which attracted over 100 people.

Fortunately, their hosts Enrico and Elke had arranged for them to stay in a veritable mansion in one of the best neighborhoods in South Berlin. Elke was its caretaker, and she had arranged its use while the owner was away. After the pace and danger of Israel, both Jeanne and John needed a quiet retreat, and the large house and gardens were greatly appreciated.

The flight back to the States was on LOT Polish Airlines, Berlin to Warsaw to Newark, and then United to Dulles where they were met by Annalisa Assaadi. At Annalisa and Nacir's home, Gracie awaited them; and after a sleepover, the couple made the drive back to Corryton via Richmond, where they had lunch with son Alan, and Graham, NC, where they spent the night with Jo Fisher. They finally got back to the little remote farmhouse on Good Friday, March 19th. They had been on the road a total of 39 days, and they had accumulated more travel miles in that month than most people accrue in a lifetime. Experientially, they had clearly lived a period beyond the scope of calendar time.

THE PEOPLE'S PIPE

Corryton in early April is in the bright bloom of springtime with temperatures in the mid-70s. Jeanne and John had a two-week break to rest, to catch up with friends and family, and to take care of the business of bill paying. John had lunch with Steve Citty to share the experiences of Israel with his closest male friend, and Jeanne had lunches out, too, with a couple of friends. Ula Rae visited the farmhouse as did John Troutner, Jeanne's son, with his fiancée Audrey. There was also news that Diana, John's ex-wife, had recently remarried. John was glad for her. Domestic life at Corryton included the use of a washer and clothes dryer and a large old-fashioned pedestal bathtub for long soaks. Such conveniences, and the privacy thereof, seemed a luxury after so many days of washing clothes and bathing from sinks in endlessly revolving bathrooms. What others in long-term residencies considered normal, ordinary, and boring was experienced as almost wonderful to the road-weary Pehrsons.

In his journal, John admitted to travel fatigue, even on their ninth day back in Tennessee. He felt sluggish and in a kind of fog. He read a book on the history of the Holy Land, but it only depressed him. How could he and Jeanne hope to bring peace to such a long existing conflict of cultures? Meanwhile, John admitted, Jeanne was the focused one. She did the forward trip planning, managed the money, and paid the bills.

A reporter from the *Knoxville News Sentinel* came to the farm with a photographer to interview Jeanne and John for the Sunday edition section on religion. The article then appeared about two weeks later. There was also a call from a freelance writer who talked about developing a piece for Oprah Winfrey's *O Magazine*. There was to be a roundup feature story in the September issue on the first anniversary of the Nine-Eleven terrorist attacks. The article intended to demonstrate ways that individuals could bring about peace. High profile people were being interviewed, and the writer thought that she could get them included. The interview was done over the phone, and the written piece was submitted to the magazine, but it was not published. John listed the four-point approach that individuals could employ to help create peace in his journal as he and Jeanne had related it to the magazine writer.

- Fasting from food and water. This helps us to let go of the ego mind and clear the static from our connection to the Divine.

- Spontaneous chanting using the vowel sounds propels us into a place "between the slices of light"

where we are fully present in the moment without
ego. In this place, we begin to remember.

- Ritual dancing to expand awareness. Dancing is
  prayer in motion. It expands our awareness. It plows
  the field of consciousness, planting seeds of inspiration.

- Love what is in front of you in the moment. This
  may be the most important practice. Love what is
  front of you in this moment. Then move to the next
  moment and love what is front of you. The rest will,
  as Sai Baba said to Jeanne in vision, take care of
  itself.

Near the middle of the month Jeanne was visiting her stepmother Peggy in Chattanooga when across the dinner table at the
country club, an envelope was passed containing a check. It was
Jeanne's share of the proceeds from her father's estate, and it was a
sizable amount enough to pay off their bills and loan debts, send
money to all five of their children, and even replace the long-suffer-
ing Gracie with a more dependable vehicle.

The next scheduled workshop events were in Pennsylvania
where the Pehrsons usually stayed with Tom and Kristen Bissinger.
There had been no time to replace Gracie since the deposit of the
inheritance check, so the aging BMW rolled over onto 288,000
miles during the drive from Tennessee. Kristen, who knew the saga
of Gracie, suggested a dealership specializing in late-model used
cars; and after Jeanne and John did their imaging, there was no
equivocation that they should buy a new car before going to Texas
for the Sun-Moon Dance. Thus the almost-new Pathfinder came
into their hands with all the amenities that had been lacking in
Gracie. Oh blessed air conditioning and cruise control! But Gracie,
who had carried them over 88,000 miles was not let go without

sentiment. They wished for the 1986 automotive senior a good retirement. And they also remembered the generosity of Perry Lane as their past, present, and future benefactor. A father's love is enduring. Mile by mile, it is enduring.

Mickey-G, the new conveyance of the Jeanne and John adventure, got them to Shiro, Texas on April 25th. John was to be a Sun-Moon dancer while Jeanne served as a Moon Mother with Brenda Sue Taylor in a dance chiefed by Neal Sutton. Neal and Elizabeth Sutton were the caretakers of the Shiro Peace-Sound Chamber located north of Houston. Neale was unique as a dance chief in that he remained in the high-powered practice of corporate law as the general counsel for a large international oil supply company. John met Neale at the New Mexico Men's Sun-Moon Dance in 1997 when Joseph retired. This SMD was to prove a very significant event. Just in terms of its dancers and supporters, it was a rare gathering of very spiritually aware individuals.

Joseph was already on the site when the Pehrsons arrived. Jeanne took their first opportunity alone to tell him about the stem of her Eagle Pipe breaking off inside the bowl. Joseph listened carefully to the full story of what had occurred, and then he responded with a radiant grin.

"The time of separation is over. What I get with both my head and heart is that the pipe is telling us that for peace to happen, we can no longer separate the masculine and the feminine. Save that pipe. One day, after you both have gone, it will be placed in a museum."

Then Joseph predicted that Jeanne would receive a new pipe, which when smoked, was never to be taken apart. This instruction was a radical departure from pipe tradition, and Joseph acknowledged that pipe purists would not like it.

Experienced dancers with long histories of association with Joseph began to arrive—Owen James from Canada; Peter Terry from England; John Stroupe and Marcus Ambrester from the Southwest; and Sally Perry, Zoe Bryant, and their Native American friend LaKotahasie from the mid-Atlantic. Joseph's own Rael family was well represented as Joseph himself danced in the West. His daughter Geraldine danced across from him in the East. Carla Jo, his niece, danced in the South, and his younger brother Benito drummed. Joseph, who had been raised Catholic at the Santa Fe Indian School, asked for a rosary to be brought to him as he intended to dance the energy of the Cosmic Christ down into the Earth. John had acquired a Jerusalem rosewood rosary near Capernaum on the Galilee outside St. Peter's Church. Not a Catholic, John did not know why he had been drawn to the rosary. Now Joseph invited John to bring his rosary into the arbor and dance the Cosmic Christ together with him. Owen James also danced with a rosary.

John had the feeling that Joseph was now extending the status of brotherhood and sisterhood to his core group as a benediction. Group members continued to honor Joseph with the title "Grandfather," but more and more, he began to refer to the men as brothers and the dedicated women as sisters. Any concept of spiritual hierarchy was being released.

The pipe story took another dramatic turn at the end of the Chief's Sun-Moon Dance. Zoe Bryant remembers her role in this way.

"As I was leaving home, Spirit told me to take the People's Pipe that I carry. I thought maybe someone there would need me to do a ceremony for them, so I packed the pipe and took it to Texas. During the dance, Jeanne said that she needed to talk to me. She said that her Eagle pipe had broken, and that she probably needed a new pipe. Well, we were very busy with the dance, so we didn't find time to sit down and visit. I actually had my car packed and was pulling out of the drive when Spirit stopped me cold and told me to *give* the People's Pipe I carry to Jeanne. Give? Not loan? Spirit kinda laughed at me and said, 'Silly, you can make another one! Jeanne is going back to Israel, and there is no time. She needs it now.'

"So before I had time to analyze the situation further, I turned the car around and went looking for Jeanne who was packing up her car. I had carried the People's Pipe for ten years, and it had been blessed by Grandfather Dubray who carried Fools Crow Medicine of the Lakota. Parting with this sacred pipe was a huge event for me. Later, I learned the whole story about the time of separation is over.

"I'm sure there are many metaphors that we could explore—the Snake pipe and the Eagle pipe being carved from the same African stone; the end of the Snake pipe's mission occurring in Israel; the breaking of the Eagle pipe again in Israel; and then the first use by Jeanne of the catlinite People's Pipe also in Israel."

Jeanne remembers Zoe saying, "When I came, I didn't know why I brought this, but now I do. This is yours." Then to her astonishment, Zoe placed the long decorated leather bag containing the pipe into her hands.

As humbling as the gift of the People's Pipe was to Jeanne, there was yet another amazing transfer of sacred objects yet to come in the same hour. Seven years prior, Joseph had given Sally Perry two belts from his Picuris Pueblo tradition. One belt carried the energy of the masculine, and the other the energy of the feminine. The belts were given to Sally so that she could balance these two energies within herself for the purpose of healing. She was told to keep the belts for fourteen years, or until she was complete with them. During the dance, Sally had a vision that the belts were to come to Jeanne so that Jeanne and John could carry them for seven years. And so, with Joseph's permission, Sally Perry presented the two gender energy belts to Jeanne.

Jeanne would wait until she was in Israel in June to join the male and female sections of the People's Pipe. The time that she chose was the hour of a solar eclipse on the 11th. The ceremony was private; and as the moon joined the sun, at that same moment, Jeanne joined the stem and bowl of the new People's Pipe as a constant symbol of wholeness and balance. The use of the "end of separation" pipe would prove to have dramatic results in Israel and later in South Africa.

THE FINDHORN GIFT

W hen Jeanne and John return to a place where they have done concerts and workshops, they are met and hosted by friends who support their work. Initially, these relationships were initiated around the Peace-Sound Chambers; but as their network expanded over the years, it included people of all metaphysical interests. The May 2002 itinerary took them to England, Wales, and Scotland and a personal encounter with the legendary Eileen Caddy of the Findhorn Foundation.

The Pehrsons were met at Heathrow by Lawrence Bloom and his friend Pippa who drove them to Herefordshire, where among the narrow country roads and hedgerows they came to the home of Peter and Ruth Terry. Later that day, Lindsay Sutton came for tea. Lindsay is the person who brought Joseph to the UK, and many stories were shared about Joseph, Sally Perry, and former Drum Dances in Wales. While they were accommodated in Peter's guest quarters, a separate two-story cottage next to the main house built in 1620, Peter was very generous in giving the couple a tour of the historic castles, abbeys, and churches of the region. Although Jeanne did a mini-workshop, the pace of their six days at the Terry's Church House Farm was very relaxed.

Midweek, Lawrence and Pippa drove them to Wales where they planned to visit Paul Benham and Jan Elliot at their Primrose Organic Farm. The farm was also the location of a Peace-Sound Chamber that Jeanne and John had awakened in May 1999. In the Chamber that night there was an impromptu concert with Jeanne and John singing, Paul playing the djimbe drum and dij, and the others joining in. The next day, the couple began a two-day Living in the Moment Workshop that was very successful. In parting, gifts were exchanged. Jan gave Jeanne a special ring that had been given to her by her mother, and there were also generous cash gifts to support their further travels.

On a Monday, the Pehrsons traveled by train to Edinburgh, and then by bus to Inverness, where they were met by their host Stella Longland. Stella's little country house was situated in a natural garden environment only a few miles away from Findhorn Bay and the world renowned center for spiritual education, the Findhorn Community. On their second night in Scotland Jeanne, Stella, and John went to the conference center to hear an introductory talk by two early members of Findhorn.

The community was founded by Peter and Eileen Caddy and Dorothy McClean in 1962 as a center for spiritual education and personal transformation. Peter and Eileen had come to the area to manage what became the four-star Cluny Hill Hotel. Later they moved into the Findhorn Bay Caravan Park, and Eileen was guided to plant vegetable gardens in its sandy soil. The vegetables that Eileen's spiritual guidance produced amazed horticulturalists by their size and quality, and a community began to form around Eileen to learn the mystical secrets of their success. In 1967 the Community published *God Spoke to Me*, Eileen's account of her spiritual guidance. At that time, the Findhorn Community was housed in caravans (trailers) and cedar wood bungalows, and its members built meditation places and a community center to meet and eat. David Spangler arrived in 1970 to help define and organize the spiritual education process, which grew to 200 weeklong courses, conferences, and programs by famous visiting spiritual teachers. In 1975, the Findhorn Foundation purchased the Cluny Hill Hotel as its center for study and member accommodations. Then other facilities were built until a huge complex that included the Caravan Park dominated the east side of Findhorn Bay. Eileen Caddy's collection of daily inspirations, *Opening Doors Within*, became a worldwide best-selling book, and today Findhorn hosts programs by the world's leading spiritual authors and teachers.

In walking the Findhorn gardens and visiting its Nature Center, Jeanne and John felt affirmed in the life that they had chosen. Findhorn's success was due to its trust in *guidance*, first from Eileen

Caddy and other individuals and then from the community at large. John wrote, "Findhorn people were willing to see beyond boundaries of conventionally accepted reality. They practiced living in the moment with a trust in the greater mission, and they practiced manifesting what they needed."

Jeanne wanted to meet Eileen Caddy, but Stella advised her that the elderly matriarch of Findhorn seldom met with visitors or ventured out in the evening. At Cluny Hill College, however, Jeanne met Linda, who turned out to be one of the three caregivers who attended Eileen. After talking about her work and expressing her heartfelt prayer to meet Eileen Caddy, Jeanne was told that Eileen attended a 6:30 A.M. morning meditation in Findhorn Village. Linda said it would not be inappropriate to attend the meditation and to bring a note for Eileen. The note was written on a beautiful card and tied to the *Between Slices of Light* CD with a red ribbon. Jeanne explained in the note a little about their work and invited Eileen to attend their talk in the Upper Community Centre that evening. The late-week short notice event drew only seven people, but one of them was Eileen Caddy herself, a gentle, white-haired woman of 83 dressed in an evening dress and gloves, who was accompanied by Linda. She stayed for the entire program and told Jeanne and John, "Oh, good. You've learned two very important lessons—obedience and self-discipline." Eileen Caddy's blessing went both ways in that the couple she had just experienced was working in the world as the embodiment of the principles that Eileen taught and held so dear. Stella told the Pehrsons that Eileen was often disappointed in the way that spiritual education had been commercialized.

One of the other seven people in the room that day was Raya Ginser from Israel. She was impressed enough with the American couple to attend their major event at Findhorn the next day. The well-attended Sound Ceremony in the Earth Lodge began at 2 P.M. with Jeanne and others singing accompanied by two didgeridoos. At one point the entire hour-and-a-half event moved to the Nature

Sanctuary for a few songs before it returned for a finale in the Earth Lodge with some amazing overtone chanting.

Raya Ginser wrote about her experience. "When I went on the next day to their sound healing circle, it was quite crowded. We were drumming and playing instruments, singing, yelling and sounding whatever came out of us. I was expressing myself and moving energy around me with my hand. In the end, Jeanne complimented me for having done good work. I felt seen for a change.

"The dream that came that night shocked me. It was a message saying, 'This was worth $20,000.' I was shocked because I felt it was a call for me to donate the money, a legendary sum to me in theory because I am very careful with money and never spend much on myself. When I heard their earlier talk, I learned that Jeanne and John were on their way to Israel, my homeland, to do peace work. During the talk, I saw a shadow above Jeanne's head, and I connected it symbolically to the negative energy of suicide bombers and fear that was occurring in Israel those days. When Jeanne was very ill, I felt sure that the shadow that I saw over her head had become tangible. Jeanne told me later that her illness and healing was a Shamanic preparation for Israel.

"I tried to contact them after Findhorn to let them know that I wanted to make the donation. I was scared, but every time I would speak with Jeanne, I would have a dream experience of freedom in my fifth chakra . . . some opening that made me know this was the right thing to do. I don't think that Jeanne and John really believed that I would give them $20,000, but after the sale of my parents' house in Israel, I sent them the money."

Raya then purchased a home in the Findhorn community area; and on one of her trips back to Israel, she and her two-year-old daughter Sufi-Priya were invited into the "For the One" Dance circle for a blessing, and today Raya still feels the spiritual connection to Jeanne and John and their peace efforts. Little Sufi-Priya, Jeanne believes, will one day play an important and positive role in the future of her mother's homeland.

Jeanne's illness that Raya referred to was severe abdominal pain and vomiting that caused Jeanne to cry out in agony. Jeanne said that she had not experienced such pain since childbirth. At times, she was profusely perspiring and in danger of losing consciousness. John was on the phone desperately trying to reach Owen James in Toronto, only to learn that Owen was in San Francisco. Finally, he got through to Owen at 5:30 A.M. Pacific time. Owen, however, was already up, and he urged John to apply hot compresses for the abdominal cramping and calming teas like chamomile for the stomach upset. He also prescribed an anti-viral homeopathic in high dosage and mega-doses of Vitamin C with lots of water. Owen was not concerned that Jeanne might have been attached by dark elementals at Findhorn, although the Findhorn community seemed always wary of such attacks. Although Jeanne finally slept through the night, she could not travel, and so their departure for the Isle of Skye was delayed.

On the Isle of Skye, The Pehrsons were reunited with Ocean and Scotty Graham who had hosted them in 1999 for the Awakening Ceremony of their Peace-Sound Chamber. The couple had met on a kibbutz in Israel in the 1980s and come back to Scotland to raise a family. They had also done the 1999 Australian walkabout with Jeanne and John. Their children Aliza, 23, and Selena, 21, came for the weekend. Jeanne was still feeling sick and went on a diet of cod liver oil and sea kelp until for the first time in a week, her perkiness was restored.

Jeanne felt up to a side trip, so she and John went to see the famous standing stones at Callanish, which required a ferry trip and an overnight in a bed and breakfast. Approaching the ancient stone circle from the north along a stone corridor, the small group included Stella Longland from Inverness, Ocean, Sandy Masson, and a few others. Tobacco and cornmeal prayers were offered, and then Jeanne lifted the old Eagle Pipe to both bless and be blessed by a shrine considered powerfully sacred for thousands of years. Their ceremony and meditation lasted for about ninety minutes.

During the next days there was a full schedule of workshops and then a Peace Concert at a church in Portree. In the next day's move from Glendale to Armadale on the southeast end of the Isle of Skye, the Pehrsons made stops to bless two future Chamber sites. Their host in Armadale was Sandy Masson whose relatively new cabin was a model of sustainable living. Her source of water was roof-collected rainwater. Her stove had only two gas burners. A small wind generator charged a battery that powered a radio and a few low wattage light bulbs strung from the ceiling. From this base, Jeanne and John did individual workshops by day and then joined for a concert at night.

The volcanic mountains around Armadale Bay, the Cuillans, were used as a backdrop for the old prehistoric dinosaur movie *The Land That Time Forgot* (1975). As the couple walked the landscape, Jeanne quipped, "If you're quiet, you can hear the pterodactyls." According to Scotty Graham, the Red Cuillans and the more jagged southerly Black Cuillans provide the best ridge walk in all of Europe.

In the first week of June, there was a flight from London to New York and then a quick turnaround for a flight to Israel. The weeks in the UK had been cool and wet in contrast to their arrival in Israel where the temperature approached 108º F with very low humidity. Their fourth trip to Israel was to last a month and be filled once again with spiritually significant events.

THE END OF SEPARATION BEGINS

When the temperature at Victor and Sharon's house at Zur Hadassa was forecast to reach 43ºC (107ºF), the Pehrsons decided to stay inside during the day and rest prior to their talk at Yaqub's Bookstore that evening. The small store was filled with about 25 people who came to hear the Americans. Their presentation was equally balanced, and John told Jeanne that maybe they were growing into the Picuris belts by honoring both male and female energies.

One night Jeanne woke up and put the People's Pipe under her pillow before going back to sleep, and she dreamed about joining the stem and bowl of the pipe during a solar eclipse. In the morning, she e-mailed Joseph for clarification. She asked about the permanent connection of the pipe's parts and also the meaning of the solar eclipse. Joseph replied from Colorado.

"Yes, keep the pipe connected together. The moon is the feminine and the sun is the masculine. There is a spiritual law that says over time everything becomes its opposite. The pipe used to be kept separated when not in use and connected when in ceremony, so now it stays connected all the time. Look in the immediate future for cause and effects of this change."

On the 11th of June, slightly more than a day following her dream of the feminine moon coming together with the masculine sun, Jeanne united the People's Pipe during the actual moments of the solar eclipse, but she did not do the Pipe Ceremony. That event waited on an intuitive sign. The sign came two days later when Isaac Holly, knowing that Jeanne was a Pipe Carrier, invited her to his home in Jerusalem to do a Peace Pipe Ceremony. Jeanne recognized this invitation as the one she had been waiting for, and she agreed on a date two weeks later.

In the meantime, the couple stayed with Hedva Stahl in the Jerusalem flat that she shared with Michael Green, a writer and translator for the *Los Angeles Times*. They especially enjoyed Hedva's Sai Baba room that was generally used for meditations and group activities. In Tel Aviv for a Power of Sound Workshop there were twenty participants with aggressive intellectual questions. By the time Jeanne was done, however, they were all in the flow of her vibrations, and half of them purchased the *Between Slices of Light* CD. Later that week there were Peace Concerts in Jerusalem and in

Haifa at the home of Brigette Kashtan. Both events were well attended.

Every day seemed to be filled with memorable events. Brigitte took the couple to Mount Carmel where the Biblical prophet Elijah won out over the priests of Bael and brought down fires from heaven. In Shacharut they attended a storybook traditional wedding deep in the Negev desert, with the bride arriving on a camel to Bedouin tents and carpets spread on the sand. There were much food, music, and singing, and Jeanne was even made an honorary bridesmaid. In a Jewish wedding ceremony, it is not only the bride and groom who marry but also the two families. One night on this trip to the far South was spent at Kibbutz Lotan, a gated and guarded community. Around that time, a suicide bomber on a bus traveling the outskirts of Jerusalem killed nineteen people including school children. Other bombings occurred, and Jeanne and John often heard sirens and the angry fly-over of military fighter aircraft as they went from place to place.

During much of the trip, both John and Jeanne were suffering from diarrhea. Although they accepted the condition as a kind of purging, or a shamanistic purification, it was unpleasant at best, and they did what they could to remedy it by diet and herbal medications. John, too, was suffering from the constant relocating. Jeanne was much more flexible with regard to finding a home anywhere she laid her head. John admitted at times to being *homesick*. There was also the recurring issue of balance between them as spiritual teachers. In many venues, Jeanne was treated as the star persona, and her natural personality allowed her to step forward in that role. With the focus on Jeanne, John had to deal with recurring bouts of second-fiddle-itis, a dis-ease that he fully realized was caused by the ego-virus. He desperately wanted a cure for what he recognized as a self-induced malady.

In Rosh Pina, Anael Harpaz hosted Jeanne and John and facilitated individual workshops for them on separate days. Anael also took them to potential sites for the "For the One" Dance. On the way back from Tsfat they stopped at the shop of another transplanted South African, Peter Isaacowitz, who makes didgeridoos, xylophones, and door harps. Peter and his 16-year-old daughter Maya performed for them on the dij, guitar, and djimbe, and Maya sang *Amazing Grace*. Afterwards, the Pehrsons invited the musicians to play with them at a Saturday Peace Concert. At the Concert, John played Peter's A-note dij and liked its sound so much that he asked to buy it. Peter chose instead to make the dij a gift. "The thought of you carrying it around the world in concerts makes me feel so good that I want you to have it. It really suits you."

That Sunday in Tsfat Jeanne and John had a remarkable two-hour meeting with Rabbi David Baruch, whom they had met on their first trip to Israel. Orthodox Jews are not supposed to hear women sing, but Rabbi David asked Jeanne to sing a spontaneous song. Afterwards he revealed to them that a school for prophets 2000 years ago had taught this kind of singing as a way to connect with God and the Divine. "Today," he said, "they would call it channeling." He also told them during this visit that the word "messiah" in Hebrew rearranges to "simchah," which means joy. So *joy* and *messiah* have the same vibration. He suggested that they might want to learn to chant the sounds of the Hebrew alphabet, and so, on their way back to Jerusalem, they got a book on Hebrew.

Finally, the day arrived for the Pipe Ceremony at the home of Isaac Holly. Thirty-two people attended. For the first time, Jeanne wore the feminine Picuris belt and John wore the masculine one. In the prologue, they told in detail about the events leading up to the ceremony and the altering of the ancient tradition associated with the pipe that would now take on the new reality that *the time of separation is over*. Witnesses to the Pipe Ceremony with the already-joined People's Pipe were both Palestinian and Jew. When the ceremony ended, Jeanne told the witnesses what Joseph had told her about cause and effects, and she encouraged them to watch the news for signs that the end of separation was indeed occurring.

Less than ten hours after the Wednesday Pipe Ceremony, water began to flow from the West, or Wailing Wall, that surrounds the Temple Mount and Dome of the Rock. The water was coming from near the center of the wall, which divides the prayer positions for men and women. The event was major news that was even reported on CNN's world service television station. Jeanne and John were told that for Jews there was special significance because water flowing from the West Wall had been prophesied in a holy book as a sign of the Redemption and the coming of the Messiah. One woman who Jeanne and John encountered speculated that it was probably just a broken water pipe that had been misinterpreted as a miracle. Jeanne reacted with a chuckle, "The prophecies didn't say *how* it would happen, only *that* it would happen."

The next day the couple walked with new friends from the Pipe Ceremony through the Muslim Quarter of Jerusalem, out the Lion's Gate to the Church of St. Anne, Mother of Mary. The church is very near to ancient pools where Jesus performed healing miracles, including the one where He told the man crippled for 28 years to take up his bed and walk. Inside the church, Jeanne and John sang their prayers, and then Jeanne went to the altar to sing alone. There she recognized the blessedness of her own mother whose first name is also Anne. Downstairs in the crypt where St. Anne is buried, Jeanne again had a powerful emotional experience.

At the close of Shabat on Saturday before their departure on Monday, the Pehrsons met Rabbi Frohman at the insistence of his wife Hadassah. The rabbi's wife had seen a shaft of light energy emerging from Isaac Holly's home during the Pipe Ceremony as she walked past. She then said to herself, "Something important has just happened here." Rabbi Frohman was considered a courageous, if controversial, Orthodox Jew because of his efforts to reach out to Sufi sheiks and Palestinians in the pursuit of peace. For some he was a hero, and for others a traitor. During their evening together, Rabbi Frohman called a seer named Nitsan to come meet the American couple. John had the feeling that Nitsan had been called to psychically "check us out."

Nitsan was so enthusiastic about Jeanne's spontaneous singing that she insisted that she and Rabbi Frohman telephone a mutual friend. The hour was late, after 1 A.M., and Jeanne and John voiced reservations about getting someone out of bed to hear Jeanne sing. Rabbi Frohman assured them, "Sheik Abu Saleh always has time for God!" And so, Jeanne sang on the telephone to the very influential Sufi sheik who exclaimed to her, "A gift from God! A gift from God! You must come visit my mosque." The sheik's mosque turned out to be in Mod'in, where the sheik was under house arrest by the Israeli military.

By the time Jeanne and John got back to the States, they admitted to each other that they were overextended with regard to their travel itinerary. They needed to work on criteria for future trips. With no staff to take care of their scheduling details, they had responded to all invitations regardless of the practical considerations. The result was many excess travel miles and a travel weariness that impacted negatively on their health. Now after only one day with Sue Mehrtens in New York following their transatlantic flight, they had to go back to the airport for a flight to Houston, Texas to pick up their car and then drive two days to get back to Tennessee. They had only a week to recover, however, before preparations for the Sun-Moon Dance at the Center for Peace. Although John had stepped down as co-chief of this Sun-Moon Dance to chief the new Sun-Moon Dance in North Carolina, he supported Steve Citty as the Alpha Dog. Including the arbor preparations and the night shifts during the dance, John actually worked harder and longer than if he had co-chiefed.

Jeanne served as a Moon Mother with Brenda Sue while Nan Citty apprenticed as a Moon Mother. Jeanne did a People's Pipe Ceremony for the dancers late Saturday afternoon, and she and John wore the Picuris gender power belts like prayer shawls or mantles. At one point in telling "the time of separation is over" story, Jeanne lost her composure and John had to pick up the narrative until she recovered. Jeanne recalls the event.

"It was the first time this pipe has been smoked in this way in the U.S.A. I wanted to give full respect to the pipe and to the ancestors. I felt vulnerable and had a challenge stepping into the fullness of where my destiny was pulling me. There wasn't a right or wrong. There was the humility of not wanting to disrespect such a beautiful purpose and ceremony. I did the best I knew how at the time, but the child in me was sad because I knew in my heart that I still had much to learn, and I judged myself by saying, 'I could have done this better.'"

Marcus Ambrester witnessed Jeanne's tears, and he gently consoled her by reminding her that there was a vast difference between the "work" and the "show." Jeanne continues to remember this moment of loving kindness.

Brenda Sue expressed concern about the break in form of keeping the pipe parts together. She feared that the pipe purists might even react in a violent way. A mixed-blood Cherokee man, however, told them that he had heard three other American Indian elders, in addition to Joseph, say that the time of separation is over with regard to gender, race, and religion. He also said that when a pipe becomes "wedded" together, it is called a "Friendship Pipe."

Two days after the Sun-Moon Dance at the Center for Peace, the couple was en route to Frankfurt via Atlanta for another round of concerts and workshops in Germany. Their first stop was in Berlin for a Peace Concert facilitated again by Enrico Hilbert and Elke. Jeanne also did a Pipe Ceremony in Enrico's flat and told the small gathering the significance of the new pipe. The message that "the time of separation is over" was then discussed as people wanted to know how they might live this new paradigm.

Moving on to Saxenhausen, the couple performed a concert at Hilde Kopesko's Peace-Sound Chamber. That night Jeanne awoke with intense abdominal pain and vomited into a plastic bag. John was upset by both Jeanne's and his own physical condition, and he wanted to return to the United States; but the next day Jeanne felt better, so they continued the schedule of workshops and private sessions in Grossropperhausen, again facilitated by Alex and Shania Racky.

The need for rest out of the spiritual teacher spotlight was served by some vacation days in Sorrento, the picturesque Italian town on the Bay of Naples. The late August weather was sunny, and the town was still swarming with German and English tourists. The plan in Sorrento was to recapture the romance that had slowly drained out of their relationship under the stress of constant travel and ceremonial demands. The first two days in paradise were an adjustment period, but then during a town-wide power outage, the couple had a romantic, candlelight supper as the only customers in a darkened restaurant in old Sorrento. With their intimacy restored, the vacation proved to be everything that they had hoped for. The next morning, they drove to Vesuvius and climbed the demanding serpentine pathway to the top of the volcano's crater. At the crater's edge, they offered cornmeal, sang a spontaneous song, and then threw a rose-quartz heart and a quartz crystal from the Grossropperhausen Peace-Sound Chamber into the volcano's abyss. John noted a sense of "Vesuvius himself." The mountain had last erupted in 1944 and was thus deemed overdue for another seismic event.

By early September they were back in East Tennessee in what John termed "the land of kudzu." Kudzu had been introduced for erosion control and then spread as a weed throughout the Southeastern United States until its rapidly growing vines had killed trees and covered power and telephone poles along most major Southern highways. Their arrival at the farm was felt like psychological kudzu. It was an infestation of responsibility: to re-provision the kitchen, to drive out the stale hot air with fans, to return calls and e-mails, and to rush back into a cycle of planning for the next Sun-Moon Dance in North Carolina and the October trip to South Africa. A decision was made to rest a few more days in support of their romantic relationship, so a deep-woods cabin was secured ten miles from Gatlinburg for the Labor Day weekend. The remote cabin was so appropriate that it even featured a large heart-shaped bathtub.

The staging of the first Sun-Moon Dance at the Watersong Chamber site in Graham, North Carolina had required the construction of a large permanent dance arbor, a large sweat lodge, a kitchen house and a dining area. While Jeanne worked from the farm to coordinate the dance crew and instruct the dancers, John was on site with David and Cheryl, Dobs, and others to complete the site preparation and to cut, split, and stack the cords of firewood necessary for the lodge and arbor ceremonial fires. At one point Jeanne called John about the support crew menu. It seemed too Spartan when she reviewed the grocery list. She suggested upgrades to keep the drummers and Dog Soldiers well fed. It was one of a hundred details to manage; but first the knee-high grass in the arbor meadow had to be bushwhacked and mowed, the dance pole cut, erected and decorated, and the meal and first-aid canopies erected. John even took time to make 15 turkey-bone whistles for the dance.

The Saturday of the dance fell on both the fall equinox and a full moon. In the first sweat lodge, John told the dancers, "Remember to trust the process. Movement expands awareness." Dancers for this dance had come from both Germany and Israel. From this dance forward, every dance that Jeanne and John would lead would be international and multicultural in scope. In sweat lodge ceremonies, when verbal prayers were offered, they would be spoken in more than a few languages.

THE SPIRITUAL DIALECTIC

I n spiritual work, the enlightenment potential is always at odds with the cultural conditioning that is recognized as the ego. Even the role of spiritual leadership is not exempt from the attacks of mind-generated despair and uncertainty. Conflicts appear that give rise to frustration, anger, pain, regret, and guilt, but it is only in this crucible of relationship that spiritual growth is possible. Great insights result from recognizing the human condition in one's self as well as in others while giving the full measure of compassion to each. If one cannot control every thought of judgment, then one must learn to forgive the error of that thought and re-confirm the presence of Pure Being which resides at the center of Self, the Self that encompasses all the parts-of-Self that appear in the grand illusion to be separate. The practice of this recognition of the undivided Divine Self is called spiritual discipline, and it is the primary attribute of the individuals whom we honor as Masters. To become a Master is to do nothing. To be a Master is to simply dwell and live from that inner space of thoughtless awareness that is termed Pure Being. All human beings are only one single breath away from having this experience for themselves . . . if they can only release the chatter of their minds and relax into the state of grace that every human culture understands as love.

Spiritual seekers often describe their journey to enlightenment as a path that requires great struggle and sacrifice. But who or what do they struggle against, and whom do they sacrifice for? Do they struggle against Evil and sacrifice for Good? Are these forces then equal, or are they merely concepts at war within the mind? And if there were no mind to form them, where then would the conflict between good and evil exist? What is the real nature of conflict as we experience it in the material world? See for one's self where conflict originates. Go to the core of it. Watch the content of one's own mind very carefully. The genesis of conflict that leads to violence and war will be self-evident. Conflict is the product of separation that is expressed as prejudice and judgmental blame in the mind of the beholder. When enough minds contain the same negative thoughts as cause, the projected effect will be death and destruction.

The above dialectic is the author's reasoning behind the movement to end separation, and it can only be accomplished by the yet imperfect human beings who have experienced it. The methods to end separation may appear to be mystical to many observers; but when enough minds transcend their inherent limitations and experience the profound sense of unity that is possible, then the cultures of planet Earth will move toward peace and abundance in a very practical way. Peace has always been a grass-roots movement, and like hope, it has sometimes been threatened by extinction. As the 21st century began on the Christian calendar, the Earth was generally at war with itself. It was so out of balance with its own nature that there were accepted scientific predictions of its imminent demise. Against this tide of pessimism and the wanton consumption of self-justifying hedonists, there were small clusters of human beings on its continental masses who sang and chanted prayers for all people everywhere. They did not impose a dogma or call themselves a religion. Their work was to create light and to use that light to push back the darkness that had descended on so much of the consciousness of the Earth. Jeanne White Eagle and John Pehrson are agents of that light as is everyone who accepts a like mission to serve humanity. This is how meaning and purpose is brought to life's experience. Interestingly, the service of Light requires no personal attributes other than devotion and self-discipline. As the song lyrics go, "Love can come to anyone. The best things in life are free."

John and Jeanne might put it another way. "All you have to do is listen to your inner guidance and inspiration, show up, say 'yes,' and be willing to do the work."

THE BLESSING OF BABA
CREDO MUTWA IN SOUTH AFRICA

T he call to South Africa had been persistent. Wherever they had met ex-patriot South Africans in Israel or in Europe who experience their work, the Pehrsons were advised to take their message to South Africa. The suggestion had also been supported by dreams and intuitive imagery. Then the door was opened wide by Stephanie Clarke, an English woman and ordained Science of the Mind minister who served a church in Johannesburg. Aside from a concert scheduled for them by Reverend Stephanie, however, there was nothing else booked in support of the trip when the Pehrsons embarked from Atlanta on the 8,150-mile flight to Capetown. The connecting flight from Capetown to Johannesburg added another 860 miles, so the in-flight travel day lasted 17.5 hours.

Africa is the Great Mother of human existence that saw hominids walk its landscape three million years ago. If one wants to go back to the roots of the tree of life, one must go to Africa. Jeanne and John felt guided to go there perhaps for the purpose of planting new seeds that would grow in the dawn of a transformative age. Symbolically, their aircraft arrived over the southern tip of the African continent just past dawn as a bright radiant sun spread like a golden fan through the clouds to the ocean below. The ocean then reflected the sun like a mirror, and the effect was momentarily blinding. The flash of intense light seemed the power of creation, and then the magnificent landscape was revealed, and the Spirit of Africa greeted the lofty observers with a rainbow. Rainbows are powerful signs to Jeanne and John because Joseph's Tiwa name means "Double Rainbow." John noted in his journal, "We wondered what miracles awaited us." If South Africa was the womb of creation, they felt then this land must always be pregnant with possibilities.

After a night's rest, the Pehrsons rented a car and drove 4.5 hours into the Maluti Mountains near Lesotho to meet Niyan Stirling at Rustlers Valley Ranch. Niyan had built Marimba House and the hosting facilities around it to take guests on sound journeys. Marimba House was in reality a Peace-Sound Chamber with a native-style thatched roof. Obviously, the Pehrsons and Niyan had much to talk about. The cottages at the ranch were round structures that resemble hobbit huts from the *Lord of the Rings* trilogy. That seemed especially appropriate since J.R.R. Tolkien grew up quite near Rustlers Valley. Niyan was not only their guide to the African spiritual experience, but he was also to prove invaluable to their future work in Rustlers Valley.

Rustlers Valley is in the heart of the Orange Free State, a hidden canyon where once stolen cattle were concealed. Ficksburg, its sandstone town, produces five hundred tons of cherries a year, or 95% of the South African crop. To the Zulu tribe, Rustlers Valley is the "Valley of the Earth Mother," and it was once considered by them to be the holiest place in South Africa. A cave in the mountain above the valley was said to be the womb where life first appeared on the planet.

Niyan, a slender man with his long blonde hair swept back into a ponytail, had once been a fashion photographer; but when his uninsured studio burned down some nine years before the Pehrsons arrived, he lived in a teepee for three years and then migrated to Rustlers Valley where he built Marimba House. In their talks, Niyan told Jeanne and John about an energy problem that existed in Rustlers Valley. Some three years before, an Indonesian man who said that he had been schooled in Native American Hopi prophecies built a medicine wheel and conducted a ceremony to change the direction of the energy flowing in a large mountain feature that resembled the shape of a dragon. Why he did this, and why he sought no counsel or permission from the resident native sangomas was unknown. His mystic mission completed, he left the valley and had not returned.

Not too long before the Pehrsons' arrival, a sangoma from Durban had called Niyan to advise him that the energy of the huge dragon-shaped mountain behind Marimba House was disturbed. "The dragon is confusing its head from its tail," the sangoma said. "Something must be done to shift the energy back again." Since a Native American ceremony had done the damage, Niyan speculated, perhaps the medicine of the two Americans who also knew Native American ceremony could restore the dragon's orientation. Jeanne and John agreed to return with the People's Pipe and the Picuris belts and to seek permission of Vusamazulu Credo Mutwa, the Zulu High Sanusi (Shaman) and of Gogo (Grandmother) Monica, the local head sangoma, to perform a re-balancing ceremony for the dragon mountain. This conduct would go a long way in establishing Jeanne and John's credibility among the Zulu spiritual leaders.

Before a temporary leave taking from Rustlers Valley Mountain Lodge, the Pehrsons introduced their Living in the Moment Workshop to a handful of people and then gave a Peace Concert later for twenty attendees. While they sang, there were flashes of lightning, and at the end of the concert, they received the endorsement of the Thunder Beings. Back in Stephanie's flat in Johannesburg, the Pehrsons learned more about Credo Mutwa, and Jeanne attempted to secure an appointment to visit him.

Credo Mutwa is as well known in South Africa as Nelson Mandela. As the Zulu spiritual leader during the struggle against apartheid, he was often the focus of controversy. When he built a "living museum" in the Soweto ghetto in 1975, he was accused by his own people of cooperating with the hated government. When he wrote books, especially *Indaba, My Children* (1964), he was threatened for disclosing Zulu mysticism to outsiders. Credo Mutwa pronounced that British colonialism had destroyed the native peoples' self-knowledge, self-love, self-respect, self-pride and self-dependency and turned them into a race of robots forever dependent on the whites. For telling the stories of his desperate childhood, and for documenting the spiritual legacy of his people, Credo Mutwa suffered a murdered wife and son and another son's death from AIDS, in addition to many personal death threats. At age 81, when the Pehrsons first encountered him, *The Father of Africa, The Awakener of the Zulu (Vusamazulu)* and *The Uplifter (Sanusi)* was a revered artist, teacher, author, storyteller, healer, priest, prophet, and keeper of the oral traditions and sacred artifacts of his Zulu nation. The gentle giant of perhaps 300 pounds was also fluent in several languages and even among degreed academics, he was referred to as "Doctor."

When Jeanne first called for an audience with Credo Mutwa, she was told that he was ill and was accepting no private appointments even though Jeanne had references from a Baba friend in Australia. Jeanne told the woman, Jane, that she and John were "supposed" to see the Zulu holy man. She emphasized the pre-destination word as she had with the registration clerk at the Deepak Chopra workshop years before, and it had the same result. Jeanne had been told that Credo Mutwa was also clairvoyant, so she had confidence that he would be aware of her intention. The next day Jeanne called back, and Jane answered. "Oh, I'm so glad that you called back. I didn't know how to contact you. Everything has been prepared for you."

Naledi, the property where Baba Credo Mutwa resides, is an exquisite piece of land below a mountain ridge with a small river running through it. Jeanne and John stayed two nights in a guest cottage apart from the main house. Jane McGlew, with her younger friend Mapula, proved to be a caretaker of the property, and both women were immediately drawn to Jeanne. Reverend Stephanie accompanied the Pehrsons for their first hour with Credo Mutwa. When the large man shuffled into the room, still suffering from a stroke affecting his left side, Jeanne and John went down on their knees and clapped softly in the traditional Zulu way of prayerful respect. The Sanusi seemed surprised by this gesture from the unknown Anglo couple.

In a soft, elegant English, he responded to them, "What can I do for you, Honorable Ones?"

Jeanne responded, "We have not come to ask for anything but rather to pay our respects and bring you our love."

The visitors then presented gifts to the Zulu Sanusi as a token of their esteem for him. He seemed very pleased and responded to them.

"Well, Honorable Ones, what then shall we talk about?"

Thus began the first of many conversations that revealed the commonality of their spiritual work. In the sharing, both Jeanne and John felt that Baba Credo communicated to them on multiple levels. Jeanne remembers this first encounter.

"I told Baba that again, out of respect, we wanted to connect with the local sangomas and the ancestors as it was their land upon which we were coming to do the Pipe Ceremony. I remember Baba smiling and saying this would be good."

In discussing the idea of "oneness" Baba Credo told them that African/Zulu words are found in many cultures around the world including Native American, Inuit (Eskimo), Japanese, Maori, Australian Aborigine and others. His point was that all human beings are one family. As in Native American ceremony, smoke has always been seen by Zulus as a medium to carry prayers to God. "But," Credo said, "God doesn't like words. We pray with feelings."

The next day at Baba Credo's request, they met him in the roundhouse of the African Cultural Village at the Naledi property where he taught them the African zodiac. Jeanne recalls.

"It was here that Baba told me that I was born under the sign of the Whale, the bringers of peace. He said that John was born under the sign of the Double Dolphin. This, for me, was a confirmation of my experience with whales in Hawaii, and our connection as a couple to the Mer people, the oceanic spirits. Baba asked us to visit him again before we left South Africa. We were told later that he liked having us around because we made him laugh."

When they departed, quartz crystal gifts from Jeanne's medicine bag were given to Jane and Mapula. Mapula, an apprentice sangoma, blessed Jeanne in return by saying, "May the elephant be small in comparison with you."

Before they could return to Rustlers Valley, there were concerts to perform at Rev. Stephanie's church and at the impressive Rudolph Steiner Hall in Johannesburg. The couple also traveled at the invitation of a new acquaintance to give a concert and relax at an Anglo artistic community. The states of undress by some of the women who lived there, however, made John feel uncomfortable, and remarks made to Jeanne by one young man about her confident personality style upset her. Poor Jeanne had stumbled into a social dynamic where her female strengths upset an already teetering applecart. The projections aimed at her were nevertheless painful primarily because they were so unexpected. Jeanne's innocence was vulnerable to attacks that momentarily pushed her off-center and set her mind to self-doubts. More often, it was John who questioned his worthiness as a spiritual leader, but Jeanne could also fall into that self-critical trap. Venturing out as they did into a world of emotional slings and arrows, it might be expected that their armor would sometimes be pierced. That social armor is most often pierced by a sharp tongue should not be surprising to those who have experienced judgmental words as weapons of mass destruction.

The Sangoma Valley is on the other side of a ridge north of Rustlers Valley in central South Africa. Sangomas are the traditional, clairvoyant healers who carry the ancient knowledge of African herbology and naturopathy. They are also trained to communicate and interact with the ancestors and the unseen spirit world. The Sangoma Village cannot be reached by vehicle as it is nestled high in the sacred caves overlooking the valley.

John's journal provides an excellent account of their first hours in the sacred native village.

"This afternoon we walked the dirt paths into the sangoma valley, stopping at a large shrine to the ancestors to light candles and offer cornmeal and tobacco, and prayers. The candles are to offer our light to the ancestors. From there, we walked through a large arroyo where a pool has accumulated water from a gentle stream. The sangomas honor this place and greet the spirit of the water by clapping hands. Up the other side of the arroyo and along a well-worn double footpath, we walked to a steep incline up the rocks to the sangoma village. The village is along the side of the mountain, under the overhang of rocks above. There, we said prayers and lit a candle at the central village shrine. It had a cross on it. Afterward, we waited for 'Mama,' the head sangoma, Monica, to invite us into her space."

Jeanne had arrived in South Africa with a broken toe on one foot and a sprained ankle on the other. Her trek up a steep incline into the Sangoma Valley was a hobble aided by a tall walking stick. Along the path they were periodically greeted by sangomas who knelt, clapped their hands, and said, "Macosi, Macosi," which translated means "the Spirit in me greets the Spirit in you." It was a way to acknowledge their common ancestors. Later, when the couple was invited to return to the sacred village, Jeanne cringed at the thought of another long distance hobble.

John's journal continues.

"We brought gifts to Gogo Monica. Gogo is the general respectful term for a sangoma. It means Grandmother. We brought sage and cedar, cornmeal, American Spirit tobacco, a cinnamon-scented hot pad from TN, and dirt from ancient Cherokee land. We also brought crystals that have traveled around the world. One packet of sage was from Israel. These were in addition to the white rice and bread that we left on the central altar.

"Monica is a large black woman with big breasts and sparkling eyes. She laughs easily and makes everyone around her feel at home. She's a wonderful archetype of the African Mother that we connected with upon arriving in Capetown. When we got around to asking permission for the Pipe Ceremony (through Niyan), she didn't hesitate in her reply. Yes, it was okay to do the ceremony. And yes, it should be done at Marimba House. But we should *start* it at the sangoma village with candles and an offering of flowers for the ancestors. She even agreed to come and participate. This was quite something since she hasn't been on this side of the mountain to do ceremony for four years. Her willingness to come was another affirmation that Jeanne is doing something good in offering the sacred pipe ceremony.

"As we were sitting with Mama Monica, I also got an intuitive flash that South Africa is important in bringing back the energy of the Mother. I've seen for a long time that if we are going to create peace on the planet, the women must play a more important role. We must bring the energies back into balance. Perhaps South Africa will play an important role in doing that.

"Monica invited us back to the sangoma village tomorrow afternoon to participate in the initiation ceremony for some new sangomas. We will also begin our ceremony at that time. The offerings to the ancestors that will be made will be the lead-in to a pipe ceremony Wednesday evening. We'll also do a sweat lodge on Wednesday afternoon.

"There was quite a thunder and lightning show tonight after dinner. The lights are blinking off and on as it passes through, bringing the rain in its wake. It will cool things down a bit, making for good sleeping."

The Pehrsons returned to the sangomas initiation ceremony the next afternoon with Niyan, and Devi, a white South African sangoma. They trekked into the mountain village just before 6 P.M. Again, John's journal provides the best word picture.

"Jeanne, Niyan, Devi, and I waited while the preparations were completed. Corn maize was being crushed into powder in a tall, thick metal container (18" high by 9" diameter) using a 1-½ inch metal rod with flattened ends—a heavy-duty mortar and pestle. Other herbs had also been crushed, all prepared to feed the fires.

Five fires had been built equidistant from each other in a circle around a large central altar upon which a sixth fire was readied for lighting. Each was built as a square fire, 1-2" branches cut to size and laid perpendicular to a base with another layer at right angles on top of them. Paper and scraps of bark placed underneath were the tinder, ready to light. Herbs of some kind were sprinkled on the top layer. Just before lighting the fire, plates of crushed herbs and little patties of cornmeal were brought out and set by each of the piles of wood.

"Each of the sangomas wore a red cape with a large white cross sewn onto it into the center. A matching headdress also carried the symbol of the unequal Christian cross. In fact, upon entering the sangoma village, an altar to the left had a tall cross. The Catholic Church has had an influence on how the religion is practiced here. These sangomas all accept Jesus as the Christ and Savior. They are themselves descendants of Abraham, who they believe is the *father of the nations* as told in the Old Testament of the Bible. So, the traditional ways of the African religion that include ancestor worship and blood sacrifice, coexist with Christianity and a belief in Jesus Christ. Very interesting.

"Jeanne and I sat on a blanket placed over a rock ledge added to and shaped by concrete. Apprentice and fully-fledged sangomas were scurrying around making final preparations. Above our heads were the branches of a tall pine tree extending outward over the path into the village and stopping about two feet above a large boulder. As the sun set behind the mountains, chickens climbed onto the boulder and flew, awkwardly, into the lowest branches of this tree, one or two falling back to the rock below on their first try. But by sunset, all the chickens and roosters had found a perch for the night. The price paid for sitting in the wrong place at the wrong time was getting chicken droppings on the top of the head. Devi and Jeanne both got baptized in this unwanted way!

"As it became darker, rats scurried out of a nearby hut and ran for alternate cover behind us. The sound of their little feet so close to us was disquieting for me. We even saw two of them run in front of us down the path to disappear somewhere in the boulder across from us. Finally, I just relaxed into these sights and sounds that blended with the nesting noises of the chickens, the Sosotho words, and the faint sounds of drumming from across the valley on the other ridge.

"We had a long wait. It was over two hours before everything was ready for the ceremony to begin. Rather than being difficult or onerous, this sitting became a meditation for me. I slipped into a reverie. My body began rocking gently back and forth with the energy of the place and the prayers that went into the preparations. I closed my eyes and found myself in vision. I saw the ancestors looking on. I went to the void. It was totally black at first. Then a golden light formed itself into a sphere and radiated luminescent, golden beams of the most beautiful light outward in all directions. The light was singing—singing itself into existence. I wondered if this vision was connected to the cave somewhere nearby that Baba Credo told us about, the place of emergence.

"The time passed quickly. The ceremony was ready to begin. Jeanne and I were guided to a blanket nearest to Gogo Monica, on her left. Jeanne sat closest, with me by her side. Devi and Niyan were next to me. The six fires were lit, one in the center atop the altar and five others arranged equidistant around the altar in a circle. Offerings of cornmeal patties, herbs and spices were made to the fire, the smoke carrying their energies to the spirits. Gogo Monica read from a Bible that had been translated into Sosotho. The teaching was about Abraham's faith when asked by God to sacrifice his son Isaac. This was extremely interesting since it seemed a direct connection to the story of the pipe, and the first people's ceremony in Israel! Singing and dancing followed. Some songs were in African, but one was in English. It was an old spiritual—*Someone's Callin' my Name*. I felt as if we were in a black church, singing, clapping and dancing to spirituals.

"As we sang *Someone's Callin' My Name,* Monica blessed us with ash from the sacred fire, and with water. She also blessed some water for Jeanne to drink ¼-cup morning and night. The blessing of the water entailed striking six wooden matches one after another and putting them into the water, and then adding some ash from the sacred ceremonial fire. Later, Monica told Jeanne that she *carried the spirit of the water.*"

The Pipe Ceremony day at Rustlers Valley began with an African variation of a sweat lodge. Manaledi, a large African woman with markings on her face, sang her prayers in the lodge with the native participants joining in. Their tradition was sung prayers rather than spoken ones, and thus the lodge lasted a hot two hours, much longer than John intended. Gogo Monica came for the Pipe Ceremony itself in Marimba House, which began after 7 P.M. Twenty-three people, including Gogo and her assistant, participated.

The intention to restore the power of the dragon-shaped mountain by reversing the flow of energy back to its natural state was known to all. The presence of the ancestors was evident during the ceremony as verified by the shouts of Gogo's sangoma assistant. Within an hour of the completed ceremony, gale-force winds blew out of the west toward the east. Jeanne and John were forced to lean into the wind as they walked down the path to their cottage, and then a hard, stinging rain pelted them. Then there was an exciting moment of awe as they recognized that the wind had shifted directions. They felt the energy shift to its natural and original orientation. Was this a coincidence? No one who attended the Pipe Ceremony thought so.

The Pehrsons had another opportunity to see Baba Credo before leaving South Africa, and now they would come to him with a message from Gogo Monica with whom they had shared ceremony. Gogo was already referring to Jeanne as CiCi, a term of endearment meaning sister, and John as Puti, or brother. Gogo also told Jeanne that the Spirit of Water was coming out of her and that she should begin to wear a sangoma's cape. She also urged the couple to stay with her in the sangoma village on their next trip. Her message to Baba Credo was, "Tell him that I am still fat." And then she laughed.

Back in a cottage on Baba Credo's grounds, their friends Jane and Mapula washed the Pehrsons' clothing and hung them in the open air to dry. There were other guests on the property including a group of sixteen Americans interested in energy healing. Some were nurses who wanted to learn about the alternatives of traditional African medicine. Unfortunately, from Jeanne and John's perspective, the Americans seemed to lack an understanding of how an elder of Baba Credo's stature should be treated. The Pehrsons also became aware of the spiritual politics surrounding Baba Credo. Sangomas of different stripes were already laying claims to Baba's medicine bundle and his many spiritual artifacts in anticipation of his passing. To the Pehrsons, they spread their wings like a pack of circling vultures.

One morning Jeanne, John, Jane, and Baba Credo with his companion Virginia, both in full regalia, together with the sixteen American energy workers all piled into four vehicles and drove to the other side of Pretoria to see the Wunderbroom, Africa's "wonder tree." The tree itself is an ancient wild olive tree that legend says was once large enough for an entire village to live under its branches. Baba Credo sat on a bench near the tree and began to teach the group about trees. His regalia must have weighed upwards of fifty pounds. His headdress was a thick band of copper or bronze over a felt base. The metal was etched with symbols, and thick bronze figures hung from each side. A heavy copper neckpiece five to six inches wide was around his neck. He told them that its etchings told the story of the Zulu people. A necklace hung to his chest with three figures representing the three aspects of God: Father, Mother, and Son. John felt it was an interesting departure from the Christian Father, Son, and Holy Ghost.

Another necklace with a green stone carved and polished into the shape of a heart signified his status as Chief. Baba said it was to remind a leader to always be strong of heart while simultaneously remaining gentle. Baba seemed pleased when the Pehrsons recounted the ceremonial events at Rustlers Valley. When they delivered Gogo Monica's message that she was still fat, Baba smiled and told them that it was the sangoma's way of telling him that she was still happy and in good health.

In a private thirty-minute conversation with Baba and Virginia, Baba told them, "It is said that those who speak with soft voices are often heard the loudest by God." They also talked about the AIDS epidemic in Africa and the ongoing conflict in Israel. On departing, the Pehrsons gave gifts of black cherry preserves from Rustlers Valley and necklaces that Jeanne had made specifically for Baba and Virginia. Baba then asked them to write to him when they returned home. If indeed, Africa had called them, Jeanne and John could have found no greater spiritual ally than the Zulu Sanusi, the great Father of Africa. All that was to follow for them in Rustlers Valley was now graced by Baba Credo's blessing.

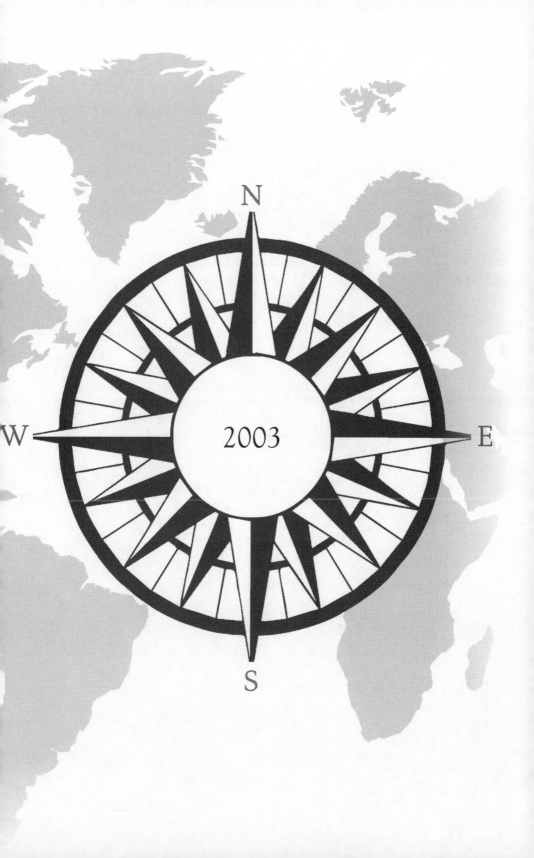

J eanne, with a sprained ankle, had hobbled through much of their itinerary in South Africa, and John had burned his left hand with a hot skillet severely enough to leave red scar tissue, so aside from the emotional drain and the travel fatigue, they should have laid up in Corryton after arriving there. They had been with Baba Credo on Saturday the 26th at Naledi; now on Thursday the 31st, they were driving to Albany, New York to fulfill a weekend commitment at the House of Mica Peace-Sound Chamber for hosts Rick and Elisa Cotroneo. They returned to the farm on Election Day, the first Tuesday in November, with the prospect of a long rest period, but first there was a family emergency.

Peggy Lane, Jeanne's stepmother, was scheduled for surgery Wednesday morning in Chattanooga, and Jeanne and John intended to be at her bedside when she came out of the operating room. The surgery went well, so the Pehrsons returned to the farm only to get another dreadful emergency call. The youngest son of an old friend had been killed in a car wreck. He was still a student at the University of Tennessee at Chattanooga, and the Pehrsons immediately returned to the city they had just left to console the parents and to stay over for the wake and funeral. Peggy, although recovering, was still in the hospital. Where, oh where, was there a place for retreat, Jeanne and John must have asked.

John felt the need to make a three-day trip to Chicago to see his oldest son Ryan. Their communication had broken down, and John wanted to restore it. He drove the distance alone through rain and some snow to visit the son he had not seen for over three years. The visit proved healing; and in addition to meeting Ryan's girlfriend, John even had Sunday lunch with his former wife Diana and her new husband Hugh. He had to admit that he liked Hugh on first impression.

At the end of November, the Pehrsons returned to their favorite diversion for fun—Disney World. They rode the theme park roller coasters with childlike abandon, ate their favorite foods, and set about attempting to put a needful world on pause, but they were only partially successful. They had seen too much, knew too much to release themselves from the urgent mission of responsibility. It was another of the aspects of serious spiritual work that no one warns you about. Once you take up the cross of humanity, you are not able to put it down. You cannot help yourself from wanting to make every hour that you live count for something sacred and yet too often unknown.

In mid-December, with the offer of Cynthia Walker's casita in Placitas, New Mexico, the Pehrsons put their worldly goods in a 5 x 8 foot rental trailer and relocated far away from the Tennessee winter. Arriving in the Albuquerque area felt like coming home in many ways since they had once had a beautiful home there. Their first meal after unhitching the trailer was green chile chicken stew at a familiar restaurant. The Sandia Mountains' watermelon-colored sunsets had a mesmerizing effect on Jeanne who wondered if Placitas—not Crestone, Colorado—should be their eventual home base. John, who felt like he had pulled up stakes in too many places, felt more adrift than Jeanne.

As Christmas approached, Jeanne was painfully inconvenienced by a December 23rd date with an oral surgeon to remove a tooth. Every two hours thereafter, she was either taking a pain pill or a penicillin tablet.

A new Christmas tradition was started in Placitas. Jeanne and John carried a Christmas card containing $50 in cash and sought an intuitive opportunity to give it to a complete stranger. Jeanne found her opportunity in a crowded mall where she handed the card to an unsuspecting young couple and then melted back into the throng of other Christmas shoppers.

John's giveaway had an unexpected feedback. John's intuition was to go to a McDonald's. Snow was falling as he got to the door;

and as he passed a twenty-something Native American young man standing outside, the man asked him for two quarters so that he could call home. John recognized that he had found his recipient, so he pulled the card from an inside jacket pocket and gave it, saying, "This is for you." John was standing in line to get a sandwich and coffee when the same young man came inside and approached him with tears in his eyes. "Thanks, man. This is going to get me home to Jemez for Christmas. Then the boy-man, the age of John's own sons, hugged him, and John hugged him back, saying softly, "You're welcome."

"You don't know what this means to me," the Indian said as he walked away, and then to John's surprise, the stranger turned around to come back and hug him a second time. "Thanks again," he said, and then he was gone.

John, who had been feeling displaced and somewhat lost, got the message. He had only given a *son* travel money. The *son* in return had given him the true meaning of Christmas. Giving is receiving. And what was the story told at Jemez that Christmas? Was it not a miracle story involving an angel? And in John's telling of the story, who is his angel but the Indian boy?

Christmas morning, Jeanne and John opened their gifts to each other and the family presents that came in the mail. In the afternoon, Cynthia fixed a turkey with all the traditional trimmings, and the Pehrsons joined the Walker family for a feast that included Jeanne's famous chocolate pie for dessert.

Cocooned in the cottage-like casita, bone tired and proverbially licking the wounds of emotional stress, Jeanne and John could hardly have imagined what the new year would bring. They could not know that the birth of the "For the One" Dance was only a few months away, and that before the year ended that the dance would be taken to both Israel and South Africa. They could not know that every spiritual training in their past had prepared them together for the realization of the "For the One" Dance, and that its actualization was thus a fulfillment of their common destiny to be powerful agents for the end of separation.

On the first day of 2003, John summarized the previous year in his journal. From the entry it is obvious that their mission was becoming more focused.

"The second year of the new millennium was a year of miracles, blessings, and accelerated learning. It brought new friends, powerful experiences and important teachings. We met elders of various cultures who shared their wisdom with us—both spoken and unspoken. We participated in some amazing ceremonies. We visited sacred places and gathered some great stories. Altogether, it is more than we can hope to share in a newsletter. Much of it will have to wait for a book. But, we'll do our best to share the highlights.

"It was a busy year. Our work with sacred sound and dance took us twice to Israel and Germany and also to Canada, England, Scotland, Wales, and South Africa. We spent half the year abroad, and half the year crisscrossing the United States. We did peace concerts, dances, ceremonies, workshops, and lots of private sessions. Wherever we went we carried two messages. 1) It's time to remember who you really are. You are the peacemakers because you *are* peace. 2) Peace will never come from *out there*. It will only come from within. If you want peace, love what is in front of you *in this moment*. Everything else will take care of itself. Then, move to the next moment and love what is in front of you in that moment. Again, everything else will take care of itself. Then, move to the next moment and love again. Instant by instant, moment by moment is how peace is created. It's really quite simple—but not often easy. This part was Sai Baba's teaching to Jeanne in 2001.

"We learned some important things, not the least of which is that sometimes the importance or impact of a particular action only comes into focus after the fact. The most important teaching we received this year happened in this way. It came through a Pipe Ceremony in Israel. The teaching was this: *the time of separation is over.*"

John was conscious that his journal was not only a factual account of the places, people, and events of his work with Jeanne, but that it was also an unfolding of his own spiritual growth. He hoped that the document would have a future use, perhaps for a book, but he also intended it as a resource for his three sons to know him better and to help them understand why he had not been present for them since he began his spiritual path.

"If I have made progress along the spiritual path, it has not been done in a straight line. Nor has it been an ever-ascending path toward the light. It has been full of pitfalls, mistakes, fears and doubts, misgivings, sharp descents into the abyss of darkness, as well as joy, flashes of insight, breath-taking visions, and amazing happenings. This is the true path. We've all been led to believe that the life of a Master such as Jesus or Buddha is constant in its progression to enlightenment. Once attained, the radiance never dims. I don't think it really works that way. The record of Sri Aurobindo's journey into the darkness gives me hope that, as a human being, my effort to become better, more spiritual, the drive to rise above the constant swings of daily life in the world, are not in vain. I do not yet know where I will end up spiritually, or how high I will go. But whatever my spiritual destination, I'd like the journey to be recorded—for my boys."

In two 490-mile round trips, the Pehrsons moved from the casita in Placitas near Albuquerque to a remote rental house in Crestone, Colorado where they had visited the previous January. They had set up housekeeping for their winter retreat by the middle of the month after visiting Joseph and Carolyn for their annual Medicine Ceremony. Housekeeping at 9,000 feet that requires kindling for a kiva fireplace, a seven-mile drive to dump garbage, and a 115-mile round trip to Alamosa for groceries is not exactly luxury. On the organizational side, there were still communications to initiate and responses to make, and dance plans to put into motion. John noted, "This relaxation can be a tense business if you don't approach it right."

Crestone, with a population of around 900, consisted of a real estate office, a post office, and a combination hardware-convenience store, and not much more. The area had attracted Hindu, Buddhist, Christian, Shinto, and Native American practitioners who had erected retreat centers, shrines, temples, and churches. The Pehrsons' rental was 7.5 miles south of town toward the Great Sand Dunes National Monument. A steady San Luis Valley wind in the high desert over a millennia of time had blown up a huge mountain of sand against the Sangre de Cristo heights. It was a natural wonder that had to be seen to be believed. Pueblo Indians considered the great dune a sacred place guarded by a Great Being.

For the winter months, with the help of friend and realtor Wooddora Eisenhauer, the Pehrsons got a great deal on the rental of the two-bedroom house. It was a beautiful adobe structure with walls constructed of rubber tires filled with insulating lava rock and then covered with adobe mud. The north side was dug into the hillside and the roof covered with dirt. Inside, sixteen pine vegas supported the roof, and south side windows and radiant heat under a painted concrete floor kept the house comfortable even in below-zero outside temperatures.

Television delivered the world news, and they watched U. S. President George Bush deliver his second State of the Union address that sounded to them very much like a declaration of war on Iraq. On the 1st of February, the U. S. space shuttle *Columbia* exploded on re-entry over Texas with the loss of its seven crewmembers. Jenny, an airline pilot who had aspirations to be an astronaut, telephoned them in Crestone with the news.

At Joseph's invitation, the couple traveled the next day to the Picuris Pueblo to witness a Deer Dance. The tribal dancers were wearing the same gender energy belts that had been given to them through Sally Perry. Later in the week John had a dream that Joseph interpreted as the Tiwa teaching about the relationship between existence and the stoppage of breath. The Tiwa of Picuris, he told John, came originally from under Sand Lake, the San Luis Valley.

On nights after the Deer Dance, John's sleep was interrupted by an involuntary stoppage of breath that awoke Jeanne. She was concerned about the high altitude of Crestone and its effects on John's heart. The recurrence of this very uncomfortable condition lasted for about two weeks. In retrospect, John thought that the period might have been one of integration as a result of Joseph's teaching about the Tiwa use of breath control. John's spiritual process was often internal. He compared it to a plant that appeared not to be growing on the surface, while in actuality, its root system was rapidly expanding.

The world news remained a daily test for both Jeanne and John to refrain from judgment. Great experiments in mass coordinated prayers for peace seemed to have failed as events moved closer to war in Iraq and a dangerous confrontation in North Korea. Each onslaught of impending violence and ongoing tragedy required the two peacemakers to re-seek their center. The circumstances of conflict were insane, so where was there sanity and hope? Isolated in a remote part of southern Colorado, Jeanne and John had to keep the faith of their convictions by holding onto the inner vibration of peace. They could not allow the politics of the mind to separate them from the human potential. This was their role, but it was often a lonely occupation of compassionate tears.

In February, the couple quietly celebrated their 8th wedding anniversary as snow fell outside the hillside adobe house. John's birthday followed two days later, and that event was expected to be low key, too. The next door neighbor, whose residence was connected to the Pehrsons' house by an interior passageway, imposed on John's good nature to come fix her kitchen sink. John was in his lounging clothes—pajama bottoms, turtleneck, and red velour pullover—as he paddled up the connecting stairs. Surprise! Jeanne had done it to him again. There were only five other people at the top of the stairs, but it was a real birthday party with food and gifts. Jeanne's gift was an Ibanez guitar in a soft travel case and a primer of how to play. John had often said that he wanted to learn to play the guitar, so now he had the means.

In a Medicine Ceremony together that week, John felt he got clear guidance. "You are *not* to get caught up in the dramas of the world. Your job is to hold the light equally for all people. You cannot do that if you are immersed in drama because you won't see it."

Near the end of February, the couple drove through some snow to take Jeanne to the Denver airport where she was flying to Seattle for a reunion with Jenny and Jenny's new husband. They had lunch with Jeff, Jeanne's stepbrother, and Judy Franklin before Jeanne's flight, and John then waited for her return with Marcus and Jennilea Ambrester at their home in Longmont near Denver.

The Pehrsons met Marcus and Jennilea at a Sun-Moon Dance when Marcus was living in Knoxville and Jennilea lived in Oklahoma. The younger couple fell in love, married, and moved to Colorado so that Marcus could pursue a master's degree in psychology at the Naropa Institute in Boulder. He would later earn his graduate degree as a transpersonal psychotherapist. Meeting Marcus in his customary clothing of that time might make an observer wonder if he had wandered off a western movie set. At 33, the blue-eyed man with the goatee beard was tall, heavy set, and dressed in indigo dyed jeans, a plaid shirt over a turtleneck, black western boots, and a funky cowboy hat adorned with a horsehair braid, hawk feather, and a U. S. Border Patrol pin. The only sign of his devoted spiritual path was the strip of red prayer cloth tied around the ankle of his right boot.

Jennilea had true grit as well. Although small, with long blonde hair and a humorous view of the world through wire-rimmed glasses, she had a job at a horse rescue shelter that required emotional solidarity and inner toughness. Dealing with an injured horse is not for the timid. John admired the younger couple for their devotion to a sacred path, and he wondered how his life might have been different if he, like them, had come to spiritual awareness in his early thirties.

When Jeanne arrived from her time with Jenny, the Pehrsons returned to Crestone. For their stored archives, John printed out his 2002 journal—all 132 pages—in a small typeface that averaged about 750 words per page, or 99,000 words. Jeanne stayed busy sewing her Chief's dress and carrying on the correspondence related to their dance and workshop schedule. One of their e-mail communications that invited people to their Sun-Moon Dances got into the hands of what can only be described as fundamental Native American purists who deeply resented any non-tribally registered person performing anything that resembled their traditional ceremonies. In this regard, these Native Americans were not unlike their fundamental Christian, Jewish, and Islamic counterparts.

The fact that the Pehrsons' e-mail seemed to place a dollar amount on dance participation outraged Indian people who then began to send angry e-mails at the rate of six or more a day. Some of the denouncers felt it necessary to express their anger day after day. Although Jeanne and John realized that they could never satisfy these critics with reasoned responses, the tone and content of the "hate mail" was disturbing.

How could they explain that the costs of staging a Sun-Moon Dance had to be shared? How could they convince the hate-mail writers that the vital support crew for the dancers was made up of devoted volunteers? How could they make the writers believe that the Sun-Moon Dance was created by a full-blooded Native American as a means of sharing the Indian spiritual experience with *all* people? How could they counter with the fact that the Sun-Moon Dance had never been promoted as an American Indian ceremony? Did fundamental religious Indians believe that only they had purified, fasted, danced, and used fire and smoke in spiritual practice? Did they not believe that all seekers of spiritual guidance had a divine right to create their own ceremonies? What was most important—the form of worship, or the sincere surrender to Spirit? And who has the right to challenge the visions given by Spirit to others? How can anyone expect the intimate practice of their spirituality to be honored if they do not honor the peace-giving practice of others in the human family?

It is not easy to live centered under the abuse of judgment. Evidently, those who had discovered the perceived sins of the Sun-Moon Dance shared it with their personal Indian networks, so the angry e-mails continued from new writers all over the country who knew little or nothing about the long-standing history of Joseph's Sun-Moon Dance. In dealing with the rush to judgment of complete strangers, John noted a Gandhi quote in his journal: "We must *be* the change we wish to see."

Jeanne recalls those difficult days.

"I remember feeling like I'd been raped. I prayed for help, asked for signs. In my dreams I kept seeing (or hearing) wisdom come from Grandpa Dubray or White Buffalo Calf Woman. One morning we awoke to find several feet of snow had fallen. I remember looking out the window in the early morning. What I saw caused me to burst into tears of joy. I quickly got John. What we both saw were white buffalo—hundreds of them—formed from the snow as it lay on the branches of the trees. It was beautiful! We still have photos of this phenomenon.

"When I came to peace with this whole situation, I took all the individual pieces of hate mail, sprinkled tobacco on them with our prayers for the writers, and then burned them."

Joseph himself counseled them that he had been confronted with the same harsh criticism when he envisioned the Sun-Moon Dance in 1983. He told them not to worry because the fundamentalists were exercising themselves as part of a ten-year cycle. In the third week of March, there was an e-mail from a leader of the American Indian Movement (AIM) denouncing them. AIM was considered the enforcement arm of American Indian resistance to cultural interlopers. Such a communication from AIM could easily be interpreted as a threat.

Joseph was prophetic in his mention of a ten-year Indian fundamentalist cycle because Lakota elders, led by Arvol Looking Horse, the 19th generation carrier of the White Buffalo Calf Woman pipe and protector of the seven sacred ceremonies given to the Lakota people, issued a proclamation that *only* Lakota natives can perform ceremonies, participate in the Sun Dance, and carry the Chanupa (pipe). The great Fools Crow had been the Lakota holy man to give the Sun Dance and the pipe to other tribes. Now Arvol Looking Horse and his group seemed to be rescinding that gift, and no outsiders would be invited to the Lakota Sun Dance that year. The Lakota elders council pronouncement sent a shock wave throughout North American Indian tribes that quickly created a theological schism. Thousands of dancers and pipe carriers had to decide who they would follow. The Pehrsons' perceived Sun-Moon Dance faux pas then took a back seat to the much larger separation issue facing Native Americans.

The last weeks of March were spent shuttling between their three separate rental storage units—two in Colorado and one in New Mexico. Seasonal clothing had to be exchanged, artifacts from their travels put away, camping gear for the Sun-Moon Dances packed, and a general sorting out done. How could they know definitively what was where? But before they could hit the highway East, the invasion of Iraq had begun, and the United States was at war.

FOR THE ONE

The Dance Begins

T he genesis of the "For the One" Dance had begun seven years before at the end of September 1996. It was a cold, rainy weekend, and Jeanne and John were doing separate three-day vision quests at the Center for Peace in Seymour. John occupied the Peace-Sound Chamber while Jeanne danced the sixteen directional paths in the open-air arbor. This was the time, previously described, that Jeanne felt ancient spirits singing through her, and she began to give voice to the vowel sounds with spontaneous melodies. The arduous fasting dance thus became a singing dance of spontaneously sung prayers that carried complex vibrational energies that yielded both visions and healing. The physical sign that the singing dance had been heard and felt was the appearance of sixteen hawks who circled Jeanne in the arbor and then followed overhead as she walked out of the arbor meadow uphill to the house as astounded witnesses watched.

Jeanne recalls. "I didn't believe enough in myself to know what I was seeing. Because of the fasting, I became less resistant and found myself being guided by the Ancient Ones with each step and each sound I sang. The dance itself began to unfold like a flower blooming. There was no thought . . . only sound, movement, and wonder."

Although the spontaneous singing of the vowel sounds evolved into Peace Concerts that Jeanne and John would give in Peace-Sound Chambers and other venues around the world, and lead to the recording of musical albums, neither Jeanne nor John had the sacred dance experience to connect these two powerful elements together. That union could come after years of Sun-Moon Dance experiences with John being appointed Dance Chief by Joseph and Jeanne serving as a Moon Mother. In participating in many Sun-Moon Dances on several continents, they both had had a long apprenticeship in both dancing and serving the dancers. As early as 1999, Jeanne was getting visionary guidance to take a "singing dance" to the people. There were, however, reservations. As a Chief, John had a four-year cyclic commitment to the dancers and to his co-chief Steve Citty in their Tennessee Sun-Moon Dance, and now John had established a Sun-Moon Dance in North Carolina. Could John keep his commitments to the Sun-Moon Dance and still support Jeanne in a new dance? And what about Joseph? How would he feel about the new singing dance? Joseph, of course, was not a master teacher who was limited by form.

Jeanne recalls her key encounter with the couple's mentor. "It was during that private ceremony with Joseph in January of 2003 that I suddenly (to my surprise) told him of a vision I had been given, years before, of a singing dance. I had been given every part of the dance except the name. Joseph immediately said, 'For the One.' I asked, 'for the one what?' He said, 'For the One' Dance. That is the name of your dance.'"

The Watersong Peace-Sound Chamber, dance arbor, and sweat lodge in Graham, North Carolina agreed to host and schedule the birth of the "For the One" Dance in April 2003. The same people who had supported Jeanne and John through the establishment of the Sun-Moon Dance there would now honor them and support them into this new dimension. Cheryl Braswell, David Stephenson, Jo Fisher, Dobs, Judith Brooks, Lance Davis, Teresa Hutson, Andy Baxter, Walton Deva, Lori Fendell, and others would be key members of the dance crew. Perry and Jeanne Robinson, Shannon Ray, Steve Citty, Cheryl Patterson, Ula Rae Mynatt, and Margarita DiVita would all add support from the Center for Peace, and Gail Cully would come from Oklahoma.

The Pehrsons drove 2100 miles to arrive in Graham on March 26th. Jo Fisher was their host, as usual. The pre-dance work went on for several days. The women set up the kitchen in "Lance house" and trusted Lance to install the sink before they would have to prepare meals. A winter ice storm had deposited tree branches all over the dance landscape and in the lakeside camping area where dance helpers would erect their tents on the coming weekend, so all that debris had to be removed and burned. John remarked as he fed the large bonfire with cedar branches that he usually singed his eyebrows around such a fire. Soon after his remark, the wind shifted and the flames kissed the right side of his face, singeing his hair and eyebrow. Jo Fisher went to a local mill to pick up two 25-pound bags of stone-ground cornmeal for the ceremonies, and other helpers brought firewood and other necessary supplies. The sage alone that was necessary for smudging occupied a ten-gallon container.

Several pounds of tobacco also had to be made available. Then there were the sheets and towels to launder and fold and bring to the dance site. Some preparations were slowed by an end-of-March rain, sleet, and snow day.

The very first "For the One" Dance proved to be very powerful for everyone involved—dancers and crew alike. When the three-day event was over, the couple believed that the dancers had come into vision and healing in less time than required in the Sun-Moon Dance. This belief raised a dilemma for both of them, but especially for John as the North Carolina Sun-Moon Dance Chief. Should they do the Sun-Moon Dance in September as planned, or switch to the new "For the One" Dance?

Jeanne wrote directly to Joseph for guidance with an account of what had occurred.

"Dearest Joseph,

First, thank you for your prayers in support of the 'For the One' Dance this past weekend. Joseph, this dance was (is) truly something that I'm still groping for words to describe. And I think that if you had not encouraged me to do the Sun-Moon Dance years ago, I would not even be able to find the few words I do have, to offer to you just now.

As the dancers danced to the pole, singing the spontaneous songs that moved through them, there were so many signs and miracles that took place, that it would be nearly impossible for the most unaware person not to be aware that something extraordinary took place.

Physical signs:

1. A perfectly shaped heart, the size of your hand, being born out of a stone person in the sweat lodge fire;

2. A perfectly shaped heart, the size of a large dinner plate, being born out of the cornmeal and tobacco prayers placed on the drum at the first beat of the drum during one of the rounds;

3. The huge perfectly shaped rainbow ring around the sun through which a hawk flew during one of the moments in the dance;

4. The birds of all kinds who kept appearing in groups of five (eagles, hawks, geese, pigeons, etc.) which we saw as the five vowel sounds permeating the songs being created by the dancers . . .

Joseph, it was magic!!!! And the drums included the People's drum (Pow-Wow drum), the African drums and all the rattles and sounds that were given as support for the dancers in their creation. It was so, so powerful.

There was another sign. We had 13 dancers. In the Hebrew tradition, this equals 'the One.' I didn't know this until we began and one of the Israelis told us. And since this was 'For the One,' the number of dancers for this first dance was perfect!!! (Among the dancers there was a 92-year-old beautiful black woman . . . what a blessing she was!!)

Here is what both John and I are wondering, and we truly need your help on this one. We're each beginning to wonder if this dance is the next level beyond the Sun-Moon Dance . . . more accurately, is this the next stage?? The Sun-Moon Dance seems to have been a springboard for this dance, and what we've learned from the dancers who have written us after the dance is that the singing to the pole moves them more quickly into a state of remembering they themselves are the hollow bones. We need your wisdom on this Joseph, as we are now wondering whether or not we are to continue with the Sun-Moon Dance or allow this new 'For the One' Dance to move into its place, with the Sun-Moon Dance having acted as the springboard and birthing channel for this new dance??

Here is what I had forgotten. I did this dance, Joseph, in 1996, right after doing the vision quest in the Bernalillo Chamber and my first Sun-Moon Dance. In fact, it was in the Sun-Moon Dance that I was told to return to the arbor and begin a dance of 16 paths, from which the spontaneous sounds were born. It was at this time that I actually was given the energy for this new "For the One" Dance, but it wasn't until four years ago in a ceremony that the actual vision of the dance came into my outer consciousness. I'm so slow and so thick sometimes!!! It has taken seven years of gestation for all of what was given me in the beginning to surface.

The physical time of the dance itself is only 2 days . . . plus the time required from the beginning sweat on Friday night when the fast begins. The physical act of dancing to the pole begins at dawn Saturday morning (after another sweat) and ends close to sunset on Sunday. So the time of the dance itself moves faster.

I don't presume that this dance should be done instead of the Sun-Moon Dance, but I am wondering (as is John, who will write his own letter to you) if this dance is the child of the Sun-Moon Dance and has been given at this time to move the masses at a pace that is in alignment with the changes that are now here. (I don't forget for one moment that we don't exist in the way we think we do [you've taught us well!], and what this dance seems to do is help us remember just that).

Please help us, Joseph, with your insights. We want to do the right thing here, and you are our dear friend and teacher. Is there a place for the Sun-Moon Dance for us now? Or are we to let it go and allow this new one to come forth instead?

Through all of this, both John and I've experienced your presence, your support and your love. You always seem to be there for us . . . You're a beautiful manifestation of Spirit. We love you deeply!

Much love,
Jeanne"

Joseph responded in his usual right-to-the-point style.

"Dear Jeanne,

"Thank you for sharing your experiences with your dance. If you do not want to do the Sun/Moon Dance, it's OK with me. Just know that whatever you do will be all right with me. I am your friend, and I just work here.

With blessings,
Joseph"

John then sent Joseph his observations and his concerns about his role in the new dance:

"Hello, my friend. Thanks for your note in response to Jeanne's comments about the dances. I anticipated your response, perhaps because it really is a question that we must wrestle with, pray about, and allow ourselves to be guided on.

Thanks for your patience in allowing us to 'process' this question with you. Putting it in writing helps to crystallize the thoughts in a coherent way.

Jeanne accurately shared the issue that has come out of her new 'For the One' Dance. But, there are a few aspects of our dialogue that might be helpful to also describe. So, I thought it might be good to 'weigh in' personally about the dilemma that Spirit is so wonderfully presenting to us (and especially to me).

There is no question that the merging of the spontaneous songs using the vowel sounds with the movement of the dance accelerates the process. Of the 13 dancers, five had previously done the Sun-Moon Dance. The consensus of these dancers was that the singing helped them move more quickly out of their 'head' and into an altered space in which issues came up, got processed, and were cleared quickly. There was less thinking. Although nobody ran up and 'hit' the pole, all but three of the dancers had a transformative experience at the pole that left them in vision on the ground. Very powerful, indeed. Of the three, one was almost 92, one was 71, and the other was very much overweight and legally blind. For this last one, she was amazed that she finished the dance—and with more strength than she started with.

I also got to try out the role of 'Sun Father' . . . the male version of Moon-Mother, as Jeanne stepped into her power as Leader/Chief.

Anyway, it was the results of the dance that was the catalyst for us to speculate that this dance might be 'the next level,' as presumptuous as that sounds in my own ears.

So, what to do about the Sun-Moon Dance in September? I've led two so far. I've got dancers who are two years into their cycle of Sun-Moon Dances and are looking forward to dancing it here again. Another factor is this, and may be just my "ego" stuff. As much as I enjoyed the role of Sun-Father, I know that I also enjoy the role of Chief. One dancer from Israel even told me how powerful it was to experience the double-paradigm shift of Jeanne as Chief and me as the nurturer. While I don't view this new role as less important than Chief, it is different, more intimately connected with the dancers' process but less involved with orchestrating the overall ceremony. So, I'm wrestling with giving up that role if we transition to doing the 'For the One' Dance. It is not yet clear to me what the correct course of action is.

In keeping with your expressed desire for each dance chief to take responsibility for their dance, I actually see possibilities for integrating some of what we learned in the FTO Dance into the 4-day SMD—using whistles sometimes and spontaneous songs at other times, for instance. On the other hand, it would no longer be a Sun-Moon Dance like you did with us. Neither would it be a 'For the One' Dance. Still, you never chiefed the dance quite the same way twice, and always told us not to get stuck in form.

Anyway, these are the other aspects of the dialogue that is going on between Jeanne and me. I'm not asking for guidance unless you feel moved to provide it. I have a sense that this is something we must puzzle through with Spirit. Isn't that the ancient way? If we really are listening to Spirit in the present moment, the past and the future guide us equally. Then, one form builds upon another to create something new, as you did with the dances.

It is enough to know that whatever we decide is OK with you.

Hugs to Carolyn. We miss you both.

> Much love and blessings,
> John"

Joseph responded to John not only as a wisdom keeper, but also as a friend.

"Dear John,

Thanks for your email.

All dances stand on their own - one isn't better or worse than another. Sun-ness is a principal idea as is Moon-ness. There is no 'better than' in the universe of ideas except here on this plane because we have the gift or curse of judgment-ness. Judgment may lead to unhappiness and dis-ease.

People will have more physical power after a dance no matter what kind it is. Why? I think it happens because of the fasting combination with movement of the physical body. I'm not sure.

I hope I'm making sense, anyway lots of love always.

With blessings,
Joseph"

There were important differences between the "For the One" Dance and the Sun-Moon Dance. As the FTOD rapidly evolved, it presented itself in new elements. First, it was a singing dance, of course, but the FTOD had two Dance Chiefs that were specified male and female. There were also to be two Firekeepers, male and female. Other different elements included two sacred fires instead of one, the placement of a water bowl between the center pole and the arbor fire, and the active participation of Dog Soldiers, Elders, and other helpers outside the arbor who played rattles, sang, and danced in-place to energize the dancers. Thus, the FTOD was not a change in form from the Sun-Moon Dance, but a new dance whose purpose was not merely vision, but profound healing.

While at Graham for the FTOD, the Watersong Chamber was used again for the recording of a second CD. The album was titled *For The One*, and it utilized cover art by Joseph Rael that was inspired by a vision Jeanne had of corn kernels on an ear of corn that were colored yellow, white, blue, and red and had facial features. The "Corn Being" with its rainbow colors represented all people, all life. The album was intended to be a story of Creation, and it began with 92-year-old elder Georgia Stone singing a gospel sounding spiritual "Prayin' Time." The remainder of the individual songs were of the spontaneous vowel-sound type with the addition of rattles, drums, flute, didgeridoo, violin, and viola. Jeanne and John were augmented by the talents of David Stephenson, Cheryl Braswell, Georgia Stone, Minda Bernstein, Blaise Kielar, Grant Freeman, and Judith Brooks. In-Chamber support was provided by Anael Harpaz from Israel, and Paul Middleton-Androsov from Wales. James Lee from Durham did the recording, mixing, and mastering.

The end of the recording session came intuitively to Jeanne and the others. "It's a good thing," James Lee said. "There are 74 minutes allotted on a CD, and you just recorded 73 minutes and 45 seconds!"

The Pehrsons stayed with Jo Fisher until April 24th when she drove them to Greensboro for their flight to New York. They had packed for their trip to Israel and loaded everything else into Mickey-G, their 1999 Pathfinder that would remain parked under the trees at Graham for the next seven weeks. After all the expenses were paid for staging the FTOD, the event was slightly below break-even. Ironic, considering all the abuse they had taken in previous months from Native American fundamentalists who accused them of selling ceremonial dances for profit.

PREPARING FOR THE DANCE

The decision to dance or to serve the dance is a serious commitment. The logistics to produce the dance takes months of planning; and for new sites where a dance arbor and sweat lodge must be constructed and a kitchen established, the advance team (who are often volunteers) normally arrive on site ten days or more before the dancers appear. For many dances in remote environs, the support crew must live in tents and bear the weather like the dancers.

For those keeping the fires, the labor is intensive as massive stocks of wood are needed for the sweat lodge and the fire at the arbor. Since the fires must be maintained around the clock, Firekeepers do not get much sleep. Dog Soldiers keep the fires during their night watch, so their sleep is interrupted, too. Everyone supporting the dancers is up at dawn, and they are not free to rest until the dancers are secure for the night.

Aside from the demanding physical aspects of supporting the Dance, the spiritual requirements are even greater. It is obvious that the Dance Chief and the Moon Mothers and the Sun Father must be centered in the crucial roles that they play in the arbor. They channel their energies to the dancers, and in very real terms, they minister to them. Their work directs the flow of the arbor's vibratory energy in its pace and intensity while they maintain total conscious awareness of what is occurring in the energy fields of each dancer. The Moon Mothers and the Sun Fathers have a high calling as counselors and protectors of the dancers. These counselors have danced themselves many times, and thus they have a deep appreciation for what is endured and experienced within the arbor. In apprenticeship, they develop the talents of a psychotherapist, but in their awareness of the metaphysical journey, they see beyond the limited mind-body dimension. What occurs in the dance is both dynamic and emotional for everyone, and yet the Chief and the arbor counselors must maintain a high degree of self-control that serves the dancers with a dedicated sense of conscious awareness of the total process.

The Drummers, who also sing, are the heartbeat of the dance. Drumming for a FTOD requires both spiritual awareness and performance endurance. They are aware as much as anyone of the dance intensity, for in taking their beat cues from the Dance Chief, they contribute directly to the energy buildup. Dog Soldiers, standing in service outside the arbor gate, get directly involved, too. Jeanne often turns to the Dog Soldiers and asks them to play specific rattles from her collection, which lie on a blanket positioned at the side of the gate. The author's experience as a Dog Soldier was that in the raised energy levels of the dance, the rattles were playing him, sometimes spontaneously for hours in succession. And at the height of the dance, all six Dog Soldiers, and the two Firekeepers as well, were lined up across the arbor gate with sacred rattles and striking sticks beating in time with the rapid drum. Their energy, total and unselfish, was pouring through the gate onto the dancers, and their faces were transfixed with huge smiles as they experienced the oneness that the dance engenders.

Strangely, after the dance, when there should have been exhaustion, there was only elation. The dancers, after being given water and food, appeared at the giveaway and sharing session with a noticeable glow. Everyone including the kitchen crew sat in the sharing circle, but it was easy to pick out those who had been the dancers. They seemed transfigured in countenance like figures who appear in the sixteenth century liturgical paintings of Botticelli and Michelangelo.

There are some basic documents that the FTOD coordinators send to dancers, dance support individuals, and to Dog Soldiers. Reviewing these basics gives an idea of what to expect. In addition, all dancers, dance supporters, and even volunteer dance crewmembers are asked to sign a liability release. This detail is a necessary legal precaution, or the expense of sponsoring the dance would be prohibitive due to insurance costs.

The Pulitzer Prize (1954) winning American poet Theodore Roethke understood that his best poetry could not be explained, only experienced intuitively. In a 1950 "Open Letter" he advised his readers, "You will have no trouble if you approach these poems as a child would, naively, with your whole being awake, your faculties loose and alert." This same advice would also serve those who would attempt to understand the meaning of the "For The One" Dance. It is not to be explained, but experienced, if it is to be understood.

Being "The One"

Every serious individual has the potential to be "the one" for somebody else in need. Most of us have had that experience of being present at some key moment of someone else's life where we sit knee to knee, eye to eye; and coming out of self, forgetting self, we give wonderful gifts. And then that person might say to us, "You're the one. You're the one who brought me this insight, brought me this love, brought me this forgiveness." We all are capable of that experience, but to live in that selfless awareness continually is a level of existence that most people have not yet achieved.

Jeanne talks about living as the unseparated One.

"What I have come to realize with great clarity is that whatever levels of me exist, there is just a single consciousness here, so therefore whatever I perceive as outside of me is really inside. This is now becoming a very active experience. On another level, I'm realizing that my responsibility is to create whatever space is necessary to recognize anyone coming into that space as 'the one.' That is why at the concluding ritual of the 'For The One' Dance, I wash the feet of the dancers to honor them as Masters. This is at the heart of our work. We reflect back to them who they really are, that each of us is Divine at the soul level, that each of us is the Creator. All this is true because there is not the many; there is just the One.

"Maybe I am the greatest student of the dance. Maybe the dance occurs so that I can remember who I really am, and all of the dancers are my teachers. Often, I am the observer of myself; and in the choices of my life, my doubts, my fears, my errors, I can have complete empathy with the other parts of Self that I encounter. No one is apart from me; no one is separate in the wholeness of Creation. This is the experience of the 'For The One' Dance. This is the experience of bliss. And when we cry, these are tears of release and joy."

End of the Movie

One of the amazing aspects of the "For the One" Dance is that every dancer, every supporter, from Kitchen Angel to Dog Soldier, has a movie-worthy personal story to share. Old and young, male and female, from far distant cultural patterns, each journey to the One is the essence of the human drama. Each traveler has had to overcome sometimes dangerous obstacles and had to endure sometimes incapacitating fears and doubts about their purpose even to exist. When seekers summon the courage to come to the Dance, however, they subconsciously accept that they enter an elemental space where vulnerability and strength are measured in equal moments. No riches or status or knowledge can protect them once they enter the circle where all are equally sacred and all are equally worthy of love. The test of endurance then is to drop all vestiges of the separate self that social conditioning has built as the ultimate illusion. In the long hours of commitment, the layers of false identity are shed like invisible skins until the center of being is experienced in the brightness of pure soul. Oh, then how the face shows bliss. Oh, then how the body knows no thirst or hunger. Oh, then how peace and joy abide.

This then is the end of the movie for every star who acts in their own drama of life. The plot may be an action adventure, a love story, a thriller, or perhaps a detour into science fiction or even horror, but always, always, a happy ending is assured. And having already seen the end of the movie, as the observers of our own dramas, we need no longer suffer stress or fear for the heroes we see on the screen, and we need not judge or condemn the plot villains who appear to torment them. We know how it all ends. Everyone comes to love. Everyone participates in the end of separation, and in the recognition of the One, we live together happy ever after. Happiness is thus a state of being, the natural state of being. Unhappiness is then the altered state, the false face of separation that creates conflict between classes, cultures, religions, and institutions. Cheer up! Put on a happy face. Don't get caught up in the drama of the movie of your life. Flash forward to the reassurance of the happy ending. For a growing number of people, the "For the One" Dance is a method, a vehicle, for the flash forward. The end of the Dance reveals the end of the individual's movie.

While Jeanne agrees that a happy ending is assured for everyone, she wants dancers to know that the enlightenment of healing separation does not always happen quickly, even with the "For the One" Dance. Dancers mostly leave the dance feeling happy and connected with Divinity. They also have a new vision, and they definitely feel lighter from having let go of a ton of disabling stuff. But Jeanne realizes that this is just the beginning of a process that changes their lives, and often this shift of consciousness is uncomfortable and even painful.

METAMORPHOSIS IN ISRAEL

The Pehrson's fifth trip to Israel was another expansion of their growing network of supportive friends who had honored them as spiritual leaders and, in some cases, as spiritual mentors. In early

May of 2003, it was neither easy nor wise to go to the Palestinian village of 12,000 that is the Mount of Olives; but at the invitation of Ibrahim Abu El Hawa and his wife Naima, whom they had met on the previous trip, the American couple came to the place well known to Christians. It was on the Mount of Olives that Jesus came to teach and pray with his disciples, and where he was betrayed by Judas and taken as a prisoner of Roman soldiers. At 61, Ibrahim was a community leader with sons and daughters and fifteen grandchildren still residing at the Mount of Olives.

On a walking tour of the village, their host took them to the garden of Gethsemane and to a Russian Orthodox church that marked the place where the historic Jesus taught his disciples what has come to be called "The Lord's Prayer." The prayer had been translated for viewing at the church in many languages including Cherokee and Ojibway, American Indian languages. At a Greek church amid a landscape of olive trees, Ibrahim pointed out that most of the caretakers of Christian church grounds were Muslims. Another stop was at an orphanage run by Polish nuns, the Sisters of Elizabeth, called the Home of Peace. Forty orphaned children, aged 3 to 17, lived there. Ibrahim's generosity to Jeanne and John also included the use of a mobile phone while they were in Israel.

On Jewish Memorial Day, the Pehrsons rented a car and went with Ibrahim to Hamakom near the Dead Sea for a gathering of about sixty Israelis and Palestinians who met to find the common ground for peace. Painful stories were shared with great emotion, and tears flowed on both sides. Then the people ate a shared picnic. Ibrahim had brought ten bags of flatbread, some 100 large pieces. After the meal, Jeanne was prepared to do a Pipe Ceremony and to talk about the permanently joined pipe as the sign that the time of separation is over. The Pehrsons expected the talk and ceremony to last no more than 45 minutes, but sometimes miracles take longer.

As the pipe was being passed, John began to play the cedar flute, and then Jeanne joined him in a spontaneous song. People next to Jeanne in the circle then began to hum in resonance with her, and within a few minutes, the humming became people singing their own songs. One by one, others joined the singing, and then someone began to accompany them on an African drum, and Rabbi Ehad Ezrakie began playing his acoustical guitar. Suddenly an American Jew named Michele got up to dance. She was then joined by a Palestinian Sufi. Before long, more people joined the dance, and a second, larger drum was heard. The celebration of Jews and Muslims dancing together ultimately included everyone, and it went on for two hours! John wrote in his journal, "There has never been a Pipe Ceremony like it, and probably will never be again. But the pipe worked its magic in healing the separation between these people. It provided a space for them to go deeper. It was a miracle!"

Their schedule of events picked up after Israeli Independence Day with a Peace Concert in Jerusalem and a Power of Sound Workshop in Tel Aviv. Both events were well attended, and the demand for their CD's was more than they had immediately available, so John and Jeanne took orders to be fulfilled before they left Israel.

On the tenth, at lunch in downtown Jerusalem with friend Michael Green, Jeanne excused herself from the table to go the ladies' room. When she returned, her face was white with pain, and she was wet with perspiration. Her diaphragm and intestinal tract had gone into spasms that wracked her in agony. Fearing a heart attack or stroke, an ambulance was called and Jeanne was rushed to the hospital. She vomited en route, which gave her some relief, but as she was being examined in the emergency room, she had another spasm causing intense pain.

Blood work and other tests, however, failed to indicate a cause. It was not a heart attack. So after five hours, Jeanne was released and advised to see an esophageal specialist for further tests. During the emergency, both Michael Green and Victor Barr had come to the hospital to translate if necessary and to offer what help they could. The day that was planned as a restful Shabat turned out to be both exhausting and expensive, considering the ambulance and hospital charges. John had his head up enough to notice the coop-eration between the Israeli Jews and Arabs working at the hospital. On Shabat, at least a third of the staff personnel appeared to be Arab. Wasn't this fact a positive case for community? Why was it never in the news?

Back at the Jerusalem apartment that night, Jeanne reached Owen James in Canada to inquire about her illness. Owen told her that he sensed no physical problems. "You have to learn to live where Sai Baba lives," he told her. "And quickly!" Both Jeanne and John believed that Jeanne's body was responding to the social ten-sions and violence that surrounded them in Israel. Day after day, they were told the personal stories of loss and tragedy. Night after night, they were gripped by the reports of further deaths from vio-lence and exposed to the vibrations of hatred and revenge that bombs and bullets beget. For Jeanne, it was felt as a severe blow to her solar plexus. In another context, the pain might be said to be caused by a psychic attack to her viscera. Psychosomatic or not, the pain was both real and debilitating, and it would not go away.

Despite Jeanne's recurring stomach spasms and John's concern for her, they continued their schedule of workshops and concerts, but they did not accept additional opportunities so that there were days of rest. One exception was the Jerusalem Celebration of Light, a large outdoor festival arranged by Jeff Goldstein for people inter-ested in energy work and healing through such practices as yoga, meditation, chi gung, and reiki. Several hundred people attended the three-day, two-night events in the Jerusalem Forest on the top of Mitzpeh Kerem, and most of them, like Jeanne and John, camped out. The Pehrsons were used to tent living at Sun-Moon Dances, but camping out in Jeanne's condition must have been a hard deci-sion. Nevertheless, the two accepted their roles as featured festival participants. Jeanne did a Peace Pipe Ceremony to begin the event on Thursday night, and then she taught the group spontaneous singing and led the singing circle both Friday and Saturday. John was also asked to address the crowd about their peace mission. Although his remarks were impromptu, they were well received.

By Sunday, Jeanne was in pain again, and John provided a heating pad for her and rubbed frankincense onto her spine. He himself was taking mega-doses of Vitamins C and A to combat an oncoming cold. Because of their combined physical distresses, they cancelled events scheduled for the Negev Desert and Sinai in the coming week. They opted for a low-profile period in the Jerusalem apartment where they could nurse themselves back to health.

An e-mail to Cheryl Braswell, one of the leaders of the Watersong Chamber community in North Carolina, is indicative of what Jeanne and John shared with their intimate friends and supporters. "DB" in the e-mail refers to David Stephenson:

> "Thanks for praying for us. It is a real help. You see, in addition to the 'attacks' that take place here on the physical level (suicide bombings by Palestinians and counterattacks by the Israelis), there are many more unseen psychic attacks taking place.
>
> "We are not yet immune from these attacks, and our bodies are feeling the effects—Jeanne's painful spasms in the diaphragm, and a miserable cold for me. We are being asked to take the next step up in our work, and quickly— to a level where we will be much less affected by these energies.
>
> "Being in Israel at this time is, you might say, the graduate level course in staying in the light while the darkness attempts to distract us. Only love and light are real, and the darkness is really our own unenlightened demons. But, it is easy to get caught in the game and perceive these energies as 'real.' Hence, the pain and discomfort in our bodies right now.
>
> "So as we step up to this new level, your prayers help give us a much-needed energy boost. We appreciate you,

and DB, and the Watersong Community. Please keep the prayers and energy coming in any way that you feel drawn.

"We don't make this request lightly because we know the seriousness with which you will receive it. So, in all the ways that it is possible to communicate, we say 'thank you' for your love and support. It helps more than we can say with words.

> Much love,
> John (and Jeanne)"

At a workshop at the home of Sarah Paz and a concert that followed, Jeanne performed through "bearable" pain, but then had to make a quick retreat to vomit. Sarah, still considered a gifted healer at age 85, worked on Jeanne until she was finally able to sleep. But by six the next morning Jeanne was awake and in misery. She had not eaten a full meal for days, and now even weak tea with honey and dry toast would not stay down. And neither would pain medications. John finally got Jeanne back to their Jerusalem basement apartment in a borrowed car. Jeanne entered like a zombie and fell on the bed, too weak to remove her clothes.

It was days before Jeanne ventured out, and then it was to the large open-air Mehane Yehuda Market called the "souk" near their borrowed apartment. The souk was a world bazaar that offered everything: fresh produce off the farm, fish from the Mediterranean, fruits, nuts, and olives in amazing variety, baked goods, luggage shops, pharmacies, CD shops blaring Middle Eastern music, clothing stalls that included sexy bras and panties, sports equipment, and prepared take-away food items. Some shops had corrugated metal front doors that could be rolled down at closing time or in case of emergency. Jeanne and John came to the market for survival items: candles, pain medication, bread, crackers, rice, humus, tahini, dried fruit, salted almonds, and the vegetable ingredients for a soup. The crowded marketplace reflected the multinational nature of Israel, and many languages could be heard as they walked throughout the sensory extravaganza of sights, sounds, and smells. Perhaps it was the threat of recent bombings in public places that caused the vendors to be so curt in their transactions. The Pehrsons mostly encountered an attitude that seemed to say, "So hurry up and get on with it!" And although there were young military guards screening people who entered the souk, the casualness that might have once existed there was absent in the body language of the crowds. Shopping the souk or anywhere else in Jerusalem was no longer a casual affair.

Their last day in Jerusalem, the couple did a presentation at Olam Qatan, Yaqub's bookstore, where they had appeared on a previous trip.

Jeanne, dressed in ceremonial regalia, did most of the talking, and there was great interest from the audience in Native American metaphysics. The bookstore owner, Yaqub, had previously attended their Living in the Moment Workshop, and he told them that the experience had led him to seek a larger space for his bookstore and to offer more transformational teaching there. It was, he said, a turning point in his life.

After a concert in Tel Aviv, the couple headed north to Rosh Pina to keep their appointments with Anael Harpaz who had been with them in North Carolina for the birth of the "For the One" Dance and the recording of the *For The One* CD. Anael wanted to bring the "For the One" Dance to Israel, and she had some locations in mind that she wanted to show to Jeanne and John. In Rosh Pina, they did a concert for a very appreciative Russian spiritual study group. Several members of the audience said, "I love you" to them after the concert, and one Russian woman named Elena offered to arrange visas for them to come to Moscow for concerts and workshops. Another day was devoted to giving a Living in the Moment Workshop. Women who had attended the Sound Workshop the previous year came back; and one of them, Rhonda

Factor, would later come to dance the "For the One" Dance and then serve the dance in the United States and other sites.

The day after the workshop, Anael took the Pehrsons to two prospective sites for an Israel "For the One" Dance. One was a kibbutz where Anael had lived for four years (1992-1996) named Kefar Hanassi, and another was a private parcel of land. The private site felt perfect to the couple, and John took twenty photographs to document it for further consideration.

It is important to note that throughout their travels, both Jeanne and John were available for personal counseling sessions to anyone in need. In some cases, a person was in crisis. In others, the person wanted access to a deeper spiritual guidance that would give them answers to the questions of relationship or to their life's purpose. Often these personal ministry relationships went on for years and resulted in life-changing realizations and new directions. These relationships were also essential in the bonding of a spiritual network that was not subject to co-dependency, but to the individual's achievement of spiritual maturity. For example, men and women of all ages and cultural orientations, stepped up to roles in the "For the One" Dance after a rigorous self-examination and spiritual apprenticeship. In serving the Dance and what it represented, the individual's process was complete when the ceremony became not so much about one's own needs, but about the needs of others that extended to all life everywhere. This then was the enlightenment that all spiritual methods hoped to achieve—the ultimate release, the ultimate freedom from the small sense of self to the Sacred Spirit that animates All.

This was Jeanne and John's personal process and one that they could share on an intimate basis with great compassion and insight because they had trod every step along that path themselves. And the scope of their journey as individuals and as a complex couple was real life with all its mistakes and family complications. They had not evolved their faith as ascetics in austerity. No, they had excelled in the material world, been married, had children, been divorced.

They were not withdrawn from us . . . they were us. Christian or Jew or Islamic or Hindu, the cultural identifications melt away in the common experiences of marriage and parenthood and an attempt to understand the meaning and purpose of our lives, no matter the circumstances. How do we come to peace within ourselves? That is every individual's question. That is the ultimate human quest regardless of the methods, religious or material, that are applied. What is life's profit if we lose contact with our own souls?

On the 6th of June while Jeanne and John were attempting to give an outdoor concert at a kibbutz where an inadequate sound system and a strong wind made their songs almost inaudible to a restless crowd of about 200, John's son Sean was graduating from art school in Chicago. There had not been enough communication for John and Jeanne to make plans to attend, and Sean was more than disappointed—he was angry. So far away in Israel, there was nothing John could say or do to alleviate the hurt.

Somehow Jeanne would rise to the occasion of their scheduled events in Israel, but afterwards, she would be near collapse and in pain. John wrote in his journal.

"It may be that Jeanne is undergoing a metamorphosis like a caterpillar becoming a butterfly. Perhaps breaking out of the chrysalis is painful as well. At the least, it involves a struggle. My hope is that she will complete this transformation soon. God knows, seeing Jeanne in pain leaves me drained also. More important, unless something changes for the better, we will not be able to continue our work."

Five days before their departure, Jeanne, John, and Anael drove to Tsfat to see Rabbi David Baruch. David, who had become a friend, met them wearing jeans, tee shirt, and a beautiful dark red prayer shawl draped over his head. He seemed to John more vigorous than he had the previous year. For Jeanne's healing, the Rabbi invited them to drink water from a cup engraved with the 72 names of God. Rabbi Baruch also suggested that Jeanne immerse herself in the Jordan River while repeating the Hebrew chant that repeats the names of God, which she did that same day. Jeanne left Tsfat pain free for the first time in 48 hours. The next day she did a workshop that required her to teach for 6.5 hours.

The following two days, Jeanne remained in Rosh Pina while John went with Judy Enteen to visit in the home of Rhonda and Chaim Factor.

Judy is an English teacher who is part of a Shamanic journeying group that included Shelley Ostroff and Daniel Mark. Later in the day they had lunch with Shelley and an English woman named Lucy Nusseibah who headed an organization called Middle East Nonviolence and Democracy. Lucy's husband was a high-ranking moderate Palestinian, and she worked with Palestinian teens and teachers in developing conflict resolution skills. At the end of their sharing, Lucy offered to take the Pehrsons into Palestinian communities and to help them locate a "For the One" Dance site on Palestinian land.

John kept a rendezvous with Jeanne and Anael at Ben Gurion Airport for an overnight flight to JFK in New York via Zurich. Jeanne was still uncomfortable and had had little sleep the previous day, but they both wanted to head for home. En route, they did a financial accounting. The trip of almost seven weeks showed a bottom line deficit of $900 that included the ambulance and hospital expenses. It was a great investment when they considered the new contacts that they had made, plus the offer by Judy Enteen to house sit in August and use her house in Israel as a workshop location. As they crossed the Atlantic Ocean once again, the Pehrsons were already feeling that the Lucy Nusseibah connection to Palestinians and the Judy Enteen offer of a home base was already pulling them back to Israel and the possibility of doing the "For the One" Dance there.

B ack in the States, the Pehrsons recovered their car in Graham; and by the third week of June, they were in Three Rivers, Michigan at the request of Ruth and Vic Eichler to do a Chamber Awakening there. John took the proximity to Chicago to go there and spend a day with sons Ryan and Sean. John attempted to heal Sean's feelings over missing his graduation, and the visit was enjoyable despite the alienation that the boys felt over their father's chosen lifestyle.

In Michigan, Jeanne's thoughts returned to Mackinac Island where she had lived for two years as a music teacher at a small college established by Moral Rearmament (MRA) in conjunction with the Up With People (UWP) program. Although Jeanne's Up with People career was 35 years in the rearview mirror, Mackinac Island was a special place for her, so the couple decided to take two overnight time-out days in an environment where no automobiles were allowed, and transportation was by horse-drawn wagon or carriage. The drive to Mackinac carried them over the St. Ignace suspension bridge that spans the strait between Lake Huron and Lake Michigan. Those two bodies of water, John observed, made the Sea of Galilee look like a pond. They left their car in the Arnold Ferry lot and took the 16-minute catamaran to Mackinac Island. Jeanne was very excited by the prospect of seeing what remained of the Up With People legacy.

That first afternoon, Jeanne found part of what she was looking for in the town's observation tower. A historic display of MRA's roots and accomplishments included pictures of the college and many of the UWP students. There was even a picture of Jeanne supervising the dining room staff. Their accommodations, the Mission Point Resort Hotel, had once been the college, so everywhere Jeanne went, there were happy memories.

On a carriage ride after dinner at the Grand Hotel, where the classic movie *Somewhere In Time* with Christopher Reeve and Jane Seymour was filmed, they met a 1984-85 UWP cast member. It seemed that many former UWP cast members made the pilgrimage to where it all began. The Grand Hotel also hosted an annual reunion of *Somewhere In Time* fans who dressed in turn-of-the-century costumes to recapture what they considered a more civil and romantic time in America. Before the couple left the island, Jeanne found the house where she had lived when she first came in 1967. The older parts of town looked the same, but much had been added to service as many as 40,000 visitors on a single peak-season day. With over 600 horses on the island and an army of street sweepers cleaning up behind them, the faint aroma of manure lingered as a reminder that the good ole days were not exactly as romantic as they seem in the movies.

Reality struck en route from Michigan to North Carolina. Checking his e-mail, John's ex-wife Diana advised him that their son Sean required immediate dental care to save his teeth, and that the ongoing procedures were costing thousands of dollars. The following month John sent the proceeds from a workshop to help with the expenses.

In Graham, Jeanne and John stayed with Cheryl and David to discuss plans for the September dances. It was decided to do the Sun-Moon Dance one weekend to meet their commitments to those dancers, and then offer the "For the One" Dance on the following weekend. David was concerned that it might be too much to ask from the support crew. The setup and recovery from a single dance usually required a full week. To work two dances back to back, well, some people might not be able to handle it. Jeanne left John in Graham to help David rebuild the dance arbor instead of repairing it. They would cut support timbers from the woods and build a more permanent structure. Jeanne had plans to see her son John, Ula Rae in Knoxville, her mother in Martin, and then she wanted some time at the Center for Peace in Seymour.

In addition to the hard physical labor required to reconstruct the dance arbor and maintain the dance grounds and sweat lodge, John assisted in David's weekend vision quest. David, Cheryl, and Walton Deva were going up on the mountain to pray for visionary guidance following an early evening Friday sweat lodge. John and four others kept a 24-hour fire vigil during the Lakota-style vision quest. On the mountain, a helper put stakes into the ground to make the four directions, and then a circle of tobacco prayer ties and cedar shavings was made around the quester to enclose the sacred space where they would remain for the duration. Then, left alone and subject to all the elements of nature without food, water, or fire, each individual offered themselves up for vision. The climb up the mountain to remote places was difficult, and the presence of wild animals like black bears and rattlesnakes was evident. Praying for guidance in the Lakota way requires both courage and endurance.

By the middle of July, Jeanne and John were in Seymour at the home of Cheryl Patterson to prepare for the sixth Sun-Moon Dance at the Center for Peace arbor. John worked with Perry Robinson, Steve Citty, and others on the dance grounds. John calculated that he had mowed, bagged, and dumped two tons of wet grass. There was also a new ramp to build from the house driveway to the basement dance kitchen, and additions to make to a small covered "grandstand" behind the arbor fire pit where supplies could be kept and where dog soldiers could rest under a tin roof.

This Sun-Moon Dance was to be a Chief's Dance, and dancers, including Joseph and his daughter Geraldine, were coming from all over the world for this event. There would ultimately be thirty dancers: Heidi Baur and Felicity arrived from Brazil, Gerd Bjorke from Norway, Stella Longland from Scotland, and two women came from Italy. Neal Sutton and Melinda Taylor had come from Texas, Minisa Crumo Halsey from Oklahoma, Michael Perlman and Joselle Gagliano from Albany, NY, and Diane Jarvi, Dorinda MacAusland, and Selena Britten-Woolf from Massachusetts. Seven members of the CFP community, including Ula Rae, were also dancing. Some dancers were accompanied by supporters who would stay on-site in tents and take their meals with the dance crew.

John served Dance Chief Steve Citty again as Alpha Dog with an experienced crew that included Dennis and Jesse Ogle, Candy Barbee, Teresa Hutson, Cindy Rae Harold, Charles Patterson, Patty Coleman, Andy Baxter, and Kevin Schriver as the "beta" dog. The new man on the team was John's son Alan.

The drummers were led by Cheryl Patterson with Marsha Fountain, Wendy Patterson, and Perry and Jeanne Robinson as beaters on the large bass people's drum. The all-important kitchen was led by Margarita DiVita with two kitchen angels—Jennilea Ambrester and Jeff Kilgore in support.

These participants are named because they reappear often in the process of taking the "For the One" Dance to Israel, South Africa, and Europe. This dance and others like it provided an apprenticeship for future responsibilities.

The dance itself was very hot and very intense. Sunday, fourteen of the thirty dancers collapsed in visionary states. The two Moon Mothers, Brenda Sue Taylor and Nan Citty, were constantly busy recovering fallen dancers with cold, wet towels. Some dancers were removed from the arbor to the recovery tent that was full at times. The Dog Soldiers as sheet-litter bearers were hard pressed as well. Monday afternoon after the dance when the participants were rehydrated, fed, and dressed in dry clothes, everyone gathered in the Peace-Sound Chamber. Joseph reminded them that what they did with their lives affected seven generations, 140 to 150 years. By American Indian standards, the energy that was created in the just-completed dance would unfold for the next generations. Joseph was reinforcing the basic teaching that each individual is responsible for their behavior and their thoughts as well.

Steve asked John to say a few words about spontaneous chanting, and then to lead the group in a chant. John took the opportunity to thank the Center for Peace for introducing Joseph to him and Jeanne and being so important to them in their spiritual

growth. He told the story of how Jeanne had been given spontaneous chanting while on a vision quest in the Center for Peace
dance arbor one cold, rainy morning, and how Ula Rae Mynatt and
Wendy Patterson had witnessed the miracle of the sixteen hawks.
He told them that he and Jeanne had been told by a Rabbi in Israel
that spontaneous chanting had been taught in the prophet's school
2,000 years ago, and that the return of the practice was the fulfillment of prophecy itself. Then the song began, and the Chamber
itself seemed to slip between slices of light into the dimension of the
Divine as the individual songs blended into one voice harmony.

Since the trip to South Africa in October, John had had the
nagging feeling that he had picked up something. It had its physical
manifestations that he first associated with something viral perhaps;
but as fatigue and dark moods became a pattern that he had to battle in order to do his spiritual work, he suspected something more
sinister. Then in the sweat lodge prior to the Sun-Moon Dance,
Brenda Sue looked at John across the fire pit and expressed a hor-
rified surprise. Later she told him that what she had seen was a dark
entity. During the dance, John tried to loose himself from what he
saw as a black, horned and fanged thing about the size of a large
grapefruit with a long tail like a salamander that attached itself to
his solar plexus. Tales from aboriginal Africa abound with the projections of witch doctors who focus harm on the invaders of their
territory. Perhaps a jealous shaman had targeted John for such a
psychic attack. Due to the long after-dance sharing, and four blanket giveaways, it was 7 P.M. before John and Brenda Sue were able
to get together in the Chamber. Brenda Sue had brought a glass of
saltwater and a sacred feather to draw the entity out and drown it.
John thought that he heard a hissing sound (tsss) as the entity hit
the saltwater. Evidently, what comes in by Shamanic means must be
turned out the same way.

The next day John spent time with Alan, and they talked music
and exchanged CD's before going their separate ways. While John
had served the Sun-Moon Dance, Jeanne had remained in Graham

at Jo Fisher's home to recover from her stomach illness. The rest had done wonders for her. When John saw her, she was beaming, fit, and sporting golden blonde hair. They had been apart for ten days, and their reunion brought back all the elements that had attracted them to each other when they first fell in love.

The date for their return to Israel and Palestine was fast approaching, but first they traveled to Mobile, Alabama for a Lane family reunion. The Lanes had been high achievers in the upper-middle-class American tradition. Jeanne's choices since 1993—ten years—were difficult for most of them to understand. John felt that he and Jeanne were seen as oddballs who practiced an impractical and unconventional world view. Political and religious subjects were thus to be avoided in favor of the social convention of "small talk." Jeanne, of course, had the memory lane of family history to walk, so she could be her smiling, effervescent self more easily than John. A day after leaving Mobile, the Pehrsons were in Atlanta for their flight to Tel Aviv via Frankfurt.

INTERMEZZO

W aking up in Mevasseret on the first full day of their sixth trip to Israel, John put the particulars in his journal.

"We are house sitting for Judy and Norman Enteen who are on vacation in the U.S. We spent the morning unpacking and setting up the space to suit us. Having a house to ourselves for a month is an odd feeling. Most people take having their own space for granted. But it is an uncommon luxury for us. So, it is a delight to be able to do little things like completely unpack my suitcase, and take all my stuff out of the shaving kit and set it up in the bathroom.

"Judy is even letting us use her car around town. So, we drove out to do some grocery shopping. Another small delight is that there is a mall with a theater just five minutes from here. Simple pleasures are often the best."

The next day friends began to gather. Victor, who with Hedva Stahl had met the Pehrsons at the airport, and Sharon, with their son Ofek, visited that evening. On Friday a person who will be called Angel for the role that she played in Jeanne and John's spiritual growth, picked them up in her car for dinner. The evening was filled with meaningful conversation, and both Jeanne and John felt a strong connection to Angel. The next evening Angel came for dinner, and two days later, she introduced John to her younger brother, who was the marketing vice president of a high-tech communications software company. The two men had a long lunch together, and John introduced the workplace applications of his workshops in a consulting role.

The Pehrsons continued to expand their contact network. Jeanne met with Sis Levine, wife of Jerry Levine, the CNN correspondent who had been taken hostage by Hezbollah in Lebanon in 1989. The two women discussed a sound workshop for children and teachers in Beit Lehem (Bethlehem). The couple also went with friends to Clil in the far north of Israel near the border with Lebanon. As guests of Dvora Pearlman and Jeff Goldstein, they participated in the Israeli version of Valentine's Day. The group did "a little energy work, a little meditation," and then a lot of dancing to recorded music selected by Jeff and his wife Leah. Hedva Stahl and Anael Harpaz also came for the fun, and little sleep was had by all. The Pehrsons did not get back to their house in Mevasseret until eleven the next morning.

Two days later Jeanne, Angel, and John continued the Israeli Valentine's celebration at the International Cultural Center for Youth on Efek Refaim. It was world music night, and everyone danced the night away. The following day Jeanne was scheduled to make a short trip with Ibrahim to meet the organizer of a free clinic for trauma victims, and John was scheduled to do a workshop. Since

John had no plans for the evening, Jeanne suggested to Angel that they should get together for the evening.

As their light schedule of concerts and workshops progressed, Angel was a frequent companion of the Pehrsons. The three of them were very comfortable with each other, and their mutual experiences in spiritual work made the time together both intellectually stimulating and emotionally fulfilling. Then there came a night after dinner out, when Jeanne and John went to Angel's apartment for dessert and conversation. At some point in their intense dialog, John asked Jeanne if she was willing to "shake" her hands and do an intuitive reading of their friend's past lives in ancient Egypt. Jeanne is a "hand shaker" in an ancient Native American tradition still practiced in the American Southwest by tribes such as the Navajo. Joseph had confirmed Jeanne as a "hand shaker" following a March 1998 Medicine Ceremony performed in the Pehrsons' Placitas home by Taita Paulino. John had not told Jeanne that he had had a vision of Angel as an Egyptian princess, or that Angel had told him in private that one of her guides was Nefertiti, the legendary beautiful wife of Ramses II. Whatever the purpose, Jeanne agreed, and in shaking her hands, she saw and described two past Egyptian lives.

In the first, Angel was dressed in simple but fine, soft clothes. She had a baby, and the baby was John's! But both she and the baby died of famine. The loss of his wife and child drove the past-life John into the priesthood. It was the same past life during which John had been groomed to take leadership of the brotherhood of priests, but he was killed for having a relationship with Jeanne that broke the rules of celibacy. If this past-life reading was not dramatic enough, the second Egyptian lifetime for Angel, as seen by Jeanne, was even more psychologically dangerous. In this incarnation, Jeanne saw Angel as an Egyptian noble woman, possibly Nefertiti, who was in love with a handsome Egyptian soldier in battle dress riding in a chariot. Jeanne said that she sensed that this soldier was John!

Jeanne's reading of Angel had far-reaching effects on her marriage and partnership with John. Whether consciously or subconsciously, it had raised the potential for jealousy in Jeanne. For John, his own vision of a past-life relationship with Angel as an Egyptian princess seemed confirmed, and he could now use it to explain to himself why he was so attracted to her. On another level, neither Jeanne nor John wanted to see their relationship with Angel as anything other than being brought together for a collective purpose—a higher purpose devoid of baser passions. Even the flickering thought of a romantic liaison had to be treated as something woefully unworthy of being considered. It was a test of the ego, and nothing more. To fear it was to accept it as possible, and that was intolerable to both Jeanne and John. They could not push Angel away. What had she done but to include them both in her life and to work for their recognition in the Israeli spiritual community where she was obviously an important role player? So what was there to do but to push the limits of the improbability? Thus, when Jeanne went north to visit Anael, the couple accommodated the practical need to work separately on occasion, and John felt free to spend more time with Angel. Later, he told Jeanne about his stimulating lunch with Angel where she shared her ideas for an experiential presentation on Deep Democracy that she was scheduled to deliver in Paris the following week. John said that Angel was happy to include ideas from his own workshop experiences. Although innocent, it was probably not a good idea to intimate to Jeanne that he and Angel made a good team.

Jeanne had a very difficult next two days. First there was a long and intense healing session with a young woman in the Israeli Army who, at age 18, had been detailed to remove body parts from terrorist bombsites. At 20, she was on medical leave with a cancerous mass in her chest that doctors suspected to be malignant. The session left Jeanne drained. Next, Jeanne learned that a Power of Sound Workshop the previous week had traumatized one of the participants. The report, without any supportive detail, nevertheless shook Jeanne and worked its way into self-doubt. Jeanne was feeling very vulnerable at the next concert and sound workshop, but the very positive feedback from both events helped Jeanne to rebound from a cautious state of mind.

The last two days of this trip were given over to a few private sessions, and John made important contacts with Daniel Kropf and with his co-workers Sharon Rosen and Birgitte Wistranz from Sweden. Sharon was a good friend of Shelley Ostroff, and Birgitte was a former member of the Swedish Parliament and a corporate board member of several organizations. Daniel Kropf is an Italian Jew residing in Israel. He is a successful businessman and entrepreneur and maintains homes in Jerusalem, Tel Aviv, and Trieste in Italy. He has business ventures in Israel, Turkey, and several other countries, but Daniel's passion is spiritual work and education. He is the founder of Universal Education Foundation, an organization devoted to incorporating spirituality into educational systems around the world. He also works to bring Palestinians and Jews together in neutral places such as Italy. His association with Jeanne and John would lead him to dance the "For the One" Dance in North Carolina, Israel, and Norway and to be instrumental in bringing it to Italy in 2007.

John's work with Daniel, Sharon, and Birgitte in Intuitive Imagery "created quite a stir," and John was elevated to star status before their departure. His new friends even arranged for John and Jeanne to receive VIP treatment at the airport.

A day after they got back to Atlanta to pick up their car, their friend Shelley Ostroff e-mailed the couple that she wanted to give them the use of her condominium at the Kruger National Park in South Africa for the week following the Rustlers Valley "For the One" Dance. It was a very thoughtful and welcomed gesture.

The next day Angel contacted them to say that she had renewed her visa to come to the United States to attend the FTOD later that month. John was excited by the idea of welcoming her at the airport.

That same day, Jeanne vomited and cried with abdominal pain. In the afternoon, feeling better, she asked for help to move her bedding to the dance arbor where she planned to do a pipe ceremony and then sleep there overnight. John awoke the next morning to rain; and although Jeanne had said, "This is between me and God. Don't check on me," he took her dry clothes and a raincoat. Despite the tension between them, Jeanne seemed glad to see him. The rain had stopped, and John hugged her and said, "Know that you are loved very deeply." Then he fed the four directional shrines with tobacco and left Jeanne to complete her private vision quest.

At the end of the week, the couple traveled from Graham west on I-40 to Swannanoa to attend the semi-annual International Gathering of Peace-Sound Chambers. Zoe Bryant and her Chamber community had worked months to repair and repaint the large domed Chamber, to fix the deeply rutted uphill gravel road to the wooded site, and to enlarge and prepare a campground below the Chamber for the many Chamber caretakers who would stay on the property during the event. Joseph spoke to the gathering, and Jeanne and John did a concert in the amazing acoustical domed space where a whisper spoken on one side of the curved roof could be heard thirty feet away on the opposite side. Troy Amastar, Teresa Hutson and Patty Coleman played drums, Jeff Goldwasser played didgeridoo, and Cheryl and David from Watersong sang. Tom Bissinger from the Pennsylvania Chamber remembered the concert as "magnificent."

John, in his journal, attempted to document what Joseph had taught them.

"Joseph was inspiring in his talks with the group. He reminded us again that, while the Tiwa-speakers are verb people, we are non-pronoun people. Nouns and pronouns objectify and separate, categorizing reality into persons, places and things. We need to dance to remind ourselves that we are the earth and sky, that there is no separation.

"The Earth is a great being. It eats the energy expended as we put in effort. While we dance, and get ready for the dance, our effort feeds the earth. As technology allows us to do things with less effort, more people are required. So, we have a population explosion. We also have storms and earthquakes of greater and greater intensity because the Earth needs that energy.

"Joseph also said that perceptual reality either expands or contracts, growing or dying. If we are not exploding, we are imploding. If we are not growing spiritually, we are dying. If we don't actively do things to get beyond ourselves and grow to the next level, we atrophy and go into decadence and degradation. We must choose between greatness and degradation.

"Our job is to inspire others. Dancing and chanting/singing are parts of the curriculum but not the objective of the work. They offer ways to achieve connection with our vast selves, our infinite selves so that we understand that there is no separation between God and ourselves. Inspiration is our product."

Back at Graham, while Jeanne was doing a "master cleanse" on a diet of lemonade sweetened with maple syrup and touched with cayenne pepper for the immune system, John, David, Walton, Dobs, Steve Citty, and others were preparing the arbor, sweat lodge, and grounds for the "For the One" Dance. One serious problem was paramount on their minds. Her name was Isabel, and she was a Category 5 hurricane with sustained winds over 160 M.P.H. that could come ashore in North Carolina and demolish the dance. For those like Daniel Kropf and Shelley, who had been inspired to travel from Israel for the dance, the looming hurricane was not auspicious.

In an effort to turn Hurricane Isabel away from North Carolina and protect the dance, Joseph had given the Watersong group a ceremony. On the Monday evening prior to the Friday start of the dance, thirteen people who had begun their day with cornmeal or tobacco prayers gathered in the Chamber. A wind came up, and sprinkles of rain began as the group moved from the Chamber and walked to a ceremonial cedar fire set, but not yet lit, by David in front of the sweat lodge. David sang the fire-building song and lit the fire; and as the group prayed and sang around the open fire, the rain became harder. Lance Davis removed his shirt, and four people held its corners to protect the flames. As the fire turned to ashes, David gathered ashes and put them with "medicine" that Joseph had given them into a sacred deerskin pouch that he had made earlier that day for the ceremony. Then the group, soaking wet, returned to the Chamber where they stood in a circle and took their turns wearing the medicine pouch around their necks and offering their individual prayers. Isabel was honored and asked to alter her path so that no harm would come to the people and that she dissipate in this process. To close the ceremony, the group then sang a spontaneous song of gratitude, and when the song was done, there was silence on the roof as the rain had ended. In the morning, it was reported that Isabel had decreased overnight to a Category 2 storm and was moving away from a landfall that would threaten North Carolina.

In the sweat lodge prior to the dance, John experienced an emotional catharsis. He pleaded with the Old Ones to help him release the pain that he was carrying, and he wept with greater and greater intensity until he screamed into his tee shirt and then vomited into the stone firepit. This catharsis for John was very complex. Much of what he was feeling could be identified, but there were other issues which remained sublimated. Jeanne, too, was experiencing an equally difficult process; and on the Monday after the dance, she cancelled their eight-day Boston tour of concerts and workshops and made plans to return to Cynthia Walker's casita in Placitas, New Mexico.

Angel had expressed interest in meeting Joseph, and so Jeanne and John asked Joseph's permission to include her in a Wah Chi Chi Hu Ceremony planned for them on the 15th and 16th of October. Jeanne, the cheap-ticket expert, went on the Internet to get a flight for Angel on the 13th so that she could rendezvous with them in

Placitas. John observed in his journal, "I am not sure what the reunion with Angel will bring being in close quarters at the casita. But I trust God/Great Spirit in guiding all of us to our highest potential."

WARNING: HIPPOS ROAM FREELY

Jeanne awoke the first morning in Placitas with the same diaphragm and intestinal tract spasms that she had first suffered in Berlin and then again in Israel in May. The attacks were debilitating, and at the height of the pain, Jeanne could barely breathe. Don Alejandro, the Quiche Mayan Elder with whom Jeanne had spent time in Guatemala, was preparing a fire ceremony in the area. Jeanne rushed to the site, changed into ceremonial clothes including a Mayan headdress, and joined the ceremony. John's imaging confirmed his own intuition that he should not accompany her. The message from the fire was that Jeanne's work in the near future was to find her HOPE again.

In a private reading after the fire ceremony, Don Alejandro assured Jeanne that there was a solution to her illness and that she would not die. Her heart was breaking, he said, because someone was coming between her and John. Later, the Mayan Elder told John, "The problem is that you need to earn some money so you can help your health. The two of you are authorities. Have faith in God and in both of you together." Despite Don Alejandro's advice, Jeanne struggled with her centering, and she talked to a close friend about the difference between service and sacrifice. Jeanne realized that her spasmodic pain was the result of an internal struggle, but it was not yet voiced. That did not prevent the tension that existed between Jeanne and John from erupting into heated arguments over often-inconsequential things.

Then on schedule, Angel arrived on the 13th, and the Pehrsons treated her to a day of exploring old Santa Fe with its Native American street vendors, fine art galleries, and shops on the historic square. On the visit to Hesperus, Colorado for the promised ceremony with Joseph, Angel and Joseph made a strong connection on first meeting. John encouraged Joseph to show Angel his artwork, and incredulously, Joseph began giving painting after painting to her—six in all. The Pehrsons had never heard of Joseph doing anything like that before, and later he also gave Angel a turquoise snake necklace and three of his books personally inscribed to her. Four days after her arrival, the couple had a parting dinner prior to the departure of Angel's flight from Denver. Jeanne presented their guest a Cherokee Friendship Bowl that she had gotten from the Cherokee headquarters in Oklahoma to symbolize the deeper level of friendship between them.

From the Denver airport, the Pehrsons drove directly to Fraser, Colorado where Jeanne's stepbrother Jeff Franklin and wife Judy, and their children Tyler (14) and Emma (11), welcomed them to a house they used as a mountain retreat. The town was only ninety minutes west from Denver and near the Winter Park ski slopes. During the next six days John recorded 49 aphorism entries in his journal. The source for these eclectic bits of advice on relationship had an acerbic bias. Witness some of their authors: Oscar Wilde, James Thurber, Mark Twain, Will Rogers, Oscar Levant, and Woody Allen. John noted, "I am aware that the quotes that I have been attracted to over the past few days say something about my own state of mind." The final quote was perhaps the most serious. It was from Heraclitus, written in the 6th century B.C. "Opposition brings together, and from discord comes perfect harmony."

Jeanne was not feeling safe in her relationship with John, and it was a difficult period to work through. At one point she told John that Spirit was not going to allow them to break apart because of what they were carrying together. They took long walks together and soaked in the hot tub together. They also played chess. Day by day their comfort zone of being together was restored. In a Cyrus reading by Sue Mehrtens long distance from Waterbury, Vermont, they were not encouraged to re-enter the business world, and Jeanne was advised to take a personal retreat during the coming winter in a warm climate close to the U.S. like Mexico or the Caribbean. Relationship issues were dealt with only in a very general way by saying that Jeanne and John's relationship was "growth provoking."

Near the end of October, Jeanne took the car for a visit with Julie Maynard, a long-time friend from their association in the World Business Academy. Jeanne had at one time been the International Coordinator for all WBA chapters worldwide, and John had started the New York City chapter and helped to organize the Washington, D.C. chapter in 1990. Julie's ex-husband, Herman, was an ex-DuPont peer of John's and a founding member of the WBA. It was Herman who had invited both Jeanne and John to the Avatar Course in Tulum, Mexico, where they first got together as a couple, and he also introduced John to Magaly Rodriguez Mossman, an important link in the development of John's interest and proficiency in Intuitive Imagery. Julie was an intimate witness to Jeanne and John's early years together.

On her way to Julie's, Jeanne had accelerated to about 75 M.P.H. to pass a large truck when one of her rear tires blew out. The trucker, seeing her emergency, sped up to give her the entire road, and Jeanne was able to bring the car safely to the shoulder of the interstate highway. Four other truckers stopped to help Jeanne change the tire. The first one Jeanne saw as Archangel Michael, the answer to a prayer. The man's name turned out to be Michael; and when the spare tire was on the car, and Jeanne thanked him, he replied as only an angel would, "That's okay. It's what the Lord put me here to do."

In Denver the next day, Jeanne had to replace all four overworn tires and the front-end struts. The loads that they carried cross-country were hard on tires, struts, and shocks. Jeanne shopped for the best deal and the best repair shop attitude and got the tires and the front-end repairs done for a price that a North Carolina shop wanted for only the front-end work alone. When John heard the news, he told Jeanne that she had pulled off a financial miracle in addition to the highway one. Now the Pathfinder was fit for the coming year of service.

On the last day of October, John spent some personal time with Joseph at his home near Hesperus and the Southern Ute Indian reservation. Joseph led John into a trance state where John was able to look at issues in his life that were causing him trauma and pain. At the end of the session, Joseph asked John what he thought about Jesus and his mission. John answered that Jesus was a reformer, that he never wanted to create a new religion, that Jesus came to simplify and purify what had been corrupted by the drive for money and power. Joseph noted the parallels in their own work of the current time.

The work of organizing the South African Dance went on by e-mail. On another front, John had a long telephone conversation with Daniel Kropf from Israel about Intuitive Imagery consulting for his companies, but most of the hour was spent on personal imaging. Shelley Ostroff called to re-confirm the use of her timeshare condominium in Kruger National Park for the week following the South African "For the One" Dance. She also planned to attend the dance.

Jeanne was busy with her responsibilities for coordinating the details of the trip to South Africa, but she had to stop in order to clean the house and begin cooking for the arrival of the Franklin family, Jeanne's relatives. John vacuumed and did what he could in support. Weighty concerns involving the day to day counseling of a distraught friend and fund-raising efforts to support dance crew volunteers who needed financial support for airfare to South Africa were also present. As the day of their departure neared, the pressures were constant, and John raced from one storage unit to another to repack the car and put together the practical and ceremonial necessities for the trip that Jeanne had detailed. Finally, on November 11th, they departed from the Denver airport. Jennilea Ambrester went with them to the airport in the Pathfinder so that she could then store it for them at her home in Hygiene, Colorado north of Boulder. John was uncomfortable. In a fall, he chipped a front tooth, and another bottom tooth broke, leaving a jagged filling exposed. There was no time for dental repair.

After a stopover in North Carolina to firm up the dance crew participation from the Watersong Chamber community, the Pehrsons left Raleigh for the flight to South Africa from Atlanta, but they were not allowed on their scheduled flight because of a new passport restriction by South Africa requiring a full, blank passport page for their visitor stamp. John had no such blank page, and the Raleigh ticket agent missed it, so the couple was rerouted to New York where they could go into lower Manhattan to the National Passport Agency and get new pages added. Jodi Brown, who was traveling with them, was left at the Atlanta airport to proceed by herself.

In New York, in a rush to make a late afternoon connection to South Africa, Jeanne and John ran the gauntlet of taxi drivers and impatient bureaucrats. A clerk told them she could not read the dates on their flight itinerary and thus would not qualify them for emergency service. She demanded that they have the airlines fax proof of their tickets before she would serve them. When Jeanne argued for reasonableness, the woman retorted, "We're closed tomorrow. If you want to get out of here today, you'll do what I say." John pulled Jeanne away and she cried tears of pure frustration. When they finally reached a real human being by phone at Delta, the agent said to John, "I wish they'd stop giving out this number. I can't fax you that information due to our security restrictions." Catch 22. Jeanne's solution was to use a black ink pen to gently go over the unclear dates on their copy of the itinerary and present themselves to a different passport examiner. This examiner did not question the itinerary, and he processed the added pages request quickly. John's amended passport came back at 3:05 P.M., and a yellow-cab driver from Senegal, West Africa got them back to JFK in just over an hour in rush hour traffic for their 5:55 P.M. flight.

Jane McGlew met the Pehrsons at the JHB (Johannesburg) Airport and drove them to Credo Mutwa's residence in Naledi outside of Pretoria. The couple had just intended to pay a brief courtesy call on Baba Credo and see him by appointment the following day, but the old Zulu welcomed them and talked with them for almost two hours. John was always reliable in recording the essence of important encounters in his journal. In these two meetings, Credo told them that AIDS was wiping out entire villages in Africa. "All I really ever wanted to be was a green grocer," he told them. His idea was to create a university of self-understanding to help people understand how to eat correctly. The fourth month after physical birth is the "God" month, the magic month, he said. The "God" months calculated to March for Jeanne, and to May for John.

On the 17th, the couple traveled to Rustlers Valley and settled into rondaval #1, one of the little round thatch-roofed hobbit hut accommodations at Frik's mountain valley spiritual retreat center that also served as a permaculture training farm. There was a great deal yet to be done: the selection of a dance site, the construction of the arbor and sweat lodge, toilets to be dug, firewood . . . a thousand details apart from the volunteers needed to get everything in place prior to the dance date. On a trip into Ficksburg with Niyan Stirling to buy construction supplies, John found that the cost of tarps to enclose the arbor was prohibitively expensive. The only solution was to ask Cheryl and Steve to bring tarps from the U.S. in their luggage.

Although Jeanne had bouts of abdominal pain, she stayed busy with organizational details and made a trip with Jodi in a rental car to buy items needed for the recovery tent. John and Niyan spent six-hour days cutting and stripping the bark off trees to make arbor poles. John could not seem to drink enough water to quench his thirst, and he had muscle aches that had to be treated with pain relieving creams every night.

Jeanne went into the Sangoma Valley with Phillipa, Niyan's companion, to visit Gogo Monica and tell her about the "For the One" Dance. Out of respect, she asked permission to hold the dance in the Zulu homeland and then invited the senior sangoma and her twazas (students) to attend.

By the 24th, a week after their arrival, all the arbor poles were blessed with tobacco prayers and set upright in a circle. The next day Jeanne returned from an airport pickup with Steve, Joško Šabiè (from Croatia), and Shelley just in time to see the arbor framework completed. The start of the dance was only four days away, but help was arriving every afternoon to complete the preparations. While Jeanne arranged with Jane for the airport pickup of the remainder of the dance crew, the arbor was being anchored against the wind, and the tarps were going up. Cheryl Braswell, Patty Coleman, Troy Amastar, Sammye Jo Harvey, Anael Harpaz, and Shulamit Urwin arrived in the rain the day before the arbor center pole was placed in an early-morning ceremony.

Both Jeanne and John tried to rest during the day prior to the Friday night start of the dance. Jeanne had mild abdominal spasms, and John was bone tired and suffering from a rib injury incurred in the arbor construction. Neither one of them had had an uninterrupted night's sleep. On Wednesday Jeanne went privately to the arbor to do a Pipe Ceremony. "I prayed for the people and for the dancers and helpers who were called to come that all would happen in a good way. I prayed for the weather that the dancers needed, and I asked the creatures of the land to be gentle with us because we were here because we were called. Foremost, there were prayers of gratitude to the ancestors and prayers asking permission of the ancestors to do the dance. The primary reason for this Pipe Ceremony is to honor the place where we dance with our most sacred prayers."

That Friday, especially, the full weight of chiefing the "For the One" Dance was upon them, and inherent was their responsibility for so many individuals—dancers and crewmembers alike—who had traveled great distances and made many sacrifices to be a part of their vision. But it was much more than duty that Jeanne and John were feeling; it was rather that Spirit now called them into an accounting with regard to their worthiness to lead such a sacred ceremony. Spirit, in effect, humbled them completely with doubts until their only relief was to release themselves to Spirit and do Spirit's will and not their own.

The dance site was a long half-mile walk from the retreat compound out into the valley with the mountains above. The dance area they selected was flat near a river that was shaded by a line of large weeping willow trees. The huge meadowlands that surrounded the arbor was pasture for roaming herds of horses, wildebeests, and a type of antelope called *blesbok*. There were thirteen dancers and the weather was perfect.

Gogo Monica brought three of her twazas to participate in the Pipe Ceremony and the dance. The chief sangoma told her twazas—Florinda, Agnes, and Amy—that the "For the One" Dance was how Africans danced in the old days, and she told Jeanne that, "My ancestors and your ancestors are now working together." She also said that there would be many more dancers participating next year when the Pehrsons returned.

At the dinner table that night after the dance was over, Jeanne told Dom what Monica had said. Dom laughed and said, "You don't have any idea what she was saying, do you?" He went on to explain that the sangoma was referring to spiritual ancestors as well as to the physical participants in the dance. Monica was saying, Dom interpreted, that this "For the One" Dance was the fulfillment of an ancient prophecy that a singing dance would come to South Africa where people of the rainbow would sing and dance as one.

Later, when Jeanne and John reported the dance to Credo Mutwa, he said, "Honorable Ones, never before has such a thing happened in South Africa." That traditional Africans had danced in sacred ceremony with whites from America, Croatia, Israel, and France represented the core ideal that it was possible to end the separation between very divergent cultures. No negotiations and no treaties played a role in the coming together. Every dancer and every crewmember came together as the human family, and they had the real life experience of being loved and accepted in that all-embracing context. No one was excluded from the sacred circle, and thus everyone was honored.

Cheryl Braswell had had a vision that she would arrive in Rustlers Valley in the rain, and she did. She also had seen herself dancing with African women, and that came true as well. Shulamit Urwin said that she received more respect for her tradition than she got from Jews in Israel. She came to dance the "High Shabat" during which old forms fall away. And indeed, they did for this orthodox woman, because by the end of the dance, she was embracing the men in celebration as easily as she was the women. Every participant had their own revelations that would carry them home with a renewed hope for the kind of peace and joy that they had experienced.

On the visit to Credo Mutwa on the Wednesday, December 3rd after the dance, those who could stay in Africa went with Jeanne and John to Naledi. Baba Credo spoke to them at length, and then he did something very generous, and very meaningful. He gave African names to the women. Anael, he named Ilanda (Flamingo). Sammye Jo, he named Nondaba (Daughter of Many Stories). He named Shelley, Juba (Dove), and Cheryl, Tolageli (The Gift That Has Been Found). To Jeanne, Baba Credo gave the name Langa Zana (Little Sun). The name was especially significant since Langa Zana was the name of a great Zulu queen who was reputed to have lived to the age of 200. She was the wife of Shaka

Zulu's father, and she saw four Zulu kings come and go and was an advisor to them all.

The Pehrsons drove Shelley to the airport where she got a rental car for herself. Shelley intended to stay in South Africa for a month more into the new year. After a warm parting, John and Jeanne headed off to Kruger Park on the border with Mozambique to enjoy Shelley's gift of her timeshare condo there. The park offered sights of many wild animals, some grazing along the golf course fairways. A sign in their suite read, "WARNING: Hippos roam freely. Do not walk around after dark. Keep your distance and do not disturb. Kruger Park Lodge accepts no responsibility for any loss due to injury or death." The hippo warning reflected the fact that hippos kill more people each year than any other wild animal in Africa.

One day the Pehrsons drove just over 200 kilometers through the park in their small Toyota Tazz rental. They saw bushbuck, impala, the tall and long-horned kudu antelope, a rhinoceros, several giraffes, monkeys, water buffalo, a family of hyenas, and a lone elephant washing itself in a river, but they saw no hippos or lions. The car, unfortunately, was not air-conditioned, and the heat flowing through the open window felt like it originated from a blast furnace.

Jeanne was quiet during the week; and when she and John sat out on the patio of their chalet after the sun had set and talked about the Rustlers Valley dance, she expressed feelings of insecurity in her role as Dance Chief. Perhaps in their own euphoria following the dance, dancers had not acknowledged Jeanne's role and given her the feedback that she needed. John tried to reassure her with the evidence of success, but Jeanne seemed stuck with doubts about herself.

There were also the uncertainties that they would have to face when they returned to the States. Where would they spend Christmas? Where would Jeanne go for her planned solo retreat, and where would John hole up in the meantime? In a few days, they would travel from the intense heat of an African summer to the snow and cold of an American Southwestern winter; from almost the longest day of the African year to the almost shortest day of the North American year. They would cross so many time zones that their bodies would remain clock confused for weeks to come.

The last two days before their flight to America were spent at Naledi. Jane, property manager and friend, caught the Pehrsons up on the news. In paying their respects to Baba Credo on the last day, the Pehrsons presented him with one of the ceremonial bowls used in the water ceremony that closes the "For the One" Dance as well as some sage, yellow cornmeal, and a copy of Anael's poems. The great Zulu wisdom keeper told them that he hoped that their dance would continue in Africa.

The long 21-hour trip back to the States was made as Jeanne and John nursed their physical ills and fatigue, and also dealt with the ramifications of an argument that they had had at Naledi about the "For the One" Dance and the Sun-Moon Dance. Jeanne said that John was "challenging" her on the content of the dance, and she became very upset. The effect, warranted or not, put distance between them as they sped across oceans in a winged silver bullet. *A Course in Miracles* teaches that we are never upset by what we think is the cause. Jeanne felt threatened, but her emotions had little to do with the conflicts over the dance.

MARGARITA'S STORY

In 1998 Margarita DiVita attended a Coptic conference in Johnson City, Tennessee where Perry Robinson was speaking. Three subjects addressed by Perry greatly interested her: relationship with Jesus, Huna Shamanism, and the Pleiades. That weekend Margarita felt that she needed a private session with Perry.

Growing up in Brooklyn, New York in an Italian family, Margarita had an odd affinity for things Native American. For birthdays and other occasions when she was asked what she wanted, she always said that she wanted something turquoise. Her daydream was that someday she would sell American Indian jewelry from a motor home on a road traveled by motorcycles. For ten years prior to 1998, she was part of the Harley-Davidson Corporation touring motorcycle road show doing exactly that—vending American Indian jewelry and traveling across the U.S.A. in a motor home. Margarita was a free spirit who could not abide the restrictions and stresses of big city life.

In authentic American Indian jewelry, Margarita felt the elemental spiritual connection that Indian craftspeople put into their creative products, and she tried to educate her buying public to that aspect. In buying Indian jewelry on reservations, Margarita also had some marvelous experiences at Native American sacred sites where doors were opened to her because of her sincere respect. But in 1998, Margarita was in transition to leave the road as a vendor and focus on spiritual growth.

Over the next two years, Margarita corresponded with Perry and received the Center for Peace newsletter and program schedule. The weekend after Easter in 2000, she came to the CFP for a workshop and decided to stay in the area and work with the Center.

"I felt as if I was coming home," she says. "In 1995, I had had a channeled reading that said that I would one day be in service to an avatar and travel all over the world showing the Oneness. Now, after twenty-one years of spiritual exploration, I realized that I was born into the box to get out of it. That's what my personal journey has been about, so now I can help others get out of the box that cultures have imposed on people for the whole of human history. We are the wayshowers, and that is the thought that I keep in my heart all the time."

In her first year at the CFP, Margarita was asked to support the July 2000 Sun-Moon Dance by helping in the kitchen. Her organizational skills quickly elevated her to head of the kitchen. John co-chiefed that dance with Steve Citty, and Jeanne was in the arbor as Moon Mother, so Margarita had her first exposure to the Pehrsons. Later that year, she had a more personal and prolonged contact with Jeanne and John when they facilitated a Community Building Workshop at the CFP. Margarita's skills in heading up a dance kitchen led her to serve other dances with John and Jeanne—some away from the CFP—and she became recognized as an important member of the ceremonial dance crews in Tennessee and North Carolina. Margarita thus headed the kitchen for the very first "For The One" Dance held in North Carolina in April 2003.

"Every time I was with Jeanne and John, the energy was so strong. I will sum it up. I believe that when I was told that I would be working in service to the avatars, I believe both Jeanne and John bring forth that energy. I got that clear, and when I tell Jeanne, she just smiles."

In May 2004, when Jeanne and John announced that they had been called to dance the "For The One" a second time in Israel and began to assemble a volunteer crew, Margarita says that she knew that she was supposed to be there. Margarita felt an intense identification with Mary Magdalene and in Mary's discipleship and in her role as a spiritual woman. Margarita had a deep sensitivity to what Mary must have suffered during the last days with Jesus in Jerusalem. She recognized that traveling to the actual sites in Israel would be emotionally hard for her.

Margarita arrived early in Israel to pull the kitchen together. Prior to the dance, she began to have intense dreams that left her with tearful feelings of not belonging. When she shared her unhappiness with dance elder and Moon Mother Ula Rae Mynatt, Ula Rae put the emotions in perspective when she asked, "Can you imagine how the Magdalene felt?"

Her advance work with the kitchen done, Margarita danced the "For The One" with twenty-five other dancers. It was a large number for the size of the arbor, and Margarita realized that her role was to allow divine love to flow through her so that peace in this troubled land might occur. In touring the Israel countryside, she was especially drawn to the ancient trees that had endured against a harsh environment, and she had a vision that "trees hold the sacredness of the land, any land."

"Whenever you are in need of some peace or guidance or wisdom, go sit with a tree because the trees are holding that wisdom."

Margarita was also moved by a trip to Qumran beside the Dead Sea where the famous scrolls were found. It was also a site frequented by Jesus and Mary Magdalene; and in an ancient cemetery in a blazing sun above the still sea, Margarita believed that she felt the energy of the Biblical characters.

At the end of the trip, the dance crew was hosted for a farewell dinner at the Knights Palace Hotel, and the Israelis encircled them and thanked them for what they had brought to their country. A well-known Muslim peacemaker, Ibrahim, who knew Jeanne and John from their Peace Concerts, opened many doors for the dance crew in Israel and showered them with food and gifts. He and his wife even hosted them for a dinner in his home on the Mount of Olives.

In November 2004, Margarita joined the dance crew for the first "For The One" Dance in South Africa. Prior to the dance, she and Jeanne and the other women in the party went to Sangoma Valley in Zulu country to visit tribal holy woman Gogo Monica and her twazas in the caves that had been used for centuries of worship. There the tribal women sang and performed their rituals with the white women in a free exchange of spiritual energies. Margarita remembers it as "a *National Geographic* moment." She could not believe their access to such sacred African places.

At the dance itself, Margarita began her apprenticeship in the arbor as a Moon Mother under the tutelage of Sammye Jo Harvey.

After supporting so many ceremonial dances of all types, and having crewed the original FTOD in the USA, and the first FTODs in
both Israel and South Africa, Margarita accepted the very
demanding role of International Dance Coordinator in 2005. And
like all her dance assignments in the past, Margarita was a volunteer
without salary and without even the promise of reimbursement for
travel expenses. Most of the international dance crewmembers paid
their own way or obtained sponsors to underwrite part of their
travel expenses. No one was making a living by taking the FTOD
to the world.

"I have a tremendous amount of love and respect for Jeanne
and John. I tease Jeanne that there is almost nothing that I would-
n't do for them; but if I say 'nothing I wouldn't do,' that's it, I'd be
out there with them all the time. I love them because they are genuine. I have seen others who facilitate ceremony, but Jeanne, and
now John by her side, encourages everyone to grow without form.
When I go to Jeanne for personal direction, she listens lovingly and
then tells me to follow my heart. I absolutely love the way Jeanne
encompasses everyone in a dance. The support people, the dancers,
everyone. No one is more sacred than the other or more important
than the other. She honors everyone, all of the time. No matter
what she is doing, she never hesitates to say 'thank you' and 'you are
appreciated.' This is the love that they both emanate. I truly honor
them. I see them as wayshowers and as peers who aren't on a
pedestal. I feel so connected to them, and I know that the work that
they are doing makes a difference. In the limitations of the physical
form, they bring God's purest love through, untainted.

"I am in total support of what Jeanne and John need, and I hope
to grow into the role of Dance Coordinator, but I will serve in whatever capacity that I am needed. Recently, I have gotten a great deal
of confirmation that I am doing what I was meant to do. My mother
(deceased) has even appeared to me and encouraged me in this
work. With her blessing, I feel both happy and fulfilled."

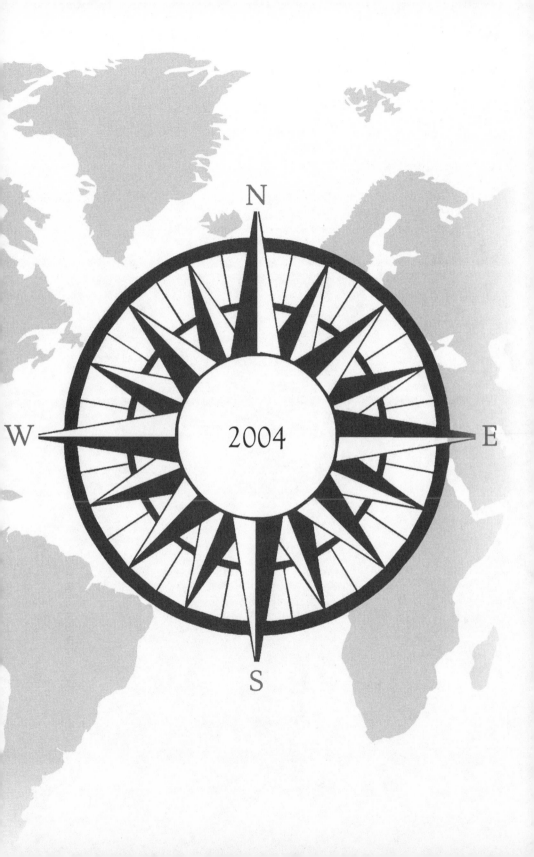

THE CRUCIBLE OF RELATIONSHIP

A few days after arriving in Graham, Jo Fisher and Cheryl organized an evening for friends in the Watersong community who wanted to hear about Jeanne and John's South African experiences. The sharing at Jo's house was a way for the Pehrsons and Cheryl to integrate what had occurred there. On the 18th they flew from Raleigh to Denver via Dallas to recover their car and visit with friends in that part of Colorado. Christmas that year was spent in Boise, Idaho with daughter Jenny and her husband Joe Ney. Jeanne and John did their Christmas giveaways in Boise where two complete strangers were handed a Christmas card with $50 inside.

In the days leading up to Christmas, Jeanne suffered from throbbing tooth pain, and she sought relief with homeopathic gum applications and over-the-counter ibuprofen. Long-term solutions to her dental problems were hampered by the constant travel perhaps more so than financial considerations. If she started with a dental surgeon, how could she keep a series of appointments? Health issues with both Jeanne and John thus continued on an ad hoc basis. Treatment was fashioned from what was immediately available because of their next travel commitment.

John had Christmas Day telephone conversations with sons Ryan and Sean, but the conversations were strained. There was a continuing blame from his sons and guilt on John's part for a father's absences since the unexpected divorce from their mother. The dynamic was psychologically predictable for children and the parents of divorce; but that did not mean that it was any less painful and troubling, and Christmas always seemed to exacerbate these emotions. John lamented that in the absence of a home, there was nowhere to gather the family for holidays and special occasions. But he also realized that a few days together would not fix deep-rooted relationship issues. In saying "yes" to what he felt called to do as a spiritual mission, he was compelled to say "no" to the conveniences and conventions of social conformity. In many ways, in choosing this difficult path, John was no longer the man who his sons remembered from their childhood.

Jeanne had avoided John's dilemma because her son and daughter did not perceive a radical change in their mother. They had been through divorce with her and been in the home with her during those critical years. They knew Jeanne so well that when she began what seemed to others like a radical spiritual quest, Jenny and John Troutner saw her lifestyle changes as just the next adventure for a very exceptional person who happened to be their mother.

Before they could head east, stops had to be made at their storage units in Colorado. Summer clothing had to be exchanged for a winter wardrobe, and there were ceremonial items to renew, and camping gear to load. There was an overnight visit with Woodora-Rose Eisenhauer in Crestone, who had just opened her own real estate brokerage, Rose Realty. There was also time for the couple to get massages from Grant Freeman, another Crestone friend. John had been suffering from what he suspected was tendonitis in his right arm from an injury that was incurred in the construction of the dance arbor in South Africa. Jeanne needed the body work, too, to help her relax. That day she confirmed that her guidance was to go to Tulum, Mexico for her private retreat. On a stopover in Tulsa, the Pehrsons stayed with friends and reconnected with other supporters in a sweat lodge. By the time they got to Tennessee on a mid-January Saturday, Jeanne had booked her flight to Cancun on a discount website.

The Corryton farmhouse had been prepared for their arrival by Ula Rae, and it felt warm and cozy as a freezing rain blew through the East Tennessee rural farmscape. Both John and Jeanne were still suffering from travel fatigue and the bodily ills that they had accumulated during the previous months. They went to town, the outskirts of Knoxville, to see movies and to have restaurant meals, but mostly they tried to rest. John described his condition as "empty and hollowed out, or just numb." Meanwhile, he described Jeanne as a "tornado of frenetic energy." Jeanne was working furiously at the computer responding to the buildup of e-mails and organizing her post-retreat schedule so that she could get away to Mexico with no dangling responsibilities. Jeanne's retreat finally began on Friday the 16th when John saw her off at the Atlanta airport.

Jeanne wrote, "Even the butterfly takes a bit of time to adjust to the light once out of the cocoon." Her adjustment after months of foreign travel and performance demands was to return to the place where she and John had fallen in love and come together on a linked spiritual path—Tulum, Mexico. The first thirty days of her retreat on the Yucatan's ocean gulf was meant for personal reflection and healing. John would join her for the last ten days. Jeanne's experience was not exactly forty days in the wilderness, but the tropical jungle by the sea where she resided qualified as an ecological accommodation.

The Cabañas Copal in Tulum was an hour and a half from the Cancun airport. The small, isolated resort had 47 cabanas and direct beach access. Jeanne's cabana had no electricity and a sand floor. Iguanas roamed free as did tropical birds and small sand crabs. The pelicans put on a daily show as they dove for fish offshore. The ocean, for Jeanne, was especially nurturing; and with no schedule to respond to, she was able to unwind and let go her concerns and cares and recharge that inner resource of stillness that allowed her to serve the purpose of her vision. No one is inexhaustible. The pressure of intensive teaching and constant ceremony in world trouble spots that were sometimes war zones had to be relieved. In addition, there was the marital tension that existed between Jeanne and John over events that had begun in Israel. John's return to a business consulting career, although lucrative enough to give them financial breathing room, was, nevertheless, a departure from their combined mission to expand the "For the One" Dance. Was this a direction being fostered by Spirit as appropriate to each individual, or was this a test of the commitment to a shared vision that she and John had nurtured for more than ten years in order to reach the realization of the "For the One" Dance? These were the questions that Jeanne faced during her weeks of sequestering.

Back on the farm in Corryton, John was not exactly a happy camper either. Joseph had told his students, "If we are moving forward, we are never in balance. That's the way we walk—first on one foot, then on the other." Without Jeanne, John felt out of balance. Often his days on the farm seemed gloomy, tiresome, and depressing. Without Jeanne, John spent many hours a day at the computer just responding to the e-mails from their support network and coordinating dance details. Since Jeanne did most of this kind of correspondence and the bill paying, John got a taste, and an appreciation, for how much time Jeanne worked every day. There was also a newsletter to write for their website.

John had planned to devote much of the month to a new system of numerology that he had been developing for more than fifteen years. Called Mystical Numerology, it was based on a new 13-month, 28-day solstice calendar; and it contained elements from Joseph Rael's work, the Quiche Mayan system of Day Lords, and Jeanne's teachings regarding spontaneous singing. John's system had developed to the point that he was doing subject tests; that is, private readings for friends, and preparing for his first workshop on the subject. He also thought that he would eventually author a book to describe his new system. Instead of a relatively long month to work on Mystical Numerology, however, John used up the energy of most days on other necessary things.

Jeanne called from Mexico to pick up his spirits, and he told her that he was looking forward to some fun in the sun with her in February. In a later call that week, Jeanne was not so upbeat, and she confessed to John that she was having self-doubts and self-worth issues. Her call had awakened John from sleep, and groggy, he later felt that he had not given Jeanne the boost that she needed, and that sense of failure "profoundly disquieted" him. Nevertheless, Jeanne sent John three "love letters" from Tulum, and he read them over again en route to Mexico in mid-February.

Reunited at Cabañas Copal, the couple sometimes walked for hours or lay on the remote beach. For their wedding anniversary, they dressed for supper and took a taxi to Maya Tulum for an elegant lobster meal served with sangria. The next day, John's 54th birthday, Jeanne gave him multiple gifts (tee shirts, Mayan calendars and books) and arranged to have a birthday cake served with six waiters singing the birthday song. At the end of her stay at Cabañas Copal, Jeanne ordered a cake with a frosting that spelled "Gracias Copal," and she gave bags of Hershey's kisses and other gifts to the wait staff in addition to pieces of the cake. Emilio, Alfonso, and Gregorio will probably remember Jeanne for a long time.

Jeanne and John traveled to Atlanta on separate flights and got back together in the baggage area where Don Boland met them. A winter storm was forecast; so instead of spending the night with Don and Kathy, the Pehrsons recovered their car and drove overnight to Corryton where they experienced a sixty-degree temperature drop from the previous day.

At the end of the first week in March, John gave his first Mystical Numerology workshop to eleven people at the Center for Peace. Both he and Jeanne were also occupied with arrangements for the Tennessee "For the One" Dance scheduled over the spring equinox later in the month. Despite the retreat to Tulum, however, both of them were still making physical adjustments. Jeanne had lost weight in Mexico but was still having intestinal problems. John had leg pain that hurt him "like I've been beaten with a rubber hose," but he did not know the cause.

The number four in numerology is about bringing things into form. It is about what John defines as "rooting an idea or an energy." It was first thought that the fourth "For the One" Dance would occur in Israel as plans were being made for a dance there in May. An invitation from the Center for Peace, however, altered the dance order and placed the fourth dance in the arbor where it had originated with Jeanne's vision there in 1996. Many of the individuals who would later serve on the international dance support crews would be participants in this dance, and Jeanne and John were already realizing that future chiefs of the "For the One" Dance would also be birthed there. It was at this dance that Jeanne, and at least two others, saw thousands of ethereal people on the hills around the dance arbor. The visionary experience was taken as a sign that there were multitudes waiting to dance, and that in the future, thousands of people would gather at dance sites just to experience the energy emanating from the arbor as the dancers sang and danced.

A long, five-round sweat lodge for dancers Friday afternoon began the event. Dancers then changed into their regalia at the arbor and were led by Jeanne and John to the Peace-Sound Chamber where they sang together in spontaneous song. When they returned to the arbor, the drums began, and they danced for about forty minutes until dusk and were then sent to their beds. Two-person teams of Dog Soldiers in three-hour shifts kept watch at the arbor entrance fire throughout the night. The dance continued all day Saturday and did not end until about 10 A.M. Sunday morning with a water ceremony in the arbor and a final chant in the Peace-Sound Chamber. The dancers were then released to bathe and re-dress for the food feast that followed. Sunday afternoon everyone, including the kitchen crew, gathered in the Chamber for a sharing circle that included a give-away blanket. Jeanne left for Corryton immediately after while John stayed behind to catch up with friends, including Shelley, who had come from Israel for the dance.

Initiatives for John to bring Intuitive Imagery to corporate managers in Israel were still being made, and he had another long telephone conversation with Daniel Kropf. Jeanne was also having long conversations with Jeff Goldstein and others to discuss arrangements for the upcoming "For the One" Dance in Israel. As March became April, springtime had come to East Tennessee, and daffodils, forsythia, and dandelions turned the rays of the sun into profusions of yellow against the greening of the rapidly growing grasses. Pear and cherry and dogwood trees began to bloom in clouds of pink and white. Most trees were still bare of leaves, but the promise of new growth was everywhere.

The first two "For the One" Dances had occurred at the Watersong arbor in North Carolina, and the third in South Africa. Now the fourth would soon be followed by yet another new location in Israel. In the time frame of thirteen months, four "For the One" Dance sites would be established on three distant continents and a regular schedule of dances would be initiated. All of this was being accomplished by a dedicated married couple without institutional staff or financial support. For heightened drama, they could be considered a homeless couple, a once bankrupted couple! And if the truth be told, they were often also an overwhelmed couple, a physically challenged couple, and a couple who constantly questioned their own abilities and spiritual worthiness to lead. In these attributes that some critics would label flaws, however, lay their strengths. They had overcome every obstacle that normally defeated the good natures of a common humanity. But the ultimate challenge to Jeanne and John was not the circumstantial adversity of forging their vision into reality; it was rather the dynamic of their own personal relationship. Perhaps all the physical ills that they had suffered in recent months had been the result of relationship anxiety. At some point for them to continue as totally present spiritual teachers, they had to address their marital discord and resolve it. Now, on the path back to Israel, the need for such a resolution would again come into bright focus.

THE "FOR THE ONE" DANCE
COMES TO ISRAEL

John preceded Jeanne to Israel by a week, leaving on April 8th. At the Newark airport, TSA security challenged the didgeridoo that John carried in a long over-the-shoulder cloth bag. Regulations, the checkpoint person said, prohibited anything on board that could be used as a bludgeon or a bat. After the instrument itself was inspected, an enlightened security manager allowed John to board with the dij as carry-on. Angel offered to meet John at the Tel Aviv airport and drive him to Mevasseret where the Pehrsons would again stay at Norm and Judy Enteen's place. She then took John to the grocery store for necessary food items. It was Passover Week, and aisles containing wheat items were covered by plastic.

Angel had already arranged for two Intuitive Imagery sessions for John to work the next day. She also had appointments for him to meet the heads of organizations who could employ John as an executive coach. At every opportunity John talked about the "For the One" Dance and invited the business people whom he met to consider dancing. He and Jeanne talked on the phone every other day, and John reported his progress in developing consulting jobs within the Israeli business community. Jeanne told John about her concerns for finding wood to build the dance arbor. Wood beams were a scarce commodity in Israel, and Jeanne said that she was seeking guidance for a solution to this problem.

John stayed busy until Jeanne arrived in Israel on the 17th. He thought that she looked "beautiful" when he saw her, and he had even begun a romantic poem about missing her. Jeanne's teeth began to pain her severely after her arrival. She reminded John that Joseph had told them that teeth problems were about relationship. Jeanne also told John that her heart was aching, too. John admitted in his journal that he was having confusing feelings regarding his time spent with Angel. It was not that they had done anything inappropriate, but a state of tension was nevertheless the result, and it was obviously injuring Jeanne.

The philosopher Bertrand Russell posed that an unbridgeable gulf existed between "knowledge by description" and actual "knowledge by acquaintance." Vicarious experience is a description of an emotional event and not the event itself, and any analysis of it is thus flawed by the gulf between. We are therefore remote witnesses to the inner life of others whom we presume to know. And if we attempt to abstract true meaning from close examination, we must realize that the best we can assume is merely a metaphor for what has actually occurred. In reconstructing lives in biography, the author is always subject to the approximations of an intellect that can only know what is given it to know. This is never so well proved as in the description of a marital relationship, even one's own.

Jeanne and John had returned to Israel with the prime purpose of establishing a "For the One" Dance there. There were additional elements to be considered—both practical, as in John's business contacts, and personal, as in their relationship issues—but their focus had to be on the dance. In their "Eagle Notes" newsletter for the first half of the year, the experience in Israel began with a quote from Jeanne, "We are the hollow bones through which Spirit blows the breath of life." It continued with this introductory paragraph.

"Israel is one of the pivotal places on the planet right now. What happens there ripples outward around the globe and touches us all in some way. The violence there has affected life in America in dramatic ways, especially since September 2001. Just so, if peace can happen in this little piece of land where the prophets of three great religions walked, it will also spread seeds of peace around the world. That is why we felt so blessed when the 'For the One' Dance became a reality in northern Israel May 4-6 in the Galilee."

Support for the "For the One" Dance in Israel came from around the world in the form of financial donations to cover travel expenses for some crewmembers and to help in the construction and supply costs to stage the dance. Dancers themselves would later contribute to these expenses, and many support crewmembers paid their own way, but the start-up of a dance like the "For the One" Dance is a significant undertaking requiring funding and extensive skilled labor.

Jeanne says that the idea for the Israeli dance arbor came while she was driving to a grocery store in Tennessee. "I said a prayer out loud," she related. 'God, what do you want the arbor in Israel to look like? We have little wood to work with.' Suddenly I noticed telephone poles connected by wire that looked like rope. I immediately got excited because I saw the potential in my mind's eye. When I got home from the store, my glance fell on the cover design of a book I had been given—*White Eagle's Sayings*. The design was the star of White Eagle. I said to John that we could build the arbor in the shape of a star and do it with rope and poles that are needed only in strategic places."

John and Joško took Jeanne's suggestion and constructed an arbor whose upright poles formed a ten-pointed star that supported the shade cloths by rope. The uncommon appearance of four eagles during construction was seen as a spiritual blessing to the site crew.

The drum for the event was especially made from a buffalo hide sent from the United States to an Israeli carpenter, Amir Baumfeld, who made a People's Drum in the shape of an infinity sign from a single piece of wood from a ficus tree. Instructions had accompanied the buffalo hide, but the drum was the first the carpenter had ever made. The stretched hide was still wet when the drum was delivered to the dance site; but by the time it was needed, it was dry, taut, and had what experienced drummers proclaimed was a magnificent sound. The drum itself was thus considered one of the dance miracles.

It is uncommon for rain to occur in Galilee during May; and yet the Thunder Beings came to the dance site soon after the directional shrines were blessed, and there was a hard rain for forty minutes, with none reported elsewhere. Tal ben Sira, the owner of the land was astounded, and she told the Pehrsons, "This was amazing! I've never had a private rain shower before!"

The Dance had 26 dancers—a large number for the size of the unusually shaped arbor. Dancers represented Israeli, Palestinian, Egyptian, American, South African, and French nationalities. One dancer was paralyzed from the neck down. His personal nurse wheeled him back and forth to the center pole. Mona Zekri, an Egyptian woman, endured a four-hour investigation by Israeli security at the border to dance. Others danced at the risk of losing their jobs.

The place of the dance is called Wadi Yanshuff, the Riverbed of the Owl, and for some of the dancers, it was indeed a look into dark places with wiser eyes. Testimonies of life-changing experiences at the dance spread through the spiritual community in Israel. The interest and excitement generated from these personal accounts prompted the scheduling of two dances, a week apart, for the following year. In a period of slightly more than three years, the Pehrsons had spent ten months in the Middle East. They had first come only to learn and observe and to see why they both had been so strongly guided to Israel. Now, with the "For the One" Dance established in the Holy Land, their purpose seemed revealed and their future path ordained.

When Jeanne and John had talked to Credo Mutwa in South Africa about Israel, he had told them, "As Israel goes, so goes the world." His insight was as much a political reality as it was a spiritual one. Israel was not only at the central flash point of the geopolitical struggle for oil resources, it was also holding the ground where violent religious ideologies merged. The very definition of God seemed to be in the balance as fundamental religious zealots made war on each other. And although the Middle East had been the focus of peace efforts by many governments, no peace seemed possible by diplomatic methods, as peace is also not made possible by armed domination.

Forgiveness had never been offered as a national policy by any party to the conflict, although forgiveness is the absolute prerequisite to the healing of revenge motivations. In the Dance arbor of the "For the One" Dance, forgiveness was being experienced, and healing was occurring as prejudicial cultural conditioning was peeled away. In the enlightenment of becoming the naked soul, dancers realize that there is no difference between themselves and the other souls who are now perceived as no longer separate. Nationalities are no longer relevant. Race and religion become insignificant. The shackles of conformity to false cultural ideas drop away, and for the first time, there is true freedom and the actual experience of joy that comes from inner peace.

This renewed human being from the dance then joins that community of the meek who are prophesied to inherit the earth. And it will not be an earth run by politicians or controlled by any theocracy, and thus those classes of individuals must oppose spiritual enlightenment in order to protect their positions and institutions. Their strategies, however, have proved over the last 15,000 years of human civilization to yield only conflict and the destructive chaos of wars. To what end? Progress? A planet divided between the relatively rich and the desperately poor? A planet whose own ecology is now in conflict with itself for survival? How have political systems and religious institutions really served the greater humanity? Great cities and complex technologies considered, how can the human species consider itself a success on planet Earth when war and starvation are still so universal in the 150th century?

The dinosaurs ruled planet Earth for an estimated 170 million years and then disappeared through no fault of their own, although some wag genius has proposed that their excessive flatulence might have caused a greenhouse effect that brought on a catastrophic ice age. Three million years ago our relatives began to walk upright in Africa. What is three million compared to 170 million? What are the Las Vegas gambling odds on human beings making it to four million? Based on human history thus far and the current conditions, the smart money is going against survival. And people place that bet every day by their behaviors. They spend like there is no tomorrow. They consume without thought of the needs of the seventh generation who will try to exist in the future continuation of humanity. They observe the suffering and demoralization of other human beings with as much psychological distance as they can manage, and they accept no responsibility for what occurs outside their own sphere of control. They consider themselves separate and independent even in times of personal distress. They feel alone even when they can flood their senses with entertainments.

Human beings choose fear over love because they believe that fear sets up the defenses that will protect them from harm. They believe that love leaves them vulnerable and subject to rejection. This principle governs their behavior regardless of all their degrees in philosophy and theology because one is their intimate chemical experience while the other is merely a system of ideas. Thus to alter the conditional orientation, the actual chemistry of the body must be changed so that fear does not override true awareness.

One method of altering this chemistry is meditative breath control or chanting (singing) combined with fasting from food and water long enough to upset the body's homeostasis by virtue of dehydration. This method of quieting the conditioned mind has been practiced by ascetics for thousands of years. Every master teacher has employed this method as a spiritual discipline. The method induces centering and focus to the exclusion of random or rampant thoughts. If movement is added to this experience, the discipline process is accelerated, and the mind and body release their limitations on the being. When this state is achieved, those who have experienced it report significant visions that directly impact their wakeful lives. This then, as a psycho-intellectual description, is what occurs at the "For the One" Dance. The method is physical and grounded in reality, but the result is purely mystical and specific to the individual.

What is uniquely different about the dances that Jeanne and John lead is that no dogma is interjected into the awareness experience of the dancers. The dance arbor is provided as a safe haven for releasing the mind-body dualism. There is no authoritarian motivation in organizing the dance and no institutional objective. That is why the "For the One" Dance can cross international boundaries and include dancers from multicultural backgrounds in the same arbor. When the object of the dance is to create a deep spiritual awareness that there is no separation, everyone, regardless of previous orientation, is included. The inclusion is in itself unique. Most organized religions practice exclusion as a dogma. They exclude everyone who does not believe as they do. If there is to be recognition of a human "family," these practices of exclusion must be abolished. Exclusion is the practice of fear, not love.

Before Jeanne and John left Israel, they traveled to the Sinai in Egypt to recuperate from the dance and to walk where Noah and Moses had walked. Their host for the week was Victor Barr. They viewed the Red Sea, and they prayed that the "For the One" Dance might be brought to Egypt, too. They were at Nuweiba until the last week of May when they returned to Rosh Pina where Jeanne did a workshop and John did a sweat lodge with Joško Šabiè and Jeff Goldstein for about thirty people in two four-round lodges followed by a communal feast. There were a few private sessions and farewells to be made; and then on June 4th, almost two months after John had first arrived in Israel, the couple departed for the U.S. Fortunately, their intuitive imagery had advised them to come early to the airport because they had to endure the most extensive baggage inspection they had ever experienced. It took four hours from arrival to being seated on the aircraft. The recent terrorist bombings in Israel had the Israeli security on full alert, and anyone with the kind of travel stamps that the Pehrsons carried on their passports was due for the full battery of inspections and interrogations.

CHERYL PATTERSON

Drum Chief

Jeanne had been encouraging, in her enthusiastic way, those of us who had a lot of experience in the dance work to go with them to Israel, especially since this was to be their first "For The One" Dance, and no one there knew the ceremony. We were going to be called the International Crew.

I don't arbitrarily decide such things, but I saw a vision of myself at the Wailing Wall and figured that I was supposed to go. I didn't know how it might materialize financially, but I told Jeanne that I would go. She invited me to chief the drum. A buffalo skin had been sent to Israel to make the drum, but we did not know if the drum would be ready, or who else would show up to play drums. There are a lot of amazing people who play drums in Israel, but we would have to train drummers to support the dance. So I had a lot of real uncertainty about my role before we left.

Two weeks before the trip, I fell off a stool while getting gear down from my closet and badly sprained my ankle. I could hardly walk at all. Instead of taking the accident as a sign not to go, I went out and got special shoes and ankle wraps. Many of the dance crew came from the Center for Peace: Perry and Jeanne Robinson, Shannon Ray (Firekeeper), Sammye Jo Harvey, Margarita DiVita, and others.

The dance experience itself was powerful. As soon as I walked on the dance ground the day that the dance was supposed to start, I leaned over a picnic table to sign a release form, and my back went out. One minute I was standing upright, and the next minute I was face down on the ground. I managed to get myself up, and I staggered down to the arbor a quarter of a mile away. The new four-day-old drum was there, but the hide was still wet. I leaned over to put my hand on the drum, and my back seized up and would not release. My introduction to the Israeli dance crew was by virtue of having everyone work on my back in an attempt to get me on my feet. At some point I realized that my physical problem was about me being with the new drum. I then told Jeanne that I needed to stay in the arbor and sleep with the drum.

So the support crew went back to the house where they would sleep and brought back my sleeping mat and stuff. I told them that I could drum the dance without food but that I would need water. At night, I stayed in the arbor with the dancers and slept with my sore back against the drum. At daybreak, I would have to crawl on hands and knees and pull myself up to my seat at the drum. People had to help me walk down the hill to the toilet, and water and food were brought to me away from the arbor at the nearby medicine tent. Sammye Jo, our Moon Mother, was sleeping and eating in the medicine tent to avoid the long trek to the house and to be near the dancers throughout the night.

The drum itself turned out to be an amazing drum. It is made into the shape of the infinity sign from a single piece of ficus tree. The tone of the drum got stronger and more beautiful with every hour of the dance. We had two djimbe drum players, and two others who played the new buffalo hide drum with me. One of the men had never played drums in his life; but when he came and was allowed to touch the drum, he began to weep with emotion. I told the Alpha Dog Soldier, Steve Citty, that I needed this man to drum, and that I would trade him one of the young strong boys assigned to the drum for this fifty-something man because his feeling for the drum was so strong.

My job was to convey to these drummers how to use the drum in sacred ceremony; how to interpret what was happening in the dance; how to know when to go faster and when to go slower . . . all the nuances of what it means to serve the dancers as a drummer in ceremony.

The drummers were wonderful. Debbie Tor, one of the Israeli drummers that I trained, chiefed the drum for both "For The One"

Dances in 2005. We sent a powerful wall of music out to those dancers. It was just amazing.

Constant drumming over a three or four-day period requires great endurance, and I have tendonitis and rotator cuff problems that require treatment. In drumming five or more dances a year, I undergo a lot of massage therapy. The pain is the price of dedication. But in Israel that first dance, my back got better each day until at the end, I could walk away. I was as amazed as anyone, and I told Jeanne, "The drum healed me!"

JOHN'S RETREAT

D uring their first week back from Israel, Angel sent an e-mail suggesting that she would rather be a Moon Mother than a dancer at the next South African Dance. Was Angel completely unaware of how her energy had come between Jeanne and John? For John's part, he repeatedly told Jeanne that he wanted "out of the game" whatever it took. The association of the three of them together had once seemed so dynamic, so promising, but their companionship now was viewed as disruptive. The third wheel on their relationship vehicle had made for too bumpy a ride, and now Jeanne and John both agreed that something had to be done about it.

It was a very painful decision to make considering what Angel had done for them in the way of networking and outright gifts. Was it her fault that she was so attractive, so capable, and so enthusiastic to be a major role player in their work? Was it her fault that she upset the delicate equilibrium in their marriage partnership? God knows, their path was difficult enough, and their relationship stressed and tested by homelessness and constant financial uncertainty. Jeanne and John had joined each other in the crucible of spiritual growth until in the amalgam they were not separate in vision or in destiny. People who saw them together in the acts of ceremony acknowledged them for their unity and harmony of spirit. They seemed to many the embodiment of the yin and yang, the male and female, in their combined potential. Jeanne and John had different personalities, but they were clearly aligned when they performed together for a spiritual purpose. This alignment had a mystical calibration that could not, would not, suffer tinkering or experimental adjustment. For the sake of this metaphysical bonding, the couple would now have to be guarded with all others who intruded on their psychic intimacy. This necessary decision, however, did not prevent agonizing soul searching by its own nature. Jeanne and John's whole spiritual philosophy was to say "yes" to everyone. Now they could not say "no" to a dear friend for reasons that were difficult for them to articulate or accept.

There was much to do in mid-year planning for the remainder of 2004, but there was also a need to get away from the environmental cues of responsibility and just have some fun together. New Orleans came up as a destination, and so they drove south for five days of Creole and Cajun cuisine, jazz music, and antebellum charm. On the last night over dinner, their conversation turned serious, and Jeanne asked John, "What is your biggest fear?" He responded, "I still fear not being good enough or strong enough to do whatever I am being called to do."

In July, John supported a Sun-Moon Dance at Zoe Bryant's Swannanoa Chamber location that was chiefed by Sally Perry. John was the Alpha Dog in a lean dog soldier crew that got little sleep over the three-day Dance. Jeanne did not attend as she was visiting her brother Tom in Alabama and attending the Lane family reunion.

Sally Perry introduced a "mud ceremony" prior to the dance crew going into the sweat lodge. The mud contained vibhuti, Sai Baba's sacred ash. As Sally stood before each person, she smeared the mud on a specific area of the body while she gave them a short reading. When she got to a bare-chested John, she put a circle of mud on his left chest above his heart and said, "Let your heart be whole." Then she put mud on his right chest and drew a streak of mud to connect it to the left side; and doing this, she said, "Let your heart and Jeanne's heart become one so that you might be free of pain." John thought her reading more than coincidental.

After the Swannanoa dance, John went to the Center for Peace to help Steve Citty cut firewood and get the dance grounds ready for the Sun-Moon Dance there later in the month. Jeanne was in Chattanooga visiting her son, John Troutner, who was going through a job crisis. Despite their agreement concerning Angel, both Jeanne and John felt under psychic pressure, and they both admitted to each other that they desperately wanted relief from this uncomfortable anxiety. Their decision was to separate for almost a month. John would spend most of August in personal retreat at Lance House, the shack-like dance kitchen and storage loft at Watersong in Graham. Jeanne would seek counseling from Sammye Jo and do whatever she had to do to shake her internal demons. These plans were then set in motion, but first John had to serve the Tennessee Sun-Moon Dance.

The Sun-Moon Dance at the Center for Peace required the usual pre-Dance hard labor and a full crew to support the twelve dancers. There were first-time dancers as well as a woman who would dance an eighth time. Steve Citty, as John's best friend, was especially sensitive to John's fragile emotional state, and he gave John the very special gift of a medicine pouch containing the great Lakota leader Grandfather Dubray's medicine. Lance Davis danced and went into vision after "hitting the pole" on Sunday. He later gave honor gifts to Steve and John as Dance Chiefs. The gifts were crisp $100 bills wrapped in a traditional red cotton cloth. Lance was known to present that kind of honor gift, sometimes in a handshake that left the folded bill in the palm of the recipient.

At Watersong, Lance had almost single-handedly built what he called the "suave palace" out of scrounged materials. The structure had plywood sheets for floors and composition plywood walls. The one-room nearly square main floor was outfitted as a camp kitchen with electric connections and cold well-water hooked up by hose to a deep fiberglass laundry sink. There was an electric stove, a microwave, and freestanding metal shelves for dishes and pantry food items, plus two refrigerators. Everything in the room looked secondhand as if acquired at a garage sale. A steep, narrow staircase led to a room upstairs that was mostly used for the storage of arbor tarps, towels, blankets, and other items needed for the Dance. Lance, who had probably never even built a doghouse, was teased about his risky staircase. Nevertheless, the cabin-shack-shanty-cookhouse, painted inside and out in shades of the Southwest, including turquoise, was affectionately named "Lance House."

Jeanne went with John to Graham, and they stayed with Jo Fisher for two nights before Jeanne deposited John and all his retreat baggage at Lance House. Jeanne took the Pathfinder back to the Corryton farm where she planned to stay. John's crude accommodation was only 150 feet from the Watersong Chamber so there was that place for contemplation. The toilet, however, was another matter. It was an outhouse equidistant from the Chamber, but in an opposite direction. A shower curtain provided privacy, but there was a gauntlet to run to get there and back that included chiggers, swarms of mosquitoes from the nearby lake, and a field of poison ivy.

John's bedroom in the Lance House loft had a sloping roof that made it difficult for him to stand without bumping his head. His bed was a queen-size mattress on the floor. When the night temperature in the space hovered at 90°, Lance and John installed an antiquated window air-conditioning unit that labored to lower the room temperature even ten degrees. The mosquitoes, however, were no respecters of either closed spaces or cooling machines, and John thus suffered sleep due to their blood withdrawals, as if the itching from the chiggers and poison ivy was not enough. If, on certain nights, John was envious of monks on retreats in distant cool caves, he could be forgiven.

John was not completely isolated. There were weekly ceremonies in the Watersong Chamber to attend with long-time friends,
and John had the use of David's small utility truck for trips into
town for groceries and other supplies. Generally he cooked his own
meals, read, and listened to recorded music. Some days he would
visit the Chamber when no one was there and play solos on his flute
and dij to enjoy the vault's amazing acoustics. He and Jeanne talked
by phone. John would take her call or call her from Cheryl and
David's house on the Watersong property a few hundred yards from
the Chamber down a dusty farm road.

When Jeanne told John that she was going to work on herself
in an ancient ceremony with Sammye Jo in the Center for Peace
sweat lodge, and that four of their most faithful male friends would
assist, John told her that he would be in the Watersong Chamber
during the exact same hours to pray for her. John understood that if
Jeanne was successful, that she would clear lifetimes of energy that
had locked Jeanne into a pattern of jealousy. In the Chamber, John
began by chanting the Om-Mani-Padme-Hum's that he felt created
a circle of protection around himself that he could then project to
Jeanne. Then for a long period, he played the dij and felt the intensity of the clearing work that Jeanne was doing. Finally, he began to
play love songs and lullabies to Jeanne on his flutes—the low D-
note flute and the higher-pitched F#. He trusted that what he did
was contributing to his wife's healing.

JEANNE'S JOURNAL 2004-2005

Jeanne's journals from mid-2004 to mid-2005 were kept in
Docket Gold Classified top wirebound stenographer pads 8 ½ x
11/3/4 inches with 70 heavyweight sheets each. She titled them
Jeanne's Journal & Book of Guidance, and the first inside page was

subtitled "Thoughts from Her/Him to me. Coming Home." The pad is stuffed with notes of various sizes, transcripts of two channeled readings by Sue Mehrtens, drafts of letters, a schedule outline, two letters from John, and two post-card sized photos of herself and John seated on the floor with friends for a Thanksgiving dinner in Jerusalem, 2001.

One top-torn graph paper from a pad notes Jeanne's thoughts about prayer. The word is circled, and then she wrote, "It isn't the result that's important. It's the act itself, the being in the sacred now that holds the significance. For it is here that the perceived separation is reconnected, and the memory, the expression of One occurs."

Again, Jeanne's journal reflects an ongoing conversation with herself in contrast to John's more extensive journaling that emphasizes the documentation of events and his feelings. Whatever their personality differences, however, the marital bond between them was strong. In her journal, Jeanne kept an e-mail love note from John dated August 16, 2004. The subject line read, "Just an old fashioned love letter."

"My dearest love,

I don't believe I've told you today how beautiful you are, and how much I love you. And even though I know this 'retreat' time is good for me, and good for us, I am missing you in lots of different ways.

"I am missing just being near you, and bathing in your glow. I am missing being able to wake up in the morning to move close and cuddle up together. I miss touching you, and hugging you. I miss talking things over with you, and doing our quick imaging sessions. I miss heading out for a popcorn fix at the movies. And, of course, I miss our love-making.

Thanks for the cards you've sent (I've received two.)

I hope you are doing well after the ceremony, and still feel light and full of new possibilities.

I'll call later.

All my heart,
John"

Many of Jeanne's journal entries are essentially conversations with herself, and they end with instructional guidance from within. Jeanne's journaling dates back to her years with Up With People when the casts assembled for daily guidance.

"We send our hordes of angels to assist you. You have but to look around to know that we walk beside you in every direction. Your heart heals for us all. When this happens, as this is happening, you see it has always been healed and perfect . . . always. You are simply learning how to remember . . . shhh now . . . breathe . . . shhh. There are signs all around you. The shawl will teach you. We're here. We're always here. Call on us. Trust us. Surrender to us. To Me. To the Me in you. Surrender. I love you. I love you . . . "

When the demands on her emotional and physical body were highest, and the needs of people in distant places the greatest, Jeanne employed her journal as a centering method, as a form of blessed assurance. The words were also prayers. In August, she wrote:

"I ask to have whatever energy is necessary to complete the task. The silence of the night, the whisper of dreams come to heal, to bless. Be in the kindness of darkness . . . let it give you the womb's love to remind you that all there is is Love. Dance with the ancestors, the family of you that lives in the shawl of love that surrounds you. Dance! And Remember . . . I love you . . . Forever. Now . . . Breathe. Shhh . . . shhh . . . shhh . . . Breathe . . . "

At the end of this entry, Jeanne drew a simple ink figure spreading a fringed ceremonial shawl out like wings.

In the early pages of this journal, Jeanne confesses a personal crisis that involved jealousy. She saw the jealousy as an evil entity, but she was not sure if the problem was in herself or in the woman whom she perceived as threatening her marriage. In this very personal matter, Jeanne sought the wise counsel of Sammye Jo, who employed an ancient Native American ceremony to rid Jeanne of the anxiety and pain that was in danger of compromising her spiritual mission. In addition to Sammye Jo, four male pillars were brought into the sweat lodge ceremony—Steve Citty, Keith Hagberry, David Hooper, and Marcus Ambrester. These men were close friends with both Jeanne and John and had shared past spiritual experiences with them in many sweat lodges and ceremonial dances. Jeanne records what occurred.

"In the womb of the sweat lodge, I went to the point of creation of separation and saw myself as a young girl who volunteered to let the drama of jealousy play itself out in her and into the world for all to experience. The jealousy took the form of a large brown speckled creature somewhere between a lizard and serpent until it reared its head and was challenged. Then it took on attributes of a demonic dragon. And so I let the energy move through me in the lodge . . . the sounds were horrendous. The four men bravely held the gates of the four directions as the energy was released. The screams and lashing out for survival were painful and beyond description. After a time, I saw the young girl. I was both—this creature and the girl. Finally, the girl, speaking in another language (Sammye Joe said I spoke five languages) told the creature emphatically that no longer would she allow this creature to live with her. (There was even an imprint in the bed of her soul where the creature lived.) She kept at this until the creature realized that the girl was speaking the truth. It was then that, with reluctance, the creature walked toward the light at the mandated bidding of the girl. As it did, it kept looking back at her as if to say, 'Are you sure this is what you want?' The girl didn't budge on her decision, and the creature kept walking into the light, continuing to turn at intervals to see the girl. The creature became softer, its heart talking with the heart of the girl until there was a tenderness of truth that blossomed, revealing that the creature was done with this particular drama. At one point, with humor, it even asked the girl (not before saying 'I did a good job, didn't I?'), 'Would you like to play another game?' The girl kept sending him into the light until what finally resulted was transformation for the creature, it remembering that it too had volunteered to play this role so all could experience separation. The game was done now, the game of jealousy. What was revealed was the love the young girl and the creature had for each other. No longer fearful or hurtful in any way, the game was done, each of these beings remembering their origin of love. The result is that something in me has changed. The imprinted place in my soul where the creature lived, once empty, began filling up with love and white light so that now there are no void places where I will allow any other such games to be played again. And now, as Sammye Jo said, I can clearly hear the ancestors when they speak—hear the Grandmothers, hear the Grandfathers. I feel new, clear, and much wiser. Wow!! God bless Sammye Jo, Steve, Keith, David, and Marcus. They showed up and said yes. Congratulations! Celebrate!"

Mythologists like Joseph Campbell and most trained psychotherapists could make much of Jeanne's allegorical narrative of her experiences in the sweat lodge, but neither class of academics could deny the human drama of jealousy that exists in all of us sentient beings. The crux of the matter is how we, as individuals, deal with jealousy and resolve it in our personal lives. Is there a method for summing up the courage to face the heart? From Jeanne's testimony, the answer is *yes*.

Book Three of her personal journal goes from page 122 to 185. At the end of whatever Jeanne confides in her journaling, she concludes with an affirmation process. Are we, as intimate readers and observers, surprised that someone so revered by others for her enlightened powers is still practicing daily spiritual disciplines? Do we assume that the ego can be completely dismissed between the ceremonial events of purification and vision? Do we imagine that the Biblical prophets were miraculously freed from the traffic of cares and concerns and disappointments that they constantly encountered on the pathway of their missions? The evidence indicates that for every mountaintop experience, there is a valley below that must be walked. It was even so for the founder of Love as the ultimate discipline—Jesus. As a God-Man, he was both tempted and denied, and even He prayed to His Father for strength and guidance as an everyday practice.

When reading Jeanne's private affirmation prayers, it is easy to imagine every honored soul seeker throughout history saying her words in their proverbial gardens of Gethsemane as they surrendered to Source and then offered instruction to their small self who doubted or felt troubled. Whatever the form of the doubt or fear— and there are millions of such forms—the root of the problem is always separation from the Source that gives rise to such forms. The solution is thus always the same. Return to Source. Remember and return.

Here is another example of Jeanne working on herself as an everyday spiritual practice.

"Every time you feel the gnawing of the emotional self, shift focus. See Me. I will help you. I am here, always. Listen. Listen. Hear the sound of Creation creating itself. Allow. Watch. See. Grow into Remembering. Remember. Shhh. Breathe. Shhh. Listen. Shhh."

WEDDING IN WALES

Jeanne came for an overnight visit during John's retreat, and they did a concert in the Watersong Chamber for about twenty people with David playing the People's Drum, Teresa Hutson on djimbe, and Cheryl on rattles. Since her sweat lodge experience with Sammye Jo, Jeanne seemed more confident and her energy level was high. After the concert, the couple had a romantic interlude before Jeanne returned to Corryton. John had yet another week to go in the "suave palace." During that week he had quality time with both David and Cheryl. He and David discussed better use of the Peace-Sound Chamber to focus the energy of sound and prayer for intentional purposes. Cheryl told John that it was important for him to chief dances because women felt safe with him. Women who had to work through abuse issues with men would be more attracted to a dance led by a compassionate man like John.

When John talked to Jeanne that week, she sounded joyful and bubbly. Plans were afoot to expand the number of "For the One" Dances with new startups in Europe and also to establish some form of non-profit organization to support the work of the dances. The need for administrative and fund-raising help was becoming absolutely necessary, or they would face "burnout" every year and its detrimental effects on their health. On the day before Jeanne rendezvoused with John at Jo Fisher's house, she wrote him what he described as "a beautiful love poem" and sent it via e-mail. The last night before their transatlantic flight to London, the Pehrsons joined David, Cheryl, Diane Draves, and Lance for a full-moon ceremony to feed the dance pole at the center of the arbor. The offering was a mixture of non-pasteurized milk, yogurt, fruit, and honey. Its purpose was to honor the Source of the Dance energy and to increase that energy by feeding it.

Spiritual rituals have been mostly abandoned in the modern Eurocentric world and their importance lost as clarifying and comforting metaphysical metaphors. Little that modern people do in everyday life is reconfirming to their core beliefs. Rituals are reconnections to Source with more tangible substance than whispered prayers. Standing in the moonlight in a ritual context creates an amplitude of power that can be felt viscerally. And if the ritual appears primitive to an outside observer, then that judgment negates the basic instinct of worship that is the very hallmark of humanity. A return to life-affirming rituals is not a backward step into primitivism but rather a return to naturalistic maturity.

On arrival in London, the Pehrsons were met by Paul Benham and Jan Elliott who then spent the day driving them to their Primrose Organic Farm in Felindre, Wales. Paul is the caretaker of the Peace-Sound Chamber there, and Jeanne and John had come to Wales to officiate at his marriage to Jan. John found it difficult to shift from the private space of his retreat to the public space of concerts and workshops. Then, too, the couple had left summer in North Carolina and Tennessee with temperatures in the low 90ºsF for the damp cool of Wales at 60ºF. Three days after their arrival, they did a Peace Concert at the Peterschurch community center, and then they traveled to Hereford to visit Peter Terry, a "mountain of a man" who lives in a house circa 1660. Peter had recently bought property in Puglia that included a structure of cupolas that form natural sound chambers. The weekend visit was casual with walks to Hereford Cathedral and meals with Peter and friends in the area.

Back in Wales, the Pehrsons planned the wedding ceremony with Jan and Paul for Saturday, the 11th of September. It was the third anniversary of the Nine Eleven attack in the United States, but the wedding date was a coincidence and not planned. John did a small numerology workshop and Jeanne a sound workshop in midweek, and then they focused on the nuptials. Primrose Farm provided a romantic country setting where tall hedgerows bordered narrow, single-carriage roads, and fall flowers were in bloom. The farm itself was on historic Celtic grounds. Arthur's Stone, a huge venerated monolith, was nearby, and the nearest church was a Norman village church circa 1143. The area certainly had romantic atmosphere if only from the legendary days of King Arthur and Merlin. Yew trees in a grove encircling a church were well over a thousand years old.

A simple arch of freshly cut willow decorated with bright orange nasturtiums provided a portal to the outdoor wedding area.

The bride and groom wore colorful attire with an East Indian flair. The originally composed vows were exchanged inside the candle-lit Peace-Sound Chamber, and then a "binding ceremony" was performed by Jeanne and John wearing the Picuris gender belts outside under a 400-year-old tree. It had rained before the ceremony, and afterward a rainbow appeared to bless the newlyweds. Paul and Jan presented the ministers who had married them with a generous honorarium that more than covered the Pehrsons' transatlantic trip expenses. Jeanne and John exclaimed "wow!" at the unexpected gesture.

There was one more couple to see—Paul and Masha Middleton in Droitwich, England—before their departure. The overnight visit near Birmingham included a lovely dinner and lunch at a 500-year-old pub the next day. Then the household was up at 2:30 A.M. for the drive to the Birmingham airport where the Pehrsons would begin their long homeward journey.

The couple arrived back at Jo Fisher's house in North Carolina just in time to greet Hurricane Ivan as it threatened Florida and the Atlantic coastline with 165 M.P.H. winds. The path of the storm in the next few days spared North Carolina, and Graham got only a gentle all-night soaking. A new roof was going up on the Watersong dance arbor in preparation for the early October "For the One" Dance. John participated in work days at the arbor site while Jeanne worked the phone and e-mails to organize the dance crew. Relationship-wise, the couple had restored their intimacy, and their focus was on the dance. In a reflective period one morning, John wrote in his journal.

"We have infinite potential but don't believe it. And so, we lock ourselves into a static future by thinking the same thoughts and taking the same actions over and over. But, we have the capacity to change things dramatically by not getting stuck. This entails movement, breaking old patterns, new thinking, and new visions. This is one of the powerful purposes of the dances that Jeanne and I lead. The dances take people out of their comfort zones, get them unstuck, and open them to new inspiration, ideas, and perceptions. Then, they can create themselves anew . . . and the whole world changes."

John decided that he would dance this "For the One" Dance. Steve Citty would stand in for him as Sun Father. There were seventeen dancers, fourteen of whom were women. Rhonda Factor and Issa Daniel Mark had come from Israel to dance. Some of the dancers had danced a Sun-Moon Dance the previous week. Candy Barbee, the Alpha Dog, had a large crew of thirteen dog soldiers that included John's son Alan. As a Sun-Moon Dance Chief, John felt the pressure of expectation as he returned to dance with Jeanne as Chief. There was also the awareness that his dance crew close friends, including his son, were watching him. John did not want to be "pushed" by the Moon Mother, or be influenced by Steve who had told him to "dance your ass off!" The physical demands of the dance no longer challenged John. His path to vision had few obstacles once he released himself to Source. On that Sunday, John fell backwards from the pole and went into a trance state. Afterwards, all that he could remember was a place of euphoria that he did not want to leave.

In mid-October, Jeanne and John drove to Waterbury, Vermont to visit Sue Mehrtens. Sue had a large house with luxurious guest accommodations unlike anything that they had seen in recent months. A visit to the Ben and Jerry's ice cream factory seemed mandatory with no apologies for the sweet-treat indulgence. The purpose of this trip was to get guidance from Sue on the organization aspects of their peace mission. What structure was best? Who would step forward to help with the overwhelming paperwork? Who would handle the financial and bureaucratic red tape of a multinational operation? Who would facilitate the fund raising, and who would handle logistics and make travel arrangements and work with event sponsors and volunteer hosts? What are the necessary roles, and how are the people with the capacity, interest, and commitment to undertake those responsibilities to be identified?

The answers to these questions had two dimensions. The first was rather straightforward with regards to organizational management, and both Jeanne and John had more than adequate career backgrounds to write a mission statement and job descriptions and develop an organizational chart. The second dimension, however, was more important than the first and was much more difficult to define. The second dimension was the spiritual one that required management by Spirit rather than management by objective. Any "For the One" Dance "organization" could not be a business that functioned or measured its success as an economic enterprise, and yet it had to be efficient and fund its own way. How was this balance between spiritually oriented service and material necessity to be achieved and then maintained? If there was a perfect model of this balance to consult for practical guidance, no one could name it. The ideal seemed still in process.

Sue, in the voice of her channeled entity Cyrus, advised Jeanne and John, "You must understand that the work you are doing is not just for yourself. It is not for the friends you make. It is not for the people who attend the dance. It is *all* of these. It is also for the planet as a whole."

Jeanne's teeth problems exacerbated when a lower molar broke in half that required an emergency visit to a University of Vermont dental clinic. Extraction of the broken molar solved the immediate situation.

Before they left the area, the Pehrsons visited Carol and Bob Frenier at their home just outside Chelsea, Vermont. Carol was an old friend from the World Business Academy. The good news for the New Englanders was that the Boston Red Socks baseball team had defeated the New York Yankees in the baseball World Series, thus ending the "curse of the Bambino" that began when the Red Socks traded the legendary player Babe Ruth to the Yankees. Boston had not won a World Series since 1918, a period of 86 years. To celebrate, nature provided a total eclipse of the moon, which tended to prove that mythology is intrinsic to social interaction and somehow related to the heavens. At least that was the theory those nights in Boston.

At a luncheon hosted by Carol, the Pehrsons were reunited with Karen Speerstra, who as the head of the business book division of Butterworth-Heinemann had published John's *Intuitive Imagery* book with Sue Mehrtens. Karen's husband John attended, and the general conversation revolved around Jeanne and John's work and the hope that books would be a by-product of their experiences.

The next weeks were spent in Corryton in preparation for the return trip to South Africa, seven time zones away. The pack-up this time was complete because the Pehrsons thought that the Corryton farmhouse was no longer to be their home base. It was needed by Ula Rae's daughter. Part of the load in the Pathfinder was left in storage with Jeanne's mother, and the car itself would be left in Atlanta with Don and Kathy Boland until their return. Don would take them to the airport for their November 14th flight.

The recent presidential election in the United States was troubling to Jeanne and John. They had voted early and witnessed an election campaign that they saw as toxic in the extreme, poisoning the country with anger, divisiveness and intolerance. In general, they were disappointed that the campaign had been waged with sound bytes on television and that the American people did not possess the attention span to demand more. Wherever they traveled in the greater world and were identified as Americans, they would be asked to explain why the United States postured so arrogantly in its foreign policies. Many American travelers abroad took measures in dress and habit not to be identified as Americans because of this condition.

THE "FOR THE ONE" DANCE
RETURNS TO SOUTH AFRICA

Reverend Stephanie Clarke met the Pehrsons at the Johannesburg airport and drove them to her flat in the city through avenues of lavender blossoms of the jacaranda trees. Again they had traveled from winter in the U. S. to full summer in South Africa. The next day Joško Šabiè arrived to help with the scheduled dances at Rustlers Valley. Jeanne and John made a visit to Baba Credo and Virginia. Baba was now 84 and still active in the campaign against AIDS. Jeanne gave a necklace that she had made to Virginia, and they gave Baba tobacco and a beaded pouch with money inside to support his work. Baba chose this occasion to give John an African name. He named John "Che Lideh," The Tall Rock.

They got to Rustlers Valley on November 19th, and Jeanne faced logistic overload when their computer could not connect to their e-mail server. It was not a malfunction of their computer. Much of their networking with the dancers and the dance crew was done by e-mails. In-country dance coordinator Niyan Stirling then pitched in to complete the coordination details. Enthusiasm for the dance at Rustlers Valley was high. Myrtle, the Irish woman who served as the restaurant's gourmet chef and manager, told them that the "For the One" Dance was the most exciting thing they had ever done at the retreat center. "And we've done a lot of things here," she added.

John and Joško got busy preparing the dance grounds down in the valley floor. Niyan's VW truck was out of service so there was no convenient way to transport tools and supplies. One morning after breakfast, the couple worked out arrangements for feeding the dance crew with Frik, the retreat owner, and Myrtle. Jeanne's day was later spent on last-minute communications to the South African helpers and arranging the details to transport the international crew to and from the airport. An uncommon rain delayed work on the dance arbor, so the men made a supply run into Ficksburg, which was in the midst of its Cherry Festival. Later, Dominic (Dom), a blonde, blue-eyed South African studying to be a sangoma, returned to the Valley where he planned to dance both "For the One" Dances. In subsequent dances, he would serve the laborious role of Firekeeper.

Once Jeanne had completed her coordination work for the Dance, she could relax and leave the outside work to John. She was finally able to sleep through the night. On Tuesday, her ceremonial activity began with a lengthy set of rituals that honored both the African sangoma traditions as well as those of her own ancestral spirits. Jeanne was aided by John, Joško, and Dom as they greeted the ancestors, lit candles, burned *mpepo* and sage, and blessed the directional shrines and dance pole with cornmeal, sacred water, and milk. Jeanne had previously gone to the arbor at dawn to do a personal clearing ceremony. As she knelt at the east shrine and touched her head to the ground, a huge bird flew so close over her head that she had felt the wind beneath its wings. Looking up to identify it, she could not see, for the bird had flown directly into the blinding risen sun.

Midweek the first wave of the American dance crew arrived in the persons of Steve Citty, Sammye Jo, Cheryl Braswell, Margarita DiVita, Troy Amastar, Judith Brooks, Melinda Taylor, and Nancy Kern. Felicity Macdonald came to dance from Sao Paulo, Brazil. The next day—Thanksgiving—Gail Cully and Sharon Creed from the U.S.A., Henry Rowan from Ireland, Brett Almond from England, Anne Klanderud from Norway, Mona Zekri from Egypt, Shania Racky (with her four-year-old son Noah) from Germany, Arifa Kaufman from Germany, and Monica Dantus from Israel arrived. In all, the people who danced or crewed the dance represented thirteen different countries. Once again, Grandmother Monica, the Chief Sangoma and her twazas came for the Pipe Ceremony and stayed to dance and then participate in the feast, the give-away blanket, and the sharing circle. Monica told the sharing crowd that the "For the One" Dance was the fulfillment of an ancient prophecy that people of the "rainbow" (people of all colors) would come together to sing and dance as "one."

The first "For the One" Dance had nineteen dancers, and the second, a week later, had fourteen dancers. Experienced Sun-Moon dancers Henry Rowan and Brett Almond told John that the "For the One" Dance experience was more powerful and profound than they had ever experienced before. Henry added in his enthusiasm, "This dance is the one." Johan, a middle-aged landscaper from Johannesburg, told the Pehrsons, "The dance is the most important thing I've ever done. It was massive!" In their third year at Rustlers Valley, it was evident that the dances were transforming individual lives and affecting the larger community that included the ancient Zulu sangomas. Niyan and Frik both acknowledged it, and they wanted to plan for future dances. For Jeanne's part, she was already thinking of bringing children into the "For the One" Dance. It was the genesis of a children's dance that would later evolve.

There is a legend known to every sangoma that in ancient times, one of the tribes in the Rustlers Valley region possessed the "key to the universe." Another tribe that was jealous of this great and powerful object sent warriors who attacked and stole the key, but subsequently they lost it due to their greed. In order to restore the key, the legend continues, it will be necessary for 2,000 people who possess spiritual understanding and unconditional love to dance in Rustlers Valley, the Valley of the Earth Mother. Only then would the dimensional gateway open again to humankind and the key be restored. In these first two dances, six of those who went into vision at the pole reported seeing thousands of ethereal people in the arbor. Niyan and Frik, talking with Jeanne and John about future dances, speculated that many dance arbors might have to be built in the valley to accommodate the potential of the dancers to come.

After the two dances were completed, a free-roaming horse entered the arbor while Jeanne was there. The pale dappled-gray horse with white socks ran directly to the center pole and then slowly circled it. Then it galloped back out the east gate bucking and whinnying. John surmised that the lingering energy of the dance must have been too much for him. In relating the encounter, they learned that the horse was named "Spirit."

As people began to go their separate ways, Jeanne and John took a group of eleven dance crewmembers to meet Baba Credo Mutwa. They greeted Baba Credo and Virginia with gifts. Baba Credo was dressed in his floor-length caftan and heavy bronze necklace regalia. He greeted the group by saying, "Honorable Ones, we have much to talk about." Then he told them that in the Zulu tradition, the visitor is God. And God has the right to ask any question. About the "For the One" Dance, he said, "By dancing, you scratch the Earth because the Earth is always itching. When you dance, the Earth comes alive, heals itself, and heals the people."

Before the Pehrsons left Johannesburg after 27 days in South Africa, they received an excited e-mail from Troy Amastar, who had already returned to the U. S. and processed the photos that she took. Several of the photos that she had taken of Jeanne and John in the arbor showed "circles of light" or "balls of energy" around their heads. Troy admitted that she had seen such orbs before in photos of spiritual events, but they had never turned up in her photos. She couldn't wait to show these photos to Jeanne and John.

THE EMERSON CONNECTION

When an understanding of the metaphysics of the "For The One" Dance occurs, those familiar with the work of Ralph Waldo Emerson will be struck by the direct spiritual connection.

Emerson, an American philosophical and literary original, left the comforts of the organized church in 1832 to teach and practice a transcendental idea that the world unfolds from the Universal Mind, which he calls the Over-Soul. Emerson taught the radical idea that divine energy is constant, and that any individual, through personal intuition, can establish relationship with it.

Emerson offered no theological system, and he was indifferent to any religions arguing over ideas about God. He did not seek devotees, nor did he proselytize. His objective was to awaken, and he viewed transcendentalists as "collectors of the heavenly spark with power to convey the electricity to others." When we read Emerson's electricity for Jeanne White Eagle's vibration, their realizations seem identical. "Salvation," Emerson said to Thoreau, "would not be a question of accepting a creed, but of acquiring insight." Insight is another term for the visionary experiences available in the FTOD method of awakening.

Jeanne and John, like Emerson, will be criticized and have their example of individual divinity misinterpreted as a self-indulgence of personality and an exaltation of ego. But like Emerson, they also experience Self-reliance as "reliance on God" and the One Mind of God as the Source of all powers and privileges. This connection that they hold in common with Emerson is the mystic's experience of higher levels of awareness.

The organizations behind modern religious practice reject Emerson's transcendental cosmology because an individual connection to the Over-Soul bypasses the social, economic, political, and moral control of their institutions. Rather than accept Emerson as a spiritual prophet, critics spin the contemporary focus to his social ideas. He is allowed to be a quintessential character in American culture as long as scholars do not take his spiritual teachings too seriously. From this perspective, Emerson may be acknowledged as a lion of literature, but never as a prophet of spiritual individualism. The idea that an individual can know God without an intercessor is too dangerous to all forms of government—sectarian or secular.

And yet, Emerson's recognition of the individual's potential for divine enlightenment is not only democratic, but it also fits the American personality that wants to push every frontier for answers to essential questions. The transcendentalism expressed by Emerson cannot be marginalized as a quaint 19th century American ideal that passed away with the rise of an industrial age. The transcendental experience has persisted, and it endures today as an unbroken Emerson legacy.

Emerson would have immediately recognized the purpose of the "For The One" Dance, and he would have first danced, and then become a Dance Chief. He would have championed the FTOD because he would have experienced it as a method for connecting to what he knew as the Over-Soul. And if ancient elders come into the dance arbor at the height of its spiritual vibration, among the great souls supporting the dancers must surely be Ralph Waldo Emerson.

In the mid-1830s, Emerson wrote about the Over-Soul in this way: "We live in succession, in division, in parts, in particles. Meantime, within man is the soul of the whole; the wise silence, the universal beauty, to which every part and particle is equally related, the eternal One. And this deep power in which we exist and whose beatitude is all-accessible to us, is not only self-sufficing and perfect in every hour, but the act of seeing and the thing seen, the seer and the spectacle, the subject and the object, are one. We see the world piece by piece, as the sun, the moon, the animal, the tree; but the whole, of which these are the shining parts, is the soul."

Time and again, Emerson speaks of "vision" and "energy" as attributes of the transcendental reality. Vision and energy as vibration is the same terminology used to describe what occurs in the dance arbor. Emerson would also have appreciated the democracy of the FTOD. No one is denied—not by social status, age, gender, race, creed, or color. There is no separation. The purpose of the dance itself is to end separation, to profoundly recognize that humanity and everything else is part of the One . . . Emerson's Over-Soul.

Like Jeanne and John, Emerson was a non-conformist. He and Jeanne and John would have enjoyed each other. Recognizing the heart connection, they would have found no need to pursue a torturous dialectic. Within a few minutes, they would have been laughing together and trading stories.

PEACEMAKERS AND THE CIA

Americans who travel extensively worldwide without official diplomatic portfolio or corporate business identification will eventually be subject to government agency scrutiny. If the Americans in question frequently travel to the political hot spots of the Middle East, Europe, Africa, and South America, where international intrigues are the everyday secret currencies, they are probably not even a little bit paranoid if they feel that they are being watched by shadowy clandestine figures connected to the United States Central Intelligence Agency.

From the perspective of the CIA, Jeanne and John must seem a threat to the world order of governments. In their small "cells" centered around Peace-Sound Chambers and dance arbors, they are organizing populations to perceive no enemies. How can there be governments without perceived enemies? If people come to believe that they are not separate from each other, what will happen to national borders and the need for a military industrial complex? With real peace, what will happen to the hierarchy of social, religious, political, and economic control?

For established institutions that obtain their power based on control, which is a form of fear, real peace and freedom threatens their authority, their status, and their incomes. Leaderships of all stripes are thus very suspicious of the peacemakers because they cannot imagine that today's peacemakers want anything more than to control their tomorrows with a hierarchy of the peacemaker's own design. The establishment cannot imagine that the spiritual experience of love can end conflict in the chaos of their fragmented societies.

Even political leaders who profess religious convictions and high clergy who wear the robes of their divine offices cannot get beyond the belief that other human beings are both sinners and enemies. Reality for them is a duality that functions on conflict, and they believe that conflict is what enables them to maintain their high positions of control over other human beings. Any meaningful activity that ends conflict thus endangers their office and their institutional hierarchy. Despite all gesturing to the contrary, prophets of peace are not welcome in this world. They are too revolutionary. They are too dangerous to the status quo. And the record shows that in one way or the other, our wayshowers of peace are usually crucified by the ruling authority.

Jeanne and John are aware, like others in the international wayshower community, that they are not always welcome by government and church authorities, and that their activities are sometimes scrutinized. Perhaps there are fat files and dossiers based on surveillances that are maintained on Jeanne and John. Certainly they have felt watched, even by black helicopters in Israel, Germany, and Norway and by surveillance aircraft in South Africa. They have also had their luggage thoroughly searched at most international airports and border crossings.

SPEEDING UP

During the period of Jeanne's 2004-2005 journal, "things were speeding up," as the couple noted in "Eagle Notes: Volume 6," dated September 2004 to January 2005. "Eagle Notes" is written in third person to "avoid any confusion around who is speaking." It is essentially a newsletter summary of their travels and experiences for supporters who receive it as an e-mail attachment or read it on the Jeanne White Eagle website.

The "speeding up" was the persistent call to stage the "For the One" Dance in distant places. Since the first FTOD in April of 2003, the dance had been taken to Israel (September) and to South Africa (November). Then in 2004, dances were scheduled for Tennessee, Israel, North Carolina, and South Africa—with Germany, Norway, and Ireland also in the planning stages. In addition, Jeanne and John continued to do Peace Concerts, occasional workshops, and personal counseling sessions as they traveled.

Joseph had told Jeanne that if you have a vision, and it is a true vision, then once it begins to take off, all that you can do is hold on for dear life. Jeanne said that she and John sometimes felt with the "For the One" Dance like they were holding on to the tail of a huge kite that was soaring in a mighty wind.

The logistics of travel planning, dance crew assembly, accommodations, and dance site facilities (arbor, sweat lodge and kitchen) were still being handled by Jeanne and John during this period. Travel coordination alone required days on the computer, and ultimately Jeanne developed great skill in obtaining the cheapest airfares and accommodations. John's usual focus was coordinating with the local sponsor on the site facilities, and where there was no arbor or sweat lodge, they had to be built. The couple also had to respond to prospective dancers and to sponsors who wanted their questions answered by the Dance Chiefs themselves. Often, the couple's e-mail correspondence required several hours a day. Without any staff support, their daily tasks could seem daunting, if not overwhelming.

The couple's most fertile ground for fear involved finances. There were no fixed budgets and no income forecasts to facilitate planning, neither short term nor long term. Jeanne and John were going to South Africa or to Israel, but how were their expenses going to be met when they scheduled the dance? They did not know. Who would volunteer to crew the dance and pay their own way? They did not know. "Is this any way to run a railroad?" old timers might ask. Well, of course not, but the FTOD train had pulled into the station on time for the last two years, and the Jeanne and John Chamber Awakening Express had been rolling since 1998. Like the old gospel song says, "The little wheel run by faith, and the big wheel run by the Grace of God." Don't try to account for it in any other way because the event ledger sheets would drive a certified public accountant stark raving mad. The numbers would only confirm that something beyond reason had occurred, and that it had occurred time and time again.

In Rustler's Valley in South Africa on November 21, 2004, Jeanne turned to her journal after being awakened about 2 a.m.

"Hearing the thunder beings and rain, my heart responds in kind. I find that I've been fearful around the money, and yet things keep happening that show me we're being supported. My heart has been heavy, but that seems to be part of my own process moving through another level of me. I remember last year that there was an issue with money, but I truly have handled it differently this year, and the door to receive has opened wider. This year we received some beautiful donations that have helped. All I need to do is trust. The thunder beings are speaking. Shhh. Listen. There are other voices speaking. Hear them. Know that I am God . . . trust Me, Jeanne. Take my hand. Trust Me. We call you. Listen. There is nothing to do but allow, observe, love, serve. The storm is over. The fertile ground awaits. Do not be afraid. I have your hand. When you are afraid, keep your eyes on Me. Listen. Shhh. The heart beats, the blood flows, the soul dances as the life force moves to the rhythm of birth. Shhh. Hear it? Rejoice now. I am in charge. There is truly nothing to worry about."

The thesis of Neale Donald Walsch's series of books, *Conversations with God*, is that God talks to everyone all the time.

The problem is that we, as humanity, do not listen. It is evident from Jeanne's journals that she listens.

Before the FTOD in Rustler's Valley, Jeanne recorded another conversation with her Divine Self in the journal. Although the focus of the process is always the same, the imagery often changes as her voice is transmuted into that of the Divine Counselor.

"I pray my being walks in full humility and integrity in this dance and that those who are truly called to dance find their way here," Jeanne petitions. Then the transmuted voice responds, "Listen. I am humming in everything around you. Listen. The trees, the water in the pipes, the silent sounds in your head. Listen. I am there. I am here. Know Me through the wind, through the sun, through the water, through the eyes, through the child's squeals and laughter. Know Me through the anxieties, fears, seeing through these veils to the truth of love. Know Me. I am here. Take My hand. Stand close, walk close to Me, lie with Me in My arms. I am never further than your breath. I am that which only knows love. I am love. I am love-ing. Always. Now . . . always. Breathe now. Listen. I am Guide-ing you. Shhh. Shhh."

Like everyone in the media-saturated world, Jeanne and John were conscious of the devastation and the shocking loss of life as a result of the December 26, 2004 tsunami in the Asian Pacific. In her private journal, Jeanne sought to deal with the tragedy in spiritual terms.

"Even in the appearance of the devastation of the tsunami, look at the name oo, ah, ee . . . center to birth to illusional death to center again . . . the circle. It is only the physical that can experience the concept of death . . . death, the doorway out of one reality into the doorway of another beginning . . . the sound of ee to the center oo to birth again ah . . . shhh, shhh . . . loving . . . lighting . . . healing . . . knowing . . . shhh."

Jeanne learned that whenever she was directing judgments toward herself that it was always a sign to slow down and be quiet. The spiritual discipline of silence and focus on breathing was practiced by distant cultures throughout recorded history. In Native American spiritual culture, the practice had been passed down by elders to ceremonial acolytes through eons that began with a Creation myth. That method of connection to Source was, and is, timeless. "Be still and know" is a universal wisdom that pre-dates the *Bible*. The truth that emerged from Jeanne's silent surrender to Source was almost always recorded in these words: "Love what is in front of you in the moment. I will take care of everything else."

The news in January that detailed the tragic tsunami losses half a world away from Colorado, where they wintered, was acting on Jeanne physically. She was internalizing the distant pain and suffering in her own body. Like everyone with access to television media, Jeanne and John watched the tourist videos as the giant waves arrived. They realized that every man, woman, and child within sight of the camera was probably dead. On beach after beach, across a thousand miles of ocean, the horrors filled the television screen with new assaults on the empathic senses every day until the viewers were numb with awe and revulsion. For most people, a sensitivity threshold would be reached, and the autonomic nervous system would be engaged to protect the viewer from excessive rumination. For Jeanne, however, the hurt would not abate. It became proximal, and almost unbearable.

On January second, the excruciating pain had been constant for twenty-four hours, and Jeanne called on John and Sammye Jo (by telephone) to help her transcend it. A first prescription was to be removed from the sights and sounds of the television reporting. Sixteen days later, Jeanne was recovered enough to write in her journal.

"It is time to let it go . . . let the pain of our precious land, people, world dissolve into the love of Spirit. It's time. It's time."

On January 21st, a day after George W. Bush's second inauguration, Jeanne wrote a letter to the President in her journal that was never mailed. She told the President that she and John had spent many months in the Middle East in the last few years, and that they had witnessed the first bombing of Bethlehem from two miles away. They saw the helicopters and planes gathering, and then the orange glow of the explosions as the bombs struck the birth town of the Prince of Peace. Through her tears, Jeanne turned to see the face of a Palestinian man. A few yards away, there was another face—the face of an Israeli Jewish friend. The faces appeared to be her own. At that moment, she told the President, she "got it." If she hurt or killed either of these persons, she would only be inflicting herself.

"I have a message to give to you," Jeanne wrote at the bottom of the page, "There is only one of us here. All there is is Love. It is time now, Sir, to move beyond the idea of war. It is time."

Throughout February and March, whenever there were financial fears, Jeanne would return to her journal to work them out. She seemed never in the psychological quagmire of denial because she even acknowledged her material dilemmas in dollar amounts. She seemed always willing in the privacy of her journal to admit to her fears and to the "old attachments," but then she processed that sense of lack into a spiritual dimension. Otherwise, how could she continue to function in the spiritual role that she felt ordained to do?

Many independent filmmakers—Spike Lee for one—made their first films by maxing out their credit cards. Their faith in what they were doing enabled them to take financial risks that were improbable or impossible for other would-be filmmakers. For the true believers in independent filmmaking, failure is not an option. The quest will not be abandoned. Is the motivation any less persistent in the soul of the spiritual artist—artist, in this sense, defined as a metaphysical physician to the human condition? Even crucifixion has been a weak deterrent against such practitioners. Money, by this perspective, then seems to be a small temporary obstacle.

The last few pages of this journal book were written in Israel, and a final page in Germany. Prior to the three "For the One" Dances that Jeanne notes, she had prayed for the dance supporters to appear—a Drum Chief, an Alpha Dog to direct the Dog Solders, and Drummers. When the dances actually began, all the support positions were filled, some by volunteers who had come from far continents after personal circumstantial miracles had made their travel possible. Jeanne constantly counseled herself to expect these miracles.

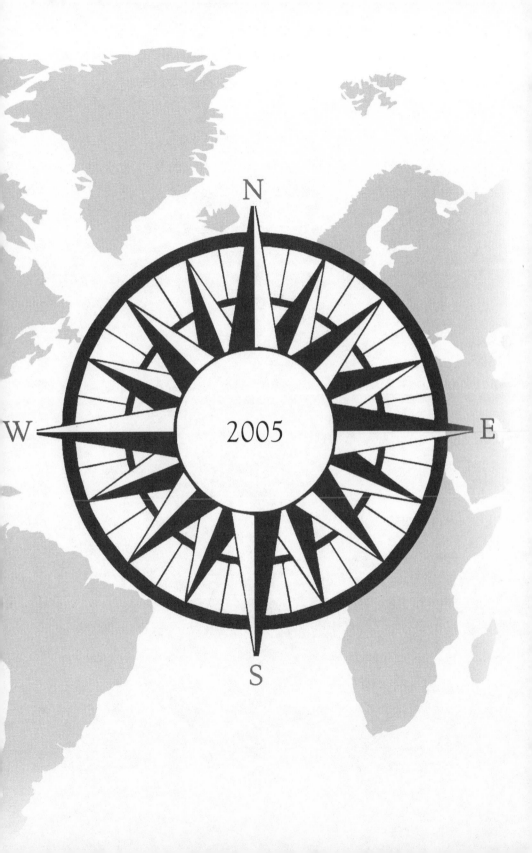

A WHOLE NEW LEVEL

T he Christmas of 2004 was spent in Crestone again, this time as house sitters that included a dog. The couple's Christmas card $50 give-aways were expanded by Jeanne in a spontaneous move to pay for a cartload of items being pushed by a young woman in a discount store checkout line. By the time the young woman reached the cashier, Jeanne had arranged with the store manager to pay for everything. The woman openly wept when the manager told her, "There is an angel in the store that wants to pay for your items as a Christmas present. There are still some good people in the world." John caught up on the event later as Jeanne was paying the bill of about $130. He was surprised by what Jeanne had done, but the giving of the anonymous gift felt very good, even secondhand.

Christmas Day, Jeanne fixed a traditional turkey dinner, and they called all five of their children. They felt that their relationship with each one was strong despite their absences. The news of the huge earthquake and the tsunamis that swept across the Indian Ocean and caused unprecedented death and destruction in its wake sobered the New Year's celebration, and Jeanne's 61st birthday on the 29th was quietly celebrated. John's gift was a massage from Grant Freeman, who was their regular Crestone therapist. Their Christmas gift to each other was a new indispensable Dell laptop computer. After it arrived, John called his son Ryan who talked him through an expert set-up of the machine.

This winter in Crestone was uncomfortable although their accommodations were excellent. There was a great deal of snow, and both Jeanne and John suffered from physical maladies that were both stress and disease related. Jeanne was sometimes in agony with stomach spasms, cold sweats, and vomiting. As an empath, both Jeanne and John wondered if Jeanne's body was reacting to the suffering of the millions of people impacted by the December tsunamis and its death toll already reported at 150,000. Owen James told the couple that Jeanne was utterly exhausted and needed to take emergency measures to restore her health. John had frequent and painful headaches that caused him to feel like he had "wasted" days.

Their last day at Crestone was the 26th of January when the generous homeowners, Jo Dee Powers and Roger Gilchrest, returned from Australia and New Zealand. After a stopover in Placitas in the casita where they had stayed before, the couple drove through blowing snow to keep their appointment with Joseph and Carolyn in Hesperus. Joseph, who would turn 70 in June, looked a bit grayer but good to them. In discussions when they told Joseph about their ongoing health problems, he said, "Look, this is what we're dealing with. We spend a lot of time in ceremonial space. When we attempt to shift gears back into normal reality with its practical demands on us, it causes problems."

John appreciated what Joseph was saying because that is what he and Jeanne were experiencing. They felt fragile, and their emotions were very close to the surface.

There was another significant conversation when they talked about the dances. Joseph told them that they come from a lineage of teachers that went back millions of years. The dances come through them from Spirit and they aren't really theirs. If the dances are anyone's, they are God's. So it really doesn't make any difference who takes the credit. He advised them to let go of the dances now, psychologically, so when the time comes to physically let them go, they will have already done it.

Later, John told Joseph that he wanted to change the name of the Sun-Moon Dances that he chiefed to the *Star Dance*. The Sun-Moon Dance, of course, was originated by Joseph, and it was Joseph who had named John as a Chief, so John was asking for Joseph's blessing out of respect. The name change was also a way of distancing the Sun-Moon Dance from Native American criticism that the Dance violated their rights and traditions. Any similarity to their sacred Sun Dance practiced by whites was considered taboo to Indian ceremonial purists. And although the Sun-Moon Dance had never been promoted as a Native American ceremony, it was perceived as such to many observers.

In the sweat lodge Joseph concluded the discussion about the dances by saying, "In the future, you don't have to even ask me to make changes in your ceremonies. I love you for who you are, and for carrying the work forward. We're the same, just different faces of the One Being. So, you don't even need to tell me in the future."

On their last morning with Joseph and Carolyn over coffee at the breakfast table, Joseph spoke about the power of growing up in a verb culture in which everything is vibration. Everything is alive. Everything is vibrating itself into being. By contrast, in a noun-pronoun culture there are animate things such as people, animals, and plants, but there are also dead, inanimate objects. Growing up in a culture (Pueblo-Southern Ute) whose world view taught that everything is alive also taught reverence for life. That's missing in our noun-pronoun society, he told them.

During this period, Jeanne recalls, "I was already letting go of the dance and needed little prompting as any good mother would begin to let go of her child more and more as the child got stronger and stronger."Nevertheless, there was still the challenge of a troubling introspection. John, too, wondered if they were strong enough, good enough, and smart enough to keep all the multiplying "For the One" Dance balls in the air. Even after years of devotion to their mission, the couple could still face a crisis of faith. And every crisis of faith also felt like a crisis in relationship. Each one had to acknowledge the fragility of the other and minister to that need in the process of passing through the valley of the shadow of doubt.

Back in Placitas, Gail Homan did massage body work on both Jeanne and John. After her session with Jeanne, Gail pleaded with Jeanne to take it easy on herself for the next few days. She felt that Jeanne was in extreme fatigue with a body that had almost completely shut down. Into February, Gail continued to work on Jeanne in sessions that sometimes lasted for two hours. Jeanne went out to few events and saw few people during this period. Then daughter Jenny, with her airline pilot's credentials, sent her mother an airplane ticket to visit her in Boise. The ticket was stand-by, and John had to wait in the airport until he was sure that Jeanne got on the flight. Someone was late arriving at the ticket counter, and Jeanne was awarded the last available seat.

That week, John agreed to provide the author with all of his journals through 2004. The author had read 10,000-word selections from the journals, but now all of it would become available. Jeanne would also provide journals, and both of them agreed to come to the author's home in Boone, North Carolina periodically for taped interviews.

Jeanne and John were scheduled to do an Awakening Ceremony at the end of February at the new Tulsa area Peace-Sound Chamber on land owned by Minisa and Jim Halsey, but Jeanne was warned by Owen James not to travel because of her health. During the exact hours of the Tulsa ceremony, however, Jeanne, John, and their close friends John and Melinda Stroupe, did a small ceremony with song and tobacco prayers to support the Chamber Awakening. When the Thunder Beings roared overhead in Placitas, Jeanne felt that everything was being done "in a good way" in Tulsa. Jeanne says in retrospect, "We realized that we were being asked to let go of the Chamber ceremonies as the communities themselves could now carry that work forward. It was hard not to be in Tulsa because Minisa had planned a beautiful celebration with people coming from around the country."

The Awakening Ceremony and Blessing was done by Minisa and Gail Cully. En route to North Carolina in March, the couple made a stopover to visit the Halseys and to perform a Peace Concert at an area Unity Church.

Since the farmhouse at Corryton was available, they went there to prepare for the first "For the One" Dance of the year at the Center for Peace. In the interim, they attended three meetings in Seymour, Tennessee, and in Asheville and Graham, North

Carolina, to organize the international dance crew. The brainstorming sessions later led to Margarita DiVita agreeing to become the "For the One" Dance international coordinator, and Patty Coleman agreeing to head up a fundraising team. The couple also did a Living In the Moment Workshop at the Center for Peace that was well attended. From full stop in Crestone in January, they were already full speed by mid-March despite their physical disabilities.

The "For the One" Dance at the Center for Peace was considered by the dance crew as one of the strongest they had ever done. The March 18-20 weekend was not springlike in the Tennessee Smoky Mountain foothills. It was wet and freezing cold, and no one in the crew tents or in the arbor could stay warm that Friday night. What perhaps was different from previous dances was the total involvement of the Dog Soldiers and helpers outside the arbor. Jeanne handed out rattles for them to play; and by Saturday afternoon, all the Dog Solders and helpers were in a line across the arbor gate playing all Jeanne's rattles, singing loud, and dancing hard in place. Sammye Jo, looking out from the arbor where she served as a Moon Mother, said that she saw some of the dancing, singing, rattle-playing crewmembers come out of their bodies. The energy that they produced was definitely powerful, and it supported the dancers inside the arbor in significant ways.

In the sharing after the dance in the Peace-Sound Chamber, dancers testified that the sight and sound of the rattle-line had moved them to greater intensity, and they were profoundly grateful for this unexpected support. In future "For the One" Dances, the new pattern was set. No more sitting around outside the arbor waiting for a dancer to hit the pole. From now on, when the drums started, everyone sang and danced, inside and out! The "For the One" Dance had graduated to a new level.

SAMMYE JO HARVEY

Months before her grandchild was born, Sammye Jo Harvey heard the child speak to her. "So this is what it is like to be a grandmother," Sammye Jo said. Sammye Jo, who is very much a Native American woman, attended the birth of the child, a girl with blue-green eyes and an Anglo's complexion. When she saw the child, she was struck with her conditioned prejudice to white people; and the child, speaking to her again and calling her grandmother, healed the mixed-race separation. Later this event was to have a powerful result when Jeanne approached her to be included in her first sweat lodge experience. Because of her granddaughter, whom Jeanne resembled, Sammye Jo was able to embrace Jeanne and form a very powerful spiritual alliance with her. She was a mentoring Moon Mother at the couple's first ceremonial dances, and all through Jeanne and John's visionary enlightenment and mission calling, Sammye Jo was there. Then, as the "For the One" Dance evolved, she served in the arbor at almost every dance.

Jeanne says this about her dear friend and confidant.

"I was not raised with any knowledge of Native American traditions, although my family has a Cherokee bloodline. At my very first sweat lodge at the Center for Peace that was poured by Beautiful Painted Arrow, I was waiting with the group to enter the lodge, and I was very nervous. Next to me stood a real Native American Grandmother, and I confessed to her that I was new to this ceremony. She said, 'You need to stay right next to me, honey.'

"A sweat lodge can be a frightening experience, but next to Sammy Jo Harvey, I felt safe. Years later, Sammye Jo told me that when she first saw me, she said to herself, 'Here comes the fulfillment of prophecy.'

"Throughout my spiritual apprenticeship at the Center for Peace, Sammye Jo turned up, and I had the feeling that she was observing me through ancient eyes to see if I was true. Later at the

Peace Sound Chamber at Swannanoa, while I was singing inside the Chamber, and she was listening at the outside fire pit, Sammye Jo says that she was convinced that I was being directed by Spirit. Today, Sammye Jo is an important Elder and Moon Mother at "For The One" Dances, and she has traveled with us to Israel, South Africa, Germany, Ireland, Norway, and Brazil."

The author first met Sammye Jo at the March 18-20, 2005 "For the One" Dance at the Center for Peace. It was both his first-time dance experience and his first tent camping ordeal since basic training in the Viet Nam War era Army. The first night of the dance was so cold that hardly any crewmember could get warm in their tent. As a Dog Soldier, the author volunteered for the midnight to three shift at the arbor fire, which did not serve sleep either. The vigil at the arbor's east gate, however, was memorable, and it provided a bonding experience with fellow Dog Soldiers. When a dancer had to use the toilet, they appeared out of the dark arbor wrapped in a white sheet. Sometimes their approach to the gate was startling. A sage smudge pot at the ready, they would be smudged both leaving and re-entering the arbor. The silent Dog Soldier then led them to the outhouse by a flashlight pointed to the ground and then waited at a discrete distance to guide them back to the gate. Jeanne and John took mercy on the Dog Soldiers and other dance crewmembers who were tenting in the arbor meadow and opened the Peace-Sound Chamber with its blissful woodstove for sleeping the second night.

During the dance itself, Jeanne called the Dog Soldiers to come to the gate entrance and take up one of the rattles in her collection. The author had never played a rattle before in ceremony; but with the drum group so close and the energy so intense, the rattle was soon playing the man. From a vantage point at the arbor entrance just behind Jeanne and John, the hours of dancing in place with the rattles afforded a great opportunity to observe what was occurring. In addition, six-member Dog Soldier teams were called into the arbor to carry dancers who had collapsed into vision back to their beds in a rolled-sheet litter. A Dog Soldier might also re-enter the arbor to take hot or cold towels to the Moon Mother who was caring for a fallen dancer. In this way, the author had many hours to witness Sammye Jo at work.

Sammye Jo was especially interesting to the author, although he knew nothing personal about her, because she had the same posture and energy of the Cherokee Grandmother and Wisdom Keeper, Jacque Red Leaf, that he and his wife loved. Pat Joynes was Red Leaf's Chosen Daughter, and Pat had been named "Morning Song" in a Cherokee Ceremony at the revered elder's lodge. The author had served as Red Leaf's ceremonial Firekeeper, and he would later be named "Smoke Rising" and recognized as a Warrior in the Cherokee tradition. At times during the "For the One" Dance, when the author looked at Sammye Jo, he had the same feelings for her as he did for Red Leaf . . . a deep, respectful love.

There was no contact with Sammye Jo during the dance; but after the sharing and the blanket give-away in the Chamber, they met and Sammye Jo asked the author to walk with her so that she could tell him a story. She said that Spirit had directed her to tell this story, but she did not know why. The story dealt with how tobacco came to be used as a sacred element in Native American ceremony. Alone on the road outside the Chamber, the author told Sammye Jo his connection to Grandmother Red Leaf and how he had learned to honor the feminine through her wisdom. Suddenly, a bolt of recognition struck the odd couple, and they both wept and embraced each other. Then Sammye Jo did something astounding, something even Red Leaf had never heard done before. She removed her sacred medicine bag from around her neck and put it around the neck of the author. The import of what she had done almost brought him to his knees. There were no more words except for Sammye Jo to say that he should keep the medicine bag until he saw her again.

When the author returned to his home in Boone, he wrote a prose poem the next day and sent it to Grandmother Sammye Jo. It is as much a testimonial to the "For the One" Dance experience as if it came from a transfigured dancer.

"After shaking ceremonial rattles for perhaps ten hours over three days, I hit the tree, and the tree's name was Sammye Jo Harvey, a Native American Grandmother. Where were the Dog Soldiers to carry me away in a white sheet? A man with an over-flowing heart should be watched lest he give himself away to the wind and disappear. But I had promises to keep, and her medicine bag to protect me, so I did not drown in the river of my own tears, although I let go of the shore and flowed with the sacred water, tak-ing nothing personally, least of all myself.

"When we as humanity hit the tree, we become the tree of pure existence, and our memory then becomes the forest of all life that sings a common song rooted in the earth and reaching for the sky. There is no other way to live except in celebration."

The author was wearing Grandmother Sammye Jo's medicine bag when Grandmother Red Leaf named him *Tsu-na-lu-gi* that sum-mer. Al Fletcher, a Dog Soldier who stood the midnight-to-three arbor watch with him at the March "For the One" Dance attended with his wife Barbara, who brought wonderful fresh fruit pies to the feast after the naming.

Grandmother Sammye Jo is Chippewa Cree in heritage and a third generation storyteller. Her strength of body and spirit is well known to dancers whom she has guided and nurtured in dance arbors all over the world. She is also honored as a significant elder among Native American people.

Grandmother Sammye Jo's medicine bag hung in a place of honor in the Joynes home until the author wore it to his next "For the One" Dance that September at Watersong. On the dance grounds Jeanne and John coached the author on how to approach Grandmother and offer the return of the medicine bag. The brief ceremonial encounter occurred outside the sweat lodge. In silence, the man offered the return of the medicine bag three times, and on the fourth time, the Grandmother accepted it from his outstretched hands. There were then smiles of recognition, and then the man walked away without the need to speak of his heartfelt emotions.

THE ISRAEL AND
GERMANY CONNECTION

J eff Goldstein met Jeanne and John at the airport and transported them to accommodations in Mevasseret. The next day they rented a car in Jerusalem for the drive to Rosh Pina. Jeanne soon discovered that their new computer would not connect to their e-mail service provider. They were told by an AOL supervisor that they had to access foreign telephone numbers prior to leaving the U. S. Thus, for the next four months of their foreign travel, they would have to depend on the e-mail computer connections of friends or Internet cafés. In Rosh Pina with Anael, coordination for the two "For the One" Dances occupied the waking hours, and 35 people had already committed to dance, including four Germans who were coming to dance during Holocaust Memorial Day. The couple gave a Peace Concert on the 29th after John and Joško had worked all day on the dance arbor. John wished that Steve Citty or Dobs were there to help.

On the Saturday before the dance, John and Joško drove a rutted rural road down to the banks of the Jordan River to select lava rocks for the sweat lodge fire. Sixty stones were needed for the multiple sweat lodges that would be held during the two dances. The roles of Alpha Dog and Firekeeper had not yet been assigned, and there was growing pressure to find experienced people to function in these essential roles. Some dances were like that. Key people appeared in the last days prior to the dance to assume the vacant positions. For this dance, Joško took the responsibility role of Alpha Dog and Debbie Tor was a first-time Drum Chief.

All 21 dancers worked hard in the arbor, and all but one went to the pole and experienced visionary releases. On Holocaust Memorial Day a siren sounded at 10 A.M. for two minutes. Jeanne then asked the four German dancers to step forward, which they did with obvious trepidation. Then Jeanne addressed the Jews and asked those willing to dance side-by-side with the Germans to step forward. The overwhelming response was a very touching moment for the volunteers as well as for everyone who witnessed it. Paul Barrett, a full-blooded Navajo from Los Angeles, who is married to an Israeli woman from Yemen, served the dance as a Dog Soldier and drummer. He returned to serve the second dance as a Firekeeper.

Jeff Goldstein was the local dance coordinator, but he got a great deal of support from the volunteer dance crew that followed the "For the One" Dance all over the world. Sonja Munz was an example. She traveled from Birmingham, England, where she is a veterinarian, to support the Israeli dance. She had also danced in South Africa. Gail Cully had come from Oklahoma. As a registered nurse, Gail filled a unique role as a lead Moon Mother. At the first dance there were 21 dancers and more than 30 helpers. In the second dance there were 22 dancers and 50 helpers. It was more than enough energy and impact to assure future years of an Israeli "For the One" Dance.

After the back-to-back dance weekends, Jeanne and John had some down time to visit with friends, but before they departed Rosh Pina, Jeanne did a well-attended Sound Workshop. Then on the 25th of May, they were en route to Germany via Athens to stage the first "For the One" Dance in Germany.

In Grossropperhausen, Alex and Shania Racky, caretakers of the Peace-Sound Chamber and the Pehrsons' long-time supporters in Germany, coordinated the "For the One" Dance. There were 25 dancers that included Jews who had followed the dance from Israel. For everyone involved in the memory of the Holocaust, courage was required. The dancers trust belied the fact that they would dance to places that they never imagined.

Jeanne and John were well known from previous trips to Grossropperhausen, and so Alex and Shania were able to enlist the support of the burgermeister, or mayor, of the surrounding villages. The town authority supplied tents for the kitchen and recovery areas and the labor of two young men to help in constructing the dance arbor and supplying firewood for the lodge and ceremonial fires. The burgermeister himself also attended the after-dance feast and sharing circle.

The first "For the One" Dance in Germany will be remembered for what occurred in the dance arbor between Anael Harpaz and a middle-age woman who experienced a historic epiphany. It is told from Anael's perspective.

Anael's Story

Many spiritual teachers who visited northern Israel came to the home of Anael Harpaz. Her warmth, generosity, and hospitality are well known in their network. When Jeanne and John first came to visit in October 2000, Anael was going through a difficult period in her personal life—a divorce—and she credits the couple with helping her through that distress.

Anael facilitated Peace Concerts and workshops by Jeanne and John, and she was a key contact and resource in their orientation to Israel. There were many gatherings of Jews and Arabs in her home.

Anael was born in South Africa, and she was emotionally affected by the prejudice of apartheid that she witnessed there. Her father was born in Palestine, and the plan that Anael heard throughout her childhood was that they were one day going home. Her entire orientation, both educationally and socially, was Jewish orthodox. When she was fifteen, she went with her school to Israel for three months just after the Six-Day War in 1967. The euphoria of the victory swept Anael up in a motivation to return to Israel, take up arms, and kill Arabs. The messages that she received constantly as a child were that her enemies were Germans and Arabs. Then after high school in South Africa, her family finally relocated to Israel.

Anael settled into life as an Israeli, performed desk job military service, got married, and had children. The loss of a child, however, pushed her deep inside herself for answers to basic questions, and thus began her first steps along a spiritual path apart from orthodox religion. When another of her children became paralyzed, Anael started to explore the nature of suffering on a spiritual level. She practiced ten days of total silence. She attended workshops. She wanted answers.

Then one astounding day in a workshop on the West Bank attended by Palestinian women, Anael experienced firsthand that suffering was not exclusively Jewish. With great emotion, Anael realized that she had been blind to another whole dimension of suffering.

"It was as if I had been standing on a plate of glass, and someone had taken a hammer and shattered it. All my belief systems fell to the ground in one day."

Anael's life-changing perspective was difficult for her family to accept; but as she engaged in peace initiatives, she became empowered to do significant things like facilitating a Peace Camp for Israeli and Palestinian teenagers in Santa Fe, New Mexico, a neutral ground far away from the influences of prejudice. Then, too, Anael found a voice for poetry, and she began to write sometimes-epic poems on the themes of peace and forgiveness. She read one of her poems at the end of a peace conference attended by the Dalai Lama and then enjoyed a private conversation with him. The long poem "Forgive – for the Children of Abraham, Sarah and Hagar" could only have been written by an intimate witness to the pain and suffering caused by cultures in conflict.

In April 2005, Anael danced the "For the One" Dance in Germany after serving both Israeli dances as a Moon Mother, with German participants on Holocaust Memorial Day. When the siren sounded to mark the Holocaust, the FTOD dancers in Israel stood silent in the arbor; and looking up, they witnessed a gathering of storks coming from various directions, who then intermingled and flew together as a formation over the arbor itself. Everyone at the dance was dumbfounded by what they considered a divine omen. The gathering of the huge birds, who are the universal symbol of birth, was in the least an unprecedented local phenomenon.

At the FTOD in Germany, Anael had a strong negative reaction to one of the German women dancers. Given her childhood conditioning of fearing and hating Germans, Anael was still a victim struggling against demons who would not yield for forgiveness. As they prepared for the Dance, Anael avoided the German woman as if she represented the Gestapo. When the dancers entered the arbor, Jeanne intuitively assigned them their rest cubicles and their lanes of dance. To Anael's horror, Jeanne placed the German woman next to her. And although she could not bear to look at the German women, Anael's prayers were not about anything other than the souls of the two conflicted sides should go to the Light.

"Enough of us being victims, and them being guilty," Anael said.

The hour that Anael hit the pole and was laid back in her arbor cubicle, she had a vision of Jewish and German souls embracing in a healing celebration. When she returned to dancing, she felt strongly guided to give her ceremonial shawl to the German woman dancing next to her. At first, Anael resisted the message because the shawl had been a precious gift to her, but at the third internal urging, she placed the shawl on the woman's shoulders. Moments later, both women were at the pole together, and Anael quietly sang a prayer that Jews say before they die. Against the sound of the drumming, only the German woman could hear it, and she sank immediately to her ground and began to weep. The dancers, including

Anael, returned to their places to wait as Jeanne and Moon Mother Sammye Jo cared for the fallen woman.

"Hearing her crying," Anael says, "I went to such a place of compassion that I wept for her."

At that moment, Jeanne beckoned to Anael and told her that the German woman needed her love, and she led Anael to the pole where Anael laid down beside the German woman, stroked her, comforted her, and blessed her as the women cried in agony together. At first the German woman did not know who was lying beside her, and then she turned and saw Anael. After that moment, they did not want to be apart from each other. Soon a drenching rain came as they danced in the wondrous release of forgiveness; and after the rain, a rainbow appeared that Anael describes as "the most amazing rainbow that I have ever seen in my whole life." The two women and all the others present accepted the rainbow as a recognition of their mutual atonement, and the German woman gave Anael her personal shawl. Later in conversation, the woman revealed that her father had served directly under Hitler. In this one instance, the FTOD had facilitated a healing of historic importance and spiritual significance. It had accomplished more than governments or religions could accomplish in all their formal pronouncements. It had changed hearts and minds on the deepest levels of being.

As a teenager, Anael was obsessed by the Holocaust, and she devoured its literature. Now she was totally released from that cultural conditioning. To make the peace of forgiveness come full circle, Anael intended to make what for her is the ultimate test—a visit to Auschwitz in Poland, the site of the infamous Nazi extermination camp during World War II.

IRELAND 2005

I n early July, the FTOD was held near Dublin at Rathe House, County Meath, Ireland. Owner Brian Garvey and his twenty-something daughter Jillian were very helpful in loaning some needed farm equipment for construction of the arbor and sweat lodge.

In seeking the placement of the arbor, Jeanne and John walked the farm fields until they encountered a sign. It was the same sign that had appeared for the placement of the Peace-Sound Chamber at the Center for Peace in Seymour, Tennessee ten years before. Too far away from any archery range for an accidental shot, there was an arrow sticking up almost vertically in the middle of a field. It was a black graphite arrow with a multicolored painted shaft. It was a "beautiful painted arrow" and proof again that Joseph was showing them the way.

The next morning when Jeanne and John returned to the site to offer cornmeal and tobacco prayers, four horses in the pasture approached them. One was a tan/yellow horse. Another was white. A third was black, and the fourth was a chestnut red. They were the colors of the four directions. What were the odds? Then, as the couple blessed the center of the arbor location, the white and black horses came near and touched their hands with their noses.

John recorded in his journal how "smooth" the energy was in the Irish dance. He and Joško Šabiè, who had traveled from Croatia, had the temporary arbor up two days ahead of schedule and thus had time to do the extra things that added to the comforts of the dance.

Èidín Griffin, an Irish friend from South Africa, was back in Ireland for a family visit, but came down to be the Alpha Dog Soldier for the dance in the company of her son Juno, age five. Alexander Racky from Germany and Nancy Kern from Texas came to be the Firekeepers. Sammye Jo Harvey, the ever-faithful Chippewa Elder from Tennessee, came to serve as Head Moon

Mother with the support of Moon Mother Shelley Ostroff and apprentice Moon Mother Sonja Munz. Dancers came from all over Europe, including Paris, and Cornwall in the UK. There were eighteen dancers—9 men and 9 women—and eighteen on the dance crew—9 females and 9 males if you count little Juno. That perfect dance balance had never occurred before, and the participants recognized it and were amazed.

The Irish dance is remembered by John for several reasons. One involved the exorcism of a male dancer who was removed from the arbor and taken into the sweat lodge for an ancient Chippewa ceremony performed by Sammye Jo to pull unwanted spirits out of the body. The strong medicine relieved the man, and he was advised not to invite the "thing" back into his body ever again.

In another case, a man was experiencing chest pain and even feared for his life. When he confided his condition to Moon Mother Sammye Jo, she was guided to ask, "How's your love life?" "It's a mess," the man confessed. Sammye Jo smiled, "Well, there you go." The man completed the dance by "running" back and forth to the pole. He amazed himself and everyone who observed him.

A third reason to vividly remember the first FTOD in Ireland was Jeanne's reaction to being there. In his journal, John writes:

"Something has come alive in Jeanne here in Ireland, as if dormant genes have been activated by her family ancestry here. I was beat but Jeanne felt energized after the dance. She went for some after-dinner camaraderie with the dancers and crew who were staying over. They sang and told stories and laughed a lot. It was a tonic for Jeanne."

In Jeanne's handwritten journal, she is effusive in describing her feelings in a stream of consciousness style. "And so, having been in Ireland for one week tasting of the coastal waters, walking in the sea, being blessed by the wind around the shore, driving through the mountains, being blessed by the lush green of the hills and the mystic faces of the mountains, hearing the subtle voices of the little ones, the wee people, bathing in the glow of Irish jigs and reels, touching and breathing my first Bodhrán (Irish drum) lesson, being guided by the ancestors to the site of the Dance . . . all this and more, so much more has brought me home again to the land of my Father, the land of my roots, my beginning."

On Sunday, after the feast and the sharing circle, the dancers pitched in to take down the arbor and sweat lodge and remove the wooden posts and tarps to storage.

THE LOVE STORY

A fter the Irish FTOD, Jeanne and John went in separate directions. Jeanne headed to Norway to spend more than a week resting in seclusion at Anne Klanderud's cabin on a lake before the scheduled Norwegian FTOD at the end of the month. John departed for Tennessee to support Dance Chief Steve Citty in a Sun-Moon Dance at the Center for Peace. It was a long-standing commitment that John would not duck because of travel difficulty, and there was plenty of that in store for him before he could rejoin Jeanne in Norway.

Flying stand-by, John spent two nights and almost three days in the Frankfurt airport. The cheap ticket turned out to be a trap because it was the German summer holiday season, and all the flights to the United States were hopelessly overbooked by more than 25 seats. In desperation, John got on an Air India flight to Chicago, one-way for $720. Steve Citty then scrambled to get John on a flight from Chicago to Knoxville for another $300. With the loss of the $138 stand-by ticket, the one-way trip cost $1158.

But escaping Germany was made even more difficult for John by having to pass through Passport Control four times after being rejected for stand-by. Each time his luggage had to be reclaimed. Then, after the fifth stamp in his passport, John got one of the last two seats on the 400-plus-passenger Air India flight. It seemed like a cattle car with lots of crying infants, but at least he was on his way. Then in Chicago, John had the dubious honor of being selected for a random security check. He wondered if his passport had been flagged because of his frequent foreign travel. Whatever, he and all his bags were thoroughly searched. Then on to Knoxville where he was met by Steve. At the baggage carousel, yet another surprise. His bags were not on the flight! John left the airport for the farmhouse in Corryton in the clothes that he'd worn for nearly four days.

Meanwhile, Jeanne was at the mountainside lake taking early morning swims. There was electricity and a cellphone for emergencies but no running water. Jeanne was aware of John's travel woes, but she was encouraged when Anne Klanderud took over all the organizational details of the Dance, and Joško, who had served the Irish Dance, volunteered to build the arbor. For the first time at a first-time FTOD, the Dance Chiefs were not also required to be coordinators and construction laborers. Jeanne told Anne that it was a "gift from God."

Jeanne's revelry at the rustic mountain cabin, however, was interrupted with a fragmentary reading from John's journals that the biographer had selected to demonstrate the dramatic nature of their relationship in the course of their demanding spiritual journey. Unfortunately, the selections included John's most privately sensed doubts and a passage where he questioned if the "in loveness" had gone out of their marriage. Jeanne should not have been exposed to that private question out of context, but there it was in the author's research document on her computer screen, and she was momentarily devastated by it. All the circumstantial anger and frustration that John had experienced in their journey had been vented and processed in his journal as a therapeutic method. Now Jeanne was seeing it all assembled without reference to the causative situations. Even if it was the equivalent of peeking into one page of a psychoanalyst's patient file on John without benefit of seeing the rest, it was still disheartening.

In Jeanne's journal of those days alone after reading the words "in loveness gone," she wrote of her tears, but she refused to ruminate on what might or might not be. She rather trusted to her spiritual practice and counseled herself.

"I thought we were doing well compared to the struggles in the earlier years. Guess I'll talk with him . . . and give it to the wind. . . to God. . . and trust that whatever happens will be perfect. The voices inside are not all yours and yet are. Simply listen. . . dance. . . the answers are not all that difficult. . . your spirit soars . . . let Me guide you . . . watch the stone people as the water caresses them, the birds who fly just above the water's surface teasing their bellies. Trust in your heart and where I take you now . . . trust . . . ing . . . always . . . ing . . . Breathe . . . things are not always as they seem. Knowing . . . ing. Love . . . ing. See . . . ing. Breathe . . . ing . . . shhh . . . shhh."

Until John returned, this was Jeanne's process every day. She did not run from introspective reviews, and she allowed her tears to mingle with the rain that sounded in the tall pines, the spruce trees, the silver birch and the aspens, but everyday she surrendered her pain to the Divine within and came to peace. And after the rain and the tears, came, too, a huge, vivid rainbow.

Back in Tennessee at the Sun-Moon Dance, John was in a familiar community of people with whom he shared mutual respect and love. He was able to relax with male friends Dobs, Marcus Ambrester, and Steve. Letting his hair down a bit was a tonic. Among the men, there was a humorous bonding vernacular that allowed John to speak without explaining as he often had to do abroad. After driving in Ireland and the UK, just the pleasure of steering his own car on the right side of the road allowed "a certain number of brain cells or synapses to shut down and take a vacation." At the Seymour dance, too, there were experienced Dog Soldiers, Firekeepers, and Kitchen Angels. John was thus not required to scrounge for supplies or micro-manage. Although, as the Alpha Dog, he still worked hard and "sweated buckets in the heat," his days at the Center for Peace were almost a holiday.

In an ironic twist, one of the dance helpers engaged John in an extended conversation about being married to a spiritually powerful woman. He wanted to know how John and Jeanne had managed it.

While John was standing in the drummers' area during the dance, Cheryl Patterson looked at him and said with surprise, "John, there's an orange glow all around your head." Brenda Sue Taylor, a mentor to both Jeanne and John during their important vision quests in the fall of 1996, heard the comment and said to Cheryl, "He frequently has light around him when he's working."

After the Sun-Moon Dance cleanup, John had errands to run, family reconnections to make, and a work session with Margarita Di Vita who had bravely volunteered to act as the FTOD International Coordinator. Then it was off to Oslo via Knoxville and Newark. Finally, John caught a break on the seven-hour flight to Oslo. One of the seats in his row of three went empty so John had the window seat and room to relax. He considered it "pretty nice for a stand-by ticket." His journal entry for that travel day ends with "Thanks, Baba."

John reunited with Jeanne at the cabin, and they had several days of rustic living before they left Norway—washing up in basins, wading in the lake, watching sunsets across the water, reading books by the fire, and making trips to the outhouse. Jeanne practiced on her new Irish drum, the bodhrán, and their only concession to technology was watching movie DVDs on their computer screen.

It is evident from John's journal that their "in love" romance was reinforced in Norway. His personal entry about Jeanne is certainly poetic.

"Jeanne stands on the moss-covered rock overlooking the lake, a soft blue and white woolen blanket around her shoulders, the sunlight glinting off the waves and her golden hair. In the distance there is thunder. We both feel a Viking ancestry in this land, something deep that lies fallow. More thunder. We wonder what awaits us in Iceland. Majestic clouds float by. Sunlight flickers through the tall pines. Colorado-blue sky surrounds the gray and white clouds. Jeanne notes the grand chorus of the wind in the trees. Across the lake, the putt-putt of a boat's gentle motor beats rhythm like a drum. There are times when I look at Jeanne and think/feel that she is growing more and more beautiful . . ."

In ways that both Jeanne and John recognize, their journey to the One is a love story. It is both their personal love story, as well as a universal love story of how it is possible for male and female energies to unite in spiritual purpose and fulfillment without sacrificing the human elements of romantic togetherness. That is not to say that married love is an easy relationship, but when it has a spiritual base, it can be both enduring and joyful. It has the potential to overcome all the obstacles of gender conditioning and even the urges of the libido.

THE NORWAY FTOD

The Norway FTOD occurred between Jeanne and John's time at the lake cabin. Anne Klanderud had selected the arbor site with the psychic approval of the Norwegian ancestors; and when Jeanne and John arrived for the Dance, they were welcomed with a double rainbow. The late summer rains in the central Norwegian mountains, however, had left the arbor grounds very wet. Birch branch beds had to be laid to keep the dancers off the ground while they rested. At the East gate, where Jeanne and John as Chiefs moved their feet in time with the drum, spruce branches had to be laid lest their steps cause a muddy sinkhole. There were fourteen dancers with Joško in the arbor for the first time as the Sun Father. The Chiefs felt that he fulfilled his role in an outstanding way.

In the absence of Sammye Jo, Shelley Ostroff became lead Moon Mother for the first time with Moon Mothers Sonja Munz, Shania Racky, and Anne Klanderud, the organizer of the dance, in support. Sammye Jo was in Colorado serving a Sun-Moon Dance, and she sent an e-mail to the Chiefs saying that she promised never to miss another FTOD. But Sammye Jo did not miss the Norway dance, at least not in spirit. She was present in the people's drum used in the ceremony. The large bass drum was made from Norwegian moose hide, and it had a strong, beautiful tone. The drum had two sides, and when one side was displayed, Jeanne and John recognized the painted symbol that covered it. It was a Chippewa Spirit symbol. On a Norwegian drum? Sammye Jo had found a way to be with them after all.

When the cabin retreat ended, there was an itinerary change. Interest in doing a FTOD in Iceland had caused potential hosts to invite Jeanne and John to stop in Reykjavik on their way back to the States. The plan was to meet the possible dance hosts and acquaint themselves with Iceland. It was viewed as a one-night stopover with connections the next day to Minneapolis, then Chicago, and finally Knoxville. Again, all on stand-by tickets.

Jeanne, however, was not sleeping well due to congestion in her chest and a deep cough that concerned John. In addition, Jeanne was robbed of rest by pain from infected teeth. Her condition necessitated a two-day delay in their departure for Iceland.

After their meetings in Iceland, there was great difficulty in getting flights out. One ticket agent suggested that they fly separately to have a better chance on stand-by. Icelandic Air had a virtual monopoly on flights in and out, and most outgoing flights were full. On the second waiting day, an agent took pity on the couple and put them on a plane to Boston. One seat was in business class and the other in economy. John suggested that Jeanne take the best position because she wasn't feeling well, and he went to the back of the plane. It was "fair play" since in a similar circumstance, John had taken the luxury ride while Jeanne sat in economy. After his

Frankfurt experience, John decided that, "there's a magic that Jeanne and I create *together* that is stronger than when we are apart."

Sitting next to Jeanne on the unexpected flight in a class beyond her stand-by ticket was Jen Randall, a young woman who works with older teens teaching conflict resolution. She had been looking for something physically challenging and experiential to use with her young people. By the end of the flight, she was determined to attend the FTOD in September at the Watersong Chamber in Graham, North Carolina. "I've been waiting a long time for this," Jen told Jeanne. In noting Jeanne's account of the meeting with Jen, John wrote, "It is amazing how it (Spirit) works—absolutely breathtaking!"

On the subject of teeth, Anne Klanderud had a very interesting observation when Jeanne began having severe tooth pain in Norway. Anne's insight was that teeth bring us to surrender. Using babies as an example, she noted that we come into the world without teeth as innocents, and we often leave the world without our natural teeth, once again as innocents. She suggested that aggression begins when we grow teeth. That is when separation begins. A baby only knows what it wants and needs, and it explores everything with its mouth until teeth come in, and the child bites someone. Then "no" is learned, and separation begins.

"FOR THE ONE" DANCE
GRAHAM, NORTH CAROLINA 2005

The people that you meet at the dance have come a long distance in psychological terms to get there. They have traveled over the roads of diverse religions, through the valleys of disease and death, down lanes of deep disappointments, and across chasms of gigantic despairs. They have come out of the shadows of pain, anger, and doubt into the light of spiritual fellowship. Their personal stories are dramatic in terms of world history, and yet they share a common enlightenment and a common dedication not to return to the mistakes of the past.

Many of the "helpers" arrive days prior to the dance, set up their tents, and do private or small group ceremonies in the Chamber or on the grounds. The kitchen begins to function to feed the early helpers as John and Jeanne come to facilitate the dance preparations.

At the helpers' supper after the sweat lodge on Thursday, grace was sung in the hand-joined circle by an Israeli in Hebrew. In the sweat lodge earlier, prayers had been said in English, Spanish, German, and Hebrew. There were people assembling from Israel, Germany, South Africa, Peru, and distant American places. Language groups were heard speaking their native tongues in the grove where tables were provided for helper meals.

Friday morning a man known to John found him in the Chamber preparing towels and sheets for the dance and asked to be a dancer. He had felt the call to dance that day. He was to be the 21st dancer. The growth of the Dance has necessitated the training of Moon Mothers, Sun Fathers, Alpha Dog Soldiers, Firekeepers, and the essential Kitchen Angels who are recognized as also contributing vital energy to the dance by feeding the dance helpers foods prepared and blessed to their function. A Spirit plate is prepared at main meals in recognition that the food itself is part of Spirit and that we are existing by grace. Although the roles differ, service to the dancers is the common cause that bonds everyone from Chief to dishwashers as equals.

There is sharing and teaching going on around the campsite, in the outdoor dining area, in the Chamber, at the sweat lodge fire pit, and at the arbor. Preparations are being made, and there are those who lead these preparations from experience; but in following an instruction or for filling a request, there is no tension, no sense of a dominant will, or the air of superiority. What is being practiced is cooperation built on a spiritual foundation of mutual compassion and respect. In this regard, a dance gathering is a model for community building on multicultural levels. No one feels excluded. No one feels inadequate. No one feels unloved. No one is outside the circle of fellowship.

Standing outside the Chamber that Thursday evening before the dance was to begin on Friday, the author observed Jeanne slipping through the twilight shadows into the arbor. She was alone and avoiding contact with those at the Chamber and in the campground. It was obvious that she had come to the arbor for a private purpose. At a distance, the author could see her make offerings to the four directions, and then she sat against the pole facing west as the sun descended below the tree line. As the day ended, Jeanne rose to do a pipe ceremony. She was asking permission from the Spirits of that specific place to dance there tomorrow. Her ceremony done, Jeanne disappeared into the darkness, and the only notice of her going was the sound of gravel on the road as she drove away.

During preparations for the Graham dance, Jeanne had two teeth pulled. After weeks on the road in pain, she finally stayed in one place long enough to consult a dentist. The doctor was appalled at the tooth infection, and Jeanne remembers her candid chairside manner when she said, "I've never lost a patient yet, but there's always a first time. We're talking life or death here. It's that serious." After the extractions, treatment for the dangerous infection began immediately. No one outside of a small circle of three or four people even knew of Jeanne's physical ordeal. Certainly the pain did not compromise her responsibilities as Dance Chief with John as they led the dance.

David and Cheryl

Cheryl Braswell and David Stephenson, Caretakers of the Watersong Chamber, came to ceremonial spirituality in a way common to many of those who dance and serve the "For The One" today. They entered the path after a successful material lifestyle had left them unfulfilled and struggling to find meaning and purpose to their lives. Unhappy, and their relationship in trouble, the married couple accepted the fortuitous gift of a trip to St. Johns in the American Virgin Islands in 1990. On St. Johns they rediscovered the innate connection to Nature, and they experienced the freedom of a relaxed, more simple lifestyle that was in sobering contrast to the stress of middle-class striving for wealth and social status. On their return to North Carolina, the couple began an earnest search for a personal spirituality.

When the couple encountered Sun Bear, Grandfather Jim Dubray of the Lakota Nation, and later Joseph Rael, Beautiful Painted Arrow, they learned the initial lessons of their connection to Nature. David was attracted to the Lakota way of being, and he was mentored by Sun Bear at Sun Dances on the Pine Ridge Reservation. For years, David carried stones and chopped wood in service to the dance, and then he became a dancer himself. By 2005, he had participated in fifteen annual Sun Dances.

"That's where the year ends and the year begins for me—July in South Dakota."

David, a powerfully built man, is deeply tanned from the sun, and he has a long braid of gray hair hanging down his back.

"The dance is where you help each other, where you discover that you are all one in the same circle. You help each other in many ways, not just in spiritual growth, but in whatever a person needs in life."

Cheryl resonated more with the teaching of Joseph Rael, and she went to his original Peace-Sound Chamber in New Mexico for instruction. She also became aware that her great grandfather was

Cherokee. She says that ceremonial dance transformed her by removing mental blocks and providing awareness that enabled true compassion.

"There is a year's worth of therapy in one weekend dance," she says. "You fast and you pray, and you feel like you're gonna die, and you don't. When you eat again and you drink again, I've never felt such respect for food and water. My first dance changed the way I saw the world forever."

Cheryl is petite with short blonde hair, and she is perky and energetic in a way that reminds you of Mitzi Gaynor in the movie musical *South Pacific*. After a long period of suffering from chronic fatigue, Cheryl can now say, "I'm passionate about life."

For years during the 1990s, Cheryl and David supported the construction of another Peace-Sound Chamber at Swannanoa, North Carolina and its programs of exploring Native American metaphysics. They helped dig the foundation for the Chamber, and three out of four weekends, they stayed in the home of the leg-endary Baxter Bryant, who with his long white beard, introduced himself to their young, spiritually precocious daughter Robin as the brother of Santa Claus.

Robin, also called BZ, had begun to ask serious spiritual ques-tions as early as age seven.

"Why do we go to church? Why can't we worship God at home?"

David and Cheryl first encountered Joseph at Swannanoa's Earth Center in an introduction by Zoe Bryant. When they were introduced to Jeanne and John at Joseph's Chamber in New Mexico, the casual encounter did not impress them. Cheryl asked, "Who are these preppy people?" They seemed like corporate-America types to her. Then, back in Swannanoa, Cheryl partici-pated in a Community Building Workshop with Jeanne and John and got to know them.

"I had never met people like Jeanne and John," Cheryl recalls.

By 1999, David and Cheryl were living on a 42-acre farm in rural Graham, North Carolina as a demonstration of their radical change in lifestyle. From job-addicted suburbanites, they were now log cabin dwellers on a "hobby farm" where all the animals, including a donkey, a cow, chickens, guinea hens, ducks, geese, dogs, and cats, were pets, and the basic diet was vegetarian.

Patty Coleman, a dance Moon Mother, telephoned David and Cheryl to say that Jeanne and John wanted to visit them. The surprise request seemed linked somehow to a strange and dangerous event which occurred before the call. Both Cheryl and BZ, in separate rooms, woke in the middle of the night. Awake and alert, they witnessed a white-hot ball of lightning dance outside their bedroom windows and then felt the tremendous booming shockwave of thunder that shook the house. David slept through the entire event, but mother and daughter came together with a single question—"What does it mean?" The expectation of something important coming was thus placed in their consciousness.

The important "something" occurred a few days later in the living room of their cabin at the end of an Intuitive Imaging session with Jeanne and John. The discussion among the small group of friends turned to the possibility of building a Peace-Sound Chamber on their farm. To their own amazement, four members of the group pledged $15,000 toward construction costs. David then selected the building site in a pasture far away from the house near their lake, and Jeanne and John marked the spot with a crystal. Jeanne and John themselves became intimately involved in the building of what was to be called the Watersong Peace-Sound Chamber, and they recorded their first CD recording, *Between Slices of Light*, there in December, 2000 with Cheryl and David doing added vocals.

The commitment to build a Peace-Sound Chamber attracted many volunteers with the craft skills to build a round kiva-like building with an interior diameter of 33 feet. One weekend a carpenter and his wife showed up unexpectedly when the technical dilemma of framing the vaulted roof had stopped progress. Over two days, the carpenter cut the difficult angles and framed the roof beams. With the problem solved, the volunteer carpenter and his wife said goodbye and have not returned.

R. J. Dobmier (called Dobs), now the principal Firekeeper at Watersong lodges and dances, met David at the Dancing Moon bookstore in Raleigh. Dobs had already met Joseph at the Swannanoa Chamber, so he devoted himself to the construction of the newest one. When the Watersong Chamber builders were told that Jeanne and John had a schedule break in August, and that they could come to Graham to perform an Awakening Ceremony, it was Dobs—going against all construction wisdom—who guaranteed completion. Dobs is a lean man with the angular face and long hair of a sun-bronzed native. He is intense and has great endurance for any work, but he can also be playful and easygoing away from his ceremonial responsibilities. At dances, he is a dynamic assistant to Jeanne and John as he sweeps negative energies out of the arbor down the corn meal line and into the fire with a feather fan. Eventually, volunteers who recognized the intention of the Watersong ceremonial grounds built a large sweat lodge for thirty or more people, a large dance arbor, and even a permanent kitchen house and canopy dining area for hosting multiple-day ceremonies.

Today, Cheryl says that her vocation is as a peacemaker. She and David do not feel that they possess the land, but that they are its caretakers. This spiritual awareness enables them to fulfill their most cherished dreams and to find peace and happiness in a new inclusive lifestyle that embraces all creatures. Life for them has thus become an activity of service rather than an acquisitive arduous marathon focused on societal expectations. And the result? They have evolved a community—a family really—with members scattered across the world who assemble for ceremony and fellowship throughout the year. Cheryl and David made the space, the place, for this to occur. And around other Peace-Sound Chambers and dance arbors on distant continents, the same phenomenon is happening. And in these centers, in their circles, Cheryl and David are recognized as family members, too.

Teresa

At the 2005 "For The One" Dance in Graham, Teresa Hutson was an apprentice Moon Mother. The night before the FTOD began, Teresa led a Fire Ceremony in the Watersong Chamber, and appropriate to the name, the ceremony was a guided meditation on the healing of the earth's water. Teresa has a youthful appearance with a slender build and long, flowing blonde hair. She laid the fire and then served the ceremony for the ten or so people, including John, who sat in a circle at the center of the Chamber.

The author and Dobs, the head firekeeper, missed the 7:30 p.m. start of the Fire Ceremony as they lingered under the mess tent for an interview. When they got to the Chamber, the doors were closed. The author, remembering the Pueblo teaching that the back is a spiritual sense organ, proposed that they stand with their backs against the kiva wall to sense the energy that was being produced inside. As they stood apart around the curve of the kiva wall, the author looked into the field opposite the Chamber's east door and saw Cheryl's three dogs—a large black and gray shepherd, a mid-sized black mixed-breed hound, and a blonde Benji—and Dobs's dog, another shepherd, lying in the grass. The four dogs were spread out equidistant some forty to fifty feet apart in the precise four compass directions. If a companion Chamber had existed next to the established one, the dogs would have sat as guardians at the four directional portals. And as far as anyone noticed, the dogs had held their positions from the start of the ceremony to its conclusion.

The next day Teresa was in her long ceremonial dress and shawl as she prepared to enter the arbor as an apprentice Moon Mother. Teresa's journey to the dance had begun eleven years previous when she studied *A Course in Miracles* in Johnson City, Tennessee facilitated by Perry Robinson. Teresa already had a degree in art from East Tennessee State University, but she was drawn to spiritual growth and began to attend programs at Perry's Center for Peace. Teresa met Jeanne and John at a CFP Peace Concert to usher in the new millennium, the Y2K night of 1999, and then she entered her first sweat lodge with them on the literal dawn of the 21st century.

When the author first met Jeanne and John at a Peace Concert in Boone, North Carolina in December 2000, Teresa was with them playing the drum. Her association with them included other Peace Concerts and participation in Sun-Moon Dances. Teresa also studied sound energy in Jeanne's workshops and by 2005 was seen as qualified to apprentice as a FTOD Moon Mother. When she is not serving the dance, Teresa is a licensed massage therapist.

Rhonda

A second apprentice Moon Mother, Rhonda Factor, had come to Graham from Israel to serve the dance. Rhonda first danced the FTOD in Israel in 2004, and again in 2005. She first met Jeanne and John at Anael's house for a Sound Workshop and then attended a Peace Concert a few days later in March 2002.

"It awakened a world within me," Rhonda recalled. "I always loved to sing, so I began to explore the sound work. It awakened within me a place of spontaneity apart from structured systems. It taught me that you can move within structure and create what you want to create."

Rhonda was born in Toronto, Canada, but her family relocated to Israel when she was twelve. She returned to North America for her college years, but her home with husband Chaim is in Israel where her children were born. In her first dance, Sammye Jo was the Moon Mother who worked with her in the arbor.

"Sammye Jo spoke to me in the language of the ancients. It was an unknown language that I strangely understood. It struck me so deeply."

In October of 2004 Rhonda had followed the FTOD to Graham and was supported by Judith Brooks and Nancy Green.

"When I put my feet on this ground, I started crying. The land just came up and enveloped me. It seemed to say, 'Oh, you're here.' Watersong is now one of the families that I belong to. And as people prepared for the dance, I saw them not in their physical bodies, but in their energy bodies accompanied by their ancestors. Wow! I never realized before how we carry our ancestors with us all the time. I am now consciously bringing my Israeli ancestors, not just the Jewish ones, to the dance."

Rhonda had a vision in 2005 shortly before the Graham FTOD that her role in the ceremonial place would be to sing songs that are codes to awaken people. She feels that what she now does in the FTOD arbor is something that she has done before.

"My maternal grandmother has asked me in vision to be the last woman in our family to embody the feminine stupidity that gives away all feminine spiritual power. Several gateways are opening now that we have to take advantage of. And we have to take advantage of them wisely. I choose to dance."

Rhonda describes her dance experience.

"The dance allows spontaneity for people who may have never allowed themselves to be spontaneous before. It is so amazing to me how the energy works with intent in the arbor. It is so soft in there, so containing, and so constant.

"In the arbor I have learned to resonate with the dancers in order to serve them. I recognize my own center from that of the other person, and then I am able to know what is going on with them and to know when they need me and when they don't. The service is about attuning yourself to the other person's needs by multi-sensual listening."

Rhonda was one of the participants who witnessed the remarkable FTOD in Israel on Holocaust Memorial Day, May 5, 2005, which was followed the next day by celebration of Israel's Independence Day. Rhonda is not in favor of the emotional intensities of these linked holidays because the focus on suffering seems to perpetuate hatreds of Germans and other perceived enemies. In the arbor that Holocaust Day when the sirens in the city went off, Jeanne allowed a round of free dancing that provided a significant release, especially for the Israeli and German dancers. As they danced arm in arm, weeping, hugging each other, Rhonda felt that years of healing took place during those moments. It was especially moving for her because at that time Rhonda's own son in the Israeli Army was assigned to the Gaza disengagement, the forced removal of Israeli settlers on Palestinian territory. It was another historical event that fostered an extreme bitterness that would require healing.

Despite the dangers and frustrations of living at the center of Middle East conflicts, Rhonda believes that there is a path to peace.

"I see a huge web being woven all around the world by the "For The One" Dance. Jeanne and John are waking up so many souls that they are creating a vortex of mass consciousness. People are waking up and saying, 'Oh, my God, I never realized. We really are one huge family. Really, there is only one of us. We have been living a cruel illusion of separation. Now it can be over.'

"No matter what your religious background, if you can come into the FTOD experience, you can know the truth of it, soul to soul."

Rhonda's experience is very instructive. Religious dogma often seems the goal of religions. Rather than allowing faith in Creation to open the doors to spiritual freedom and an understanding that transforms all behavior into acts of love, dogmas divide humanity into groups at conflict. For there to be peace, this separation must end.

Judith

Judith Brooks is an attractive brunette who has served the dance in various ways. She went to acupuncture school and lived in Albuquerque for six years where she observed Native American ceremonial dancing at the Jemez Pueblo. She made Pueblo friends while working as a massage therapist at a spa and was invited to Christmas mass and the Eagle Dance at Jemez Springs.

Although she had heard about Joseph and his Peace-Sound Chamber, she did not meet him until she attended a gathering of Chamber caretakers in 2003. Now, every year Judith attends Joseph's "mystery school" to learn more about Native American cosmology.

Judith has a somewhat adventuresome background. She trained volunteers for Habitat for Humanity in Nicaragua during the Contra War.

Friends introduced Judith to the Watersong Chamber in 2000; and when she came to a Sun-Moon Dance, not knowing anything about it, she was drafted by Steve Citty and trained as a Dog Soldier. At the very first "For The One" Dance, Jeanne asked Judith to serve on the drum. It was a good fit because Judith had been a drummer in her high school marching band. Judith played the People's drum and rattles on Jeanne and John's second CD—*For The One*.

Judith was one of the first volunteers to go to South Africa on the FTOD support crew. Her favorite experience there was with Gogo (Grandmother) Monica and her Zulu sangomas in their ceremonial caves. The two groups of women sang their ceremonial songs to each other and became bonded in a way no social anthropologist could imagine. If a way were made possible, Judith would devote herself full-time to spreading the FTOD with Jeanne and John all over the world.

Steve

Steve Citty's mother, who died when he was fourteen, told him that the *Bible* was a metaphor, a story of his life, and that he was all its characters. Living in Roswell, New Mexico, far from the mainstream, she had nevertheless read Edgar Cayce and listened to Unity Church clear-channel radio broadcasts from Kansas City. In her way, she prepared Steve for the day when he entered a Unity Church after the Vietnam War to say, in his own words, "Hello, God. Remember me? It's been a long time since we talked. I'll make you a deal. Tell me what you want me to do, and I'll do anything. Just make it clear to me."

A cable television supervisor in Rome, Georgia at the time, Steve had come to Unity after exposure to telephone dial-up readings of *The Daily Word*. Within weeks of attending Unity, Steve was asked to sponsor the youth programs of the church, which he did for the next eight years. Steve also re-associated himself with the study of Silva Mind Control, a course that he had taken in the early 1970s. For many spiritual seekers, Silva Mind Control was a doorway to silencing the conditioned mental reflexes of fear.

While at Unity, Steve was also exposed to *A Course In Miracles*, and then, through a female companion, he made a serious study of Jewish mysticism—the *Kabbalah*. Another area of exploration was energy work, and Steve studied with several teachers until he was able to establish an energy healing practice for himself up and down the East Coast. Today, he specializes in chair massage and has corporate as well as private clients.

Steve believes that he has an understanding of how healing works. From the ages six to ten, he was confined to a wheelchair. As a child, the first thing that his doctor told him about his legs was that he was going to heal perfectly. True to the intention, when Steve was a young man being examined for military service, a doctor looking at his X-rays said, "You have healed perfectly."

In 1994, Perry Robinson, whom Steve had met at conferences where they both appeared on the program, invited Steve to come to The Center for Peace to participate in a Drum Dance given by Joseph Rael. Although Steve was skeptical about any event that exploited Native American ceremony, his respect for Perry brought him to the dance. After the Dance, although Steve had not experienced any dramatic visions, his 25-year quest for spiritual awareness was made evident. He woke up! Everything that he had learned in the past came together as if he were truly breathing for the first time. When he told Joseph his revelation, Joseph said, "Now you need to do the Sun-Moon Dance."

That next summer Steve's wife-to-be, Nan, wanted to dance the Sun-Moon Dance, and so Steve was asked to serve in a support role. When the couple parked their car, another couple was next to them unloading their items for the dance. The other couple was Jeanne and John. While the women danced, the two men began a significant bonding.

Steve, a former helicopter reconnaissance pilot with heavy combat experiences in the Viet Nam War, is a no-nonsense character with an acerbic wit. From the moment they met, Steve was teasing John about his always perfectly-combed hair and his behavioral rigidity. Steve made John laugh and helped him to relax. The two men soon discovered that they could talk to each other about anything and everything. For being outwardly so different, they became mutual confidants and affable comrades in an adventure that they could not possibly have imagined when they met. Steve says that he feels that his relationship to John is karmic; and although he has a sibling brother whom he loves, he feels that he and John are closer.

"One of the reasons that John drags me with him all over the world is because I make him laugh."

The thing that Steve remembers about his first experiences with John was how much John was like a sponge, absorbing information. John seemed so innocent, and in innocence.

A year later, in July 1997, Steve and John were dancing the Sun- Moon Dance at Joseph's arbor in New Mexico, and Steve visited with Jeanne and John in their impressive Placitas house above Albuquerque. It was at this time that Joseph named Steve and John as co-chiefs of the Tennessee Sun-Moon Dances. Accepting this commitment meant that they would be doing serious spiritual work together for the foreseeable future. The men were shocked that Joseph was retiring from dance leadership and appointing them to carry on his vision. Some men wept. Steve says he went dumb for five minutes before he told Joseph, "Yes. Yes, with help."

Three years later at their third annual Sun-Moon Dance in Seymour, Tennessee, John woke Steve at five o'clock in the morning complaining of chest pain. "Can you do some massage work on me?" John asked. Steve says that when he rubbed the sleep out of his eyes and saw John's gray facial color, he immediately said, "You're going to the hospital." John's resistance was futile against Steve's insistence; and at the hospital, it was confirmed that John had had a heart attack, and measures were taken to minimize the cardiac damage. Steve was left to chief the dance by himself.

When John recovered from the heart attack, he wanted to turn the Sun-Moon Dance over to Steve. The Sun-Moon Dance commitment, however, is a four-year cycle. A dancer dances one of the four cardinal directions each year, so Steve held John to supporting their dance for a fourth year. After that, Steve encouraged John to get a dance of his own started in North Carolina, and he promised to support John in those dances, which he ultimately did as a Sun Father in the arbor or the Alpha Dog Soldier outside. When Jeanne's vision gave birth to the new "For The One," Steve continued to be a major support person, and he has traveled to South Africa and Israel in the volunteer FTOD crew.

"If I wasn't married with responsibilities for a teenage son, I'd be with Jeanne and John at every dance," Steve says.

"We are being breathed in and out by Spirit. Spirit is constantly breathing us out for a crystallized moment. In that moment of crystallization, we experience existence, and then we shatter in the light and fall back into Spirit. We are constantly being recreated."

In Israel, where Steve served as the Alpha Dog, dancers told him after the FTOD that in the dance arbor, they had felt safe for the first time in their lives. The feeling of safety amazed them. Then someone asked him, "What are you going to do if terrorists show up with guns?"

Steve answered, "I am going to offer them water."

In remembering Israel, Steve says, "We will not fight. Our job is to live and to bring life to those places."

Steve Citty continues to chief the Sun-Moon Dance and the Hollow Bone Dance—a dance without drums or outside support—annually at the Center for Peace in Seymour. He feels that the vibration of these dances continues to support all such dances wherever they occur. And whether or not he travels with Jeanne and John, his link to them, and to Joseph Rael, is never broken.

Sharing

At the end of a FTOD, after the dancers have rehydrated, eaten their honoring feast, and changed into everyday clothing, there is an assembly in the Peace-Sound Chamber for sharing. The sharing begins with a give-away. Blankets have been spread at the center of the Chamber, and each person—dancers and helpers alike—places a meaningful item on the blanket. Then, the youngest and the eldest in the group are invited to select an item first. When they have picked, the others wander around the fringes of the blankets seeking an item that beckons to them.

At Watersong following the September 2005 dance, there were 68 people participating in the give-away. When all the items had been selected, the participants were invited to identify their respective gift and tell the recipient something about it. The glad noises of these exchanges filled the Chamber for the next half hour.

Often there is a second, or even a third, give-away by a dance participant or helper. It might be a dancer announcing an engagement to marry, or a happy married couple celebrating their relationship (and sometimes a relocation) with a give-away of personal and household items as diverse as decorative knick-knacks, kitchen appliances, television sets, jewelry, and clothing. At Watersong that day, Jo Fisher gave away precious items from her mother's home, including quality pieces of art. She said that she could not see these familiar things go to strangers, but that she could gladly give them away to members of this Watersong family. A few weeks after Jo's generous sharing, her aged mother died; and the Watersong family, with Jeanne and John, were on hand to support her.

When the excitement and laughter of the give-aways is over, Jeanne invites anyone in the Chamber to share their experiences of the dance. Dancers are cautioned not to relate their visionary experiences outside the counsel of the Chiefs, or perhaps Senior Moon Mother Sammye Jo, for a period of three months because feedback has demonstrated that visions are often understood in increments over an extended period of time. Jeanne also cautions that the sharing of visions before they have time to gestate and become fully born drains the energy out of them. "It is like giving a young plant too much sunlight," she says. "The plant would wither and die. This can happen when a vision is shared too soon."

The testimonies of those sharing are both moving and humorous. Here is a collection of quotes gathered from the September Watersong dance.

"A fly flew into my ear while I was in the arbor. I panicked when I couldn't get it out. Then it hit me. The fly's struggle was showing me that the way out was to stop struggling. I no longer have to suffer in order to heal."

"The dance is different for me every time. The Moon Mothers have such a gentle way of helping you go down. And, oh God, how I love those cold, wet towels!"

"I had no idea what I was getting into. Spirit had to trick me into healing."

"I am so impressed with the depth of the hearts of the other dancers and the helpers. The fire was like a deep red heart through the night."

"A part of me was at the center pole, and I was running to myself in the experience of oneness."

"I felt very weak on Saturday, but I was inspired by the other dancers to do the impossible. I was amazed at my own strength. The surrender was so sweet."

"I gave up a part of my ego, and I hope that I can permanently leave it behind."

"I had first-time fears. When other dancers cried, I cried. When they laughed, I laughed. For me, it was the proof of oneness."

"I came to the dance to offer my little crumb of service, and I now go away with the whole bread factory."

"I bonded with something greater than myself. This is my third dance. I have danced the infinite dance of death and rebirth, death and rebirth. I now understand what it means to say, 'It is a good day to die.' I have the gift of purpose without death as a preoccupation. I now understand that I live for the moment of the dance."

"I came to the dance and got fed the spiritual food that I needed."

"For me, it's the beauty. I drew strength from your support. I felt safe and was able to explore."

"I was on a massage table on Thursday and agreed to dance without any knowledge of it. On Friday in the arbor, I was asked to give up my medical companion dog, who is always with me. It was the hardest decision of my life. But then, I endured the dance. I hit the pole twice. It turned out to be the greatest experience of my life."

"I never thought that I would see this Chamber filled with so many people when we built it six years ago. At my church, I introduce you white Chamber people as my grandchildren. You should see the eyebrows go up. Now my grandchildren are becoming more numerous all the time."

"I feel the return of feminine energy, a balance of head to heart. An end of violence. I am so proud to see the young people here."

"I am dealing with anger. I've been around it so much in my culture. My life seems hijacked by the emotions of anger. I want peace."

"As a Dog Soldier, I was aware that the Moon Mothers were so conscious of the dancers—all 21 of them!"

"I experienced the Moon Mother space as sacred. I had no idea how powerful it was to walk the dancer's path and to serve them."

"The criteria for an apprentice Moon Mother or Sun Father is this—can they love a complete stranger, and whatever happens, remember to love again?"

BRAZIL

The "For the One" Dance at Watersong had been a large one. The 21 dancers were supported by over 50 people on the crew and support staff. This dance was also a training dance. Inside the arbor Jeanne, John, and Sammye Jo guided the activity of four apprentice Moon Mothers (Patty Coleman, Margarita DiVita, Rhonda Factor, and Teresa Hutson) and a new Sun Father (Walton Deva). The Pehrsons were well aware that at the rate the FTOD was growing, they would need a reservoir of experienced people to draw from for the worldwide crew. This training was also necessary for the purpose of identifying new dance Chiefs who would take over dances in coming years. This eventuality was already in Jeanne and John's consciousness.

Another reality learned was that the kitchen is the heart of the dance. If the kitchen didn't work well, then neither did the dance.

The kitchen at this FTOD, by all reviews, was the golden standard by which all future dance kitchens would be measured. The Kitchen Archangels were Anael Harpaz and Sonja Munz (from South Africa). Their support staff included Cheryl Braswell, Kathy Bright, and Lance Davis among others. Sonja decorated the entire eating area outside Lance House, including the tables and the overhanging trees. The Kitchen Archangels themselves wore strands of sparkling stars formed as halos on their heads and glittering fairy dust on their faces. Their style and enthusiasm was completely justified by the grand buffets that they served. Their abundant and creative health-conscious dishes were imbued with a loving spirit that was both felt and appreciated by the hungry crew. Most importantly, the transition from the dance arbor to the food service area was seamless because of the energy that the kitchen angels had established there. Grace was given to begin each meal as the entire crew formed a hand-linked circle. Then the oldest elder and the youngest person present were invited to go first in the outdoor buffet line. When the food had been first arranged on the long table under the canopy roof, small samples were taken from each dish to make a Spirit Plate that was then laid in the nearby woods. This offering, this consideration, was a conscious symbol to acknowledge the Source from which all blessings flow.

On the Wednesday after the weekend FTOD, while the Pehrsons were still at Jo Fisher's home, Jo's aged mother, Lonnie Powell, died from heart failure. Jeanne and John consoled Jo, helped with arrangements, and cleaned the house for the arrival of Jo's three grown children. The Pehrsons would stay with Cheryl and David when Jo's children arrived for the funeral. At Jo's request, John played his flute while people gathered in the chapel for the funeral service. Georgia Stone, the black octogenarian gospel singer sang the opening song, and Jeanne sang *Amazing Grace* at the graveside. The participation of Jo's Watersong family at the evangelical Baptist service probably seemed a bit odd to the regular congregation, but it was a great consolation to Jo and her family. Before leaving Jo the following week to attend the 5th Peace Congress of the Peace-Sound Chamber Caretakers near Nassau, New York, the Pehrsons met with Cheryl Braswell and Tracey Turner-Keyser, a psychiatrist, to plan for a "For the One" Youth Dance as a 24-hour event in mid-October. This was a new direction but one that had been persistent in the collective dance community consciousness for months. At the recent FTOD, three children had been present with their parents, and Jeanne had been approached by them about staging a dance for young people. Jeanne and John discussed the importance of the Youth Dance en route to New York.

The highlight of any gathering of the Peace-Sound Chamber Caretakers is the opportunity to be with Joseph and to experience more of his teaching. In New York, many words that Joseph spoke were either quoted in John's journal or paraphrased. One of Joseph's insights was that rational decisions exclude the presence of Godly decision-making from the Higher Mind. Joseph urged the caretakers to give everything up to the Higher Mind and then not worry about what the Higher Mind wants to do with it. It is the rational mind that wants to control, wants to play God. The rational mind and brain separates. It separates us from God and the Higher Mind. When Joseph told the assembled group, "You are giants," John believed that Joseph was releasing them and urging them to do great things. "It's *your* time now," he said. "It's time for you to take responsibility. It's my time to spend with my children."

On their return to North Carolina, Jeanne began work on getting their flight reservations and visas for the November trips to Brazil and South Africa. John worked on e-mail letters to prospective dancers and FTOD sponsors in both countries. On the weekend of September 30th, Jeanne and John began a private FTOD at Watersong in Graham. Sammye Jo was in the arbor, David poured the opening sweat lodge, and their dance was further supported by Cheryl, Sonja Munz (who stayed an extra week to help), Teresa, Andy Baxter, Fernando Rubio, Margarita, Lance, Judith, Nancy Green, and Grandmother Georgia. Everyone performed multiple tasks. David said in the Sunday morning sweat lodge that Jeanne and John's faith in the crew to do what was right took them to a new level of spiritual empowerment.

Into October, while the Pehrsons stayed with Jo, Jeanne worked tirelessly every day on their travel and dance arrangements for Brazil. Jo gave a generous gift to underwrite some of the crew's travel expenses; and Jeanne was able, after hours of searching the web, to get cheap tickets for herself, John, and Sammye Jo.

Much of what Jeanne did for the dances went unrecognized. And even after some dances, when she had given her all and was exhausted, dancers glowing from the FTOD experience walked past her, oblivious to what she had sacrificed to serve them. And there were times, in retrospect, when Jeanne was saddened, and even depressed, by her seeming invisibility at the end of a dance. Too often, a dancer's gratitude went to the Moon Mother who had nurtured them in the arbor, or to the Dog Soldiers who had carried them from the pole to their beds and then brought the cold towels to soothe their feverish brows. Did they not understand that without Jeanne there would have been no dance at all? Perhaps the rational mind blamed Jeanne as the chief perpetrator of their ordeal. Standing in the East gate, she had directed their fates in the arbor. She caused them to thirst and to dance beyond endurance. Jeanne had been the torturous focus of spiritual authority, and now that there was release, triumph, water and food, perhaps the dancers shied away from their former taskmaster by the same reflex that causes students to avoid their disciplinarians no matter how beneficial. We appreciated the teachers who made us work the hardest only in mature retrospect. We too often failed to acknowledge them when we were in their classrooms. In time, of course, FTOD dancers come to fully appreciate Jeanne's role in their growth.

The first "For the One" Youth Dance occurred on the 14th and 15th of October, about a week prior to the Pehrsons' departure for Brazil. Tracey Turner and her husband David Keyser were the facilitators and sponsors of this initiative that they hoped would help the troubled children and teens with whom they worked. All except three of the 13 children who danced were considered "at risk" because of severe abuse and parental neglect. These children aged 7 to 17 had been removed from their homes by the courts, and generally they lived in group homes. The dance itself at the Watersong arbor was shortened to an overnight two-day period, and was served by an experienced FTOD crew.

John reported that the dance for these troubled kids produced more heavy energy than an adult dance. The children danced hard, and their emotions sent shockwaves of pain through the adults. The dance seemed to have a real therapeutic value for some of the at-risk kids and was healing for the non-abused children as well. This initial experiment encouraged Jeanne and John to schedule FTO Youth Dances for ages 13 to 21. The first would be in Graham in March 2006, and the second the following October in South Africa.

Tracey Turner-Keyser, in a communication that she sends to the parents of her children and teen clients, says this in recommending the "For the One" Youth Dance.

"My belief is that this is the best way to get 'out of your head' and 'into your heart' where a person can recognize their emotions and feelings and begin to process whatever needs processing. I take advantage of many tools to help my clients move in this direction. I have found a powerful and wonderful opportunity (tool) to offer to a select few of my 7 to 17-year old clients—the "For the One" Youth Dance. I feel the progress they have made to date and continue to make will be solidified and accelerated as a result of this dance experience."

The Pehrsons arrived in Sao Paulo, Brazil, one of the earth's five largest cities at over 20 million people, on the 21st. The FTOD sponsors were Felicity and Andrew Macdonald, and on the next day they arranged for Jeanne and John to talk about the dance and sing spontaneous songs at an informal gathering of about 15 people.

Here they also met the two men who would head the drum group. Later, at the open-air market, Jeanne purchased small clay bowls to present to the dancers during the water ceremony.

Andrew and Felicity had been married for 35 years and been in Brazil since 1973. Andrew was a war baby born in England of Scottish heritage. His career as a cotton broker first took him to India for eight years before relocating to Argentina and Brazil. Felicity was born in Argentina, raised in its British community, and schooled in England. Both speak with an English accent. Their large home in a gated community on the south side of Sao Paulo sits on a hill. Below, there is a new Peace-Sound Chamber, a sweat lodge, and a tennis court mostly given over to ceremonial use. The Chamber is a wattle and daub construction of bamboo and stone mudded over with adobe. The roof is thatched with coconut fronds. The FTOD site, however, was located on the Macdonald's *sitio*, a mid-size farm located about two and a half hours from the city. The beautiful landscape was rugged, and steep, and challenging dirt roads had to be negotiated to reach the arbor. Cattle and a few horses had free range in the large fenced spaces.

Some of the dance crew who had met Felicity when she danced the FTOD in South Africa planned to come to the Brazilian dance as preparations at the arbor site began. On Saturday night, the 29th, the Pehrsons did a blessing ceremony for the new House of Peace Chamber. Afterward, Felicity had arranged for a Brazilian tribal dance called a Toré to be performed by a young shaman on the court below the house. Jeanne and John gave gifts to T'Kayná, the shaman, and his assistant Maria Lucia and were surprised that gifts had also been prepared for them. John was given a native pipe and tobacco and Jeanne a necklace. The honor gifts were well received on both sides.

The dance preparations were made more difficult in its remote mountain setting by a rain that continued on and off throughout the dance, but an ingenious system of tarps kept the rest cubicles dry for the dancers. On the afternoon of the second dance day,

Jeanne had a painful episode of back pain that scared John. Between dance rounds she rested, but fifteen minutes into the new round, Jeanne suddenly doubled over in pain and had to be helped from the arbor by Sammye Jo. John took over as Chief, but rested the nine dancers after another thirty minutes so that he could go to Jeanne. He found her flat on her back, soaked from the rain, lying in Sammye Jo's lap near the drum. The Moon Mother was already pressing warm stones from the ceremonial fire on Jeanne's chest and back to help relieve the pain, but Jeanne seemed not there. Her eyes were blank as if she had left her body. Both John and Sammye Jo began to speak to her, to coax her back to life.

Much later, after Jeanne had recovered enough to do a powerful pipe ceremony at the end of the dance, she and Sammye Jo talked about what had occurred. Jeanne said that she had stepped into a white light and that she had seen a round portal that she might easily have decided to walk through and thus die to her body. Sammye Jo then told the couple that she had a vision of a past life when Jeanne died in her arms. While Jeanne was in the light, Sammye Jo said that she was praying, "Oh God, don't let this happen again!"

A Dog Soldier named Ronnie, who had observed Jeanne's collapse and recovery, said, "I saw this happen to my mother. She died and was given the chance to be reborn into the same body with the same memories. Jeanne has just been reborn!" Ronnie's mother had not only survived cancer but also the great Indian Ocean tsunami the previous December.

Jeanne remained very fragile for the remainder of the dance, but John, Sammye Jo, Sonja Munz, and the others in the crew worked hard to give the dancers what they needed for a powerful dance. By the time of the water blessing on the final day, everyone felt honored, and Felicity and Andrew's hopes for the dance seemed fulfilled. To aid Jeanne and John's post-dance recovery, the host sponsors gave the couple the use of their mountaintop retreat, a large house at 6000 ft. located near The McKinsey Institute. The house came with a live-in staff—a husband and wife, and their 11-year-old daughter. When the Macdonalds were not in residence, an outbuilding on the property with bedrooms, toilets, and showers was rented to mountain hikers so that year-round employment was provided for Celso and Luciana, the caretakers. John and Jeanne had a precious five days at the retreat before Felicity came to drive them to the airport for their flight to Paris where they would make connections for a subsequent flight to Johannesburg. When a group of cub scouts came for the weekend to camp in the outbuilding, Jeanne and John offered them a mini-concert. The scout leader told them the next day that John's flute playing and Jeanne's singing had been very meaningful to him and to the children as well. "I was flying," he told them.

THE END OF BLOOD SACRIFICE

The long, long day from Sao Paulo to Paris to Johannesburg came to its final destination at the end of a bumpy dirt track that led to Rustlers Valley Mountain Retreat. Jeanne, John, and Sammye Jo arrived by rental car just in time to watch the earth's rotation raise the light aurora and then the full moon itself over the dramatic Zulu mountain homescape. It was a vision of the ages that had stopped spear-carrying hunters in their tracks to look up in awe as now these modern travelers did.

Jeanne made an important observation to John when they were talking about the occurrence of visionary experiences in the sweat lodge and in the dance arbor. There were times, John admitted, when no visions occurred in the course of a given ceremony. Jeanne compared seeing visions and energy auras to being on the outside of a picture looking in and seeing all its wonderful colors, shapes, and designs versus becoming the picture itself. Her point was that when an individual moved fully into power and became the power, there was no further need for visions to confirm its presence or reality. "You just *are* the power," she said. "Then the feedback becomes the result of what you do. You move *inside* the power and thus become less aware of it."

As it was done in Israel, American buffalo skins were provided to make a People's Drum for the FTOD. Carol Beem from Oklahoma donated this skin, and John and Niyan stretched it over the rims of African kiaat wood. Kiaat is used for the making of marimbas, and it is commonly called "the singing wood." The drum was double-sided, and it proved to have a deep, resonant voice with a palpable energy when played. But first a birthing ceremony was held in the starseed hut below Marimba House to awaken the People's Drum. Sammye Jo directed the ceremony and Niyan, Dom DeBruin, Jeanne and John stood the four directions. After prayers, the buffalo rawhide umbilical cord was cut and buried on the north side of the hut. Sammye Jo also gave Niyan, the drum maker, a piece of the cord to put into his medicine bag. Then the drum was played for the first time; and as the five ceremony participants began to play, other drums outside the hut joined them. The new drum symbolized a union of North American ancestors with African ones, and it would be sounded in this valley to energize the vibration of oneness deep into the Earth Mother. That evening, once the drumming began, it continued well into the night on the pure joy of the drummers.

Jeanne rose early one morning and drove down into the valley meadow where she did a private pipe ceremony at the dance arbor. Jeanne did solo, unobserved ceremonies to prepare dance arbors and other ceremonial spaces wherever she went. This dawn, however, after she had smoked the pipe, she vomited, lost consciousness, and fell to the ground. Her next conscious recognition was of being surrounded by curious cows. Jeanne recalls what happened next.

"Before leaving the arbor, I was careful to honor the pipe as I took the ashes, blessed the shrines, fireplaces, and the Center Pole, and then sang as I wrapped the pipe back up in its sacred blanket. I was extremely weak while doing all of this, but I felt in integrity with the whole process. I knew something powerful had just happened. I had been given a glimpse of what the upcoming dances would be, having just cleared something so they could take place. The ancestors were loving and gentle with me. We were in this together fulfilling an ancient vow."

Somehow, although desperately weak and feeling "out of body," Jeanne got herself back to her hut and collapsed on the bed. John, who had attended an early morning planning breakfast, discovered his wife in this condition with the vomit still evident on her discarded shirt. Jeanne was able to relate what had happened to her, and John crawled into bed and held her until she felt able to function again. Episodes like this worried John, and he thought back to something Carolyn had told Jeanne when they were last with Joseph in Colorado. Jeanne did not want to hear it, but possibly they would have to release the FTOD to other chiefs for the sake of Jeanne's physical survival. Their current world travel schedule was obviously hard on her, and the number of dances was growing. Since Jeanne was incapable of giving anything less than her full devotion to any dance or sweat lodge or pipe ceremony, then the only solution was to schedule less for her to do. That, of course, was tantamount to asking a mother to give up one of her children.

Native workers had been hired to complete the new arbor, and they had also had to erect a pole fence to keep the cows from eating the thatch off the new sweat hut. For a change, John was not required to labor in the construction of a dance arbor. Niyan told him that he had paid sufficient labor dues. There were other necessary chores, however. In the division of labor, John did the couple's laundry and kept the floors wherever they resided either vacuumed, scrubbed, swept, or raked. Free from arbor construction, John was pressed into airport runs. The faithful crew from all over the globe were assembling. Mona Zekri was arriving from Egypt. Teresa Hutson, Andy Baxter, and Cheryl Braswell arrived from North Carolina, and Anael Harpaz and Rhonda Factor from Israel. Sonja Munz was meeting Joško Šabiè, and Brett Almond from England coming in the next day.

As the tarps went up on the arbor poles, a herd of eland, estimated between 75 to 100, came to graze in a far pasture northeast of the arbor. Dom, a sangoma, said that the eland brought the spirit of the Bushmen people to the valley. Bushmen have been proven by DNA testing to be the original human beings of Africa.

Sangomas had come to the last two dances and danced part of a day or attended a pipe ceremony, but this dance three initiated native sangomas from three separate tribes, who were trained by Gogo Numzimani, were staying for the entire dance. This was very significant given South Africa's history of apartheid. The FTOD was acting as a healing bridge between races as it was intended. With Dom and another sangoma, Nonty, African traditions were well represented.

Around noontime on Saturday of the dance, Jeanne called on Sonja Munz, who lived in England but was South African born, to take her place as Chief for one round of the dance. John did the same for Brett Almond, and in this way the Pehrsons began preparing others to chief future dances. On Sunday, at the conclusion of the water ceremony that ends the dance, after Jeanne had honored all the dancers and crew, she herself received the water blessing from John. Then spontaneously, all the dancers and crew surrounded Jeanne and gave her an ovation of love and tearful appreciation to the thundering accompaniment of the drums. In the sharing circle that followed later in the day, dancers spoke of the healing power of dancing with the sangomas and the release of past racial tensions. Dom testified that he was the visionary witness of many souls who crossed over from darkness into the light of the ceremonial fires.

On Thursday Dom and two other sangomas offered to "throw the bones" and give John a reading. Much of the reading was given over to health issues, but at the end the sangomas saw that John was ready for the *isentwazo* ceremony that graduates a twaza into recognition as a sangoma. Two days later Gogo Numzimani, in the presence of Gogo Mzinyati and Dom DeBruin, read the sacred bones for Jeanne. She, too, was seen as ready to be initiated as a sangoma in the ancient ceremony. Jeanne knew enough about the ceremony, however, to have reservations about accepting it. Jeanne tells the rest of the story.

"When this was announced to me, I immediately asked Gogo Numzimani, 'Does this involve blood sacrifice?' She smiled and said 'yes.' I felt something flip upside down in my stomach. And then I gathered the courage to say in as gentle and respectful way as I knew how, 'Gogo, is there a way to do this ceremony without blood sacrifice? I believe that I have come here to do it differently, to show a new way. Because I believe we are evolving to a place that is beyond sacrifice. At the same time I don't want to offend your people, because important bridges are being built here. What shall I do?'

"Gogo Numzimani looked at me with such loving eyes, as did Gogo Mzinyati. The consensus was that we would all pray about it. John, afterwards, also spoke with Dom about the dilemma of blood sacrifice. To me later, Dom suggested that perhaps dear Credo Mutwa would show himself to us and give me an answer.

"As it turned out, Credo made a six-hour journey in the African heat to visit with John and me, near what had been his home near Pretoria. He had also come to see a medical doctor who told him that he was not to visit with anyone. His wife Virginia later told us that Credo's comment to the doctor was, 'If I do not get to see these people, I will be very angry.' At which point, he left and came to us. It was in this visit that I shared with Credo the dilemma I was having. John and I had already decided that we would happily gift a goat to feed the people, but to have it sacrificed on our behalf and to have its blood used upon us in ceremony was something we were both uncomfortable with. (I had even reconciled inside myself that if this is what Spirit wanted me to do, then I would be the one to take the animal's life. I would be the one who would take full responsibility). Credo smiled and said simply what John and I had already surmised . . .that a blood sacrifice was not necessary, and that a goat for the people as a gift would be a good thing. And so, this is how it was done.

"It wasn't until we had returned to the United States that I received an e-mail on Gogo's behalf, saying that no longer would the initiation ceremony for the sangomas involve blood sacrifice. I cried when I read this. Centuries of tradition were being changed. I still am humbled by all that occurred."

The second FTOD in Rustlers Valley in 2005 was unusual in that, for the first time, more men than women danced—a ten to three ratio. Male ancestors who were seen at the pole by John and others included a tall black African warrior with spear and shield and an equally impressive Native American Medicine Man and Chief in full regalia that included an eagle feather headdress and a painted face. Brett Almond, who danced, had a rough experience at the pole as John and Sammye Jo pushed him to come into his full power. At one point, Brett shouted to Sammye Jo, "I don't want to be here!" To which she replied, "Well, I guess it's a good day to die!" Brett then fell to the ground, and Sammye Jo began stabbing him with an imaginary knife until she pronounced him dead. Then the Moon Mother set about Brett's rebirth, stage by stage until she called the Medicine Man (that she saw Brett to be) back into his body. "Come back," Sammye Jo intoned. "Come back. You have work to do here. We need you." John recorded Sammye Jo's method in his journal.

"Afterward, Sammye explained to me that in ancient days, the Medicine Man in her tribe would take people into a cave where they would fast for several days from food and water (like we do in this dance). Then, he would give them medicine to slow their heart and body down to simulate the dying process. He would take them through a rebirth into their full power. So, what she did with Brett was a variation on this ancient process. Brett will likely be one of the first new Chiefs of the 'For the One' Dance. He does have work to do. We do need him to step into his full power."

The male dancers worked very hard, John reported. All but two completely surrendered at the pole and allowed themselves to shout, scream, and cry. John knew from personal experience how much courage was required for the men to do this.

In looking to the next year, Jeanne was already planning to return to all the arbors that they had danced in 2005—twelve dances in seven countries. But other places beckoned, too—Egypt, Croatia, Italy, Haiti, Hawaii, Iceland, and more. Was it even possible for the Pehrsons to physically dance in thirteen countries in a single year?

When the visit with Credo Mutwa and Virginia was concluded at Naledi, Jeanne altered their return flight and car rental arrangements so that they could travel with Dom to Kwazulu Natal Province for their appointment with Gogo Numzimani. Dom, initiated as Gogo Gerre, was still a novelty in Africa. When they stopped in a gas station en route, the blonde, blue-eyed white man in the traditional sangoma robes attracted attention. Still many of the blacks that they encountered greeted Dom with honor, saying, "Takoza, Gogo" and clapping their right hand over their left in a heartbeat rhythm. Others asked in disbelief, "Are you a sangoma?" At such times Dom would give them his infectious smile and hold up his wrists that were adorned with the symbols of his office. "You don't get these at Pick 'N Pay," he would tell them. Five or more times people asked Gogo Gerre for healing medicines and ceremonies for themselves and family.

On arrival at Gogo Numzimani's ceremonial grounds, the Pehrsons went into the ancestor's house or *macosini* for an extended ceremony to announce their arrival. There was drumming and singing in the background as they did prayers and clapped their hands to call the spirits. Then they lit white candles and placed them on the altar. All this was preparation for the secret Isentwazo Ceremony to follow the next day. Although Joško and Mona were also visiting the sangoma campground, they were not allowed to witness the ceremony that initiated Jeanne and John as titled sangomas. The initiation did not magically give the Pehrsons the knowledge of plant medicines and the complex ceremonies that twazas take years to learn before they become sangomas. Rather, it was a recognition by the African spiritual community of the power of Jeanne and John's work.

In an Oceanside sacred Mandau Ceremony, Jeanne and John were initiated to the Mer People. The Tkoza sangomas from Swaziland believe themselves to be descendants of the Mer People. Gogo Mzinyati and Dom sought to introduce and connect the Pehrsons to the oceanic spirits so that future communications with the Mer People would be made easier.

It took 31 hours to get from Johannesburg to the Raleigh-Durham airport. Cheryl and David were on hand to greet them and take them to their bed at Jo Fisher's. They left Africa in 90 degrees of bright sunshine to arrive to freezing rain and overcast in North Carolina. Adjustment over the next weeks would again be difficult, and how could they explain it to friends and family over a Christmas that was less than ten days away? How could they hope to convey what they had just experienced in Brazil and South Africa without sounding either braggadocio or hallucinatory? Once children had asked their fathers returning from combat in the Second World War, "What did you do in the war, Daddy?" What was the possible reply? There were no words to relate their experience to the understanding of anyone who had not been there. Jeanne and John faced the same psychological dilemma. How were they to respond to the innocent question, "And what you have guys been up to lately?"

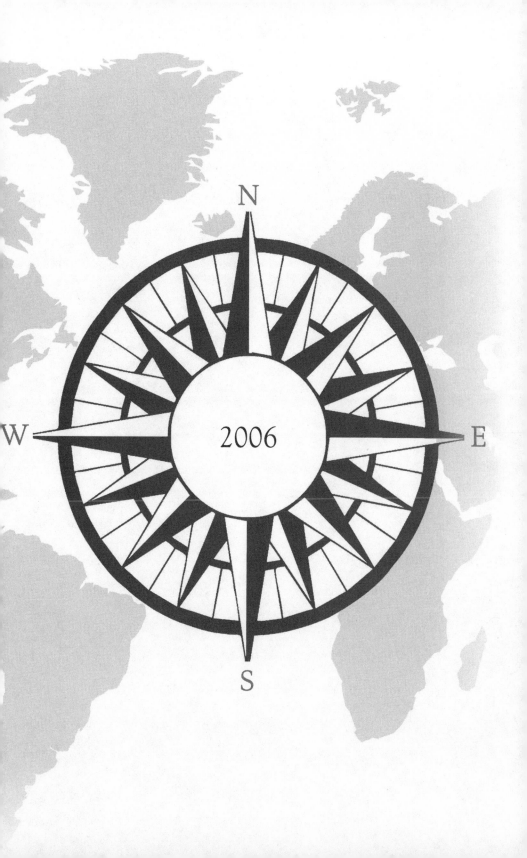

THE YOUTH DANCE

There are multiple antecedents in Jeanne and John's personal histories that would give rise to a "For the One" Youth Dance. John had the teenage experience of being consigned to the Bonnie Brae Farm for Boys through no fault of his own. He entered that atmosphere of what today would be called "at risk" teens a month before his fifteenth birthday, and he remained there until he graduated from high school. If John was not a tough kid before he went to Bonnie Brae, he soon became one. But despite the labels put on Bonnie Brae boys, John bloomed as a talented leader in the regular high school of the nearby town. Another impetus for John's concerns about young people was the fact that he was the father of three sons who had also been subjected to parental divorce. If he often felt inadequate to serve the needs of his own boys, that did not mean that he was not acutely sensitive to their situation.

In their first year together as a couple, Jeanne and John worked together with teens in an ad hoc organization that began by opening the door of their home for empathetic dialogs. Jeanne tells the story from her perspective that led to the advent of the "For the One" Youth Dance.

"In the early 1990s I found myself with the challenges that any parent goes through when their children have reached the teen years. And my two, though exceptional in so many ways, were also typical in their ability to bring challenges onto the home front. What I can say is this. I adore teens. I always have . . . challenges and all. There is something about the raw energy of the teen that moves my heart in a way no one else can. And something I find interesting is that most of the revolutions on the planet throughout the centuries have been started and carried on by those in their teens and early twenties.

"It was in 1992 that a police officer knocked on my back door and asked if I still wanted to start an organization for teens, an idea that I had presented to him several months before. If so, there was another woman who might be interested in helping me do this. Her name was Olga Franklin. And so, on a wing and a prayer, Olga and I pulled together several like-minded individuals of the community, including members of the police department in Signal Mountain, Tennessee. It wasn't long before we found we had created a non-profit organization called 'Up On The Mountain.' My partner John soon came along and became an integral part of the organization.

"As it turned out, we created a place for teens to come where they could be heard, accepted for who they were and given alternative skills for dealing with anger and any other issue they might be struggling with in their lives. We were not associated with their school, with their parents (outside of receiving parental permission for their being present at our meetings), with a church, with the police (other than having two on the board), or any other organized group. We were neutral, and we were safe. And so once a week, teens began to gather in John's and my home. Jenny brought in the first one. His name was Jason. After that, the rest began to flow.

"John and I simply listened. We ate pizza, drank juice, and listened to their stories, to their ideas, to their hearts. More and more kids began to come. It was amazing and quite beautiful to watch what was happening. The kids were always full of surprises, too. One night (not their regular meeting night) we heard a car horn in our driveway. It was around 10:00 P.M. We opened the door to find a Volkswagen stuffed full of teenagers, all of whom had been brought up the mountain to our home by one of the teens who came to the weekly meetings. He wanted all of his friends to meet us. We're still amazed at the number of people they squashed into the VW.

"Over time, our board created a few outings that included camping trips and rock climbing. It was truly gratifying to watch these young people stretch and grow. Had John and I not moved away when we did, the organization, I have no doubt, would have continued to grow and to flourish. In our absence, though, it ceased to exist. But the relationships with the kids did not. We continued to get calls and letters months after.

"All my adult life I have enjoyed being with teenagers. I was sad when Up On The Mountain no longer existed. I was sad because my path seemed to be pulling me in the direction away from teens. The ceremonial life has been fulfilling, and it is exactly what I was being guided toward. But through it all I have yearned to work and be with teenagers again. So guess what?? Through divine providence or simple perfect timing, a couple of years ago people began to ask me to do dances for the youth . . . a 'For the One' Youth Dance. With the impetus, encouragement, and support of the Watersong Community in North Carolina, as well as Tracey Turner-Keyser, a psychiatrist who works with troubled youth, and her husband David Keyser, a medical doctor and retired lieutenant commander in the U.S. Navy, the first 'For the One' Youth Dance (ages 7-17) took place in October of 2005. In March of 2006, the first full FTO Youth Dance for those 13 to 21 happened. Both were so powerful and such major successes that FTO Youth Dances were scheduled to go global.

"The bottom line is that I feel everything coming full circle. I cannot imagine anything more powerful than providing a singing dance for the young people of our planet . . . giving them a productive way to clear out the angers and hates, that they might sing and dance back into the memory of the mass consciousness the fact that we are not separated . . . that we are part of each other and must care for each other in a loving way if we are to survive."

A Mother's Story

Sue Spies grew up on a farm in Zimbabwe, and her concerns for the environment led her into the study of Permaculture. Today she works on community and school food gardening projects where she teaches and implements a nutritional food source for those who have been historically malnourished. Sue both writes and illustrates the training materials that she uses. She is also a frequent contributor to *EnviroKids*, the junior magazine for the South African Wildlife and Environment Society. Sue came to Rustlers Valley with a team of facilitators working on the annual Permaculture Design Course, and there she encountered the "For the One" Dance. Here, with permission, is a mother's perspective of seeing her sixteen-year-old daughter dance the "For the One" Dance and the daughter's first-person story as well.

"In December 2004, three of my friends danced in the For-The-One Dance at Rustlers Valley in South Africa. I listened to their enthusiasm for what they'd experienced, but, somehow I just didn't get the message. Admittedly, at the time I was about to start facilitating a course at Rustlers, and my mind was on my task at hand, not on what they were talking about. At that time I met many of the crew, and what struck me was their peaceful energy and grace. I have seldom seen so many radiant people in the same place at the same time.

"A year later one of my friends, Èidín, was going to be the Alpha Dog (the person who takes care of on-site logistics) and she asked if my daughter Danette, aged 16, and I would come along to Dog Soldier. I agreed, and so did my daughter, albeit with some reluctance because it was the beginning of her much-needed December holiday and, like most teenagers, she would much rather have had time to chill out and do as little as possible.

"I had no idea what to expect. I answered the call knowing it was the right thing to do at that time. Èidín asked me to help out in the kitchen. The kitchen team starts feeding the rest of the crew the day before the dance; but we could only get to Rustlers on the day of the dance.

"By the time we arrived, the arbour was already built, and Èidín's team had built a lean-to kitchen a short distance from the arbour. People were milling around, busy with things. Jeanne, John, the Sun Father and the Moon Mothers were getting the dancers ready. Each dancer has their place in the arbour, which is a shelter around a centre pole.

"The sweat lodge is near to the entrance of the arbour, and the Fire Keepers were tending an enormous fire that would heat up the stones for the first sweat. The crew have a short sweat first, then the dancers have a full sweat to commence the process. They also have a sweat each morning before the dancing starts.

"Danette and I soon had tasks to do, and I did wonder what on earth I was doing there. I felt as though I had entered another world. I thought, in those first few hours, that I should just take my daughter by the hand and escape, but, fortunately, I didn't, because the next ten days were undoubtedly one of the most significant experiences either of us has ever had—for me, as a mother, and for Danette, as a young person on the brink of adulthood.

"The Dance Chiefs, Jeanne and John, create a sacred, safe space for the Dance. The Sun Father holds the male energy for the dancers. The Moon Mothers hold the female energy for the dancers. The drummers keep the rhythm for the dancers. The Firekeepers help to transmute the energy generated. The Dog Soldiers do what has to be done—smudging, fetching, carrying and making sure whatever supplies are needed are on hand. Each person has a role to play to help the dancers dance their dance.

"The purpose of the dance is healing and to bring about a remembrance (putting back together) the realisation that We are One. Each dancer dances his or her own dance; their processing and healing helps others to heal and process. They dance for us all, because We are One.

"I have been blessed with many remarkable, deeply spiritual experiences in my life, and yet what I encountered during that first dance astounded me. In one of the meditations that I had during a course many years ago, I received a message that "the only pain we feel is the pain of separation," and on the first day of the dance, this knowledge had finally made the transition from head-knowledge to heart-knowledge. I have never experienced the unity and union that I experienced then.

"In the kitchen I chopped vegetables to the beat of the drums. Although the other kitchen crew and I were separated from the dance, I felt completely part of what was happening. I felt totally connected to what was happening in the arbour. It was deeply transformative.

"I was a bit concerned about how Danette was responding. She'd been exposed to my spirituality for her whole life. I'd taught her breathing and meditation techniques for longer than she could remember, but she'd never embraced any of these practices fully. It had always been 'mom's thing.' During the dance, at some point, most dancers collapse and process their 'stuff.' I wondered what Danette thought of what she was seeing; some dancers cry, scream or even babble. Each person's process is different.

"I did see people respond to her, though, and I saw her connect with people in a way that I'd never seen before. I could see that she had a deep understanding of what was happening, however, and I saw a yearning in her eyes. At some point I said to her, 'You want to dance, don't you?' She looked coy and said, 'Maybe,' which is teenage-speak for 'you betcha!'

"I knew money was the issue; she knew I didn't have the support funds readily available. I said the same thing that everyone always says—if you are meant to dance, then you will dance. Then I realised that her father's annual maintenance payment was about to be made to me; and when I told her that this was essentially her money, and she could pay for her dance support herself, her apparent hesitation vanished.

"No one as young as Danette had ever danced the full dance, and yet Jeanne and John had no hesitation in saying it was okay. As the second dance drew nearer, I began to realise more and more how significant Danette's dance was going to be. The night before the dance I hand-stitched a dance skirt for her; it was a meditative process because I knew this was a coming-of-age ceremony for her.

I knew this was a symbolic step for both us—for me to let go and for her to step into her own power.

"I don't have the words to describe my feelings when she stepped into the arbour to take her place, or as I watched her crouch down to go into the sweat lodge, which is the beginning of the dance for the dancers. I watched her self-consciously take her first dance steps, and I ached to tell her it was okay, but the crew outside the arbor are not allowed to make any contact with the dancers. She was one of three female dancers; the other ten were all men (which was a remarkable ratio!).

"It was the most beautiful thing to see. One of the Moon Mothers put a shawl around Danette's waist, and immediately her dance changed. Suddenly she was like a graceful fairy, skipping to and fro. She was dancing!

"I asked Danette if she wanted me to be there when she fell into her process, and she said, 'absolutely!' I worried that I would be in the kitchen at the time, so Èidín and I had an agreement that if I was, she would come out of the arbour and wave her arms frantically so that I could dash over.

"I knew many of the dancers in the second dance—old and new friends. This time my experience was much deeper than the previous weekend. As I worked in the kitchen, I sensed a minute or so before a dancer went down that it was going to happen, and sure enough, as I'd sensed, the heart-beat drumbeat could be heard. I wondered if I'd know when it was Danette, and I did. By the time Èidín was waving her arms, I was already halfway to the arbour.

"I stood at the entrance, holding onto a pole, watching my precious girl sob her heart out, tears flowing down my face. I knew what she was dealing with, and I knew it had nothing to do with me; this was her stuff. I knew I had to let go and not try to fix anything, not try to stop her from healing. Sammye Jo, the Moon Mother, called me over as she was singing to Danette and gesticulated for me put my hands on Danette's back. She was facing away from me, and I wondered if she even knew I was there (she did).

After a while Sammye Jo sent me away, and Èidín, another Moon Mother and some friends took me to the medicine wheel where I could finish letting go.

"I knew her process was not over, and when she fell again the next day, I was there. That time I didn't collapse into tears. I could join the other Dog Soldiers to carry her back to her place, and she knew I was there; she held onto one of my fingers. And then I knew that she had danced her dance.

"When the crew joined the dancers for the last celebratory dance, I danced with my daughter, no longer the young girl, but now, instead, the young woman. For her it was a coming-of-age and for me a transformation from mother to mentor.

"As I write this now, it has been three months since the dance. I look at this remarkable young woman who is so confident. She knows who she is, and she is brave, tenacious, and doesn't take life too seriously. Letting her dance, letting her go, letting her BE has been the most profound step I could take as a mother.

"For the first time this year (2006), there is a dance for the youth of South Africa. I encourage other parents to let their children dance their dance. There are few opportunities for young people to go through a symbolic change from child to adult. In African traditions, there is the Abakewta for young men. In the Jewish tradition there is Bar Mitzvah. In the western tradition there is nothing."

Danette's Story

"When I met the dancers from the dance in 2004, it felt I was meeting people from a different world—they were so different from other people. As I've grown up, Mom has always spoken about spiritual stuff, but it was always her thing, not mine. I didn't think I would ever be part of something like the dance. Little did I know!

"When Èidín asked me if I would help in November 2005, I was reluctant because I didn't know what it was about, and I was scared of the unknown. Mom asked me if I would help if she helped; and because I wasn't going to be alone, I decided I would try something new. When we got there, I had no idea what I should do. I kind of just slotted in somewhere.

"I was a Dog Soldier in the first dance. We basically had to do what had to be done—whatever was needed; fetch water; smudge the dancers, the crew, the arbour; help in the kitchen; watch the fire at night. I made lots of friends.

"One of our jobs was to carry the fallen dancers back to their places, and sometime on the second day, I started helping with the carrying, too. I was nervous at first, scared I'd do the wrong thing, but after that, I felt as though I was helping to kind of mother them.

"I really enjoyed the drumming and the rattles that the Dog Soldiers played. I realised afterwards that the drums really do help you to keep going. When my feet were really sore, I kept going to the beat of the drums.

"I don't know when I decided I would dance. I was concerned about the dance support money, and then mom said I could use dad's maintenance, and so I said 'yes.' I think it's one of the best things that I've ever done.

"In the beginning I was very self-conscious and didn't know what to do. Then one of the Moon Mothers told me to just let go, and when Cheryl gave me a shawl to wear, I was fine. I just danced my dance. I felt like a fairy or an angel when I was dancing, like I was flying. I was sometimes aware of other people, especially my neighbours, but most of the time I was in my own space, doing my own thing. I felt as though I was alone in the mountains.

"I never really thought about not eating and drinking. I got a bit thirsty on the Saturday afternoon and Sunday morning. It felt as though I couldn't go on, but I persevered. At the beginning of the dance, they told me that hunger and thirst are choices, and knowing this helped me get through it. I kept saying to myself, 'I choose to be full.' It worked.

"We were in the arbour for two nights. The first night the sky was stunning, and because Rustlers is so far from town, the stars were bright, clear, and stunningly beautiful. The second night it was raining, and the sound of the raindrops on the tarpaulin was so loud that I couldn't sleep very well.

"I remember in the dance that Brett from England was also dancing, and at one point I burst into tears, and he was there for me. I was hugging the pole, and I couldn't really move, and I was dealing with stuff to do with my dad, and I guess he just picked up what was happening with me. He left his dance path and held on to me, and I didn't want to let go, but the Sun Father, Joško, walked me back to my place, and I sat down for a while.

"When I fell for the first time, I was lying on the ground, and Sammye Jo was singing to me. I knew Mom had come into the arbour to be with me because her scent is familiar to me (not because she hadn't showered!). Somehow our senses are heightened at that point.

"Afterwards, when I was being carried, it felt so nice. It felt as though I was in a huge feather bed, or a waterbed. It was so cool. The Moon Mother who sat with me when I fell, Mona, was 'my' Moon Mother. She kept humming, and when I started crying, she cried with me. She lay down next to me, and that helped me to let go—because she was just there with me. I still hum that same tune that she hummed to me, sometimes without me even realising it.

"I'm so glad I danced. There are things that our parents can't do for us, and the dance helps us do it for ourselves. It's helped me open up more, to be who I am, and it helped me grow up a little. I have become a bit more responsible, somehow. I'm more aware of what is going on around me now, and I've learnt a really, really hard lesson, and that's to let go of 'stuff.' It's helped me to come to terms with the fact that my dad is really far away, and there's nothing I can do about it.

"My relationship with my mom has grown because we were both part of the dances. We were close before, but now she's basically my best friend. I miss the people from the dance. I made special friends. Forever friends. The dance crew feel like my family to me. I also learnt from Jeanne that just because someone isn't there physically, they can still be there in your heart. This is the big thing that I learnt through the dance—that we are all One. There is no separation.

"If you hear the call to dance, then do it. It's true that if you are meant to do it, the money follows."

EGYPT 2006

In their Spring Update, 2006 e-mail, the Pehrsons described their "For the One" Dance experience in Egypt in these terms.

"Nadia is her name. She's sixteen years old and is a Bedouin Arab who lives in the Sinai in Egypt. She has taught herself to speak more than five languages fluently, including English, German, French, Hebrew, and Italian, plus fragments of such languages as Polish, Lithuanian, Norwegian, Afrikaans and more. The Bedouin are at the bottom of the economic scale in the Middle East. They are the true Nomads, who, for centuries, have adapted to life in the desert. It was Nadia's father, Ahmed, and others of his Zina tribe who not only helped us build the dance arbor for the "For the One" Egypt Dance, but it is they who cooked and cared for us throughout the dance experience.

"We were in the high mountain sandy desert of the Sinai away from trees and water, accessible only by camel and four-wheel drive vehicles. The closest village was a beautiful little intimate resort community next to the Red Sea called Dahab, an hour's drive from the dance site. The dance site?? It found us. While driving in the high mountains, praying for direction on where the site should be, Jeanne looked up at one point to see the perfect image of a whale in a nearby mountain. We immediately stopped and looked down. There on the ground, in the midst of the white barren sand was a single kernel of bright yellow corn. This was the sign we had looked for. This is where the dance was to take place.

"The dance arbor itself was built of a circle of Bedouin tents, with a center pole of six small tree trunks bound together, covered with palm leaves. Mona Zekri, with help of family and friends, was the brave soul who brought the dance to Egypt. She did an extraordinary job of bridging cultures and laying the groundwork for this event to occur. She enlisted Ehab Farid, whose skills in leading safaris and understanding of the desert and its people, turned out to be an angel in disguise . . . providing us with all that was needed to manifest the dance in the deep desert.

"Ten countries were represented in this singing dance, each playing a powerful role in fulfilling the dance's purpose: to bring people together of all nationalities, religions and political views, creating an experience, through song and movement, where we can remember our interconnectedness to each other and all life."

Two weeks after the completion of the dance in the Sinai, there were terrorist bombings in the Red Sea resort town of Dahab where the dance crew had assembled to stage the dance. One massive bomb destroyed the restaurant next door to the café where they had held their planning sessions.

Another perspective of the "For the One" Dance in Egypt is provided by Rhonda Factor. Rhonda, from Israel, had danced and then Moon Mothered dances in North Carolina, Israel, and South Africa. In Egypt that April she was called to dance with a very deep purpose. This is her account.

"It was very clear to me that my dance began weeks before my actual arrival in Egypt. My thoughts and emotions were filled with a desire to help energetically clear a way for deeper peace between Jew and Arab, Israeli and Egyptian. It was also clear to me that I was being called to Egypt to help clear away the pain between our peoples, as well as to help souls caught between planes who were unable to move forward in the spiritual realms.

"Several days before leaving for Egypt, knowing I would be dancing in Egypt, one of my dearest friends called to tell me that she had dreamt that her first husband, who had been killed in 1973 in the Israel-Egyptian 'Yom Kippur War' had shown up at her doorstep. In the dream, she and her present husband welcomed him, and the three of them proceeded to discuss how they would live altogether and even began to plan how to expand their house.

"I promised to energetically take all of them into the dance arbor for healing.

"Soon after, I had a similar conversation with another friend whose first husband had been killed during the Six Day War in Egypt. I asked if she would like me to 'bring' them into the arbor, and she heartily agreed. The dance itself was held high in the Sinai mountains, far away from civilization. We started out as six dancers, with five of us making it through to the end of the dance. I had brought my shawl with me, the one I had made as an apprentice 'Moon Mother.' It is fringed on all four sides with satin ribbons. All the ribbons were strung on with focused intent by myself, my family members and close friends. Many of the ribbons also represented my grandmothers and grandfathers—my entire lineage.

"The dance started off very strong. The cool desert air, the isolation of the dance arbor surrounded by tall sandstone mountains and the subtle desert energy, all contributed to my allowing myself to surrender and be present with what was surfacing from within me.

"At times I felt the weight of the world upon me. I could barely take a step. At others I felt such joy and exhilaration at just being alive. At others I felt a million years old—a wise old grandmother had crept up to teach me the deeper ways. At other times I could see how I tend to retreat from the world when I feel overwhelmed.

"At some point, I began to feel the deep sadness, grief, and despair of my people. I felt all of the persecution, but most of all, I felt how we have come to cling to the tragedy and claim it as who we are. I was angry, sad and in deep despair. I took my shawl and began to run back and forth from my place in the arbor to the pole with tears streaming down my face. I began to bury the ribbons of my shawl in the sand at the pole, to 'rebury' all of my ancestors, this time in a good, reverent way, knowing that many of who had come before me had been left to die in fear and pain with no burial. At that point, Jeanne came over to me, wrapped me in her shawl, and said, 'Here is my shawl, my ancestors will carry you.'

"I then began a dialogue between myself and my ancestors. I told them that I recognized their pain and loss. I told them I grieve, too. I also told them that it is time for us all to move forward—to a place where we can live in peace within and without. I showed them Jeanne's shawl and said: 'There are others who have suffered as we have and have found the strength and courage to move forward and to build a better future for the next generations.' I was referring to the grave injustices and massacres perpetrated against the Native Americans, Jeanne's ancestors.

"When it was time, I picked my shawl out of the sand and proudly put it over my shoulders—this time with honor and pride. At that point, I felt an enormous upsurge of energy. I looked back at my place in the arbor where my sleeping bag was and saw hundreds, if not thousands, of people—my people—waiting to pass through. I directed them to go towards the pole, and they began to file by me, into and beyond the pole to pass onward. They just kept coming and coming, passing through and passing through. I now knew that my ancestors were working and living through me. It was an awesome feeling, a privilege on so many levels.

"I have witnessed much healing occur since that dance, including deep personal healing between one of my girlfriends and an Egyptian woman, something unthinkable for her before. To me, it is a miracle that I am privileged to witness. There are more aspects of my dance that still germinate inside me. I feel that the message I have related above can be an example of the possibility of healing and reconciliation to others.

"I, for one, am deeply grateful for the privilege to be involved in the 'For the One' Dance family. I thank Jeanne White Eagle for her vision and the courage to manifest it and her husband and partner John Pehrson for his strength and loving steadfastness and both of them for their deep wisdom."

REFLECTIONS OF A NEW CHIEF

B rett Almond was managing a complementary medical practice in Norwich, England before he founded a holistic Internet mail order company in 2000 that has become a leading and award-winning business in its field. On the day of his 25th birthday in 1993, Brett did a Corn Dance with Joseph Rael, and he experienced it as an initiation into a new way of life. In 2003 Brett asked Jeanne to write an article about the power of sound for his spiritual website, and he then began to read Jeanne and John's periodic newsletters that detailed their travels and dance experiences.

When the couple came to Wales in mid-2004 to do a Sound Workshop, Brett attended and met them face-to-face for the first time. After the workshop, they talked about the upcoming South African dance, and Jeanne suggested that Brett come and experience the dance for himself. Brett replied with the usual excuses—family commitments, the expense, the time off from work, etc. Jeanne expressed empathy and then spoke the now legendary words that have brought so many people into the dance community . . . "just think about it."

Brett thought about it. "I wanted to go, no doubt, and then a few miracles happened, and I made it. For me it was like a calling. It felt like I had made an appointment before I was born to meet up with all these people and dance in South Africa in November 2004. It felt like coming home."

Some months later with the dance in Israel coming up, Brett got an e-mail from Jeanne and John saying that he would be a good Alpha Dog for that dance . . . "just think about it."

"My thinking process got going," Brett recalls, and with a few more miracles—bang—I was in Israel Alpha-Dogging the dance." Then in Israel at Anael's house in Rosh Pina, Brett remembers Jeanne saying that it would be lovely if he could apprentice as a Sun Father in Ireland. And before Ireland, there was Germany, and they could do with some help in Germany if Brett was available . . . "just think about it." Brett put his fingers in his ears and started singing loudly, "La, la, la" like a child trying not to hear. But joking aside, Brett says that Jeanne's phrase is a symbol of something. "The people don't need to be called, they just need permission and this phrase gives permission. The dance itself actually does the calling."

After the 2005 "For the One" Dances in Israel, at the request of the biographer, Brett wrote about his insights. In addressing future readers, he said, "It is so nice to share these things with people who understand!

"The 'For the One' Dance literally relieves/cleanses us of our sins, of our darkness, the things that get in the way of being who we truly are. It also cleanses nations and all life.

"This dance is a fast track to the centre of the universe. The pole is the centre of the universe. It doesn't represent it; it becomes it. It becomes the place from where all life is born. As we connect with it, we are reborn. As you hit the pole, you hit the centre of all creation. You hit the meaning of life full on and you die into love. Life carries you. This dance truly has this power.

"The arbour carries the archetypal energy of a single cell. It is the same as a tadpole egg, or a human egg cell being fertilised by a sperm. If you look at the arbour from above, you see a round cell with a centre to it, and people come in to fertilise it.

"As we dance, we fertilise, and we give birth. We enter the miraculous white flash of creation. In this instantaneity we actually enter the centre and heart of all things. This is why the 'For the One' dance *rips up the rulebook*, because in this place there are no rules, there is only potential. That is why this dance is so powerful, because it has the power to birth universes. It is at the heart of all creation. That is why it contains the power to change the world and bring world peace. That is within its capabilities.

"As a single cell grows, divides and multiplies, so can the arbour divide and multiply. Thus I feel some clues to how more than one arbour can fit together can be found in how cells divide and multiply. This may be the connection with the multiple arbours."

More than a year later, as he was preparing to be named a "For the One" Dance Chief at the September dance in North Carolina, Brett reflected on his recent personal path.

"As you do some of the key roles around the 'For the One' Dance, you are forced to learn quickly by the power of the ceremony that you encounter. After my first dance as Sun Father in Ireland, I went into an altered state and had a very powerful and challenging time bringing myself back from an ancient part of me. It was a huge development. When I told Jeanne what had occurred, she laughingly told me, 'Oh, we forgot to tell you about that part!' I learned that as you take on more prominent roles, the demands on your integrity become greater, and you need to evolve quickly. Major growth opportunities can be intense.

"As a Chief, I think it is important to take great pride and pleasure in other people's astounding breakthroughs. In thinking about the prophecies from both South Africa and Israel, that we will one day all come together to sing and dance in celebration of our oneness, I realise that I have now taken up residence inside the prophecy along with everyone else that is part of the dance. It is no coincidence that this prophecy emerged from widely divergent cultures, and that its truth is being realised every time we dance 'For the One.'"

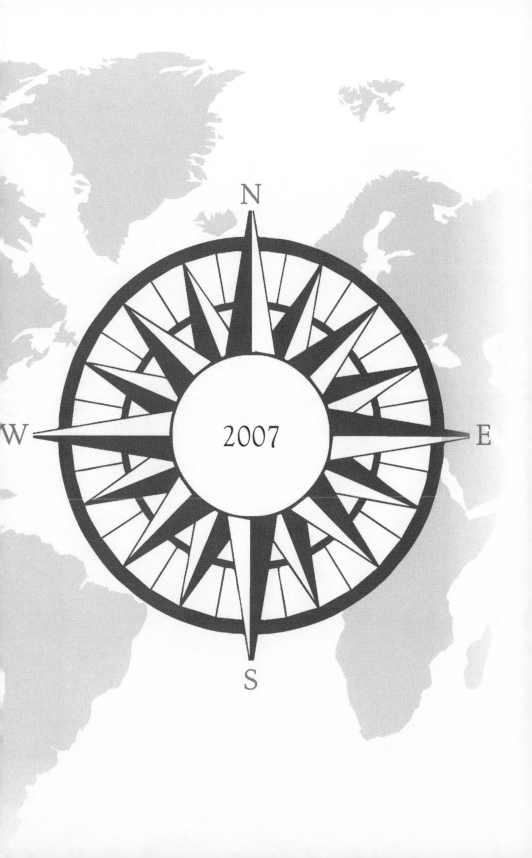

THE JOURNEY CONTINUES

I n their journey, Jeanne and John have not strategized as organizational managers. The record clearly shows that they have often ventured forward without the resources to rationally justify their bold visionary moves. They acted on the faith that if their direction was appropriate, then the means to take the next step of their journey would be provided, and so it has been since they came together as a couple in 1993. By any measure, what they have accomplished in country after country across six continents is both significant and amazing.

The continuing evolution of the journey for the One in 2006 and 2007 was an expansion of the "For the One" Dance through the creation of new Dance Chiefs and the unfolding of the "For the One" World Youth Dance along the same pathways where the Pehrsons have previously traveled. But first came the necessary trainings.

The first ten-day "For the One" Crew and Chiefs' Training began on November 28, 2006 at the Watersong Sound Chamber and Arbor in Graham, North Carolina, USA. The hosts for this landmark event had also been present when the "For the One" Dance was first danced in April 2003. They were Cheryl Braswell, Judith Brooks, and Dobs Dobmier. Twenty-six men and women showed up and said yes to the growing global mission. All of them had already served on various international crews for dances in the United States, Israel, South Africa, and Europe. They comprised a core group of individuals who had paid their own way to every place of service. Most came from the United States, but Israel was represented by Anael Harpaz and Rhonda Factor, England by Brett Almond, and Germany by Alex Racky.

During the training, Jeanne and John shared the lessons of their long journey. They counseled about cultural differences and local protocols because as participants in an international dance, each member of the crew—particularly the chief—becomes an ambassador for peace and good will. The crews were also taken through the Community Building Experience that Jeanne and John had taught internationally for years. The experience can be difficult for participants as they are forced to dig deep into their own psyches and purge out any conditioning of cultural bias that might adversely affect their group dynamic roles. Psychotherapists must undergo a similar training in order to be aware of negative aspects of their own personalities that might arise in providing therapy to patients. The emotional revelations from the group interaction of this process clear away the barriers to harmony and cooperation. At the end of the process, the crewmembers gain new skills in conflict resolution which are crucial in working within complex communities that include the ad hoc crews themselves.

The Crew and Chiefs' Training also had to deal with the practical rigors of organizing a dance. In new locations where limited development resources and labor power placed a premium on creative imagination, problem solving had to be raised to an art form that elevated both dedication and faith. Many attending the initial training had been witnesses to on-site miracles, but the reinforcement of those stories retold set the precedents for future successes when circumstances appeared impossible to the rational mind.

Jeanne and John also advised the new chiefs and their crewmembers to seek internal guidance about where they should go and what they should do, just as they themselves have done for so many years. As the FTOD founders, the two leaders were encouraging the chiefs and crew to follow their own vision, guidance, and faith in the grace of Spirit rather than to depend on the prerogatives of a formal hierarchical organization. This instruction alone set the FTOD movement apart from others that depended on top-down authoritarian management.

Jeanne says, "Maybe it's about how we treat each other as we create the experience."

As a couple whose mission had subjected them to the crucible of financial destitution, travel overload, intense spiritual processes, and abject uncertainties, Jeanne and John had a lot to say about the delicate relationship balance between male and female. If there was to be an end of separation between peoples, the battle between the sexes was the first enlightened peace treaty to be signed. Peace at the intimate level of husband and wife, however, was only emblematic of the greater matrix of human sexuality and the honoring of both the male and the female aspects of creation. The gender dynamic of the FTOD requires a conscious centering of those serving within the dance arbor. It is a sensitive area that requires candid discussion and an awareness built on understanding.

Traveling as they do, chiefs and crewmembers often find themselves as guests in a dance sponsor's home. There is an art to the practice of being a good guest whether the accommodation is an apartment in Berlin or a Zulu hut in mountains above Rustler's Valley. Jeanne and John share their experiences in this regard as an orientation that fosters happy experiences. Small gifts collected from previous travels are always welcome by hosts as is the willingness to do household chores, including the laundering of bed linens. Among the author's treasured gifts from Jeanne and John's visits are a pebble from where Jesus walked near the Sea of Galilee and an elephant tail bracelet from South Africa. A bar of Swiss chocolate, however, was eaten rather than displayed.

Over the years, especially since the advent of the World Wide Web and laptop computers, Jeanne has become an expert at obtaining the lowest airfares possible albeit by flying stand-by. She shares her practical secrets and then obviously delights in telling the miracle stories of being upgraded to Business Class on long, long transcontinental flights. On stand-by tickets, that's impossible!

The second Training for Crew and Chiefs occurred in South Africa in November 2007. Twenty-eight men and women completed the rigorous ten-day event that ended with the three-day fasting dance where participants rotated through the various roles from Chief to Kitchen Angel. By the end of this training, the total roster of experienced Chiefs and Chiefs-in-Training rose to twenty, with another 34 individuals qualified as key role players. A third training was already being organized for June and July of 2008 in northern Germany.

Jeanne reminds all participants that, "the real training comes in working the dances in the support positions that builds to the responsibility of the whole. The 'For the One' Dance is a medicine dance, a healing dance on all levels . . . physical, emotional, and spiritual. Chiefs must be prepared to minister to all those needs even within cultures quite different from their own."

In 2007 the FTOD continued to evolve. The individual processing within the Dance was becoming quicker and deeper. Dancers were going to the arbor pole sooner in the energy build-up, but the process was more gentle as the east entry gate fire had been replaced with a large water bowl. This profound shift in established practice came about in an unusual way, and it illustrates how openness can overcome the prejudice of fixed positions.

Water had already been well established as a sacramental element in the ceremonial dances. At the end of the FTOD, after a three-day water fast, a Dance Chief washes the dancers' feet and then offers them their first taste of its life-giving nature. In the South African dances where Zulu Sangomas participated, sprinkled water was used by them in the same way that sage smoke and corn meal were used in ceremonial purification and blessing. By 2006 international crewmembers Teresa Hutson and Dom DeBruin began using water in this way at African dances where they served. This profound enhancement in the role of water was thus foreshadowed for the dramatic events that occurred at the North Carolina Watersong Dance in September 2007 where Jeanne and John were chiefing.

The day prior to the Watersong Dance, the North Carolina State Fire Marshall placed a statewide ban on open fires due to serious drought conditions that might precipitate dangerous forest fires.

Normally the firepit that heats stones for the three separate sweat lodge ceremonies and the east gate dance arbor firepit consumes perhaps two cords of wood in a three-day continuous open burn. Now these fires were illegal. Participants from several countries were already gathered and established in tents adjacent to the farm lake, so what was to be done? How could a dance that seemed so dependent on fire energy go on when its open-pit fires were outlawed? As in other apparent crises, Jeanne sought privacy to do a Peace Pipe Ceremony to ask "for clarity in what Spirit wanted to happen in regard to the Dance."

Jeanne's pipe has always been an instrument of focus and vision. Her vision on this occasion was to see water in the east gate firepit that was connected to the sweat lodge fire pit by a cornmeal line. In the future, when fire was again permitted, the sweat lodge fire and the water bowl at the east gate would thus be balanced as energy vortices.

Jeanne later said, "The water is talking as strongly as the fire."

To solve the immediate problem of no sweat lodge for this dance, Jeanne envisioned the dancers going into the Watersong lake, stepping deep into the bank mud and then immersing themselves in the water.

This immersion, Jeanne felt, was a releasing of prayers and the receiving of blessings. Instead of the sweat lodge ceremony, which was water-related by steam, Jeanne saw the people going to water as her traditional Cherokee ancestors had done for centuries. Cherokee traditionalists still go to a natural water source every morning to purify themselves and to pledge themselves to righteousness in the new day.

Thus, the only fires for those dance days at Watersong were the sixteen candles that Jeanne was guided to place in the four directions around the arbor. A cornmeal line connected the central arbor pole to the east gate firepit, which now contained a three-gallon clay water bowl. Then the cornmeal was extended to the lake to create a powerful symmetry. To affirm the transition from fire to water, the iconic water bird—the blue heron—flew over the arbor at the end of the group Pipe Ceremony, and Thunder Beings were heard at another significant moment as if applauding the Dance's changing form.

The Watersong FTOD in 2007 thus served as a bridge to connect water at the dance arbor directly to the fire at the sweat lodge. This dance-evolved element was implemented in the next scheduled FTOD, which occurred in Ireland. Now, at FTOD ceremonies, two Firekeepers and two Waterkeepers share responsibility for serving the energy link between the two powerful elements; and wherever possible, the firepit and door of the sweat lodge are positioned to face the east gate water bowl in a direct cornmeal power line.

Bosnia

Jeanne and John have willingly gone into places where human despair has threatened to extinguish the potentials for the genuine joy that loving hearts can bring. The ethnic wars in the area formerly known as Yugoslavia demonstrate the dehumanizing effects of terrorism and torture. The couple had been to Croatia in August 2000 with the Sun-Moon Dance and had established relationships there. They had heard the Balkans war stories concerning the three cultures in conflict—Serbs, Croatians, and Muslims—but nothing prepared them for what they encountered in Bosnia on their 2007 visit. Survivors of the contemporary holocaust had urged Jeanne and John to bring the "For the One" Dance to Bosnia in an attempt to end the insanity of neighbors hating neighbors. People in desperate financial circumstances, who lived in houses still pockmarked with shell holes, volunteered to provide land for the dance arbor and to cook for the international crew who would assemble as a working symbol of hope. As individual stories of horror and spiritual need were related to Jeanne, she seemed to weep continually. John struggled to contain his emotions as he documented what they witnessed in his journal. Both the victims and the perpetrators now shared a geography of loss and shame. The countrywide atmosphere, however, was still heavy with inflammatory sentiment that had the potential to ignite into further misery.

Despite the logistics and security challenges that a FTOD presented in Bosnia, Jeanne and John agreed to schedule a 2008 event there.

Youth Dances

"For the One" Youth Dances began as a way of helping severely abused children, ages 11 to 16, to make breakthroughs in their therapy. The initial dance of this type was held at Watersong in October 2005. Jeanne now sees this specialized dance as a healing vehicle for children who have experienced severe trauma during times of war or natural disaster. Parents are now required to serve their child during this dance, and they receive a training in their role prior to the event. In Bosnia, for example, where so many young girls were raped, a FTO Youth Dance there would serve a significant purpose.

The primary youth dance that has evolved, however, is the "For the One" World Youth Dance for the extended age group 13 to 21. The purpose of the dance is to provide "young people of all cultures a way to eliminate prejudice, resolve interpersonal or interethnic conflicts, and promote peace at the grass roots level." The first dance of this type was held near Cape Town, South Africa on December 7-9, 2007.

November and December 2007 had been a very active period with four South African dances preceded by the ten-day Crew and Chiefs' Training. The "For the One" Dances were held on successive weeks in Johannesburg, Rustler's Valley, and Cape Town, with the FTO World Youth Dance ending the month-long run. It concluded the fifth consecutive year of South African dances.

The Rustler's Valley event proved to be a daunting challenge when in September 2007 a devastating fire destroyed the Rustler's Valley Guest Lodge, Restaurant, Marimba House (the meeting facility), and most of the homes and guest cottages in the area. The dance arbor and the sweat lodge that were on the grassy plain away from the structures, however, survived. Jeanne and John were in Ireland preparing for the FTOD there when they received the alarming news from Niyan Stirling. No one wanted to cancel the Rustler's Valley Dance, but immediate support was needed from the worldwide FTOD community. The start of the Dance was only nine weeks away.

Crew, Chiefs, and dancers made no hardship excuses and said "yes" to hold the Dance. They lived in tents, bathed outdoors camp-style, and suffered the heat and the insects, but they helped to restore hope to Rustler's Valley.

"And don't forget the powerful storm that blew away our tents," John recalled. "It rained so hard and so long that it burst a nearby dam. No one will forget that!"

The first "For the One" World Youth Dance was the culmination of a dream to create a space where both black and white teens from within South Africa who lived in the aftermath of Apartheid might experience healing. The vision for this Dance then expanded to the world as Anael Harpaz told Jeanne and John that four Israeli and Palestinian teenage girls who were involved in healing their own cultural conflicts wanted to attend. The couple also learned that a twelve-year-old Croatian boy and his mother were doing what they could to finance the trip to Cape Town, and that a fourteen-year-old German girl and her mother were holding bake sales to pay their airfare.

With so many end-of-the-year dances requiring financial support, the only way to help these distant teens attend the Youth Dance was to appeal by e-mail through the FTOD network. Jeanne's appeal went out in early October, and it was answered in a miraculous way—a $5,000 gift that went immediately to finance the teens' travel.

A letter sent to Jeanne and John from the Israeli and Palestinian girls following the Dance demonstrates its efficacy. Signed by Adi, Feirooz, Shoshan, and Hazar, it reads in part:

"We would like to thank you for helping to make it possible for us to go through this amazing experience. It was truly a great opportunity to meet new and wonderful people, especially the teenagers from different parts of the world, and to have the opportunity to heal through this process.

"The biggest surprise was to discover that the Arab and Jewish cultures are so similar compared to the other cultures we met. In the beginning we were shocked by everything about the dance. A week later we had our own experience, and realised the deep healing that it brought to us and the others.

"There are no words to express how meaningful this trip has been for us in that we have learned to appreciate our own lives after learning from the Black youth about their lives. Despite the terrible conditions they live in, their joy is contagious. We feel hopeful about our situation after learning how life was here just a few years back. Having Anael with us made our journey more meaningful as she intermingled the stories of her childhood as a white South African child who experienced the separation so strongly. It has helped us to get a better understanding about the changes that have occurred here and brings us hope.

"So we wanted to say thank you from the bottom of our hearts for making this possible for us. There are no words to say how much we appreciate this and we are sure it has added to our journey towards peace."

A Black South African youth nicknamed Lucky, who grew up in the violent streets of the Soweto township, followed the dances from Johannesburg to Cape Town both as a dancer and as a faithful hard-working member of the crew. In a Christmas 2007 e-mail, he wrote Jeanne and John to say, "I will never forget all who played part in transforming my life." He then asked for support to obtain a passport and visas so that he could crew dances elsewhere in the future. In a later e-mail, Lucky expressed his personal insights in a free-flowing, almost poetic form.

"Throughout the ages, humankind has been visited by rare individuals whose sole purpose is to remind us of who we are and what we are here for through spiritual uplift-ment of humanity. We are masters, saviors, messiahs, and some are divine mothers and fathers.

"Let us dance like gurus, like living saints. Let us dance the dance of gods, dance for enlightenment, salvation, realization, liberation, or awakening that we don't have to be separated in all aspects. Let us not say it or do it only in ceremonies but let us be love. Let us practice all that in this lifetime as the holy ones from the past are with us. Let us be grateful that we are not alone and respect that by in every thing we say, do, or meditate about, let us set posi-tive intentions of one world for us all. I love you all."

Readers might want to pause at the statements of these FTO World Youth dancers and consider the ramifications of their per-spectives when they become leaders in their respective societies. A nation influenced by them would not be exclusive in the way of past prejudices, but inclusive in the realization of our common human-ity. Theirs would not be a positional zeal fired by religion or politics, but rather a passion for the interconnectedness that they experi-enced in heart-to-heart multicultural relationships.

Organizational Roles

The years 2006 and 2007 were a transition period for Jeanne and John to pass responsibility for chiefing established "For the One" Dances to others so that they could reduce the demands of their travel schedule, focus on the World Youth Dance, and respond to calls to establish dances in new areas. They also wanted to be more available to train and counsel the growing international dance crews.

In previous years their constant global travel by air and their crisscrossing of the North American continent by car had made their bodies pay the price. There was a record of exhaustions, and even collapses, along the way because they were unable to say "no" when called. This cycle of work-till-you-drop activities caught up to Jeanne on the eve of the Watersong "For the One" Dance in early September 2006. The symptoms began the previous week when Jeanne was supporting John's Star Dance, a dance evolved with permission from Joseph Rael's original vision of the Sun-Moon Dance. Jeanne suffered a gallbladder attack so severe that John feared that the pain would cause his wife to have a heart attack, and that she might actually die.

Jeanne was supported by Reiki treatments, massage, acupuncture, and many prayers, but the terrible pain persisted. On Thursday evening, hours before the FTOD was to begin on Friday, Jeanne finally agreed that she could not chief the Dance with John and allowed herself to be rushed to the Alamance Regional Medical Center in Burlington, NC. Her lungs were full of fluid, and she was diagnosed with severe pancreatitis. Started on oxygen and morphine, her pain was off the scale, and the medical staff told John that she nearly died.

Back at Watersong, there were twenty dancers and a crew of near fifty who had assembled from England, Haiti, Ireland, Israel, South Africa, and the USA. Nearly comatose at the hospital, Jeanne asked John to return to the arbor and lead the Dance.

Cheryl Braswell stepped in to chief the female role, with the support of Sonja Munz, Patty Coleman, Sammye Jo, and Ula Rae Mynatt. The entire crew extended themselves to a very fragile John who fulfilled his non-stop Chief duties.

"I wish that I had been able to rush to Jeanne's side at the end of each day, but that was not the case. I couldn't see her until the Dance was over on Sunday afternoon. It made my discomfort hugely greater."

Jeanne spent half of September in the hospital. Later she would have gallbladder surgery and be under strict medical orders to observe an intense recovery period of months. She was thus unable to accompany John on the next scheduled dance in Ireland. To lighten John's emotional load, Brett Almond from England and Sammye Jo Harvey from the USA chiefed the Ireland Dance.

The horrific event of Jeanne's collapse tested the dedication and ability of the crews and chiefs in training. They proved to be more than equal to the sudden responsibilities of leadership, and thus they validated the faith, trust, confidence, and love that Jeanne and John felt for them.

To support the new Chiefs and their dances, Jeanne and John remain involved in fundraising and in improving international coordination. They had performed these functions on the fly for many years. Jeanne, remember, had traveled worldwide with Up With People for more than ten years and had also been the World Business Academy International Chapter Coordinator. John, too, had multiple organization skills as a long-term DuPont executive and as a WBA Chapter organizer. No one was better trained to work the telephone and e-mails, and some days their entire energy was spent in this way. But by 2006 volunteers had stepped forward to take responsibility for some of the management burdens.

Margarita DiVita, from her base at the Center for Peace in Tennessee, became the International Dance Coordinator, and Patty Coleman, from her home in Asheville, North Carolina, became the International Director of Fundraising. Both women had danced and crewed FTOD dances across the globe, and both had taken the initial crew and chief training at Watersong. With the addition of the Youth Dances, Robbie Warren in Charlotte, North Carolina, stepped forward to serve the role of the "For the One" International Youth Coordinator. It was a modest start to a staff; but as other volunteers emerged to function as in-country coordinators in specific dance locations, the pressure for Jeanne and John to do "everything" was eased. This network support coverage in established places thus allowed the founding couple to develop new locations for the dance and to focus on making the FTOD available to young people. In workdays and miles traveled in 2007, if Jeanne and John were attempting to reduce their pace, the record did not show it. When needs were presented, they continued to say "yes" even when the needs led to places as dangerous as Bosnia.

In the future, Jeanne and John feel like they have individual books to write when their travel schedules are less demanding. Jeanne wants an opportunity to tell her personal story as a legacy to her children and family. John, of course, has his continuing personal journal that he hopes to one day edit from more than a million words into something manageable that his sons can read. Then, too, John wants to complete his Mystical Numerology system and document that in book form.

Somewhere along this journey, as age sometimes dictates, they want to settle down, find a home of their own, and welcome their children and grandchildren as well as other visitors into the warmth of their understanding. Before their travel mission began, Jeanne had been a natural homemaker with all the decorating and cooking skills to transform a house into a place of favorite memories for future grandchildren. And imagine the stories that Grandmother Jeanne and Grandfather John could tell on their front porch about Australia, and India, and Israel, and South Africa, and Brazil. So much to share about a powerful vision that began with Jeanne and then swept the world.

Much of this biography has been "about" Jeanne from the point of view of John's extensive journals. And although Jeanne has had the opportunity to express herself in her own voice, it is only fair that John have the last word. And so he does.

"Looking back, I am struck by the power of vision to carry us—Jeanne's vision. It has carried us from country to country around the world. At the outset, many people thought we were crazy dreamers who would soon crash and burn. But we never did. The power of Jeanne's vision carried us. We've never been without a meal or a roof over our heads. I hope people will take note of that. This power of carrying is true not just of Jeanne's vision, but of all visions. More people need to find the courage to follow their own visions.

"Of course, the other important thing to note is that this vision of the 'For the One' Dance is a woman's. That's important. Women should take heart. My belief is that women have an important role to play in bringing the earth back into balance and healing. Jeanne is a great spirit, it's true, but great spirits grow into their roles. They are most defined by their courage to swim upstream against the current of mass consciousness. Everyone has this potential.

"This journey has been a transformation for me as well. It has been full of adventure, exhilarating highs, and abysmal lows. Along the way, I've redefined my own sense of power. I know much better who I am. And that has allowed me to support Jeanne in her visionary role. It hasn't always been easy. But it has been worth it. All over the world, I get feedback—primarily from women—about how strong I am perceived while simultaneously how supportive I am of Jeanne. This is using male strength in a different, perhaps more ancient way, as the compassionate warrior. It is very powerful, and yet so many men are threatened to be in support of a strong woman, as if the woman's success demeans their own. This is a shame. I hope my part in this journey will give more men the courage to change."

AFTERWORD

O ne of the lessons of spiritual stewardship is that proselytiza-
tion is both unnecessary and unwarranted. Since there are so
many sectarian vocabularies that attempt to define and explain
spiritual enlightenment, and so many dogmas and theologies that
claim to know the mind of God, the wise prophet does not posture
himself or herself into that dialectic. The spiritual steward goes
about spiritual practice without benefit of mass audience or organization; and if recognition comes, it comes on the lips of others and
not from the prophet. The prophet understands that his or her
function is one of service, and service does not require recognition.
How then is the wisdom of prophets to be conveyed? It is conveyed
to the questioners who pose serious questions. The prophet then
answers each questioner according to their need and level of understanding. If a group of implied questioners gather and ask the
prophet to speak to their collective needs, he or she must attempt
to serve them.

But how is one to know the nature of a prophet? How can one
trust? It is said that to sit in silence in the presence of a prophet is
to know. To listen in the silence is to know. And then, when the
prophet speaks, does the prophet separate one people from another,
or does the prophet teach the divine unity of all creation? If specialness is assigned to any race, creed, or religion, then the prophet is
false. Prejudice is not a virtue of enlightenment. Prejudice is the
cause of separation that denies God as Creation. There is no peace
of any kind where separation exists due to prejudice. The historic
record of humanity proves this statement as fact.

We all see that the human disease of conflict is apparent in ourselves and in the world. There have been many remedies proposed
and tested, but there has yet been no cure. Why? Why is humanity
still so fragmented? Why do we divide ourselves into patterns that
produce chaos, war, and self-destruction? Like the song asks,

"When will they ever learn?" *They* are not *them*. *They* are *us*. When will *we* ever learn? Some people do. There is yet hope. And there are methods that lead to understanding and even to an enlighten-ment that produces more prophets, more masters who teach an end to separation.

In documenting the lives of Jeanne and John Pehrson, I do not advocate that we revere them as saints, and they themselves would not allow it. I do, however, recommend that we pay serious atten-tion to the visionary method practiced in the "For The One" Dance as a multicultural way of coming together as human beings and experiencing the peace that can change our common destiny. We need to study war no more. We need to end separation. We need to sing and dance together in the harmony of the unified Soul.

ABOUT THE AUTHOR

M onty Joynes is primarily a novelist and screenwriter. In non-fiction, he was the narrative author and photo editor of *The Celestine Prophecy: The Making of the Movie* (2005) with James Redfield, and the author and editor of *Conversations with God: The Making of the Movie* (2006) with Neale Donald Walsch. In fiction he is best known for his four novels in the Booker Series (*Naked Into The Night, Lost In Las Vegas, Save The Good Seed,* and *Dead Water Rites*), which deals with an Anglo character's entry into the culture and metaphysics of contemporary American Indians.

Monty has written and edited professionally in magazine and book publishing for more than 35 years. He also has writer-director credits in two short films, and he has written seven feature-length screenplays currently under option or in various stages of production consideration.

Monty and Pat, his wife and Producing Partner, live in the Blue Ridge Mountains of North Carolina, USA. They have three daughters and six grandchildren.

The research and writing of *Journey for the One* involved the couple's full-time devotion for two years. Nearly one million words of the subjects' personal journals were considered. Extensive interviews were conducted with the subjects themselves and with nearly 100 others involved with them. The author also served the "For the One" Dance twice as a Dog Soldier and Elder in 2005 and 2006.

HOW TO ORDER

C opies of *Journey For The One: The Biography of Jeanne White Eagle and John Pehrson* may be purchased at the $18.95 cover price, plus shipping. North Carolina residents should add 6-¾% sales tax.

On the world-wide web place orders at
www.jeannewhiteeagle.com where
payment is available via PayPal.

By mail, order at:

One Journey Publications
P. O. Box 5738
Asheville, NC 28813 USA

By e-mail: blueearth48@bellsouth.net

Donations to support the "For The One" Dance and the "For The One" World Youth Dance are welcome at the same sites, as is information on becoming a dance participant or a crewmember.